T. S. ELIOT IN CONTEXT

T. S. Eliot's work demands much from his readers. The more the reader knows about his allusions and his range of cultural reference, the more rewarding are his poems, essays and plays. This book is carefully designed to provide an authoritative and coherent examination of those contexts essential to the fullest understanding of his challenging and controversial body of work. It explores a broad range of subjects relating to Eliot's life and career; key literary, intellectual, social and historical contexts; as well as the critical reception of his oeuvre. Taken together, these chapters sharpen critical appreciation of Eliot's writings and present a comprehensive, composite portrait of one of the twentieth century's pre-eminent men of letters. Drawing on original research, *T. S. Eliot in Context* is a timely contribution to an exciting reassessment of Eliot's life and works and will provide a valuable resource for scholars, teachers, students and general readers.

JASON HARDING is Reader in English Studies at Durham University and Visiting Research Fellow at the Institute of English Studies, University of London. His publications include *The 'Criterion': Cultural Politics and Periodical Networks in Inter-War Britain* (2002) and *T. S. Eliot and the Concept of Tradition*, co-edited with Giovanni Cianci (Cambridge, 2007).

T. S. ELIOT IN CONTEXT

EDITED BY

JASON HARDING

CAMBRIDGE
UNIVERSITY PRESS

CAMBRIDGE UNIVERSITY PRESS
Cambridge, New York, Melbourne, Madrid, Cape Town, Singapore,
São Paulo, Delhi, Dubai, Tokyo, Mexico City

Cambridge University Press
The Edinburgh Building, Cambridge CB2 8RU, UK

Published in the United States of America by Cambridge University Press, New York

www.cambridge.org
Information on this title: www.cambridge.org/9780521511537

© Cambridge University Press 2011

First published 2011

Printed in the United Kingdom at the University Press, Cambridge

A catalogue record for this publication is available from the British Library

Library of Congress Cataloging-in-Publication Data

T. S. Eliot in context / edited by Jason Harding.
p.   cm.
ISBN 978-0-521-51153-7 (Hardback)
1. Eliot, T. S. (Thomas Stearns), 1888–1965–Criticism and interpretation.
1. Harding, Jason.   II. Title.
PS3509.L43Z87256 2011
821'.912–dc22
2010038357

ISBN 978-0-521-51153-7 Hardback

In memory of Sir Frank Kermode (1919–2010)

Contents

Illustrations

Contributors

CHARLES ALTIERI, *University of California, Berkeley*

MASSIMO BACIGALUPO, *University of Genoa*

RICHARD BADENHAUSEN, *Westminster College*

C. D. BLANTON, *University of California, Berkeley*

DAVID BRADSHAW, *Worcester College, Oxford University*

JEWEL SPEARS BROOKER, *Eckerd College*

JOHN XIROS COOPER, *University of British Columbia*

MICHAEL COYLE, *Colgate University*

MARTIN DODSWORTH, *Royal Holloway, University of London*

RACHEL BLAU DUPLESSIS, *Temple University*

JENNIFER FORMICHELLI, *Boston University*

DAVID FULLER, *Durham University*

SIMON GRIMBLE, *Durham University*

JASON HARDING, *Institute of English Studies, University of London*

HUGH HAUGHTON, *University of York*

EARL K. HOLT III, *independent scholar*

PETER HOWARTH, *Queen Mary, University of London*

MARK HUSSEY, *Pace University*

MANJU JAIN, *University of Delhi*

MICHAEL LEVENSON, *University of Virginia*

BENJAMIN G. LOCKERD, *Grand Valley State University*

WILLIAM MARX, *University of Paris Ouest Nanterre La Défense*

TERRI MESTER, *Case Western Reserve University*

MICHAEL O'NEILL, *Durham University*

MARJORIE PERLOFF, *Stanford University*

RACHEL POTTER, *University of East Anglia*

STEPHEN REGAN, *Durham University*

STEPHEN ROMER, *University of Tours*

ERIC SIGG, *independent scholar*

BARRY SPURR, *University of Sydney*

ANNE STILLMAN, *Clare College, Cambridge University*

HANNAH SULLIVAN, *Stanford University*

ADAM TREXLER, *University of Exeter*

JEROEN VANHESTE, *Dutch Open University*

PATRICIA WAUGH, *Durham University*

PETER WHITE, *independent scholar*

MICHAEL H. WHITWORTH, *Merton College, Oxford University*

Acknowledgements

I would like to thank Ray Ryan for commissioning this book for Cambridge University Press and Maartje Scheltens, Sarah Roberts and Hilary Hammond for seeing it through production. I am grateful to my research assistant Alistair Brown for compiling the index with the financial support of Durham University. Assistance with various chapters has been provided by Robert Brown, Jim McCue, Jeremy Noel-Tod, Gareth Reeves, Sir Christopher Ricks, Ronald Schuchard and Thomas Staley. Rachel Blau DuPlessis's chapter benefited from the research assistance of Michael Kreger, holding an Iris and Gene Rotberg Undergraduate Research Humanities Award, Temple University, and from the hospitality of the National Humanities Center.

Abbreviations

ASG	*After Strange Gods.* London: Faber & Faber, 1934.
Brooker	*T. S. Eliot: The Contemporary Reviews*, ed. Jewel Spears Brooker. Cambridge University Press, 2004.
CFQ	*The Composition of 'Four Quartets'*, ed. Helen Gardner. London: Faber & Faber, 1978.
CPP	*The Complete Poems and Plays of T. S. Eliot.* London: Faber & Faber, 1969.
E&A	*Eeldrop and Appleplex.* Tunbridge Wells: Foundling Press, 1992.
EAM	*Essays Ancient & Modern.* London: Faber & Faber, 1936.
FLA	*For Lancelot Andrewes.* London: Faber & Gwyer, 1928.
ICS	*The Idea of a Christian Society.* London: Faber & Faber, 1939.
IMH	*Inventions of the March Hare: Poems 1909–1917*, ed. Christopher Ricks. London: Faber & Faber, 1996.
KEPB	*Knowledge and Experience in the Philosophy of F. H. Bradley.* London: Faber & Faber, 1964.
L1	*The Letters of T. S. Eliot*, vol. I, *1898–1922*. Revised edition, ed. Valerie Eliot and Hugh Haughton. London: Faber & Faber, 2009.
L2	*The Letters of T. S. Eliot*, vol. II, *1923–1925*, ed. Valerie Eliot and Hugh Haughton. London: Faber & Faber, 2009.
NTDC	*Notes Towards the Definition of Culture.* London: Faber & Faber, 1948.
OPP	*On Poetry and Poets.* London: Faber & Faber, 1957.
SE	*Selected Essays.* Third enlarged edition. London: Faber & Faber, 1951.
Southam	*A Student's Guide to the Selected Poems of T. S. Eliot* by B. C. Southam. Fourth edition. London: Faber & Faber, 1981.
SP	*Selected Prose of T. S. Eliot*, ed. Frank Kermode. London: Faber & Faber, 1975.

SW	*The Sacred Wood.* Second edition. London: Methuen, 1928.
TCC	*To Criticize the Critic.* London: Faber & Faber, 1965.
UPUC	*The Use of Poetry and the Use of Criticism.* Second edition. London: Faber & Faber, 1964.
VMP	*The Varieties of Metaphysical Poetry,* ed. Ronald Schuchard. London: Faber & Faber, 1993.
WLF	*The Waste Land: A Facsimile and Transcript of the Original Drafts,* ed. Valerie Eliot. London: Faber & Faber, 1971.

Introduction

Jason Harding

T. S. Eliot's work demands contextual commentary. The celebrated obliquities of his poetry are extraordinary. Studded with allusions, echoes and parallels to previous poets, these poems revel in a dislocated syntax which wilfully abstains from logical articulation. Similarly, his prose is habitually densely layered, making continual play with source materials and canvassing, in intricate and nuanced detail, a multitude of contemporary literary, cultural, social, economic, philosophical, theological and political issues that have now, for the most part, receded dimly into the past. In truth, his voluminous outpouring of poems, essays and books from 1905 until his death in 1965 cannot be divorced from the circumstances of their immediate composition and reception. The sheer erudition required to take full measure of Eliot's corpus can erect a formidable barrier between him and new readers. For this reason, a vast secondary criticism has grown up to expound and explicate this difficult, often provoking, work. However, for four decades after Eliot's death, a large amount of important archive material was routinely closed to researchers. We are now at the dawn of a new era in Eliot scholarship. The projected appearance of textually accurate and contextually annotated authorised critical editions of Eliot's prose, poetry, letters and plays will undoubtedly transform the landscape of Eliot studies. This collection, too, takes its place as a timely contribution to an exciting reassessment of Eliot's life and works, offering a valuable resource for scholars, teachers, students and general readers alike.

T. S. Eliot in Context is carefully designed to provide an authoritative and coherent examination of those 'contexts' deemed essential to the fullest understanding and appreciation of Eliot's work. It explores a broad range of subjects relating to his life, work and career; key literary, intellectual, social and historical contexts; as well as the critical reception of his works. Great pains have been taken to ensure that each chapter is clear, precise and succinct. Although written by a team of experts who have done

I

original research in their respective fields, this is not a collection dictated solely by the needs of academic specialists. Those readers looking for adjudications on what Professor X has said about Professor Y and Professor Z will be mostly disappointed. And yet, taken together, these chapters provide an up-to-date engagement with current developments in Eliot scholarship, and also with the wider terrain of Modernist Studies. Each chapter is self-contained and can be profitably read on its own, but it is hoped that the aggregation of chapters and sections builds into a comprehensive, composite portrait of one of the twentieth century's pre-eminent men of letters.

Contributors have been permitted some latitude in establishing the 'context' addressed in their chapter: this has led to a fascinating array of approaches, even, on occasions, to fruitful differences of opinion. Debate and disagreement is an essential ingredient in the ongoing conversation about Eliot's achievement and reputation. While consciously avoiding stage-managed controversy, *T. S. Eliot in Context* fully acknowledges the forthright expression of informed opinion. Some chapters present biographical and historical information known only to specialist scholars, others subtly reweave contextual material that has previously been examined by numerous commentators. In every case, as Anne Stillman rightly points out, the critic-as-guide must display wise tact in the course of their exposition and elucidation, encompassing a due respect for the enigma of what cannot be known or stated in bold declarative terms. This book is certainly not intended as a short cut or a substitute for reading and thinking about Eliot's writings; rather, our ambition is to stimulate further individual responses, sharpening critical appreciation and thereby enhancing the pleasure of encountering Eliot's texts. As Martin Dodsworth observes, after the critics have had their say, there is always more to be said about a body of work so inexhaustibly rich and challenging as T. S. Eliot's oeuvre.

T. S. Eliot in Context is organised into five sections. Part One, 'Life', might be seen as turning upon Eliot's gnomic statement – with Henry James in view – that it is 'the consummation of an American to become, not an Englishman, but a European'.[1] A recent BBC *Agenda* documentary has amply demonstrated the complex facets of this public, if extremely private, man. He was a scion of the New England intellectual aristocracy. In the early nineteenth century, his paternal grandfather transplanted an educational fervour mixed with religious duty to the Midwestern frontier, where Eliot grew up in a maternal environment dominated by the example of this illustrious patriarch. After an education at genteel

Harvard, touring its seedier environs, he was irresistibly drawn to Paris at a particularly crucial stage in his intellectual formation, and then to London, where he settled into the conventions of middle-class sobriety by day – as a teacher at private schools, City banker, ultimately a gentlemanly publisher – albeit indulging his mildly bohemian tastes after working hours. In time, he came to articulate mythologies betokening a strong desire to belong to imagined communities – to an 'Englishness' founded on an ideal of class-based and religio-cultural stability, and to the larger geographical and spiritual fraternity embodied by an undissociated 'mind of Europe'. That this lifelong advocate of the 'unity of European culture' lived through two ruinous European wars culminating in a Communist iron curtain drawn over half of the Continent is an inescapable context for revisiting these ideals. Part Two, 'Forms', brings us closer to Eliot's public roles. As an intellectual, he was a combative pundit equipped with a suave but imposing rhetorical armoury (deploying a corrosive irony). He was a publisher who worked in a climate of heavy censorship and a prolific literary journalist who appeared regularly in a remarkable variety of periodicals. Upon founding his own critical review, the *Criterion*, he commissioned regular bulletins on the latest innovations in the visual arts, theatre, dance, music and radio broadcasting. His work as a successful dramatist and as a BBC broadcaster in particular, unsettles misleading accounts of Eliot as an aloof 'Modernist' (a term he never embraced). By contrast, the chapters in this section reveal a more complicated picture of a man who continuously reached out to diverse audiences in search of a common culture.

'Modernism' is not a term that appears in the chapter titles of the section characterised as 'Literary Cross-Currents'. Since Eliot's distinction lies primarily in his achievement as a poet, secondarily in his influence as a critic, his polemical (somewhat opportunistic) re-evaluation of the literary canon is located quite properly at the heart of this collection. These fresh chapters significantly revise standard accounts of Eliot's literary borrowings and his critical prejudices. Above all, they demonstrate the dynamic ways in which Eliot's confrontation with 'tradition' is manifested in his poetry. A recurrent theme is the exploration of how his prodigious reading is put to excellent use – quite deliberately, though at times issuing through subterranean layers – in the combustible furnace of his transformative imagination. His compulsion to search the literary past for those elements that could be made to speak to the present is not patient scholarship, but the work of a poetic practitioner. It goes hand in hand with an acute, if abruptly dismissive, awareness of his difference from contemporaries; some of these were erstwhile fellow travellers, others antagonists who formed the whetstone on which he sharpened his own razor-sharp literary self-consciousness. This section sifts literary history, uncovering fertile allusions in Eliot's idiosyncratic readings of Shakespeare, Dante and the Classics. Moreover, by resituating this intense engagement with the literature of the past not only among trends in the scholarship and criticism of the day but also in the light of his own instrumental aesthetic goals, these chapters reinflect received knowledge: Eliot's penchant for seventeenth-century and French symbolist varieties of metaphysical 'wit', for instance, was tempered by a sense of their extravagance or narcissistic limitations; just as his fastidious recoil from Romantic self-revelation and from sub-Romantic forms of Georgian pastoralism did not prevent him from acknowledging a profound debt to the practice and theory of individual Romantic poets, or from sponsoring as editor and publisher a number of 'Georgian' poets. This ambivalence in his literary relations is also apparent in his dialogues with his friend Ezra Pound and with his Bloomsbury acquaintances, as in the respectful distance he maintained from the most advanced cadres of the European avant-garde.

Part Four, 'Politics, Society and Culture', tackles head-on several controversial subjects. These chapters remind us that if Eliot's values and beliefs are not ones that are commonly held in high regard today, they were sophisticated responses to specific socio-cultural conditions, as well as to extreme political and economic crises. What emerges from this section are the continuities and transitions in Eliot's thought, rather than sudden reversals or conversions. While hostile critics have latched on to Eliot's occasionally unguarded or intolerant public pronouncements, these chapters reveal the degree of scepticism, at times radical, with which he held a point of view. From his earliest exposure to the competing theories of positivism, pragmatism and relativism during his undergraduate and graduate studies in philosophy, social science and natural science, Eliot was impressed by a need to impose social order on metaphysical and epistemological flux. His commitment to the Anglican Church identified that branch of it which cherished exacting ritual observance without entailing submission to the dogma of papal infallibility. The right-wing conservatism of his political convictions and his regrettably condescending remarks about (free-thinking) Jews and women are investigated here in chapters which combine sensitivity and empathy with a tough-minded willingness to judge those aspects which are unpalatable. Finally, Part Five re-examines Eliot's critical reception: from the polarised response of contemporary reviewers to his slim volumes of poetry and prose, which prepared the ground for his later institutional canonisation, to the fascinating creative dialectic of admiration, rejection and emulous rivalry exhibited by contemporary and subsequent poets. The cold eye frequently cast on Eliot by younger generations of critics and scholars, keen to clear a new space on university syllabuses drawn up by his academic epigones, is viewed in this section in the broadest perspective of the evolution of English Studies from its beginnings to the present day. The closing chapter is a virtuoso meditation on the variegated legacies operative in contemporary literary criticism and cultural theory which take Eliot as their acknowledged or unacknowledged point of departure. If we sometimes like to believe that we know so much more, or know so much better, than the writers of the past, *T. S. Eliot in Context* offers compelling testimony announcing that Eliot himself, to quote his key essay 'Tradition and the Individual Talent', is still an indispensable part of 'that which we know' (*SE*, 16).

NOTE

1. T. S. Eliot, 'In Memory of Henry James', *Egoist* (January 1918), 1.

PART ONE

Life

CHAPTER I

St Louis

Earl K. Holt III

Home is where one starts from

(*CPP*, 182)

A writer's art, T. S. Eliot proposed, depends 'on the accumulated sensations of the first twenty-one years' of his life.[1] Born in St Louis on
26 September 1888, Eliot spent more than sixteen of his first twenty-one
years there. Reminiscing about his early life on a visit to his birthplace in
1953, the poet said: 'I am very well satisfied with having been born in
St Louis: in fact I think I was fortunate to have been born here, rather
than in Boston, or New York, or London' (*TCC*, 45). Eliot had been
invited to St Louis to address an audience gathered to celebrate the
centenary of Washington University. The university had been co-founded
by (and initially named after) his celebrated grandfather the Reverend
William Greenleaf Eliot. Acknowledging the profound and continuing
influence of what he called his grandfather's 'law of Public Service', Eliot
observed that 'it is no doubt owing to the impress of this law upon my
infant mind that, like other members of my family, I have felt, ever since
I passed beyond my early irresponsible years, an uncomfortable and very
inconvenient obligation to serve upon committees'. Although his grandfather died a year before he was born, Eliot noted that 'as a child I thought
of him as still the head of the family' (*TCC*, 44).

William Greenleaf Eliot came to St Louis in 1834 at the age of 23,
shortly after graduating from Harvard Divinity School. He had been
offered a year's board and lodging in St Louis by a small group of
transplanted New England Unitarians. Before accepting their invitation,
however, he had announced to a friend that he would 'remain and lay my
ashes in the valley of the Mississippi'.[2] He kept that pledge, giving a
lifetime's service to what on his arrival was little more than a frontier
outpost, but which before his death had become the most populous city
in the American Midwest. Under his leadership, the Unitarian Church of

9

the Messiah grew to be one of the largest and most influential in this rapidly growing city. His grandson remarked that the Unitarian Church, St Louis and Washington University represented to him 'the symbols of Religion, the Community, and Education', adding that it was 'a very good beginning for any child, to be brought up to reverence such institutions, and to be taught that personal and selfish aims should be subordinated to the general good which they represent' (*TCC*, 44).

Today, Unitarians do not think of themselves as evangelists, but William Greenleaf Eliot was proud to recall that he was ordained as an evangelist in Boston before setting out for what was then the American frontier. He personally initiated the founding of Unitarian churches along the Mississippi valley from New Orleans to Milwaukee. Many were financially supported by himself or by his congregation in St Louis. Evangelism in the city itself meant the creation and maintenance of institutions of charity, education and culture; some concerned with the alleviation of poverty or suffering, all designed to contribute to the moral and spiritual uplift of the community as a whole. The Reverend William Greenleaf Eliot acknowledged that St Louis was mainly populated by those who had come west to make money. The mission of his ministry was to increase not the material but the moral and spiritual capital of the community, and in so doing he proved himself to be ingenious in converting private wealth into endowments for institutions whose aims were for the common good. A noted businessman of the time commented that if he could have had the Reverend Eliot as a business partner, together they would have made the greatest fortune west of the Alleghenies. The influence of William Greenleaf Eliot's personal ministry and character was legendary. He is a notable example of what Daniel Howe has called 'The Unitarian Conscience'.[3] A memorial plaque commemorating him now hangs in Eliot Hall of the First Unitarian Church of St Louis. It reads: 'His best monument is to be found in the many educational and philanthropic institutions of St Louis to which he gave the disinterested labor of his life. The whole city was his parish and every soul needing him a parishioner.' Reflecting both his extreme personal modesty and his deep sense of Christian discipleship, at his request William Greenleaf Eliot's gravestone was inscribed simply with his name, the dates of his life (1811–87) and the words 'Looking Unto Jesus'.

T. S. Eliot, then, was born into the single most important family in the history of American Unitarianism. Collectively, the Eliots form a veritable *Who's Who* of Unitarian biography. Two of the poet's cousins, including his contemporary Frederick May Eliot, served as presidents of the

American Unitarian Association (their combined terms in office spanned almost half the twentieth century). Two of his uncles were prominent Unitarian ministers: one of them, Thomas Lamb Eliot, nearly duplicated in Portland, Oregon, the achievements of William Greenleaf Eliot in St Louis. Thomas Lamb Eliot's daughter married the Reverend Earl Morse Wilbur, a leading Unitarian historian and founder of the Starr King School for the Ministry, the Unitarian seminary in Berkeley, California. One of Thomas Lamb Eliot's sons, William Greenleaf Junior, became the minister of the same Portland church his father had served for over fifty years. The distinguished association of the Eliots with the Unitarian Church in America, as ministers and laity, male and female, could be extended almost indefinitely.

T. S. Eliot's father was not a minister. Henry Ware Eliot was born in 1843, the second of William Greenleaf Eliot's fourteen children (only five of whom survived to adulthood). It never occurred to the Reverend Eliot that any of his sons would not become clergymen and he expressed his disappointment at Henry's decision to go into business, angrily exclaiming that his son's education was wasted, 'except that it has made a man of you'.[4] Henry built a successful career, however, with the St Louis Hydraulic-Press Brick Company, rising to become president and chairman, thereby providing not only enough money to contribute generously as a philanthropist, but also to sustain the ambitions of a son who wanted to be a poet. He was aged 45 when Tom was born, his seventh and youngest child. There seems to have been a distance between them. It is not a caricature to see this separation as the natural estrangement between the businessman father and his artistically minded son. Henry died in 1919, just as his son was beginning to establish a reputation as a poet. Tom regretted that his father had died thinking he was wasting his life writing poetry.

Henry Ware Eliot had married Charlotte Champe Stearns in 1868. Charlotte was a Boston Unitarian of formidable intellectual and artistic abilities. She was a natural scholar who resented the educational restrictions placed on women in that era. She did, however, publish a large body of work, both poetry and prose, mostly in Unitarian periodicals. She understood her son's artistic talent and defended *The Waste Land* to bewildered family members, although she expressed the wish that 'with its suffering and struggle, it was an interim poem and would be followed by a poem of fulfilment'.[5] She was a leader of various social reform movements in St Louis and was active in women's organisations, in particular the Wednesday Club, which featured speakers on literary and cultural topics. It was the kind of social gathering to which women would

come and go talking, among other things, of Michelangelo. Aside from
her somewhat unexceptional poetry, Charlotte wrote a detailed biography
of William Greenleaf Eliot, which she dedicated to her children with the
inscription 'Lest They Forget'. Her son Tom did not.

Eliot's decisions to join the Anglican Church and to adopt British
citizenship in 1927 are among the most debated elements of his biography.
It is clear he was abandoning the denominational faith of his Unitarian
parents, grandparents, cousins, uncles and aunts; yet he retained the
spiritual and especially the moral imprint of this profound family legacy.
In important respects, Eliot's baptism was less a repudiation of his
religious past than a rebaptism and reconfirmation into the Christian
heritage of his St Louis Unitarian family. The scholar and critic Grover
Smith has observed:

Eliot was nothing without his Unitarian upbringing – it was his salvation from
philosophy, from Buddhism, and from the Church of Rome, and even in a
curious way from Anglo-Catholicism as well. He could not be *quite* sceptical,
quite godless, or *quite* authoritarian. So he moved through stages that brought
him back to his grandfather's ideal of the exemplary life. This is hard to
document, but I think the *Quartets* show it.[6]

In like fashion, the aspiring English man of letters never forgot that his
roots were deeply planted in the soil of the American Midwest. In 1930,
Eliot informed Marquis Childs of the *St Louis Post-Dispatch* that the first
sixteen years of his life spent in St Louis beside the Mississippi River
had 'affected me more deeply than any other environment has done'. He
went on to say that in middle age these early impressions intensified; for
example, the memory of taking photographs of a buffalo in Forest Park,
of being taken as a child by his nursemaid to a Catholic church near his
home, and of the steamboats on New Year's Day. Eliot concluded that
'there is something in having passed one's childhood beside the big river,
which is incommunicable to those who have not'. In spite of the years he
had spent outside of St Louis and outside of America altogether, Eliot
claimed 'Missouri and the Mississippi have made a deeper impression on
me than any other part of the world'.[7]

Eliot's first sixteen years were spent at 2635 Locust Street (long demolished), located just a few blocks from the Church of the Messiah, where
he attended Sunday school and where two of his sisters were teachers.
Behind the back garden of this boyhood home, concealed by a high brick
wall, were the school grounds of Mary Institute, a preparatory school for
young women, one of several St Louis institutions that had been

Figure 1   Church of the Messiah, St Louis, Missouri.

founded by his grandfather. The ailanthus tree planted on these grounds reappeared in *Four Quartets*, as does the Mississippi River, the 'strong brown god' (*CPP*, 184) that had made such a deep impression on him as a child. Eliot himself graduated from Smith Academy – the boys counterpart to Mary Institute – in 1905. The year before he left school, he had attended the grand St Louis World's Fair. Originally scheduled for 1903 to celebrate the centenary of the Louisiana Purchase, but delayed to accommodate greater national and international participation, the fair opened on 30 April 1904 and ran for eight months. With exhibits from nearly all of the then forty-five American states and from sixty-three nations, it was in every respect the largest exposition of its kind to that date. It brought the world to St Louis. The Olympic Games were held on grounds adjacent to the fair. In retrospect, the world's fair was the city's last great hurrah, for Chicago had already eclipsed St Louis, just as the railroads had overtaken the riverboats as the primary vehicle of commerce by the turn of the twentieth century.

The name of Prufrock-Littau, which Eliot apparently saw on the sign of a St Louis furniture store, is another of those footfalls that echoed in his memory, like the yellow St Louis fog that he likened to a cat 'that rubs its back upon the window-panes' (*CPP*, 13). Eliot's second wife Valerie told James Olney that she would never forget her visit to St Louis in 1959, when her husband 'almost became a schoolboy as the train approached the station'.[8] Valerie informed Olney that when the newlyweds had taken a flat in Kensington Court Gardens in London, Eliot, who was aged 58, remarked that it was the 'first home I have had since I left St Louis'.[9]

Some enthusiasts think the poet is buried in Westminster Abbey, where a plaque in his memory is to be found in Poets' Corner. In fact, his ashes lie in St Michael's Church at East Coker in Somerset, not far from where his ancestors had resided in the seventeenth century. Close to Eliot's commemorative plaque in St Michael's are three tall stained-glass windows, images of the Christian graces – Faith, Hope and Charity – which are remarkably similar to three stained-glass windows that used to be found in the Unitarian Church of the Messiah in St Louis and which Eliot had known as a boy. Designed by the architects Peabody & Stearns of Boston, this building was destroyed by fire and is now a vacant lot, bringing to mind Eliot's musing in 'East Coker':

> In my beginning is my end. In succession
> Houses rise and fall, crumble, are extended,
> Are removed, destroyed, restored, or in their place
> Is an open field, or a factory, or a by-pass.
> Old stone to new building, old timber to new fires,
> Old fires to ashes, and ashes to the earth   (*CPP*, 177)

NOTES

1. 'Turgenev', *Egoist* (December 1917), 167.
2. Earl K. Holt III, *William Greenleaf Eliot: Conservative Radical* (St Louis, MO: First Unitarian Church of St Louis Press, 1985), p. 24.
3. D. W. Howe, *The Unitarian Conscience: Harvard Moral Philosophy, 1805–1861* (Middletown, CT: Wesleyan University Press, 1988).

4. Henry Ware Eliot Sr, unpublished memoir entitled 'A Brief Autobiography', William Greenleaf Eliot Papers, University Archives, Department of Special Collections, Washington University Libraries. Henry explained his decision not to become a Unitarian minister: 'Too much pudding choked the dog' (*L1*, 820).

5. See Herbert Howarth, *Notes on some Figures behind T. S. Eliot* (Boston, MA: Houghton Mifflin, 1964), p. 35.

6. Grover Smith, letter to Earl K. Holt III, 16 August 1987.

7. T. S. Eliot to Marquis W. Childs, 8 August 1930, reprinted in *Seeking St Louis: Voices from a River City* (St Louis, MO: Missouri Historical Society Press, 2000), pp. 555–6.

8. Valerie Eliot, 'A Photographic Memoir, with a Note by James Olney', *Southern Review* (autumn 1985), 988.

9. See James Olney, 'T. S. Eliot Memorial Lecture', *The Placing of T. S. Eliot*, ed. Jewel Spears Brooker (Columbia: University of Missouri Press, 1991), pp. 60–76.

Figure 2	Rockport, near the Dry Salvages, New England.

CHAPTER 2

New England

Eric Sigg

T. S. Eliot often called himself a New Englander. His relationship with New England, however, had a double quality: positive and negative, inherited but also personal, giving him a source of inspiration but failing to provide an environment that would sustain his poetic career. Although Eliot grew up in a large family in St Louis (see Chapter 1 above), his ancestors had lived in New England for more than two centuries. Eliot remembered that his family 'guarded jealously its connexions with New England'.[1] They did so by preserving their loyalties and traditions, but also by renewing their contact with the region. When Eliot was a child his family began to spend summers at Cape Ann on the Massachusetts coast. They built a large house at Eastern Point commanding a view of Gloucester Harbor, which Eliot called 'the most beautiful harbour' on the New England coast.[2] He spent each summer there from June until September and learned to sail a small catboat skilfully along the coastline. His experiences inspired the images of red granite, pine forest and blue ocean that appear in *Ash-Wednesday*, 'Marina' and 'Cape Ann', in the closing lines of 'The Love Song of J. Alfred Prufrock', in *The Waste Land* – 'The boat responded / Gaily, to the hand expert with sail and oar' (*CPP*, 74) – and above all in 'The Dry Salvages'. He particularly recalled the Atlantic Ocean off the New England coast as one of the great natural forces which 'impressed my childhood imagination'.[3]

The Eliots educated several of their children in New England. In 1905, T. S. Eliot was sent to Milton Academy in Massachusetts for a preparatory year before he enrolled at Harvard University. He would study at Harvard until 1915, completing his bachelor's and master's degrees and research for a Ph.D. in philosophy (he failed to take the viva and did not receive his doctorate). At Harvard, Eliot learned Sanskrit, read Dante and the Elizabethan dramatists, discovered John Donne, the metaphysical poets, Jules Laforgue and the French symbolists, and began to write poetry himself. When dissatisfied with the academic surroundings at Harvard, he took to the city of Boston – a pattern he would repeat in Paris and London – venturing into the poorer areas and using what he observed there in his poems. Eliot titled drafts of three sections of what would become 'Preludes' after the Boston districts of Dorchester and Roxbury (see *IMH*, 334–6). Much later he recalled his discovery that 'the sort of experience that an adolescent had had, in an industrial city in America, could be the material for poetry'. In fact, 'the possibility of fusion between the sordidly realistic and the phantasmagoric' could transform what had hitherto been regarded as 'sterile' and 'intractably unpoetic' (*TCC*, 126) into poetry.

Aside from their poetic value, Eliot's urban explorations also supplied an antidote to the genteel society of Harvard and Boston, in which he moved as an undergraduate with relatives in the city. He had many relatives in the main branch of the Eliot family, which had remained in New England and which counted among its members a mayor of Boston, the current president of Harvard, prominent Unitarian ministers, and an array of literary and academic figures.[4] As he acquainted himself with realities that genteel Boston society chose to keep at a distance, Eliot felt uneasy with what he saw as a morally complacent and only superficially cultured society. In 1918 he wrote that 'the society of Boston was and is quite uncivilized but refined beyond the point of civilization'.[5] Several poems in Eliot's first collection – 'The Love Song of J. Alfred Prufrock', 'Portrait of a Lady', 'The Boston Evening Transcript', 'Aunt Helen', 'Cousin Nancy', and 'Mr Apollinax' – satirise the remoteness of Boston society from contemporary life, criticising a tendency to turn away from what was new, unfamiliar or unpleasant. Other early poems treat difficult, urgent subject matter that genteel Boston would not willingly recognise. 'Preludes', 'Rhapsody on a Windy Night' and 'Morning at the Window' address themes of poverty, sordid surroundings, insistent sexuality and hopeless urban distress. For Eliot, poetry needed to comprehend not only what was civilised but also what was primitive: 'it is certain that primitive art and poetry help our understanding of civilized art and poetry'.[6] Moreover, he argued that 'the subject-matter and the imagery of poetry should be extended to topics and objects related to the life of a modern man or woman'. In seeking such 'material refractory to transmutation into poetry', contemporary poets should employ 'words and phrases which had not been used in poetry before' (*OPP*, 160). *The Waste Land*'s mixture of music hall and metaphysics realised this poetic theory concretely, depicting degraded behaviour and personal despair as emblematic of modern existence. In this poem and in *Poems* (1920), Eliot

contradicted the genteel canons of taste he had encountered in New
England, which believed that art was better and higher if it was refined,
idealised and sanitised.

Eliot's rejection of the genteel view of art corresponded to a moral
scepticism and a questioning of religion, especially of the Unitarianism
that provided the dominant moral tenor of Boston and New England.
Eliot had grown up in a family highly conscious of its Unitarianism.
In Boston, the historic home of Unitarianism and of Eliot's family, his
grandfather, the Reverend William Greenleaf Eliot, was ordained at the
Federal Street Church in 1834, with the foremost Unitarian preacher in
the United States, Dr William Ellery Channing, in attendance. As Earl
K. Holt III has shown in Chapter 1, the Reverend Eliot established the
single most important family in the history of American Unitarianism.
Yet T. S. Eliot himself maintained a critical stance towards Unitarianism.
Dismissive of what he viewed as its humanitarian rationalism, he went
so far as to express a hatred of its cheerfulness and optimism. It was
fundamental to Unitarianism that human nature was essentially good
and could be perfected through conscious, diligent cultivation; indeed,
Unitarians decreed moral self-improvement to be the paramount duty.
Unitarians held Christ to be the paradigm, a human being who, by
perfecting his moral nature, had become divine. They believed that with
lifelong effort, ordinary humans could achieve this perfection. Eliot
rejected these doctrines, and later opposed them with the orthodox
Christian dogmas of Original Sin and the Incarnation.

In a 1919 review of *The Education of Henry Adams* (whose author was a
distant cousin), Eliot piercingly criticised Unitarianism and some aspects
of New England culture. He argued that Adams's 'very American curiosity was directed and misdirected by two New England characteristics:
conscientiousness and scepticism'. Inherited from the Puritans, conscience imposed 'the heavy burden of self-improvement' on Adams.
'Conscience', wrote Eliot, led Adams to recognise the shortcomings of
his education, which had omitted 'a vague variety of things he ought to
know about'. Eliot remarked that Adams was also

aware, as most Bostonians are, of the narrowness of the Boston horizon. But
working with and against conscience was the Boston doubt: a scepticism which is
difficult to explain to those who are not born to it. This scepticism is a product,
or a cause, or a concomitant, of Unitarianism; it is not destructive, but it is
dissolvent ... a great many things interested him [Adams]; but he could believe
in nothing ... Wherever this man stepped, the ground did not simply give way,
it flew into particles.[7]

Here Eliot analysed his own background and its influences on his character and development. The 'fractured atoms' of 'Gerontion' (1920) and the
fragments 'shored against my ruins' of *The Waste Land* (*CPP*, 39 and 75)
offer parallels to the 'Boston doubt' that caused solid ground to fly into
particles. Revealingly, Eliot called this Unitarian-inspired scepticism dissolvent, echoing his many poetic images of the destructive power of water –
for instance, the drowned Prufrock, the 'worried bodies of drowned
men' (*CPP*, 31) in 'Mr Apollinax', Bleistein's subaqueous vision, and the
drowned Phoenician sailor of *The Waste Land*. The 'dissolvent' quality of
scepticism recurs in Eliot's poetry and criticism, which are marked by a
preoccupation with emotional, mental and cultural dissolution. This
scepticism contributed to Eliot's artistic self-consciousness, which he
defined as his sense of the artist 'as an Eye curiously, patiently watching
himself as a man'.[8] In Eliot's writings, this artistic eye – resembling the
Unitarian moral conscience, which carefully monitors, controls and corrects both thought and conduct – shifts its scrutiny from the self to
something more encompassing, comprehensive and – in a key departure
from Unitarianism – supernatural.

The Unitarian doubt stemmed from the commandment to engage in
self-improvement, taking the form of self-cultivation through moral self-
questioning. 'Are these ideas right or wrong?' (*CPP*, 20) asks the speaker
in 'Portrait of a Lady'. Evaluating one's own feelings, thoughts, motives
and conduct against a standard of moral perfection almost inevitably
results in self-condemnation. In this way spiritual autobiography, an
aspect of the morality (shading into self-absorption) of New England
Unitarianism, emerges in Eliot's poetry. However much he desired to
clothe his poetic creation in impersonality, his poetry discloses a strongly
confessional element. In the Unitarian manner, Eliot criticised his own
conscience and spiritual progress from an external moral viewpoint. With
candid self-disclosure, Eliot's confessional impulse exposed the painful,
halting steps in his spiritual development. Correlatives to the divided,
fragmentary, dissolving mind appear in every period of Eliot's poetry and
criticism: whether in the 'dissociation of sensibility' (*SE*, 288) splitting
apart the mind of Europe after the Middle Ages; Prufrock's 'hundred
indecisions' (*CPP*, 14); or the speaker in *The Waste Land* who could
'connect / Nothing with nothing' (*CPP*, 70).

The failure of the personality and the soul to cohere, to assume
identity, troubled Eliot's imagination. This fragmentation finds one
analogue in Eliot's images of remnants: Prufrock's 'butt-ends', the
broken, soiled and decayed objects, polluted water and infertile land,

and the litter and waste that furnish an almost limitless stock of Eliot's poetic imagery. At the human level, personal dissolution finds its images in Eliot's representation of people by synecdoche or parts disconnected from the body – smiles torn from a passer-by and eyes last seen in tears. His most recurrent image combines the remnant and the body part as human remains, the bones (and jaws, skulls, corpses) found almost throughout Eliot's verse. Yet if waste in the physical world corresponds to a sense of waste in the life of the self, and if images of an imperfect, broken world realise the sensation of the self coming apart, these images functioned differently in early and later stages of Eliot's career.

In Eliot's early poetry, images of damage and ruin served as a corrective to Unitarian optimism, which he viewed as falsely denying the reality that evil and sin, or even hardship and decay, existed in the world. Eventually, however, the Unitarian habit of moral self-development would lead Eliot in a different direction. His conviction that evil and sin did exist in a fallen world and that they corrupted natural life compelled his discovery, or creation, of a divine reality. At first obsessed by seeing death in the life around him, Eliot passed through this morbid lens to a transfigured vision of life in death. His criticism of the world came to assert the primacy of the supernatural over the natural life. Writing of Charles Baudelaire, Eliot expressed an aspect of his own spiritual dilemma: 'Either because he cannot adjust himself to the actual world he has to reject it in favour of Heaven and Hell, or because he has the perception of Heaven and Hell he rejects the present world: both ways of putting it are tenable' (*SE*, 423).

It is a short step from the cultivation of the conscience to self-consciousness. Eliot once called the artist 'the most conscious of men'.[9] Of poets, he asserted: 'The business of the poet is to be more conscious of his own language than other men, to be more sensitive to the feeling, more aware of the meaning of every word he uses, more aware of the history of the language.'[10] In a remarkable passage in a late essay, Eliot invoked superior consciousness not simply as an artistic quality, but as something that gave access to a kind of power. Writing of *The Adventures of Huckleberry Finn*, Eliot observed that 'Huck is passive and impassive, apparently always the victim of events; and yet, in his acceptance of his world and of what it does to him and others, he is more powerful than his world, because he is more *aware* than any other person in it.'[11] It is common for characters and narrators in Eliot's poetry to suffer as victims of events without gaining any increase in power. Yet Eliot also wrote of moments when perceptual insight gave rise to a new awareness that became a means to power – not a power to act, but the power to see and therefore to comprehend. Eliot's early poetry offers instances of this combination of detached passivity with superior awareness, if not yet of its power: Prufrock's 'visions and revisions' (*CPP*, 14); the speaker in 'Preludes' who 'had such a vision of the street / As the street hardly understands' (*CPP*, 23); and, in *The Waste Land*, a memory of 'Looking into the heart of light' (*CPP*, 62) and Tiresias who 'foresuffered all' (*CPP*, 69).

It is not often a fruitful task to search Eliot's writings for ideas corresponding to those of Ralph Waldo Emerson, the great nineteenth-century New England sage. Yet in drawing attention to a moment of heightened awareness that accompanies a passive acceptance of the world, Eliot seems to arrive at an insight resembling Emerson's transcendent moment when he loses consciousness of self in an encompassing vision of nature. It is true that for Eliot nature does not provoke these visionary moments. Yet if the cause differs, the effect of the expanded awareness that Eliot proposes seems to resemble the state of selfless perceiving described in Emerson's essay 'Nature':

In the woods, we return to reason and faith. There I feel that nothing can befall me in life, – no disgrace, no calamity (leaving me my eyes), which nature cannot repair. Standing on the bare ground, – my head bathed by the blithe air, and uplifted into infinite space – all mean egotism vanishes. I become a transparent eye-ball. I am nothing. I see all. The currents of the Universal Being circulate through me; I am part or particle of God . . . I am the lover of uncontained and immortal beauty. In the wilderness, I find something more dear and connate than in streets or villages. In the tranquil landscape, and especially in the distant line of the horizon, man beholds somewhat as beautiful as his own nature.[12]

As Emerson's 'I' becomes his eye, personal identity falls away, to be replaced by an identity between the self and what it sees in nature. If rather different forces call forth Eliot's visionary moments, those moments resemble Emerson's when self-consciousness – confined, narrow and exclusive – is transformed into consciousness of something beyond the self – comprehensive and powerful. By losing consciousness of self, the self gains power over consciousness, assuming a superior point of view, as in the vision in 'Burnt Norton' of 'the still point of the turning world' (*CPP*, 173).

Eliot's transcendentalism, if it can be called that, was a long time coming. His urban explorations as a Harvard undergraduate seem to have set the process in motion. At the same time, his sceptical discontent with Boston society led him to question its genteel proprieties and its Unitarian pieties. The Boston of his time also fell short in a practical way. In the nineteenth century New England enjoyed a dominant cultural position in the United States, and Unitarians in particular set a high value on literature. By the time Eliot arrived at Harvard in 1906, however, he was disappointed to find no literary models there. 'There were no American poets at all', he recalled.[13] 'I cannot remember the name of a single poet whose work I read' he observed, adding that 'the only recourse was to poetry of another age and to poetry of another language'.[14]

Eliot once remarked: 'One great test of a society is the kind of art it produces.'[15] In his eyes, New England failed that test. He claimed that Boston's literary importance as a 'provincial capital' had peaked in the 1850s. He went on to say that unless a provincial city could attract a 'continuous supply of important men' its importance was temporary.[16] When this supply ended, the metropolitan centre regained its ascendancy. In Eliot's view, the ideal for an aspiring writer was a leisured existence in a civilised metropolis where he could be exposed to the 'exchange of ideas and critical standards'.[17] Eliot did not find these qualities in the New England of his day, which was still in some respects a colonial culture, long accustomed to receiving its literary and artistic standards from England and from Europe. Eliot's striking claim that 'it is the final perfection, the consummation of an American' to become 'a European'[18] emerges as a product and a critique of this colonial cultural inheritance. Boston having ceased to be a vital literary centre, Eliot's metropolitan theory of literary production made his choice to pursue his literary career in London almost foreordained. He took this step against his family's objections, but it was not an uncommon one for American writers. Eliot differed from most of his fellow literary expatriates by staying abroad permanently, as Henry James had done. In 1918, Eliot wrote that James did not come to Europe merely to improve himself, because 'the soil of his origin contributed a flavour discriminible after transplantation'.[19] Eliot concluded that James's transplantation had improved the flavour of his writing, and gave it its chance; he undoubtedly hoped his own transplantation would work in a similar way.

A literary success almost without precedent would eventually follow Eliot's settlement in London (see Chapter 4). Yet there is evidence that his transplantation imposed a high personal cost. It also seems to be the case that during the dry literary period that followed publication of *The Waste Land*, distance from his American origins caused some temporary withering of Eliot's poetic imagination. After 1927, however, memories of New England would begin to offer fresh inspiration and to give access to a lyric impulse. In 1959 he said of his poetry that 'in its sources, in its emotional springs, it comes from America'.[20] The life-giving waters of Eliot's complex New England inheritance provided an essential creative spring.

NOTES

1. 'Preface', *This American World* by Edgar Ansel Mowrer (London: Faber & Gwyer, 1928), p. xiii.
2. 'Publishers' Preface', *Fisherman of the Banks* by James B. Connolly (London: Faber & Gwyer, 1928), p. vii.
3. 'Address', *From Mary to You* (centennial issue [December] 1959), 136.
4. These far-flung family connections included Noah Webster, the Lowells, Henry Adams, Herman Melville, Nathaniel Hawthorne and John Greenleaf Whittier. See Eric Sigg, 'T. S. Eliot and the New England Literary Family' (forthcoming).
5. 'The Hawthorne Aspect', *Little Review* (August 1918), 49.
6. 'War-Paint and Feathers', *Athenaeum* (17 October 1919), 1036.
7. 'A Sceptical Patrician', *Athenaeum* (23 May 1919), 361–2.
8. 'The Preacher as Artist', *Athenaeum* (28 November 1919), 1253.
9. 'War-Paint and Feathers', 1036.
10. 'Ezra Pound', *Poetry* (September 1946), 337.
11. 'Introduction', *The Adventures of Huckleberry Finn* by Samuel L. Clemens (London: Cresset Press, 1950), p. x.
12. Ralph Waldo Emerson, *Nature* (Boston: James Munroe, 1836), pp. 12–13.
13. Quoted in 'Tradition and the Practice of Poetry', *Southern Review* (autumn 1985), 878.
14. 'Ezra Pound', 326.
15. 'A Commentary', *Criterion* (April 1932), 471.
16. 'Was there a Scottish Literature?', *Athenaeum* (1 August 1919), 681.
17. 'Hawthorne Aspect', 49.
18. 'In Memory of Henry James', *Egoist* (January 1918), 1.
19. 'Hawthorne Aspect', 47.
20. 'Interview with T. S. Eliot', *Writers at Work: The Paris Review Interviews*, second series, ed. George Plimpton (Harmondsworth: Penguin, 1977), p. 110.

CHAPTER 3

Paris

William Marx

'I cannot bear to think of your being alone in Paris, the very words give me a chill. English speaking countries seem so different from foreign. I do not admire the French nation, and have less confidence in individuals of that race than in English' (*L1*, 12). Those are T. S. Eliot's mother's words in April 1910, after her son had told her he would spend a year in Paris following his graduation from Harvard. Although her reluctance was plain to read, he went nonetheless. In every respect, it was a decisive year. When Eliot departed for Paris, he felt a real temptation to become a French poet. When he returned to America a year later, he had decided against this move. What had happened? Eliot's mother provides a clue, for Eliot was 'alone in Paris' for two reasons. First, as his mother makes quite clear, he had broken with his American cultural background. Second, it was not easy to create new ties in his host country. In a letter of 1914 to his friend Conrad Aiken, Eliot admitted that his stay in Paris occasioned 'one of those nervous sexual attacks which I suffer from when alone in a city' (*L1*, 82). It was no accident that the poems contained in his first collection, *Prufrock and Other Observations* (1917), examine the theme of urban dereliction after the manner of two French poets, Baudelaire and Laforgue.

In Paris, Eliot's loneliness was more complete than it would be in London, because it was also cultural – a point many critics have overlooked. Although Eliot was more than simply an American in Paris, he was not, nor could be, an insider. The countless elements he borrowed from French culture and literature could not keep their original meanings and function, for in such cultural transfers every reading is to some extent a misreading. If one must have all the keys to unlock a foreign culture, the real barrier between France and the United States might not be the Atlantic Ocean, relatively easy to cross, but the English Channel, which much more radically separates Anglo-American from French culture. This is what Mrs Eliot said. Crucial though it was to his development, Eliot's engagement with France was hardly unambiguous. Or to put it more precisely, it was crucial because it was based on, or gave rise to, exceptionally fruitful misunderstandings. When describing some of the most stimulating discoveries Eliot made during his Parisian sojourn (October 1910 to July 1911), it is important to remain attentive to possible dissonances. Since several of these encounters (with the visual arts, music, theatre, dance) are treated elsewhere in this collection, the focus here will be on three fundamental discoveries of a more literary or philosophical nature: those associated with contemporary French literature, Bergson's philosophy and the Action Française. It will be seen that Eliot's mother had some grounds to worry about her son.

Eliot's reading and experiences in Paris were to have profound consequences for his entire writing career. It would be too simplistic to say that they were really determining factors, if one means a mere relation of cause and effect. Things did not happen that way. No contact can take place if it is not prepared or desired. Eliot would never have chosen to live in Paris if he had not already made the intellectual journey through his reading in 1908 of Arthur Symons's *The Symbolist Movement in Literature*, or through Irving Babbitt's Harvard classes on 'literary criticism in France, with special reference to the nineteenth century'. Not only did Eliot know he would find something in French culture that would suit his interests, but he had, as it were, already found it. As a young man he was strongly attracted to France. His mother regretted his decision to 'specialize later on French literature' (*L1*, 12). Eliot recollected that when 'it came to foreign writers' he was 'all for the French'. He went on to remark that during his 'romantic year' in Paris 'I had at the time the idea of giving up English and trying to settle down and scrape along in Paris and gradually write French.'[1] Far-fetched as this scheme might now appear, it would have seemed less so at the time when American expatriate writers such as Edith Wharton and Gertrude Stein resided in France. While Wharton and Stein wrote in English, other writers had attempted a complete linguistic switch: Natalie Clifford Barney, Stuart Merrill and Francis Vielé-Griffin had settled in France and had become fully assimilated Symbolist poets. Eliot therefore had living examples of successful literary emigration before him.

Still, why should Eliot plan a literary career in Paris rather than Boston, New York or (where he eventually settled) London? Many American writers had flocked to Chicago or New York. Moving to Paris was a more radical instance of what Jean Bessière has called 'the general unprovincialization of the artistic enterprise'.[2] In 1934, Eliot wrote: 'Younger generations can hardly realize the intellectual desert of England and America during the first decade and more of this century ... The predominance of Paris was incontestable.'[3] Paris was widely viewed during this period as 'the capital of the literary universe, the city with the greatest literary prestige in the world'.[4] It was the literary capital par excellence. Eliot himself recalled in a French wartime publication: 'Mais ce n'est pas un accident qui m'avait conduit à Paris. Depuis plusieurs années, la France représentait surtout, à mes yeux, la *poésie* ['I did not arrive in Paris by accident. For several years, in my eyes, France meant above all *poetry*'].[5] For him poetry meant French Symbolism descending from Charles Baudelaire, which he had come to know through Symons's book. In the work of Jules Laforgue, Tristan Corbière, above all, in Arthur Rimbaud and Stéphane Mallarmé, Eliot discovered one of the highest and strictest conceptions of poetry ever formulated: 'the world is made to end in a beautiful book', as Mallarmé put it in 1891.[6] This young American looked to French Symbolism as a way of renewing the English poetical tradition (see Chapter 21).

However, when Eliot arrived in Paris Mallarmé had been dead for more than a decade and Symbolism, in spite of some noteworthy survivors (including the movement's most celebrated critic, Remy de Gourmont),[7] was largely a thing of the past. He had arrived in the midst of a post-Symbolist era when the Parisian literary world was in the process of wholesale reconstruction, divided, without any clear leadership, between a vast array of movements. Broadly speaking, two dominant trends were beginning to emerge. The first, represented by Naturism and Unanimism, tried to go beyond Symbolism by sticking close to the realities of modern urban life, expressed through an unsentimental lyricism. Eliot found these experiments 'disappointing'.[8] Although his poetry treated the same urban milieux – fogs, gas-lamps, cafés, crowds and loneliness – examined in the work of Jules Romains, a leading figure of Unanimism, Eliot preferred to take Baudelaire and Laforgue as his masters. The other main trend was more anti-Symbolist or anti-Romantic. Under the banner of a *renaissance classique*, 'neoclassicism' was fighting a rearguard action against the 'decadence' of Symbolism, seeking to restore the great models of seventeenth-century French classicism: notably François de Malherbe and Jean Racine. From 1907 periodicals such as *Le Divan*, *Les Guêpes* and *La Revue Critique des Idées et des Livres* coupled this literary cause with political groups espousing monarchist reaction, the most prominent of which was Charles Maurras's Action Française. Powerful as the influence of Maurras's movement would be on Eliot, his support was never unequivocal.

The middle way between these polarising post-Symbolist trends was provided after 1909 by the monthly magazine *La Nouvelle Revue Française* (*NRF*), which was connected with a new Parisian publishing house founded by Gaston Gallimard and would become arguably the foremost French twentieth-century literary magazine. Through a remarkable coincidence, during his stay in Paris, Eliot took lessons in French conversation from Alain-Fournier, who was then in the process of writing his cult novel *Le Grand Meaulnes* (1912) and whose brother-in-law, Jacques Rivière, was the young secretary (later the chief editor) of *La Nouvelle Revue Française*. Although Eliot met Rivière only once during his stay in Paris, the *NRF* would become for him, as indeed for a whole generation of French writers, an exemplary literary journal (and a model for his own quarterly review, *Criterion*).[9] Back in America, Eliot took out a subscription to *NRF*. However, from his days in Paris he would have become familiar through its pages with two of the most important French poets of the twentieth century: Paul Claudel, whom Eliot recalled as 'already a great poet in the eyes of a younger generation',[10] and the future Nobel laureate Saint-John Perse, whose *Anabase* he translated in the mid 1920s (see Chapter 21). From 1922 until 1927, Eliot was the English correspondent of the *NRF*, and he was strongly influenced by the magazine's aesthetics, which advocated a modern classicism (to be distinguished from Maurras's 'neoclassicism') uniting such diverse writers as Paul Valéry, Charles-Louis Philippe, André Gide, Jacques Maritain, Julien Benda and Ramon Fernandez in a broadly Symbolist heritage.

It is worth recalling that when Eliot immersed himself in the intellectual life of Paris he was a visiting student. At the Sorbonne, a number of outstanding scholars were trying to promote the search for scientific objectivity in fields where subjectivity had been the dominant approach: for example, Pierre Janet in Psychology, Émile Durkheim and Lucien Lévy-Bruhl in Sociology, and Gustave Lanson in Literary Studies. This reformation of the teaching system was controversial but gave the Sorbonne an intellectual excitement that fascinated the young Eliot. He did not scorn Lanson's reverence for literary facts, once remarking that 'Shakespeare's laundry bills' (*SE*, 33) could provide a useful tool for the literary critic. In *The Sacred Wood* (1920), Eliot had quoted with approval Gourmont's injunction for the critic to 'Eriger en lois ses impressions personnelles' ['Establish as laws his personal impressions'] (*SW*, 1) and a penchant for scientific-sounding critical concepts – 'objective correlative', 'dissociation of sensibility' – may owe something to the climate of ideas he encountered at the Sorbonne.

However, it was not at the Sorbonne but rather listening to Henri Bergson's lectures across the rue Saint-Jacques at the Collège de France, that Eliot experienced his most stimulating academic studies in Paris. Bergson was then at the height of his celebrity. Open to all, his 5 o'clock Friday lectures were fashionable events that were attended in droves. When there was a danger that the lecture hall would be full, society ladies asked their chauffeurs to come early and reserve a seat. Between 13 January and 17 February 1911, Eliot slipped through the crowds to attend seven of Bergson's twenty weekly lectures. Considering how assiduously he took notes, Eliot clearly did not attend these lectures out of mere curiosity. Bergson's lectures addressed the nature of Personality. Against theories that postulated a multiplicity of states of consciousness that could not be unified, Bergson proposed a much simpler model. He pointed out that 'states of consciousness are only views taken by consciousness on a flowing continuity which really cannot be divided' and sought to demonstrate that 'the main personality disorders' – in particular, forms of 'psychological dissociation' – could be explained on this model.[11] According to a contemporary who attended these lectures, Bergson frequently borrowed ideas from his earlier books, such as this observation about memory from *L'Évolution créatrice* (1907):

In fact the past is kept automatically. No doubt it follows us at any time in its entirety: whatever we have felt, thought, wanted since our infancy is there, leaning over the present which is going to join it, pressing against the door of consciousness, which would like to leave it outside.[12]

In his notebook, Eliot wrote down these lines in French. He also underlined this sentence: 'Past, present and future are one, which abstraction decomposes.'[13] This calls to mind the opening of 'Burnt Norton' where 'Time present and time past / Are both perhaps present in time future / And time future contained in time past' (*CPP*, 171). And Eliot jotted down this approximation of the reflections on self by the eighteenth-century British philosopher David Hume: 'I always stumble on some particular perception. I never can catch myself.'[14] It is natural to compare these notes with Eliot's poetry, the evocative power of which lies in its ability to depict and place side by side with all their heterogeneousness different states of consciousness, allowing the reader full scope to speculate upon their mysterious continuity. According to Bergson, the greatest novelists make us believe in a character's reality by revealing it as composed of a thousand diverse impressions in conflict. In *Introduction à la métaphysique*, Bergson implores the novelist not to describe characters from the outside, but to produce an *interior* 'coincidence with the person itself'.[15] Eliot followed this lesson in his own poetry. He later spoke of his 'temporary conversion to Bergsonism' during his year in Paris.[16] For Christmas 1912, he gave his mother a new English translation – *The Introduction to a New Philosophy* – of Bergson's book. The English philosopher and critic T. E. Hulme, a significant influence on Eliot, also published a translation of this work in 1912.

However, Bergson's influence was soon to be countered by Eliot's acquaintance with other French writers. This could explain why he didn't attend all the lectures. Bergson's success was not achieved without controversy. His most prominent opponent was Julien Benda, who published virulent attacks on Bergson shortly after Eliot had left Paris, but which Eliot encountered in *Belphégor* (1918).[17] An uncompromising intellectual, Benda's rationalism and materialism were deeply opposed to the irrationalism and spiritualism in Bergson's writings. An attack on Bergson from the political right also attracted Eliot's attention. This right-wing anti-Bergsonism issued from Catholic (more particularly neo-Thomist) sources and was sometimes associated with anti-Semitism (Bergson was Jewish). In 1910 two newspapers, *L'Opinion* and *L'Action Française*, published harsh critiques of Bergson by 'Agathon' (the pen-name of Henri Massis and Alfred de Tarde) and by Pierre Lasserre. Eliot was familiar with these writers. He placed Lasserre's assault on French romanticism, *Le Romantisme français*, on the syllabus and reading list for his 1916 Oxford Extension 'Course of Six Lectures on Modern French Literature'.[18] In spite of their different political beliefs, Eliot recruited both Benda and Massis as contributors to the *Criterion*.

It was perhaps through Lasserre's work that Eliot became acquainted with the Action Française; at first a right-wing political newspaper, later a movement inspired by Charles Maurras, which flourished in France after the turn of the century and which was active in the Latin Quarter at the time Eliot resided there. In 1910 Eliot witnessed some of the violent demonstrations of the Camelots du Roi, the youth organisation of the Action Française. Eliot also had privileged access to the theories of the Action Française through the intermediary of his boarding-house companion Jean Verdenal, who was interested in the opinions of Maurras and his followers. Verdenal's letters testify that Eliot was aware of Maurrassien attacks on the *'critiques scientifiques'* (*L1*, 21) of the Sorbonne professors.

It is a well-known fact that Eliot dedicated *Prufrock and Other Observations* to the memory of Verdenal, who died serving as a medical officer during the First World War.

The Action Française advocated monarchism and neoclassicism; it used Catholicism as a political tool and was decidedly anti-Semitic. Pope Pius XI condemned the movement in 1926 (the ban was lifted in 1939). Although Eliot's famous 1928 proclamation that he was a 'classicist in literature, royalist in politics, and anglo-catholic in religion' (*FLA*, ix) seems to echo the spirit of Action Française, we must not underestimate the differences, indeed the clear divergences, between this declaration and the actual beliefs espoused by Maurras. Such a trio does not appear in Maurras's own writings, although it corresponds to a summary of his doctrines – '*classique, catholique, monarchique*' – proposed by Albert Thibaudet in an article published in the *NRF* in 1913.[19] Crucially, this trio is not directly translatable to a British context: the concept of classicism had never been as crucial in the history of English literature as it was for French criticism; any declaration of royalism made in Georgian England had none of the incendiary power it had in Republican France; nor was the status of Anglo-Catholicism in Britain interchangeable with the position of the Catholic Church in France. Eliot had to adapt and transpose the doctrines of the Action Française to make them applicable across the English Channel. His originality appears most clearly in his conception of classicism. Although he knew the anti-Romantic polemics popularised by Lasserre and Maurras (and shared some of their hostility), Eliot publicly repudiated the 'neoclassical' aesthetics associated with the Action Française.[20] His own classicism was not to be confused with either the 'neoclassicism' of the Action Française, fashionable before the First World War, nor the 'modern classicism' inspired by Rivière's *Nouvelle Revue Française* during the interwar period. Rather, Eliot's classicism was a creative aesthetic as well as a programmatic slogan, which was not incompatible with the formal experimentation exhibited by *The Waste Land* or James Joyce's *Ulysses*.

After less than a year in Paris, exceptionally intelligent though he was, Eliot came to appreciate the insurmountable difficulties that prevented him from becoming a French poet. Being 'alone in Paris', however, without ties of any kind, allowed him to cultivate a characteristic independence of mind: in spite of – perhaps because of – a variety of French influences, he developed a new conception of Anglo-American modernist literature. Mrs Eliot had worried too much about her son.

NOTES

1. 'Interview with T. S. Eliot', *Writers at Work:* The Paris Review *Interviews*, second series, ed. George Plimpton (Harmondsworth: Penguin, 1977), pp. 94–5.
2. Jean Bessière, *La Patrie à rebours: les écrivains américains de la generation perdue et la France, 1917–1935* (Lille: Université de Lille III, 1978), p. 135.
3. 'A Commentary', *Criterion* (April 1934), 451.
4. See Pascale Casanova, *La République mondiale des letters* (Paris: Seuil, 1999), p. 41.
5. 'What France Means to You', *France Libre* (15 June 1944), 94.
6. Stéphane Mallarmé, *Oeuvres completes*, vol. II, ed. Bertrand Marchal (Paris: Gallimard, 2003), p. 702.
7. Eliot modelled the 'perfect critic' in *The Sacred Wood* on Remy de Gourmont (see *SW*, 1–16).
8. 'Commentary', 451.
9. For Eliot's memories of Rivière, see 'Rencontre', *Nouvelle Revue Française* (1 April 1925), 657–8.
10. 'Foreword', *Contemporary French Poetry* by Joseph Chiari (Manchester University Press, 1952), pp. vii–xi.
11. See Henri Bergson, *Mélanges*, ed. André Robinet (Paris: Presses Universitaires de France, 1972), pp. 845–6.
12. Ibid., p. 848.
13. Notes on the lectures of Henri Bergson, Houghton Library, bMS Am 1691 (130), fol. 7, Harvard University. Permission to cite this unpublished material is granted by Mrs Valerie Eliot.
14. Ibid., fol. 6.
15. Henri Bergson, *Oeuvres*, ed. André Robinet (Paris: Presses Universitaires de France, 1959), p. 1394.
16. *A Sermon* (Cambridge University Press, 1948), p. 5.
17. In *The Sacred Wood*, Eliot remarked of Benda's *Belphégor* that 'Much of his analysis of the decadence of contemporary French society could be applied to London' (*SW*, 44–5).
18. For details, see Ronald Schuchard, *Eliot's Dark Angel* (Oxford University Press, 1999), pp. 27–32.
19. See Albert Thibaudet, 'L'Esthétique des trois traditions', *Nouvelle Revue Française* (March 1913), 355–93.
20. 'The term "neo-classicism" is not ours, and is not particularly commendable; for all "neos" indicate some fad or fashion of the moment, and it is not our concern to be fashionable.' 'A Commentary', *Criterion* (June 1927), 359–60.

CHAPTER 4

London

C. D. Blanton

LONDON! The needy villain's gen'ral home,
The common sewer of Paris, and of Rome;
With eager thirst, by folly or by fate,
Sucks in the dregs of each corrupted state.

(Samuel Johnson, 'London')[1]

How many? Count them. And such a press of people.
We hardly knew ourselves that day, or knew the City.

(*CPP*, 127)

By the time T. S. Eliot affixed his name to a poem entitled 'London' in 1930, he had maintained residence in this 'common sewer' of eight million 'dregs' for a decade and a half. He had abandoned a career in philosophy and a job in banking for the curial poses of an 'agèd eagle' (*CPP*, 89): director of Faber & Faber, oracular editor of the *Criterion*, the Pope of Russell Square. He had rendered his adopted 'Unreal City' (*CPP*, 62) as *The Waste Land* and assumed guardianship of a poetic movement well on its way to canonical orthodoxy. Accidents of birth aside, few figures could better voice the city's accent, and fewer still could claim to have mastered its poetic corruptions and virtues so thoroughly.

In 1930, however, Eliot borrowed the stance of another poet to describe the capital, introducing a limited edition of Samuel Johnson's 'London': 'among the greatest verse Satires of the English or any other language'.[2] In part, Eliot's essay attempts a mild self-correction, moderating his curt dismissal (offered in 1921) of those dissociated sensibilities condemned to a fractured experience after the English Civil War. Having lost 'a mechanism of sensibility which could devour any kind of experience' (*SE*, 287), poets like John Dryden and Johnson had compensated by writing satires, achieving a social 'precision' unavailable to later centuries. Eliot remarked that the Augustan satirist 'said what he wanted to say, with that urbanity which contemporary verse would do well to study; and the satisfaction I get from such lines is what I would call the *minimal* quality of poetry'.[3]

33

In Eliot's idiosyncratic estimation, this ambiguous lower threshold, where poetry becomes good if not great, satirical rather than sentimental, maintains both intensity and detachment. If it fails to reintegrate disordered experience, it also acknowledges the loss and imagines a form of sociability in its place. But the key word here is *urbanity*, a term packed with surreptitious allusive force. Before Johnson, Dryden had defined 'urbanity' as a refinement of manner, an elegant strain of wit: it lightens satire's touch but sharpens its political edge.[4] Eliot seizes upon the etymology of the word to wrench his critical language into a more precise meaning. In Johnson, he finds 'the most alien figure' among the poets of a 'rural, pastoral, meditative age', yet one almost inviting in his unsociability: 'a townsman, if certainly not a courtier; a student of mankind not of natural history; a great prose writer; with no tolerance of swains and milkmaids'.[5] If Johnson takes his place in London's 'gen'ral home' uneasily, the city itself offers a way of putting unease to use. In that paradox lies a strategy for partial reassociation: for Eliot, urbanity substitutes the city for a poetic subject, trading the experience of one for that of many and using London itself as a sensory prosthesis.

Eliot's urbanity is not merely a matter of carefully cultivated distance from American origins, English pastoral concerns and the uncounted press of demotic voices; it also implies a cultural identification with the polis. As Wyndham Lewis understood, the satirical mode that Eliot drew from figures like Johnson 'can only exist *in contrast* to something else', eliciting the counter-intuitive conclusion (for Lewis) that Eliot is also 'democratic *in spite* of himself'.[6] No less than tradition itself, Eliot's London provides a medium 'in which impressions and experiences combine in peculiar and unexpected ways' (*SE*, 20). It creates a new and collective mode of intentionality, an impersonal and only sporadically conscious fact shared thoughtlessly by millions: 'not what one man thought, but what several millions thought – what *nobody* thought really, in a sense, but what a great multitude passively sheltered in their consciousness'.[7] In this respect, the city in which Eliot lived and wrote for half a century is less a setting than the very substance of his work, the concrete form of a turbulent unconsciousness – his urbanity less a pose than an unwilled bond. In 1921, the same year that Eliot declared that 'poets in our civilization, as it exists at present, must be *difficult*' (*SE*, 289), he had fixed on this same notion of urbanity in an essay on Andrew Marvell: 'this modest and certainly impersonal virtue – whether we call it wit or reason, or even urbanity – we have patently failed to define. By whatever name we call it, and however we define that name, it is something precious and

needed and apparently extinct' (*SE*, 304). Despairing of an exact definition, Eliot ended the essay on a deliberately foreign note: 'C'était une
belle âme, comme on ne fait plus à Londres' ['It was a beautiful soul, such
as one no longer finds in London'] (*SE*, 304). The line enacts the very
thing deemed absent, dredging up and dislocating an alien phrase in the
act of claiming estranged residence. This is the contradiction of Eliot's
London: somehow distant and set apart, even at home.

In 1945, J. H. Oldham's *Christian News-Letter* published a series of
supplements debating the Beveridge Plan, the scheme for post-war reconstruction that laid the groundwork for the welfare state. Originating from
meetings of 'The Moot' (an ecumenical discussion group organised by
Oldham and including Eliot), the exchange opened with a brief essay
entitled 'Full Employment and the Responsibility of Christians', signed
by 'Civis'. Eliot responded with a challenge to Civis's conflation of
Keynesian economics with Christian doctrine, over the signature of
'a small businessman' named Metoikos [resident alien].[8] The pseudonym's
edge lies in its ironic identification with the underclass of Athenian
immigrants and slaves: deprived of full citizenship, without property or
political rights, *metoikoi* are defined by what they lack, belonging nowhere
in particular. Even the wry substitution of the Greek word for the Latin
insists upon a kind of homelessness, a translation between traditions.
In context, what Eliot's usage was primarily meant to underscore was
not his foreign origin (he had been a British subject since 1927), but
his larger resistance to the incursion of temporal claims into the realm
of religion. As with so many of Eliot's allusions, however, the figure of
Metoikos draws on a longer history of the term's use in his work, already
several decades old by 1945.

In a letter of July 1919 pondering what he would soon come to call
tradition, Eliot described a still inchoate '*historical sense*, which is not
simply knowledge of history, a sense of balance which does not deaden
one's personal taste, but trains one to discriminate one's own passions
from objective criticism'. The idea of a 'civilisation which is impersonal,
traditional ... and which forms people unconsciously' (*L1*, 378) would
assume greater force months later in the essays 'Tradition and the Individual Talent' and 'Hamlet and His Problems'. Privately, however, Eliot's
professed motivation remained more modest: 'But remember that I am
a *metic* – a foreigner, and that I *want* to understand you, and all the
background and tradition of you' (*L1*, 379). In 1919, as in 1945, Eliot's
sense of tradition is, among other things, an attempt to accommodate
the problem of the *metic*, turning alienation to advantage. From its first

attempt to channel the mind of Europe for 'English ears' (*SE*, 13), the
individual talent shows itself by not quite belonging, by its capacity (as
Robert Crawford puts it) 'to maintain two opposite, mutually reinforcing
stances, to be an insider and an outsider at once'.[9] The dual figures of civic
and metic, rooted and yet rootless, thus form the ground of an uneasy
dialectic that denatures both positions, forcing each into definitional
interdependence. But this tension also constitutes the polis as a unity
reducible to neither term, quietly invoking the city as the larger structure
within which relative terms of insider and outsider overlap. The metic, as
Jean-Michel Rabaté notes, 'derives his being and significance' from the
city as fully as the citizen, both politically and existentially.'[10] In Eliot's
private usage, then, the position of the metic does not preclude that of
the civic, but rather presupposes it, gathering both identities as aspects
of a larger whole.

In public, however, Eliot was already prepared to adopt the civic's
stance. Also in July 1919, under the title of 'A Foreign Mind', he used a
tart review of another resident alien to ponder 'the question of the form
of existence enjoyed by Mr Yeats'. Perplexed by the arcane nature of a
volume of the older poet's essays, Eliot attributes its eccentricity to a
difference 'not only personal, but national': 'Mr Yeats has spent altogether
a great deal of time in England and acquired here a degree of notoriety
without being or becoming an Englishman.' Consistently, Eliot trans-
poses the language of nation into that of 'existence'. Ultimately, he
ascribes Yeats's foreignness less to an exotic Irish tradition than to the
fundamental otherworldliness of its most prominent representative: to a
position 'not "of this world" – this world, of course, being our visible
planet with whatever theology or myth may conceive as below or above
it'.[11] Given Metoikos's own higher loyalties, the pose is ironic, but for
Eliot it underscores a contorted logic of cultural belonging, built upon
the intensity of perceptions made available in an unfamiliar place. For
Eliot, Yeats's foreignness is a function of neither language nor passport
(British in 1919, unlike Eliot's own), nor even the number of years spent
in London (where Yeats had settled before Eliot's birth), but rather
the simple refusal to acknowledge the concrete facts of the world he
inhabits. Unlike the metic in the city, Yeats registers little of the strange
place around him, and accordingly loses the urbanity that estrangement
makes possible.

Only weeks before reviewing Yeats, Eliot had approached the question
of foreignness more straightforwardly, contrasting the arrival of Henry

Adams in Liverpool with that of Henry James, another patrician en route to London. Eliot notes the imperviousness of Adams's 'American mind' to the 'appearances, aspects, images' that so fascinated James, 'experiences which are at once sensuous and intellectual', detached from the sentimental reflections of other places and poised to cultivate new senses in their stead.[12] Eliot's notion of residence is in effect a theory of sensations like these. Like Yeats's foreignness, Adams's stifling intellection eludes the worldly senses altogether, neglecting the profuse disorder that unconsciously binds the metic to the city, but also renders it legible. For Eliot, as for James, the metic recuperates a measure of lost experience by cultivating the unfamiliar.

Eliot's metics thus claim an authority derived from deracination, adopting a political language forever mediated by strangeness. But the cognates of metic and metoikos also recall another lurking etymology. In 1896, visiting Athens to see the first modern Olympic Games, the literary critic and political theorist Charles Maurras pondered the nineteenth-century city built on the ruins of its depopulated ancient predecessor and formulated the 'integral nationalism' that, on his return to France, guided the emergence of a new reactionary political movement.[13] With the founding of Action Française, Maurras combined monarchical sympathies, neoclassicist tastes and political Catholicism into the ideology that Eliot later borrowed to declare himself 'classicist in literature, royalist in politics, and anglo-catholic in religion' (*FLA*, ix). In the aftermath of the Dreyfus Affair, Maurras had placed the category of the *métèque* (a slur capacious enough to include foreigners, Jews, Protestants and republicans) at the centre of political debate. Eliot's own familiarity with Maurras, dating from 1910 and his reading of *L'Avenir de l'intelligence*,[14] culminates in his public defence of Action Française in the *Criterion* in 1928 against papal condemnation, and even his language confesses a debt to Maurras's reactionary politics. But there is an irony here. Whatever the depth of Eliot's complex form of reaction, it is worth noting that his persistent self-identification as *métèque* systematically inverts the force of Maurras's slur. As metic or metoikos, Eliot deliberately invokes an exclusionary language (with which he retains an unmistakable sympathy), only to count himself regularly among its outsiders. Eliot's politics require the metic in order to imagine a polis at all.

Indeed Eliot's London is a city of metics. From the first lines of 'Gerontion' and the extravagantly foreign tenants of its speaker's 'draughty house' (*CPP*, 38) to the 'first-met stranger' (*CPP*, 193) of

'Little Gidding', his 'body on a distant shore' (*CPP*, 194), Eliot's verse
swarms with interlopers, each activating the tension that Christopher
Ricks has cannily described as 'prejudice' – both a mode of unqualified
judgement and a persistent epistemological gap between impoverished
experience and the rich but unknown history that explains it. The thick
accumulation of negatives – 'neither', 'Nor', 'Nor' (*CPP*, 37) – that
introduce 'Gerontion' negotiates the disparity between a figure stripped
of all senses – 'I have lost my sight, smell, hearing, taste and touch'
(*CPP*, 38) – and a city peopled with strays displaced from other geographies: 'And the Jew squats on the window sill, the owner, / Spawned
in some estaminet of Antwerp, / Blistered in Brussels, patched and
peeled in London' (*CPP*, 37). Even the cruel anti-Semitic caricature
presents but the first among aliens, sounding a harsh keynote that
determines the sequence of stereotypes that follow – Mr Silvero,
Hakagawa, Madame de Tornquist, Fraülein von Kulp, De Bailhache,
Fresca, Mrs Cammel. Possessing an agency (whether bowing among
Titians or shifting candles) which Gerontion himself lacks, each of these
figures presents an aspect or image that underscores the city's resistance
to being known. In *The Waste Land*, the exotically ambiguous figures of
Madame Sosostris, Mrs Equitone and Mr Eugenides answer to the same
refrain; even Phlebas the Phoenician reproduces the paradox of the
Eliotic *métèque*, rhyming the 'You' of the poem's opening – 'You!
hypocrite lecteur! – mon semblable, – mon frère!' ['You! hypocrite
reader! – my twin, – my brother!'] (*CPP*, 63) – into a matter of doubt,
'Gentile or Jew / O you' (*CPP*, 71).

There is more to this effect, however, than a catalogue of displaced
names and lost origins. Like the 'Men and bits of paper, whirled by the
cold wind' in 'Burnt Norton', Eliot's Londoners seem to exist in transit,
entering and exiting the city on 'metalled ways / Of time past and time
future':

> Eructation of unhealthy souls
> Into the faded air, the torpid
> Driven on the wind that sweeps the gloomy hills of London,
> Hampstead and Clerkenwell, Campden and Putney,
> Highgate, Primrose and Ludgate.   (*CPP*, 174)

Wrenched from other places and cast into an aggregation where no one
quite lives, these ghastly souls are seemingly borne into phantasmagoric
gloom. This underworld image of London has origins in the nightmarish
visions of Dante and Charles Baudelaire, even in the haunted streets of

James Thomson's *The City of Dreadful Night*. In Eliot's version, however, spectres assume concrete form, concentrated in the financial district of the City:

> Unreal City,
> Under the brown fog of a winter dawn,
> A crowd flowed over London Bridge, so many,
> I had not thought death had undone so many.
> Sighs, short and infrequent, were exhaled,
> And each man fixed his eyes before his feet.
> Flowed up the hill and down King William Street,
> To where Saint Mary Woolnoth kept the hours
> With a dead sound on the final stroke of nine.   (*CPP*, 62)

Obscured by layers of allusion, the literalism of this passage's topography is easily missed. As the crowd mimics (but strangely inverts) the river's motion to flow over the bridge and up the hill, it converges in the heart of the City, where the church of Saint Mary Woolnoth stands at the intersection of King William and Lombard streets, near the Bank of England, the Stock Exchange and Eliot's own office at Lloyds Bank. Significantly, Eliot's sly annotation to the 9 o'clock chimes of Mary Woolnoth – 'A phenomenon which I have often noticed' (*CPP*, 77) – stages one of the poem's few unmediated appeals to experience. But that experience situates the poem's perception within the mass of commuters, a faceless class of clerks and typists. The strength of the association depends in turn on another elided detail. For Eliot's deathly crowds are summoned not merely from Dante's underworld, but also from the London Underground's Bank station, which at the turn of the twentieth century had displaced the eighteenth-century crypt of Nicholas Hawksmoor's Baroque church.

The passage is not unique. *The Waste Land* maps the city it inhabits, co-ordinating symbolic superstructures with an infrastructure lying beneath them, ultimately connecting London to the distant points from which strangers arrive. Mr Eugenides's Cannon Street Hotel thus adjoins Cannon Street station, built on the site of an old Hanseatic trade mission to link the Underground with stations south of the Thames and trains to the Continent. The song of the Thames daughters names the commuter stations – Richmond and Kew to the west, Highbury and Moorgate to the north – that connect the suburbs of Greater London to the City proper. The barges off Greenwich and the Isle of Dogs conjure up the East End docklands. Indeed, the poem consistently imagines London as a series of strategic entry points through which commodities (human and otherwise) pass. Each topographical element thus marks a node in the mundane network that subtends the City, creating a persistent allusive undertone that devolves its historical high culture into pedestrian mass experience. But these secondary references are almost never specified explicitly. Unlike James Joyce's Dublin, Eliot's London traffics in associative geographies which are rarely articulated but which carry much of the poem's force: routine patterns of entry, exit and exchange invested with elusive significance.

To the degree that Eliot's commuters are metics, the City's monuments are adapted to new purposes. In his May 1921 'London Letter' to the New York *Dial*, Eliot insinuated as much when he discussed a proposal to demolish nineteen City churches:

Probably few American visitors, and certainly few natives, ever inspect these disconsolate fanes; but they give to the business quarter of London a beauty which its hideous banks and commercial houses have not quite defaced. Some are by Christopher Wren himself, others by his school; the least precious redeems some vulgar street, like the plain little church of All Hallows at the end of London Wall. Some, like St Michael Paternoster Royal, are of great beauty. As the prosperity of London has increased, the City churches have fallen into desuetude; for their destruction the lack of congregation is the ecclesiastical excuse, and the need of money the ecclesiastical reason. The fact that the erection of these churches was apparently paid for out of a public coal tax and their decoration probably by their parishioners, does not seem to invalidate the right of the True Church to bring them to the ground. To one who, like the present writer, passes his days in this City of London (*quand'io seniti chiavar l'uscio di sotto*) the loss of these towers, to meet the eye down a grimy lane, and of these empty naves, to receive the solitary visitor at noon from the dust and tumult of Lombard Street, will be irreparable and unforgotten.[15]

Juxtaposed against modern monuments to finance, these condemned churches stand in cross-reference to the City geography of *The Waste Land*, projecting the double vision of a day worker at lunch. The line quoted from Dante's *Inferno* – 'quand'io seniti chiavar l'uscio di sotto' ['When I heard the door below being nailed shut'] – figures the financial district as a prison, associating the City's 'Falling towers' (*CPP*, 73) with Count Ugolino's 'all'orribile torre' (*CPP*, 80). The same reference appears in Eliot's note to line 411, reimagined as one of F. H. Bradley's 'finite centres' of perception: 'My external sensations are no less private to my self than are my thoughts or my feelings' (*CPP*, 80). Elsewhere, Eliot folds the same churches into a momentary urban ode:

O City city, I can sometimes hear
Beside a public bar in Lower Thames Street,
The pleasant whining of a mandoline
And a clatter and a chatter from within
Where fishmen lounge at noon: where the walls
Of Magnus Martyr hold
Inexplicable splendour of Ionian white and gold.   (*CPP*, 69)

Setting fishmen in Billingsgate Market against the poem's Fisher King, the passage mobilises several senses at once, while Eliot's laconic note isolates a visual impression from the smell of the market and the sound of the mandoline: 'The interior of St Magnus Martyr is to my mind one of the finest among Wren's interiors. See *The Proposed Demolition of Nineteen City Churches*. (P. S. King & Son Ltd.)' (*CPP*, 78).[16] The note invokes the report, commissioned by the Bishop of London, which inspired Eliot's reflections in his 'London Letter'. It also implicitly marks a series of associations on which the poem pivots. Of the hundred City churches damaged or destroyed by the Great Fire of 1666, fewer than fifty survived to the twentieth century. For centuries the tower of Magnus Martyr had stood at the northern end of old London Bridge. Destroyed in 1666, rebuilt by Wren but ravaged again by fire in 1760, Magnus Martyr (like Mary Woolnoth) was one of the nineteen City churches slated for demolition, anachronisms in a modern commercial district depopulated of parishioners.

Eliot's annotation unobtrusively conjures up both the present church and its serial incarnations: the lost original (1666); Wren's interior (1676) long since damaged (1760), and soon to be lost entirely (*c.* 1921). But the poem transfigures such historical details as detached sensory fragments, from the Great Fire – 'Burning burning burning burning' (*CPP*, 70) – to the destruction of old London Bridge – 'falling down falling down falling down' (*CPP*, 74) – to the proposed demolition of City churches – 'Falling towers' (*CPP*, 73). Such cryptic echoes travel beneath hearing, but cumulatively they add London to the poem's litany of cities: 'Jerusalem Athens Alexandria / Vienna London / Unreal' (*CPP*, 73). London's inclusion among fallen capitals simultaneously ennobles and evacuates the City, but the repetition of 'Unreal' countenances a larger claim. For Eliot, the student of Bradley's philosophy, the idea of reality bears technical weight, denoting 'simply that which is intended' (*KEPB*, 36), thus specifying a mode of philosophical attention (a sort of urbanity) yet to be paid to the City. By consigning London to its metics – Johnson's 'dregs of each corrupted state' – Eliot imagines a London made real.

NOTES

1. Samuel Johnson, *London: A Poem and The Vanity of Human Wishes*, with an introductory essay by T. S. Eliot (London: Frederick Etchells and Hugh MacDonald, 1930), p. 24.
2. Ibid., p. 15.
3. Ibid., p. 16.
4. See 'A Discourse Concerning the Original and Progress of Satire' (1693), *Essays of John Dryden*, ed. W. P. Ker (New York: Russell & Russell, 1961), pp. 75, 84.
5. 'Introductory Essay', *London: A Poem*, p. 15.
6. Wyndham Lewis, *Men Without Art* (Santa Rosa: Black Sparrow Press, 1987), pp. 89, 57.
7. Ibid., p. 66.
8. 'Full Employment and the Responsibility of Christians', *Christian News-Letter* (21 March 1945), 7–12.
9. Robert Crawford, *Devolving English Literature* (Oxford: Clarendon Press, 1992), p. 223.
10. Jean-Michel Rabaté, 'Tradition and T. S. Eliot', *The Cambridge Companion to T. S. Eliot*, ed. A. D. Moody (Cambridge University Press, 1994), p. 212.
11. 'A Foreign Mind' (review of *The Cutting of an Agate*), *Athenaeum* (4 July 1919), 552.
12. 'A Sceptical Patrician', *Athenaeum* (23 May 1919), 362.
13. See Charles Maurras, 'La Ville moderne', *Athinea: d'Athènes à Florence* (Paris: Librairie Champion, 1919), pp. 284–96.
14. *L'Avenir de l'intelligence* was one of the six texts recommended by Eliot as exemplifying a 'modern tendency' of 'classicism'. See 'The Idea of a Literary Review', *Criterion* (January 1926), 5.
15. 'London Letter', *Dial* (June 1921), 690–1.
16. According to Eliot's student John Betjeman: 'The whole district smells of fish, but inside the church [Magnus Martyr] there is an abrupt change.' See *The City of London Churches* (London: Pitkin Pictorials, 1965), p. 22.

CHAPTER 5

Englishness

Simon Grimble

Still I feel that I don't understand the English very well.

(*L1*, 61)

In September 1914, writing from Bloomsbury, just prior to going to study at Oxford, T. S. Eliot gave his cousin Eleanor Hinkley his impressions of the English. In particular, he contemplates their habits of reserve, a sense that their personalities remained in some sense out of sight, partly because they seem to be 'conventional'. Eliot portrays himself as perplexed by this:

I don't know just what conventionality is; it doesn't involve snobbishness, because I am a thorough snob myself; but I should have thought of it as perhaps the one quality which all my friends lacked. And I'm sure that if I did know what it was, among men, I should have to find out all over again with regard to women. (*L1*, 61)

Eliot cheerfully admits here to his own 'snobbishness', a keen if anxious sense of social superiority, but he is mystified by this other category of 'conventionality', with its capacity to make the identity of others inscrutable and to make those who are not conventional (that is, Eliot and his friends, but implicitly Americans in general) unsure about where they stand in relation to these baffling people. Eliot's conclusion is that 'Perhaps when I learn how to take Englishmen, this brick wall will cease to trouble me.'

Clearly, Eliot does not expect this 'brick wall' to disappear but merely to become something he might be able to take for granted. But in September 1914 he has not yet reached this point, insisting 'it's ever so much easier to know what a Frenchman or an American is thinking about, than an Englishman. Perhaps partly that a Frenchman is so analytical and self-conscious that he dislikes to have anything going on inside him that he can't put into words, while an Englishman is content simply to live'. Eliot goes on to link this lack of self-consciousness with a kind of gentlemanly ease, which can then also be utilised for patriotic and military purposes ('that's the way they have been fighting in France'). On the other hand, 'the French way has an intellectual honesty about it that the English very seldom attain to. So there you are' (*L1*, 62). The liveliness of his engagement here shows the depth of his involvement in these necessarily broad-brush and comparative issues. Eliot was himself clearly so 'analytical and self-conscious' that he disliked having 'anything going on inside him' that he couldn't 'put into words' and yet the inscrutability, the impersonality perhaps, of the English clearly also allowed room for a more private, less observed self, which could mean that one could be, on the one hand, 'content simply to live' and, on the other, be prepared for the kind of unostentatious self-sacrifice that Eliot discerned in English conduct during the newly begun First World War (of course, this rather aristocratic way of thinking was soon to be challenged by the demands of the next four years of trench warfare). And yet, Eliot's very liveliness and openness seems to continue to be in some ways characteristically *American*: he is here the candid descendant of Ralph Waldo Emerson's *English Traits*, another American abroad in England.

Perhaps the key element here is that these various national identities are seen by Eliot as, in a sense, alternatives to each other which one could, in effect, *choose* between. At this time, Eliot had already lived for a year in Paris. He had considered the possibility of becoming a poet who lived permanently in France and who wrote in French (see Chapter 3 above). That idea had been abandoned on the grounds that it seemed a romantic, vaguely bohemian longing that had to give way to the demands of familial responsibility and, at this stage in Eliot's life, the call of an academic career in philosophy. But the notion of choosing an alternative country and language, rather than making an accommodation with those to which Eliot was native, had already been broached. To Eliot's mind, one could decide which country to affiliate oneself to, rather than passively accepting the terms of what one was born into. This was to prove to be the pattern of Eliot's life: in the long term he affiliated himself to England by marrying in 1915 an Englishwoman, Vivien Haigh-Wood; by dedicating himself to the pursuit of his literary career in London; by becoming a member of the Church of England (a *national* church, unlike the forms of Christianity that existed in America, with its separation between church and state, or the universalism of Catholicism) in 1927; and by becoming a British citizen in the same year. Eliot would continue to live in England until his death in 1965, although he visited America frequently in the last thirty-five years of his life and seemed, to some observers, more conspicuously at home there. The Scottish writer and translator Willa Muir met

Eliot in America in 1950 and noted that, 'Tom Eliot is much more human here than in England'.[1] Muir's term recalls the question asked by the Dutch historian Gustaaf Renier in his 1931 book *The English: Are They Human?*: one might say that Eliot had chosen, through these decisions, to become less human, in other words, to become English.

In that sense, Eliot brought the question of national belonging into the realm where he existed as a writer: the realm of choice. One could decide to be English, just as one could decide that 'April is the cruellest month' (*CPP*, 61) or that 'The existing monuments form an ideal order amongst themselves' (*SE*, 15) or that contemporary history was indeed 'an immense panorama of futility and anarchy' (*SP*, 177). But of course, Eliot was rather singular in making these decisions. Ezra Pound never gave up his Americanness, in spite of his hostility to its culture. William Carlos Williams saw Eliot's adoption of Englishness as a kind of betrayal – he famously said that the publication of *The Waste Land*, with its deracinated and also somehow academic vision, 'set me back twenty years' in his attempts to find 'a new art form', one which was 'rooted in the locality which should give it fruit'.[2] There was a kind of reversed Americanness about Eliot's decision. Since its foundation, America had been a country open to immigration; to become American was certainly something that one could aspire to and realise – it was an elective identity. To become English, on the other hand, was in one sense impossible. One can choose to become, with state approval, a British subject, as Eliot did, and in that way a full member of the nation of the United Kingdom of Great Britain and Northern Ireland, with concomitant rights of participation in the political process. However, as England was not a state in 1928 (and it is not one now), one cannot become *English* by any procedural mechanism. Instead it is a question of approximation: partly of inheritance (having English parents confers Englishness on their children, even when they are raised outside of England), partly a matter of everyday life (as with any foreigner in England realising that 'I am becoming very English in my tea-drinking habits / awkwardness in class-relations'). But in this precise sense, for Eliot to become English, rather than British, was a kind of category mistake (the kind of entity that horrified Eliot's 'rage for order'): he was trying to become something it was, technically, impossible to become.

Of course, this is to push the argument too far. Since England was not a state during Eliot's lifetime, there was no test one had to pass in order to become English. Instead, Eliot was entering into a matrix of under-standings, more or less implicit, where much was taken for granted but where the ability to distinguish oneself from English culture, while at the same time maintaining its outward forms, could, in fact, be an advantage. Certainly, the boldness, the certainty, with which Eliot addressed English culture gave him an authority most of his English literary contemporaries could not match. Part of that authority came from a sense of being free of both the history and the cultural assumptions he was now addressing. After first meeting Eliot, Ezra Pound wrote to Harriet Monroe, the editor of *Poetry* (Chicago), to say that 'it is such a comfort to meet a man and not to have to tell him to wash his face, wipe his feet, and remember the date (1914) on the calendar'. Part of his emphasis was on the cleanness of Eliot's break with the past: he was unmarked by history and particularly by the compromises and confusions of English history.[3] For Pound, Eliot was therefore better able to make a break with the dead weight of the recent poetic and cultural past. Piers Gray has characterised Eliot's position in English culture as that of the stranger or outsider who has something of the perspective of the anthropologist, visiting distant lands but gifted with an exterior objectivity:

free to judge his new culture, assert its 'true' values and even introduce dimensions of alien cultures – with which, of necessity, he is familiar – to his trusting hosts. And indeed it is no accident, therefore, that so much emphasis should be laid upon theories of objectivity by the stranger himself: objective correlatives, impersonal theories of poetry, scientific analogies, tradition itself, all sustain the very ideals of which, as the stranger, he himself is an embodiment.[4]

Eliot's position as an outsider can be compared with Philip Larkin's experience of living in Belfast, as presented in the 1955 poem 'The Importance of Elsewhere'. Larkin writes that when 'Lonely in Ireland, since it was not home, / Strangeness made sense'. The final quatrain, however, contrasts this experience of 'difference', which makes the poet feel both 'in touch' and 'separate, not unworkable', with his present situation:

> Living in England has no such excuse:
> These are my customs and establishments
> It would be much more serious to refuse.
> Here no elsewhere underwrites my existence.[5]

There is a sense in which Eliot in England was also 'separate, not unworkable'. He could make his way in his career as a poet and man of letters, and become an authority, while English competitors would have a greater sense of England's 'customs and establishments', which it would be 'much more serious to refuse'; as if that refusal would be tantamount to an act of betrayal, even treason. Eliot was freer to make judgements about English customs and establishments, freer to revise them or abandon them, because he had the authority of the outsider; the outsider who could present himself *as* authority, but an authority that comes from elsewhere, an authority that is therefore not fully explained nor understood but who can formulate and bring to order existing anxieties. There is, of course, a degree of isolation for the outsider: displaced and not completely understood, he has no home in this world and must improvise a commercial existence. For Eliot, this meant working at Lloyds Bank and later for the publishing house of Faber & Faber, but writing was also one of his trades: in his poetry and criticism he was involved in the commodification of himself, in selling versions of himself to an audience, but he also had to take pains to look distinct from commercial culture in order for that carefully cultivated authority not to disappear.

It was not easy for all of these tensions to be held in balance. It was clearly not possible to remain the outsider or the anthropologist: after a time Eliot became a leading member of the literary establishment he had helped to unsettle. In that sense, the alien culture became one that Eliot himself was partly responsible for and implicated in. Eliot became fully aware of this. In January 1918 he had contributed his essay 'In Memory of Henry James' to the *Egoist*, which had begun with the brazen line, 'Henry James has been dead for some time' (it had been less than two years since James's death in February 1916), seemingly dismissing James and the literary culture he represented. But following that opening gambit (and it *is* a gambit), Eliot turns to a more thoughtful consideration of James as a cosmopolitan American resident in an England that is also clearly part of, rather than distinct from, a wider Europe: 'It is the final perfection, the consummation of an American to become, not an Englishman, but a European – something which no born European, no person of any European nationality can become'.[6] In this view, both James and Eliot are the true inheritors of the finest and most durable aspects of European civilisation, because they are unmarked by the petty nationalisms that divide Europe (and that also, at the time of Eliot's writing, have transformed Europe into a theatre of war, while the cultural scene has been pervaded by nationalist propaganda on all sides).[7] In this sense, however, England can be pictured as a stepping stone, an entry point, a giant port town for an American abroad, whose use of England can then possibly be equally instrumental. The high culture of England can therefore provide just some aspects of the 'heap of broken images' (*CPP*, 61) that *The Waste Land* describes (even if Eliot would come to sit on top of that heap), placed alongside the rest of international civilisation that it calls on, with all of its ancient and modern, eastern and western aspects. But by assimilating himself to English culture, Eliot would not be able to maintain such feelings of distance or qualified superiority. Even by the time of the publication of *The Sacred Wood* in 1920, Eliot was confessing, although perhaps in veiled terms, identification with one particular recent English critic who could pretend to be neither an anthropologist nor an outsider:

> Arnold is not to be blamed: he wasted his strength, as men of superior ability sometimes do, because he saw something to be done and no-one else to do it. The temptation, to any man who is interested in ideas and primarily in literature, to put literature into the corner until he cleaned up the whole country first, is almost irresistible. (*SW*, xiii)

What Eliot is considering here is the turn in Arnold's career from being a poet to becoming a public moralist, even perhaps a 'sage', who had turned from a primary concern with 'literature' to the more general cultural and social health of the nation. Eliot is, ostensibly, regretting this turn: it is a waste of Arnold's 'strength' and it is not, by implication, a mistake that Eliot is planning to make himself. Instead, his emphasis is on the austerity and professionalism needed for the task of renovating the state of literature in England, rather than being foolishly, regrettably, accidentally, drawn into putting 'literature into the corner until he cleaned up the whole country first'. Eliot seems to be suggesting that there was a kind of aristocratic amateurishness about Arnold's resignation to this actually Herculean and impossible task: there was certainly a touch of 'nobility' about it. But what this moment also seems to suggest is that Eliot was imagining similarly absurd ideas in himself: his family's Unitarian background had certainly prepared him for a life of selfless and public spirited endeavour. But this very desire necessarily involves getting your hands dirty, and therefore prevents the possibility of remaining as Pound's young man of 1914, who had 'washed his face' and 'wiped his feet'. Furthermore, Eliot also seems to be confessing that it is England that he cannot altogether get clear of from this point forward, that it is its problems that he will have to, at least in part, engage with and think through. In that sense, Eliot is in the process of adapting himself to the demands of becoming a descendant of Matthew Arnold's public moralist; that is, in the idiom of the twentieth century, an intellectual. Through his ventures as an editor, as a literary and cultural critic, and as a publicist for the values he was trying to promote, Eliot increasingly became a public figure, eventually a sufficiently representative spokesman to be entrusted with the task of giving wartime radio broadcasts on the BBC.

In all these roles, Eliot managed to become more and more prominent in Britain and internationally, especially during and after the Second World War, but he also began to meld partially into the background, to acquire, if not to build, the 'brick wall' of conventionality and privacy that he had noticed as an English trait upon his arrival in London in 1914. He had acquired the forms of upper-middle-class social life: he spoke with the accent of 'received pronunciation', dressed in a conventional suit, carried a furled umbrella, and was a member of gentlemen's clubs. His Englishness now had some fairly precise markers, gesturing towards the adoption of elements of that Arnoldian inheritance mentioned above. It must be admitted that this reflects only an extremely *partial* version of the broadest experiences of English life in the period from 1914 to the year of Eliot's death, in 1965. It does not embrace the experiences of women; or of the working class (over three-quarters of the population during the interwar years); or of various regional identities, especially in the industrial north of England; or even of immigrants like and unlike himself. At the same time, Eliot did reflect an England that was marked by strongly centralising trends, to which the two world wars gave a particular impetus, handing a power to the state that Matthew Arnold could only have wondered at. The BBC accent that Eliot arrived at was also the desired accent for many English people during this period: it was a collective construction, designed to distinguish the speaker both from aristocratic tones of voice and from other 'lower' tendencies, just as Eliot's speech and identity were a more radical and willed personal construction.

But the main reason that Eliot made such a personal investment in England was for the privacy this very Englishness allowed. The forms of southern, upper-middle-class Englishness that he assumed enabled Eliot to adopt another one of his masks. Richard Sennett has observed that 'wearing a mask is the essence of civility. Masks permit pure sociability, detached from the circumstances of power, malaise, and private feeling of those who wear them'.[8] So, the adoption of such a mask allowed Eliot to circulate, comparatively frictionlessly, in various English worlds – of banking, of literary life, of publishing. But because it was a mask, there was at least the possibility that it could be temporarily discarded, put aside, therefore leaving room for other identities to exist beneath. This means that Eliot could occasionally express some considerable distance from English preoccupations: in a letter of 1945 to the *Christian News-Letter*, he signed himself 'Metoikos', Greek for 'resident alien'. In this instance, Eliot was showing his distance from, as well as a possible fear of rejection by, the English, in ways that could be said to be shadowed in his poetry. In 'East Coker', Eliot imagined an end to the social and commercial worlds to which he had become a part:

> O dark dark dark. They all go into the dark,
> The vacant interstellar spaces, the vacant into the vacant,
> The captains, merchant bankers, eminent men of letters,
> The generous patrons of art, the statesmen and the rulers,
> Distinguished civil servants, chairmen of many committees,
> Industrial lords and petty contractors, all go into the dark,
> And dark the Sun and Moon, and the Almanach de Gotha
> And the Stock Exchange Gazette, the Directory of Directors,
> And cold the sense and lost the motive of action.   (*CPP*, 180)

Just as Eliot used Englishness to move frictionlessly through these worlds, from his religious perspective all these worlds will slide equally frictionlessly into the dark of 'the vacant interstellar spaces'. Eliot was both able to employ Englishness and to contemplate its disappearance with cosmic equanimity. In that sense, the concerns of England could be projected on to a universal screen, where they are pictured as both representative and transcendable, in some sense unimportant.

Eliot's example allows us to gauge the force of Donald Davie's (admittedly rather blanket) characterisation of the difference between English and American poets, as well as the difference between English and American identity:

The Englishman supposes he is trying to operate in some highly specific historical situation, conditioned by manifold contingencies (hence his qualifications, his hesitancies, his damaging concessions), whereas the American poet, conditioned since the Pilgrim Fathers to think in utopian terms, is sure that he is enacting a drama of which the issues are basically simple and permanent, and will be seen to be once we have penetrated through their accidental, historical overlay.[9]

In Davie's terms, Eliot had managed to enter into the 'manifold contingencies' of England and had even participated in the qualifications, the hesitancies and the damaging concessions. But underneath this (or perhaps above it), Eliot was also inclined to think he was 'enacting a drama of which the issues are basically simple and permanent'. This inner structure of mind, then, informs the ways in which Eliot writes about England: London becomes a universal city in *The Waste Land* – closer to Babel, Sodom and Gomorrah than to, say, Birmingham. At the same time, Eliot can demonstrate a tin ear when discussing the social fabric of Britain. In 'The Function of Criticism', he asserts that, 'The possessors of the inner voice ride ten in a compartment to a football match at Swansea, listening to the inner voice, which breathes the eternal message of vanity, fear and lust' (*SE*, 27). The possessors of the inner voice may do just that, morally speaking, nevertheless sports fans in south Wales in the period were far more likely to be going to a rugby match than a football match. But as his career progressed, Eliot's choice of England hardened into what he had become. In his wartime poem 'Defence of the Islands', he shared and amplified national anxieties for an American public, declaring himself one 'for whom the paths of glory are / the lanes and the streets of Britain' (*CPP*, 201), even if many other 'elsewheres' of time and place shadowed those very paths.

NOTES

1. Quoted in Peter Ackroyd, *T. S. Eliot* (London: Hamish Hamilton, 1984), p. 301.
2. William Carlos Williams, *The Autobiography of William Carlos Williams* (New York: New Directions, [1951] 1967), p. 174.
3. *The Letters of Ezra Pound 1907–1941*, ed. D. D. Paige (London: Faber & Faber, 1950), p. 80.
4. See Piers Gray, *Marginal Men: Edward Thomas, Ivor Gurney, J. R. Ackerley* (London: Macmillan, 1991).
5. Philip Larkin, *Collected Poems* (London: Faber & Faber, 1988), p. 104.
6. 'In Memory of Henry James', *Egoist* (January 1918), 1.
7. For an example of a vitriolic wartime attack on Prussian culture, see Ford Madox Ford, *When Blood is their Argument* (London: Hodder & Stoughton, 1915).
8. Richard Sennett, *The Fall of Public Man* (Cambridge University Press, 1974), p. 264.
9. Donald Davie, *Thomas Hardy and British Poetry* (London: Routledge & Kegan Paul, 1973), p. 186.

CHAPTER 6

The idea of Europe

Jeroen Vanheste

After the First World War, in which 16 million people died, and before the outbreak of the Second World War, in which even more would die, T. S. Eliot strove for a reconciliation of past divisions by emphasising 'the idea of a common culture of Western Europe'.[1] This idea of Europe as a cultural unity was promoted in the literary review *Criterion*, which he founded in 1922 and edited until its demise in New Year 1939. In fact, throughout the 1920s there existed an informal network of like-minded European periodicals, including the *Criterion* in Britain, *La Nouvelle Revue Française* in France, *Europäische Revue*, *Neue Deutsche Beiträge* and *Die Neue Rundschau* in Germany, and *Revista de Occidente* in Spain. Prominent European intellectuals such as Eliot, the Viennese poet and playwright Hugo von Hofmannsthal, the German novelist Thomas Mann, the German professor of literature Ernst Robert Curtius, the French philosopher Julien Benda and the Spanish philosopher José Ortega y Gasset contributed regular essays to these reviews. Although the views and opinions of these European intellectuals often diverged, they shared a common conception of the importance of the European cultural tradition. As a reviewer in the *Criterion*, discussing an essay by Mann published in *Die Neue Rundschau*, put it: 'Intellectual differences may be the cement of international friendship, provided there is mutual respect and a common consciousness of a fundamental common tradition.'[2] Eliot referred to this common tradition as 'classicism': this chapter explores his changing perception of the European cultural heritage.

From its inception, the *Criterion* was European rather than British in scope. In a letter to Curtius, Eliot explained that the aim of his review was 'to raise the standard of thought and writing in this country by both international and historical comparison' (*L1*, 710). In order to achieve this aim, Eliot sought to recruit overseas writers who shared his European perspective. He found examples of pan-European intellectual co-operation in the past. Writing of the Elizabethan Anglican divines Richard Hooker and Lancelot Andrewes, Eliot admired their 'breadth of culture, an ease with humanism and Renaissance learning, which helped to put them on terms of equality with their continental antagonists ... they were Europeans' (*SE*, 343). Looking back on his editorship of the *Criterion* in a 1946 radio broadcast entitled 'The Unity of European Culture', Eliot emphasised this European dimension. 'In starting this review,' he explained, 'I had the aim of bringing together the best in new thinking and new writing in its time, from all the countries of Europe that had anything to contribute to the common good' (*NTDC*, 115). Indeed, the *Criterion* quickly established relations with men of letters across Europe. A good example is the German scholar Ernst Robert Curtius, an expert on modern French literature who published essays on Marcel Proust and Honoré de Balzac in the *Criterion* and who translated *The Waste Land* into German in 1927. Curtius considered himself a '*civis Romanus*' and a 'German Roman': he was a cosmopolitan who had contacts with many European men of letters, including André Gide, Paul Valéry, Charles du Bos, Hofmannsthal, Eliot and Ortega y Gasset. In a *Criterion* editorial, Eliot wrote of Curtius that he was 'one of those men such as Gide and Larbaud in France, Hofmannsthal in Austria and Ortega y Gasset in Spain, who have steadily laboured in the interest of the European spirit'.[3] Eliot later recalled that 'no name is more representatively that of the *European* man of letters, than the name of Ernst Robert Curtius'.[4] Curtius himself, looking back with nostalgia on the cosmopolitan spirit of the 1920s, reminisced:

But how many paths and encounters there were in the spiritually relaxed Europe of the time! Rilke translated poems by Valéry, who showed them to me in manuscript. At [Max] Scheler's I saw the first issue of Ortega's *Revista de Occidente*. Valery Larbaud introduced [James] Joyce in France. Sylvia Beach's bookstore, 'Shakespeare and Company', was an international meeting-place ... A Europe of the mind – above politics, in spite of all politics – was very much alive. This Europe lived not only in books and periodicals but also in personal relations.[5]

Sometimes these personal relations were formal, at other times they were friendships cemented by the exchange of letters over many years. Eliot met Curtius only twice, but they corresponded for over thirty years. Although their relationship cooled somewhat in later years, their friendship survived. In a letter Eliot wrote for a *Festschrift* in honour of his friend, published shortly after Curtius's death, he declared: 'I owe him a great debt ... for it was he who first brought my work to the notice of the German public.'[6]

Crucial to the European orientation of the *Criterion* were the regular reviews of foreign periodicals that appeared from 1923 onwards. Eliot actively sought to establish a network for intellectual exchange between comparable European reviews. He recalled:

the existence of such a network of independent reviews, at least one in every capital of Europe, is necessary for the transmission of ideas – and to make possible the circulation of ideas while they are still fresh. The editors of such reviews, and if possible the more regular contributors, should be able to get to know each other personally, to visit each other, to entertain each other, and to exchange ideas in conversation ... their co-operation should continually stimulate that circulation of influence of thought and sensibility, between nation and nation in Europe, which fertilises and renovates from abroad the literature of each one of them. (*NTDC*, 116)

It is important to remember that this intellectual co-operation was established on the basis of a shared cultural tradition. Eliot asserted:

The Criterion was only one of a number of reviews similar in character and purpose, in France, Germany, Switzerland, Italy, Spain and elsewhere; and my own interest in making my contemporaries in other countries known in England, responded to the interests of the editors and contributors of these other reviews.[7]

Numerous foreign periodicals were discussed in the *Criterion*, especially *Nouvelle Revue Française*, *La Revista de Occidente* edited by Ortega y Gasset, and *Neue Deutsche Beiträge* edited by Hofmannsthal, which shared a comparable approach to European culture. Aside from its foreign reviews section, the international outlook of the *Criterion* was apparent in the chronicles of foreign literature, which described the contemporary literary and cultural activity in France, Germany, Italy, Spain, Soviet Russia and America. (Eliot contributed a similar chronicle discussing contemporary English letters to the *Nouvelle Revue Française* between 1922 and 1927.) All this demonstrates that the *Criterion* was one of several prominent literary periodicals which shared an interest in a common European culture. These reviews, and the men of letters who wrote for them, can be seen as constituting an informal network in which topics of a general cultural interest could be examined. This network flourished during the cosmopolitan 1920s but was damaged by developments in foreign affairs during the 1930s and partly by the *Criterion*'s shifting editorial orientation.

Classicism was central to Eliot's conception of the European cultural tradition. He used the term in his 1926 *Criterion* editorial manifesto, 'The Idea of a Literary Review', to represent both the common tendency exhibited by core contributors to the *Criterion* and also a more general trend in modern letters:

I believe that the modern tendency is toward something which, for want of a better name, we may call classicism ... there is a tendency – discernable even in art – toward a higher and clearer conception of Reason, and a more severe and serene control of the emotions by Reason. If this approaches or even suggests the Greek ideal, so much the better: but it must inevitably be very different.[8]

Eliot's later contributions to the *Criterion* reinforce the remark that this classicism has no exclusive association with classical antiquity. Rather, he uses the term to denote a belief in reason, established standards of excellence and the importance of the cultural tradition. The Aristotelian model provides just one example of how this classical ideal has presented itself throughout European history. The criterion of the *Criterion*, then, was essentially an assertion of intellectual, moral and aesthetic standards that transcend the subjectivity of the individual. They are to be discovered through the use of reason and by considering the lessons taught by the greatest achievements of the European cultural tradition. It is in this sense that Eliot, Hofmannsthal, Ortega and Curtius can be called European classicists.

In the essay 'Restoration of the Reason', published by Eliot in the *Criterion* in 1927, Curtius declared:

[Classicism is] the organization of the human domain by means of Reason that assigns values, imposes standards, decides and directs. This reason created valid forms in the thirteenth and the seventeenth centuries. Our task is – not to resuscitate these forms artificially, but to revive the spirit which created them, and so to create a form of Reason proper to the twentieth century. Only so will we overcome the various types of radicalism ... and attain that objective which is the most important of all today: the reconstruction of the European man.[9]

In several of his editorials for the *Criterion*, Eliot elaborated upon this conception of a shared European tradition. In 1923 he remarked it was a fact '*all* European civilizations are equally dependent upon Greece and Rome – so far as they are civilizations at all', adding that 'if everything derived from Rome were withdrawn [from English culture] – everything we have from Norman-French society, from the Church, from Human-ism ... what would be left? A few Teutonic roots and husks. England is a "Latin" country.'[10] In an editorial of 1927 Eliot discoursed at length the subject of 'The European Idea' as 'one of the ideas which characterizes our age'.[11] He gestured towards the essays of Paul Valéry as a source of further elucidation on this subject. In his 1922 public lecture 'Europe',

Valéry characterised those peoples as European who had undergone the shaping influences of Greece, Rome and Christianity:

These, it seems to me, are the three essential conditions that define a true European, a man in whom the European mind can come to its full realization. Wherever the names of Caesar, Caius, Trajan, and Virgil, of Moses and St Paul, and of Aristotle, Plato and Euclid have had simultaneous meaning and authority, there is Europe. Every race and land that has been successively Romanised, Christianized, and, as regards the mind, disciplined by the Greeks, is absolutely European.[12]

In his magnum opus, *European Literature and the Latin Middle Ages*, Curtius concurred that the 'bases of Western thought are classical antiquity and Christianity'.[13] Revealingly, in a *Criterion* editorial Eliot took Joseph Wood Krutch to task for associating Europe with the ideals of the Renaissance and the Enlightenment rather than the Christian Church. 'He [Krutch] does not appear to think', complained Eliot, 'that Christianity had very much to do with the development of European civilization, except to obstruct it.' Eliot went on to ask: 'Is Mr Krutch able to rewrite the history of Europe in such a way as to show that his "European man" whom he admires was evolved and maintained in spite of Christian culture, and not by means of it?'[14] Eliot was particularly irritated by Krutch's assertion of Dante's bigotry, for Eliot admired Dante as an outstanding product of European culture: 'in Dante's time Europe ... was mentally more united than we can now conceive' (*SE*, 240). Eliot's later poetry and criticism emphasised Europe's Christian foundations rather than its classical heritage.

Still, Eliot's classicism can be interpreted as a form of European humanism. It was the expression of an ideal that is represented by the humanism of the Greek city states, by the Christian humanism of Erasmus, as well as the civic humanism of the French *philosophes* of the Enlightenment. For all their differences, these forms of humanism share a similar idea of human nature as relatively autonomous, undetermined and equipped with free will. Humanism takes reason to be man's highest faculty. Furthermore, humanism stresses both cosmopolitanism and cultural continuity. In his 1932 essay 'Humanismus als Initiative' ['A Humanism of Initiative'], which Eliot considered 'one of the best and most reasonable expositions of a "humanist" attitude that I have ever read',[15] Curtius claimed that although historical manifestations of humanism are mutable and conditioned by their time, together they form 'ein Wesensmerkmal des Europäismus' ['a distinguishing characteristic of

Europeanness'].[16] It may seem remarkable to associate Eliot with humanism, given his criticism of Irving Babbitt's American New Humanism in essays written in the late 1920s. However, Eliot did not reject all of humanism, rather those interpretations of it as 'the *alternative* to religion' (*SE*, 472) or those placing emphasis on an optimistic view of human nature deriving from Jean-Jacques Rousseau. Eliot was a Christian humanist in the spirit of Erasmus rather than a modern secular humanist like Curtius or Ortega. In fact, in the 1929 essay 'Second Thoughts about Humanism', Eliot argued that humanism can be a useful supplement to religion, one which 'makes for breadth, tolerance, equilibrium and sanity' and which 'operates against fanaticism' (*SE*, 488). The following year, in 'Religion without Humanism', Eliot even went so far as to warn of 'the danger, a very real one, of *religion without humanism*', since without humanism 'religion tends to become either a sentimental tune, or an emotional debauch; or in theology, a skeleton dance of fleshless dogmas, or in ecclesiasticism, a soulless political club'.[17]

Eliot's views on the complex interrelations of religion, humanism and the European cultural tradition continued to develop in the 1930s. His hopes for a revival of European humanism following the First World War were checked by political developments in Spain, Italy and Germany. In 1946, Eliot recalled a 'gradual closing of the mental frontiers of Europe' (*NTDC*, 116) that had accelerated throughout the 1930s. Many of the important European periodicals which maintained a relationship with the *Criterion* were unable to continue their work in the same way. *Die Neue Rundschau* in Germany, *Neue Schweizer Rundschau* in Switzerland, *Revista de Occidente* in Spain and *Il Convegno* in Italy were all forced to close or to change their editorial direction drastically. In his final editorial 'Last Words' in 1939, Eliot regretted this disintegration of the 'European mind':

> Gradually communications became more difficult, contributions more uncertain, and new and important foreign contributors more difficult to discover. The 'European mind', which one had mistakenly thought might be renewed and fortified, disappeared from view: there were fewer writers in any country who seemed to have anything to say to the intellectual public of another.[18]

Eliot's commitment to the Church of England in 1927 exacerbated his critical differences with secular humanists like Curtius, Ortega and Benda. Curtius first publicly criticised Eliot in an article of 1929 published in *Die Literatur*. In 1949 he lamented that Eliot's 'open-minded Europeanism of 1920 remained an unfulfilled promise' owing to his 'intellectual anglicization ... a de-Europeanization'.[19] In 1932, Ortega's analysis of contemporary democracy in *The Revolt of the Masses* was criticised by a reviewer in the *Criterion* for its apparent rejection of 'the religious solution'.[20] Moreover, contributors to the *Criterion* – notably the French neo-Thomist philosopher Jacques Maritain and the English historian Christopher Dawson – sought to demonstrate the inseparability of the 'idea of Europe' from Christian civilisation. Eliot's two major works of social criticism, *The Idea of a Christian Society* (1939) and *Notes Towards the Definition of Culture* (1948) underscored the Christian roots of European culture.

Recent criticism has too often neglected Eliot as an exponent of the values of the unity of European culture. The *Criterion* was an integral part of a European network of cultural reviews that strengthened the literary and intellectual exchange, as well as the correspondence and friendships, between the countries of Western Europe. If the 1925 Treaty of Locarno and the sharing of the 1926 Nobel Peace Prize between the French and German foreign ministers, Aristide Briand and Gustav Stresemann, were evidence of a political rapprochement, then the *Criterion*'s espousal of classicism contributed to a cultural 'springtime of the mind', in the words of Ernst Robert Curtius.[21] However, this classicism failed in its ambition to reunite European culture and the promise of the 1920s would be superseded by the ultra-nationalism of the 1930s. After he joined the Church of England, Eliot's conception of humanism was increasingly inflected by Christianity, even if his firm commitment to the 'idea of Europe' or the 'mind of Europe' was constant from the early essay 'Tradition and the Individual Talent' (1919) to the late 'The Man of Letters and the Future of Europe' (1944). Eliot always stressed the unity of European culture, rejected nationalist divisions, and worked tirelessly for the reconstruction of this shared cultural heritage.

NOTES

1. 'A Commentary', *Criterion* (April 1926), 222.
2. A. W. G. Randall, 'German Periodicals', *Criterion* (October 1926), 804.
3. 'A Commentary', *Criterion* (October 1932), 73.
4. 'Brief über Ernst Robert Curtius', *Freundesgabe für Ernst Robert Curtius*, ed. Max Rychner and Walter Boehlich (Bern: Francke Verlag, 1956), p. 26.
5. Ernst Robert Curtius, *Essays on European Literature*, trans. Michael Kowal (Princeton University Press, 1973), p. 170.
6. 'Brief über Ernst Robert Curtius', p. 25.
7. Ibid., p. 26.
8. 'The Idea of a Literary Review', *Criterion* (January 1926), 5.

9. Ernst Robert Curtius, 'Restoration of the Reason', *Criterion* (November 1927), 396.
10. 'Notes', *Criterion* (October 1923), 104–5.
11. 'A Commentary', *Criterion* (August 1927), 97.
12. Paul Valéry, *History and Politics*, trans. Denise Folliot and Jackson Matthews (London: Routledge, 1963), p. 322.
13. Ernst Robert Curtius, *European Literature and the Latin Middle Ages*, trans. Willard R. Trask (London: Routledge, 1953), p. 596.
14. 'A Commentary', *Criterion* (April 1936), 458–9.
15. 'A Commentary', *Criterion* (October 1932), 74.
16. Ernst Robert Curtius, *Deutscher Geist in Gefahr* (Stuttgart: Deutsche Verlags-Anstalt, 1932), p. 168.
17. 'Religion without Humanism', *Humanism and America*, ed. Norman Foerster (New York: Farrar & Rinehart, 1930), pp. 105 and 111.
18. 'Last Words', *Criterion* (January 1939), 271–2.
19. See Ernst Robert Curtius, 'T. S. Eliot als Kritiker', *Die Literatur* (October 1929), 11–15, and Curtius, *Essays on European Literature*, p. 397.
20. Frank McEachran, 'Books of the Quarter', *Criterion* (October 1932), 144.
21. Curtius, *Essays on European Literature*, p. 169.

PART TWO

Forms

CHAPTER 7

The role of intellectual

Michael Levenson

T. S. Eliot planned for a place in the public sphere, well before he enjoyed its mixed blessings. Questions of cultural power and literary influence appeared in his letters soon after he arrived in London, and his developing career cast the issue of the public intellectual in a revealing light, because it so quickly raised the question of what constitutes a 'public'. Within the small universe of experimental modernism, he soon established a name, a voice and a reputation. His work on the *Egoist*, his essays in the *Athenaeum* and the *Times Literary Supplement* (see Chapter 10), and his friendships (above all, with Ezra Pound) gave him a minor but significant stature. Yet the anonymity of much of this critical writing and the wartime circumstances, while providing occasions to enter the arena of critical judgement, kept his early reputation narrow.

Eliot's academic studies in philosophy involved a wide course of reading in anthropology, comparative religion and psychology. Even after abandoning his doctoral dissertation in 1916, he kept an interest in a range of intellectual and technical disciplines. This analytic turn for conceptual thinking combined with a facility for polemical writing: both would assist his rise to prominence. Eliot understood the social power of concepts. Strategic definitions, outflanking arguments and the tone of philosophical authority secured his reputation. In 1919, Eliot published two key essays, 'Tradition and the Individual Talent' and 'Hamlet and His Problems', which established the sound of a public voice. Much of the initial effect of these essays turned on refinements of tone and rhetoric. The essay on *Hamlet* adopted a tactic that would become familiar: the sharp refusal of a cultural commonplace uttered with authoritative conviction. 'Few critics', Eliot famously began, 'have ever admitted that *Hamlet* the play is the primary problem, and Hamlet the character only secondary', before going on to say that 'far from being Shakespeare's masterpiece, the play is most certainly an artistic failure' (*SE*, 141, 143). The audacity of the attack on *Hamlet* is one sign of growing confidence, but equally striking are the terms of the critique. The play's apparent inability to express its emotions in art is what Eliot took to be its weakness, yielding the celebrated phrase 'objective correlative' (*SE*, 145). The technical aura of the term helped distinguish the essay from conventional journalistic fare and furnished a memorable shorthand term that promoted a maturing reputation.

The growing attention to his poetry, especially the controversy it excited, prepared Eliot's entry into active intellectual discourse. But the publication of *The Sacred Wood* (1920) marked a new stage in the history. In bringing together reviews and essays from the last few years, the volume established two aspects of his public voice that would develop throughout his career: a fluent consciousness of the literary past and also a readiness to confront rival critics. 'Tradition and the Individual Talent' laid out a view of literary history as a simultaneity – 'the whole of the literature of Europe ... has a simultaneous existence and composes a simultaneous order' (*SE*, 14) – and part of Eliot's bid for critical authority depended on the mastery (or the aura of mastery) of the whole performance. The skill in quotation, particularly from a minor or forgotten work, became a familiar device: as a polemicist, Eliot frequently argued by simply enlarging the field of view. What about John Marston? Have you forgotten George Chapman? Equally, he deployed a conceptual tactic: claiming that a crucial distinction had been lost or that an assumption had gone unacknowledged. In the essay on 'Four Elizabethan Dramatists' (1924), he writes in characteristic tones:

Contemporary literature, like contemporary politics, is confused by the moment-to-moment struggle for existence; but the time arrives when an examination of principles is necessary. I believe that the theatre has reached a point at which a revolution in principles should take place. (*SE*, 109)

On one side, then, stands the resource of historical breadth, and on the other side, the appeal to a deeper truth, a more profound principle. 'Comparison and analysis' are Eliot's terms for these essential 'tools of the critic' (*SW*, 37); in practice, they show themselves as a polemical recourse to context and concept. Notably, both manoeuvres become forms of attack on 'individualism', the individualism that takes shape as Eliot's bitter adversary, and also as his resource for establishing a public posture.

The reliance on 'the accidents of personal association', on 'impressions' and 'purely personal' (*SW*, 7) reactions – this is what continually irritates Eliot into opposition. Romanticism is one name for this disabling complex; it becomes a target in the early essays, because it always 'leads its disciples only back upon themselves' (*SW*, 31). A more recent danger Eliot warns us against is the specialisation of knowledge, because

> when every one knows a little about a great many things, it becomes increasingly difficult for anyone to know whether he knows what he is talking about or not. And when we do not know, or when we do not know enough, we tend always to substitute emotions for thoughts. (*SW*, 10)

The demand for thought to control emotion is recurrent, pronounced and significant. For Eliot emotion is individualising. It can only register the narrow contingency of selfhood. Ideas, on the other hand, belong to a world of exchange, negotiation and transaction – an essentially social world. The creation of a public role depends, then, on moving from the private sphere of emotion to the public domain of thought.

A further implication follows from this emphasis. Ideas do not simply generate a public world; they produce an arena of controversy. As Eliot puts it, thinking of Julien Benda and Matthew Arnold as examples: 'A man of ideas needs ideas, or pseudo-ideas, to fight against' (*SW*, 46). This antagonistic conception of the public realm impels, and underlies, Eliot's career as an intellectual. Sometimes the target is a rival critic (often John Middleton Murry during the 1920s); sometimes academic scholarship, the 'highbrow effect which is so depressing' (*SW*, 72) (Eliot has Gilbert Murray in mind here); sometimes the general state of journalism; sometimes the 'ordinary man'. In opposition to these forces, Eliot not only locates himself but also a select community of initiates. He continually provokes the public he addresses, placing readers in uneasy positions, forced to choose between initiation into a cultural elite or acceptance of benighted ignorance. Does his audience belong to the 'three thousand people' who can respond to Ben Jonson, or the 'ten who have read the *Masque of Blackness*' (*SE*, 159–60), or are they merely 'ordinary' readers, whose experiences are 'chaotic, irregular, fragmentary' (*SE*, 287)?

In the important essay 'The Function of Criticism' (1923), Eliot takes on Murry's defence of a revived Romanticism, founded on the principle of the 'Inner Voice'. Eliot crisply responds: 'Why have principles, when one has the inner voice?' (*SE*, 29). He articulates a counter-principle, namely that of Outer Authority, whether it appears in literature, politics or religion. Within his emerging career of public declamation, what is notable about 'The Function of Criticism' is its constellation of values marked out by 'order' and the 'outside'. Also notable is the archness of tone and the coy refusal to define central terms. Eliot was always impatient with mere verbalism and vague speech – with the loss of connection between words and objects, which he had diagnosed in the poetry of Swinburne, where 'you find always that the object was not there – only the word' (*SW*, 148). Yet his own polemics not only acknowledged but also deployed the indeterminacy of central concepts and the tactical power of imprecision. In the closing lines of 'The Function of the Criticism', Eliot mock-modestly admits he hasn't defined 'truth, or fact, or reality' and has proposed only a 'scheme into which, whatever they are, they will fit, if they exist' (*SE*, 34).

A further significance of 'The Function of Criticism' lies in its evident enjoyment of open dispute. Even as he satirises his opponent, Eliot thanks and praises Murry as the one critic who has shown the seriousness of the problem. While others hush up the noisy difficulties of the day, Murry forces them into view. David Goldie and Jason Harding have shown how this polemic – sustained over several years, and at once sharp and playful – was decisive to the maturing of Eliot's views.[1] Murry offered him an opportunity to depict post-war modernity as an unavoidable forking of paths – 'what Mr Murry does show is that there are at least two attitudes toward literature and toward everything, and that you cannot hold both' (*SE*, 26). Importantly, this contention allowed Eliot to hone techniques on which he would rely for the next three decades. The insinuating admiration – 'To Mr Murry I feel an increasing debt of gratitude' (*SE*, 26) – as well as the barbed wit and heavy sarcasm – 'The possessors of the inner voice ride ten in a compartment to a football match at Swansea, listening to the inner voice, which breathes the eternal message of vanity, fear, and lust' (*SE*, 27) – are potent weapons. But then they abruptly give way to an even-toned voice which can affect the fatigue of plain speech: 'The sense of fact is something very slow to develop, and its complete development means perhaps the very pinnacle of civilisation' (*SE*, 31). Eliot's discourse is as much a display of tone as of content. Central to this campaign of outflanking rivals is a willingness to move quickly between registers, to ascend to cool magisterial judgement and then to drop into combative mockery.

His editorship of the *Criterion* was just as important as the shock effect of *The Waste Land* in securing Eliot's prominence. The journal's distinguished contributors belonged to no party line, but the editorial framing (including the editorial 'Commentary') encouraged a tendency towards what Eliot describes as a 'classical, reactionary and revolutionary' outlook.[2] These terms are only superficially contradictory. They reflect the subtle and demanding relations of past and present in Eliot's public address, a call that was neither for revivalism nor for a slowing in the pace of change. He consistently held that the only way to live up to tradition was to engage radically with the present, and to do so in the name of 'classical' and 'reactionary' values.

By the mid 1920s, Eliot found himself an object of public attention, even fascination. His religious conversion in 1927 was no doubt an intensely personal event, but it was also a public relations coup. The famous avowal of 'classicist in literature, royalist in politics, and anglo-catholic in religion' (*FLA*, ix) became a tag associated with his celebrity. Eliot later spoke ruefully of the 'facility with which this statement has been quoted' (*ASG*, 27), but he had always been conscious of reputation as a resource – he once proudly informed his mother that he had had 'more *influence* on English letters than any other American has ever had, unless it be Henry James. I know a great many people, but there are many more who would like to know me' (*L1*, 331). His conversion to Christianity created a new buzz of chatter, which Eliot deplored and exploited. For growing fame led to new opportunities for conspicuous speech, including an invitation to deliver the Charles Eliot Norton lectures at Harvard in 1932/3, where he emphasised the place of poetry within the ongoing life of a community: 'The poetry of a people takes its life from the people's speech and in turn gives life to it; and represents its highest point of consciousness, its greatest power and its most delicate sensibility' (*UPUC*, 15). At the same time, though, Eliot notes the power of an intellectual synthesis that can be performed by an individual critic, remarking that 'every hundred years or so, it is desirable that some critic shall appear to review the past of our literature, and set the poets and the poems in a new order' (*UPUC*, 108). It is clear that Eliot understood himself as such a defining figure. Even as he called for Outer Authority, he worked to establish an authoritative voice of his own.[3]

Eliot's visiting professorship in the United States in 1932/3 marked a crossing point in his career as a public intellectual. The Harvard lectures confirmed his transatlantic pre-eminence. But he then travelled to the University of Virginia, where he delivered his most notorious public utterance during a series of lectures later collected as *After Strange Gods* (1934). In the 'Preface', Eliot noted that his subject had not been 'literary criticism', rather that he had 'ascended the platform only in the role of moralist' (*ASG*, 12). Eliot was still relatively new to the role of public lecturer; his consciousness of the 'platform' would mark his speech from this point forward. At the same time, the turn from literature to morality indicates the broadening reach of his claims upon his audience: the 'literary' distinction between Romanticism and Classicism is replaced by the contrast between Orthodoxy and Heresy. In these uncompromising terms, displaying more sarcasm than irony and less playfulness than vehemence, Eliot denounced several major contemporary writers, among them D. H. Lawrence and Ezra Pound. Most controversially, he defended a 'homogeneous' culture and 'unity of religious background', concluding that 'reasons of race and religion combine to make any large number of free-thinking Jews undesirable' (*ASG*, 19–20). This remark, the source of so much outrage, has often been taken as an unfortunate effect of Eliot's personal crisis at this time, especially his decision to separate from his first wife. But whatever the immediate cause, the statement reflects the rhetorical unsteadiness and the elusive mobility of his later public discourse. Eliot did not reprint this series of lectures; his career has remained troubled by their existence. But if we see the event as anomalous, we miss one of the most revealing features of Eliot's later writing; namely, its artful play between extremity and retreat. As his positions in the 1930s grew more 'reactionary and revolutionary', Eliot worked to refine a discourse of extremity. The flurry over his anti-Semitic remark in *After Strange Gods* taught at least this lesson: that radical opinions, if they were to be placed before the public, required the most studied presentation.

In 1931, Eliot intoned a severe judgement on the entire culture of modern secularism:

The World is trying the experiment of attempting to form a civilized but non-Christian mentality. The experiment will fail; but we must be very patient in awaiting its collapse; meanwhile redeeming the time: so that the Faith may be preserved alive through the dark ages before us; to renew and rebuild civilization, and save the World from suicide. (*SE*, 387)

The question that Eliot faced was how far to go in promulgating the language of doom and apocalypse, especially at a time when liberal democratic states faced the challenges of Communism and Fascism. Eliot regarded liberal democracy itself as insufficient to withstand totalitarianism; indeed, it could easily prepare the ground for a totalitarian state. The choice in the 1930s, as Eliot saw it, was between Christianity and totalitarianism, an inescapable choice given the failure of liberalism. The implication, which Eliot was quick to draw, was that religion cannot separate itself from the worldly crisis; it must engage in the struggle for political and social renewal. As he put it in the opening of his address to the 1933 Anglo-Catholic Summer School of Sociology: 'any programme that a Catholic can envisage must aim at the conversion of the whole world' (*EAM*, 123).

However, even as he calls for a Christian solution to the social problems of the world, Eliot keeps a careful distance from raging political debates over government powers and policy. In 1937, as the Spanish Civil War drew many young intellectuals to fight on behalf of the anti-Fascist Popular Front and incited others to take up strong positions on the conflict, Eliot called for abstention, observing that 'those who have at heart the interests of Christianity in the long run ... have especial reason for suspending judgement'.[4] Repeatedly, the suspension of judgement is Eliot's response to pressing international controversies. But rather than see this as a sign of disengagement, we should recognise it as his deliberate attempt to choose both his platform and the terms of his intervention. In a BBC radio broadcast entitled 'The Church's Message to the World', Eliot made it clear that if he doubts the wisdom of fighting in Spain, he has no doubt about the campaign for a Christian society, urging that the Church 'must struggle for a condition of society which will give the maximum of opportunity for us to lead wholly Christian lives, and the maximum of opportunity for others to become Christians' (*ICS*, 93).

In 1939, Eliot published a series of lectures delivered at Cambridge University, under the title *The Idea of a Christian Society*. Here he offered extreme attitudes under the circumspection of abstraction. The lectures propose that the Church has the final authority over the nation, a society of faithful believers and of a self-conscious elite – a Community of Christians. But the description of details in these lectures is studiously thin, with all its radical implications – for democracy, for religious diversity, for freedom of thought and social critique – left implicit.[5] Behind these lectures can be heard the sharp-edged proposals which circulated among Eliot's small group of interlocutors. But when the ideas go public, they give way to suave generality. On the eve of the Second World War, Eliot acknowledges the Fascist and Communist critiques of democracy and foretells an ever-deepening emergency that, one way or another, Christian or secular, will end in social revolution. But the mix of radicalism and rhetorical banality allows Eliot to maintain the dignity of public eminence, even as he implies the overturning of cherished values.

The term 'democracy', as I have said again and again, does not contain enough positive content to stand alone against the forces that you dislike – it can easily be transformed by them. If you will not have God (and He is a jealous God) you should pay your respects to Hitler or Stalin. (*ICS*, 63)

These sentences epitomise one aspect of Eliot's public posture on the eve of the war. Democracy is drained of history and specificity; it stands not as a form of political life but as a 'term' no longer serviceable. The real struggle is an eternal conflict between the extremes of faith and paganism. Ten years earlier, Eliot had asserted that 'Dante and Shakespeare divide the modern world between them; there is no third' (*SE*, 265). Five years before that, Romanticism and Classicism had divided the field. This habit of Manichean dualism persists in the deep structure of Eliot's thought. He sets aside democracy as lacking 'positive content', but in fact his later rhetoric depletes the content of all his major terms in favour of the abstract form of an either/or. *The Idea of a Christian Society* gives no determinacy either to the new Christian nation or the pathway leading towards it; it offers no more than an outline, avoiding the risks of specificity ('too many free-thinking Jews') while laying claim to the power of an 'Idea'.[6] Eliot observes: 'What I mean by the Christian State is not any particular political form, but whatever State is suitable to a Christian society, whatever State a particular Christian Society develops for itself' (*ICS*, 12). These phrases are characteristically revealing: no 'particulars' need be mentioned, because they must adjust to 'whatever' form a given society will take. Even at this high pitch of generality, Eliot comes to the threshold of outrage: 'However bigoted the announcement may sound, the Christian can be satisfied with nothing less than a Christian organisation of society' (*ICS*, 33–4). But the force of these lectures depends precisely upon approaching, and then receding from, the scandalous limit. Unlike *After Strange Gods* and the threshold-crossing Ezra Pound, in the late 1930s Eliot perfects the trope of hypothetical extremity ('If you will not have God') that is at once provocative and bracketed, startling but abstract.

The public intellectual 'T. S. Eliot' was at the same time a poet, dramatist and literary critic. Even as he stirred the cauldron in lectures, essays and in his editorial Commentaries for the *Criterion*, he continually reminded his audience of his eminence. It served as a frame around his opinions. Absorbed within the writer's deeper vocation, his contentious views lost some of their sting. The poems from *Ash-Wednesday* (1930) and the drama beginning with the pageant *The Rock* (1934) belong to the discourse of the committed Christian. As the drama develops, especially in *The Family Reunion* (1939), and as the poetry reaches the complex meditations of *Four Quartets* (1943), the question of faith becomes both urgent and difficult, a compound of belief and doubt. Agony lives in the midst of conviction. The public posture is thus divided between the abstract hypothetical assertions of Christian regeneration and the literary enactment of religious struggle, loss, humiliation and revelation. If this makes it difficult to extract an *intellectual* position from Eliot, he wanted nothing less.

The last turn in Eliot's public career was marked by a drawing back from the teasing of extremity he employed throughout the 1930s. His social criticism in the 1940s muted talk of an approaching apocalypse that would bring an end to a society 'worm-eaten with Liberalism' (*ASG*, 13). Eliot's major critical publication of this period, *Notes Towards the Definition of Culture* (1948), abandoned a call for the Christian reorganisation of society or the conversion of the non-Christian population, emphasising instead the functional interdependence of all elements of collective life. The goal of the community should be to achieve a harmony of units (family, religion, nation) and powers (the power of the Church and the local parish). 'Centripetal' and 'centrifugal' forces must come into equilibrium, in order to produce an 'ecology of cultures', a balance of competing pressures: Catholic and Protestant, aristocratic and democratic, nationalist and regionalist, and even (in a footnote) the Christian and the Jew (see *NTDC*, 82).

In the later 1940s and the 1950s, Eliot gave a series of lectures and addresses that rely upon this same language of consolidation and harmony. Strong positions are relinquished (his early impatience with Milton is replaced by a serene acceptance). Irony, sarcasm and polemic fade from the sound of his voice. Of those twin weapons of criticism, comparison and analysis, the latter loses its edge, while the former spreads wide in generous appreciation. The public discourse is now founded not on the language of hard choices, but on an accommodation of the diverse history of European literature, with all its varied instances finding their place within the broad tradition. The irony that remains is largely self-directed. In the 1956 lecture 'The Frontiers of Criticism', delivered to an audience of 14,000 people in a baseball stadium in Minnesota, Eliot gently chaffs his own phrase-making ('objective correlative') and literary provocations (for example, the notes to *The Waste Land*). His provoking early critical opinions are now moderated. In one respect, the late tone is a mark of serenity, even resignation. But viewed from another aspect, it represents a different way of tending to reputation. The lofty vantage point of these last lectures look back on Eliot's career itself as a kind of monument. The aging critical voice again speaks from the platform, but no longer with ferocity or in the name of social extremity. Eliot now recalls those ferocious years in mild, waggish tones, but this, too, is a way of preserving their significance. The self-distance and self-mockery are also styles of self-assertion.

NOTES

1. See David Goldie, *A Critical Difference: T. S. Eliot and John Middleton Murry in English Literary Criticism, 1919–1928* (Oxford: Clarendon Press, 1998), and Jason Harding, *The 'Criterion': Cultural Politics and Periodical Networks in Inter-War Britain* (Oxford University Press, 2002), pp. 25–43.
2. 'A Commentary', *Criterion* (April 1924), 231.
3. In two 1929 reviews of *For Lancelot Andrewes*, Edmund Wilson marvelled at Eliot's position as 'perhaps the most important literary critic in the English-speaking world. His writings have been brief and few, and it is almost incredible that they should have been enough to establish him as an intellectual leader' (Brooker, 158) and F. R. Leavis also remarked upon the fact that Eliot's 'influence has made itself so profoundly and so widely felt in so short a time' (Brooker, 153).
4. 'A Commentary', *Criterion* (January 1937), 290.
5. In his subtle and persuasive chapter on Eliot's career as a public intellectual, Stefan Collini notes how 'The spiky ironies and wilful obliquities of the early essays are increasingly displaced by a blander, flank-guarding discursiveness.' See *Absent Minds: Intellectuals in Britain* (Oxford University Press, 2006), p. 323.
6. Cf. Collini: 'it is noticeable that Eliot made much of the invocation of principles in general, and rather less of the content of any actual principles'. Ibid., p. 310.

CHAPTER 8

Publishing

Jason Harding

Frank Morley once claimed that T. S. Eliot was appointed to the board of directors at the publishers Faber & Gwyer as a sound businessman; he was a banker who had worked for eight years in the City of London. Morley was exaggerating, but he correctly suggests that Eliot's literary reputation was not in itself sufficient to persuade the board to employ him in the autumn of 1925. Eliot himself recounted that his name had been passed to Geoffrey Faber as a literary adviser during a dinner at All Souls College, Oxford, by his friend, the journalist and man of letters Charles Whibley. Faber had recently joined Lady Gwyer's Scientific Press, a publishing house specialising in medical textbooks and periodicals (most notably, *The Nursing Mirror*) and he was planning to reorganise the firm as a general publisher. Eliot recalled a nervous interview in the spring of 1925, when he successfully convinced Faber of his usefulness to the new venture. It meant release from his work in a basement office at Lloyds Bank and Eliot described it as the best piece of salesmanship he had ever undertaken. Faber in turn persuaded any sceptical colleagues that Eliot's editorship of the highbrow quarterly review the *Criterion* would bring the firm prestige as well as extensive connections among British, American and European writers and intellectuals. Initially employed as a non-managing director at £400 per annum, Eliot told Faber that he 'did not have in mind an exact correspondence between the publishing and the review', but that he wished to avoid 'publishing a book by some writer who had been consistently and steadily damned in the review' (*L2*, 610).

A lifelong friendship between Faber and Eliot ensued. It is worth remembering that Faber, a published poet (Eliot praised Faber's 'fine heroic note' in a review in the *Egoist* in 1918),[1] a formidable scholar with a first in Oxford 'Greats' and estates bursar of All Souls, did not automatically defer to Eliot's literary judgement. Eliot described Faber as a good chairman of the weekly Wednesday book committee meetings, which took place around a large octagonal table strewn with readers' reports

Figure 3   24 Russell Square, London.

and bottles of beer, lasting (according to Morley) from 'lunch till exhaustion'.[2] It was here that book proposals were discussed and decisions regarding publication were taken. Faber was attentive to the advice offered by his fellow directors, tolerant of their humour and even their practical jokes, but he was very much chairman of the board, not averse to putting his colleagues in their place if the occasion demanded it. Yet this was the exception rather than the rule: the atmosphere at 24 Russell Square, the large Bloomsbury town house transformed into the offices of Faber & Gwyer, was gentlemanly in the manner of a Victorian family business.

From his top-floor room, a snug garret with sloping ceilings and a view across Woburn Square, Eliot set about establishing the finest English poetry list of the twentieth century. Aside from the onerous duties of editing the *Criterion* as the firm's flagship literary journal and – until its demise in 1939 – a recruiting ground for potential Faber authors, Eliot carefully cultivated and advised several generations of writers, as his voluminous publishing correspondence from four decades (occupying 120 box files) attests. Given his remarkable success in the field of English poetry, it is perhaps surprising that his beginnings as a publisher were less than auspicious. His first recommendations in the field of French literature, translations of Jean Cocteau's *A Call to Order* and Henri Massis's *Defence of the West*, were commercial failures. The money lost on them made him cautious about pressing recommendations, for he fully understood the importance of financial imperatives. Moreover, his earliest, rather unremitting initiatives in building up the literary side of Faber & Gwyer upset several of his London acquaintances. Richard Aldington was annoyed that Eliot's proposed series of critical biographies on European men of letters curtailed his own involvement with Routledge's Republic of Letters series, while Leonard and Virginia Woolf were surprised and distressed to discover that Eliot had persuaded Herbert Read to defect to Faber & Gwyer from their Hogarth Press.[3] They did not welcome this new rival in the niche publishing field of advanced modern poetry, and they were entitled to feel aggrieved, as the London publishers of both *Poems* (1919) and *The Waste Land*, when they saw, without warning, Eliot's *Poems 1909–1925* announced in Faber & Gwyer's first catalogue.

There is no doubt that Eliot himself was the firm's most important and, in the long term, most lucrative acquisition as a poet. His slender output of new poetry appeared at strategic intervals, starting with 'The Hollow Men' in *Poems 1909–1925*. The Ariel Poems pamphlet series was the vehicle for 'Journey of the Magi' (1927), 'A Song for Simeon' (1928), 'Animula' (1929), 'Marina' (1930) and 'Triumphal March' (1931), attractively illustrated with the artwork of E. McKnight Kauffer and Gertrude Hermes. 'Burnt Norton' made its first appearance in *Collected Poems 1909–1935* and consolidated his reputation as the pre-eminent poet of his generation. Although Eliot exercised a great measure of control over the appearance, arrangement and distribution of his work, he was often an inattentive proofreader (hard pressed by other responsibilities), contributing to the instability and unreliability of successive editions, including his *Selected Essays* (where 'Tradition and the Individual Talent' is misdated to 1917) and the *Collected Poems 1909–1962*, in which there are several errors and unauthorised final emendations. Over these decades his writing was so much in demand, and was issued so many times and in so many forms, that he could scarcely keep up. Unlike many poets, his work was never in danger of going out of print. Even under exigent wartime publishing conditions, including paper rationing, 'Little Gidding' was published in 1942 in a print run of 16,775 copies. The 1959 paperback edition of *Four Quartets* had a staggering print run of 58,640 copies.

The halcyon days of Eliot's work as a publisher followed the withdrawal of Lady Gwyer's interest and the reorganisation of the firm on 1 April 1929 as Faber & Faber (a name selected for euphony, since no second Faber was active on the board). Joined by his American friend and occasionally sparring partner Frank Morley, Eliot was (ir)reverently dubbed the 'Pope of Russell Square': many luminaries of modern literature were drawn to Faber by the gravitational pull of his presence. Championing controversial figures was to be an important part of his achievement and of his legacy as a publisher. They included writers of his own generation such as James Joyce, Ezra Pound and D. H. Lawrence, and younger writers such as Samuel Beckett, Djuna Barnes, Henry Miller and Lawrence Durrell. Eliot was determined that the firm should publish Joyce's 'Work in Progress', and sections from it, *Anna Livia Plurabelle* (1930), *Haveth Childers Everywhere* (1931) and *Two Tales of Shem and Shaun* (1932), appeared as pamphlets. In July 1931, Joyce signed a contract with Faber for the rights to the completed work, although it would be eight further years before *Finnegans Wake* was finally ready for publication, following innumerable editorial tribulations which put a strain on the friendship between Eliot and Joyce (who lamented the failure of 'Feebler and Fumbler' to publish a UK edition of *Ulysses*).[4]

Pound found a sympathetic new London publisher. Eliot introduced a 1928 Faber edition of his friend's *Selected Poems* and commissioned, copyedited and wrote 'blurbs' for subsequent works. In 1937, Eliot reported to the book committee regarding Pound's idiosyncratic *Guide to Kulchur*: 'We asked for this and we have got it. It is only a damned kulchered [*sic*] person who will be able to find his way about in this book, but for the perceptive there are a good many plums, and for the judicious who know how to trim the boat with their own intelligence there is a good deal of wisdom.'[5] At times, Pound could be exasperating; obstinate and arrogant on matters that left his publisher vulnerable to the laws of libel. Eliot's secretaries recalled the time and effort that went into managing this difficult author. Still, Eliot's loyalty as a friend and as a publisher was crucial in keeping Pound's presence before a wary poetry public. His blurb for the *Pisan Cantos* spoke with quiet authority of these cantos as 'both more lucid and more moving than some of their predecessors, with the same technical mastery but a new poignancy of human speech'. The catalogue continued: 'Such an achievement is all the more extraordinary, because of their having been written under conditions which, for most men, would have stifled inspiration and prevented composition' – a reference, that is, to Pound's incarceration in an American prisoner-of-war camp outside Pisa, as a consequence of his broadcasts for Fascist Italy.

The 'Pope of Russell Square' gave countless business lunches and tea-and-cake audiences to aspiring writers. He was instrumental in launching the 'Auden Generation' of Oxford poets, who were nurtured in the *Criterion*. Auden himself was launched in *Poems* (1930), and although Eliot occasionally found him to be supercilious, Faber were to be the chief purveyors of 'Vin Audenaire' (as a 1937 advertisement put it) for more than three decades. With the young Stephen Spender, Eliot took an avuncular interest, offering him practical advice on how to build up a reputation. Principally, Eliot emphasised the need for an emerging poet to foster a select readership and to avoid publishing too much (Spender's literary and political criticism appeared elsewhere). In 1933, Spender's first Faber collection was introduced by a blurb which claimed: 'If Auden is the satirist of this poetical renascence, Spender is its lyric poet.' This sentence incited the Cambridge critic F. R. Leavis to complain, 'Whoever was allowed to write it knew nothing about poetry'[6] – but the ignorance was his, for the blurb was written by Eliot. Louis MacNeice was also corralled into Faber's stable of Oxford poets. His debut was accompanied by another magisterial blurb: 'His work is intelligible but unpopular, and has the pride and modesty of things that endure.' Years later, in an obituary note on MacNeice, Eliot drew attention to the differences between the gifts of 'several brilliant poets who were up at Oxford at the same time'.[7] Distaste for Cecil Day Lewis led Eliot to differentiate between the respective merits of that Oxford collective poet satirised as 'MacSpaunday' in Roy Campbell's Faber volume *Talking Bronco* (1946).[8] Day Lewis remained with the Hogarth Press.

Cambridge poets did not fare as well as Oxford poets at Faber in the 1930s. Leavis's protégé, Ronald Bottrall, was dropped following the publication of *Festivals of Fire* in 1934, which led to several awkward letters of rejection, particularly given Eliot's principle (later stated publicly) of sticking with poets 'through thick and thin however disappointing the response of reviewers and readers'.[9] This explains why Eliot sometimes took years in coming to a firm decision on the long-term promise of a young poet, preferring to test them out in the *Criterion* before recommending book publication. Charles Madge, a young Cambridge poet, turned out to be one of Eliot's less inspired choices, and although Faber published William Empson's second collection, *The Gathering Storm*

(1940) – deliciously epitomised by Eliot's blurb as a development from 'the most brilliantly obscure of modern poets' – Empson would later send Eliot the 'most insulting letter which I have ever received'.[10] Empson wrongly alleged that his publisher had failed to promote his work. Eliot was so annoyed that he directed future correspondence to his younger colleague Peter du Sautoy. (Thankfully, cordial relations between Eliot and Empson were restored.) James Reeves, who had collaborated with Empson on a Cambridge student periodical, was invited to tea at Russell Square and given reviewing work for the *Criterion*, but as a poet he remained outside Eliot's fold. He recalled that Faber published the most 'fashionable poets', adding that this imprimatur 'had an enormous cachet attached to it'.[11]

Eliot's attention, of course, was not focused solely on poets fresh from Oxford and Cambridge. The case of George Barker is illustrative in this regard. In 1934, Eliot was so excited by his first reading of Barker's poetry that he touted his talent – sometimes using the word 'genius', although circumspectly[12] – to potential benefactors, including Lady Ottoline Morrell and Virginia Woolf. His efforts to raise funds and find employment for Barker were not uncharacteristic of his generous dealings with a number of impecunious waifs and strays: he usually gave them terse, often severe, criticism on matters of poetic technique, but tempered this with encouragement. He offered Barker practical advice on the selection and arrangement of his poems in a volume and on the need to continue to develop as a writer, suggesting that he seek to clarify his 'difficult' poetry in order to communicate better with his audience (although he was told to ignore the popular market). Barker was included – together with Auden, Spender, MacNeice, Yeats, Pound and Eliot himself – in Michael Roberts's *Faber Book of Modern Verse* (1936). This was a canon-forming attempt to delineate the 'new bearings' in English poetry, and in American poetry too, since it also featured Marianne Moore, whose *Selected Poems* had been published by Faber the previous year, introduced by Eliot's subtle analysis of Moore's metric. (In 1945, Eliot acquired Wallace Stevens for Faber, another key American poet.) By establishing a canon of modern/ist poetry, Roberts's anthology eclipsed its rival, W. B. Yeats's eccentric selection in the *Oxford Book of Modern Verse* (also 1936). In 1939, Eliot's patronage of an anthology drawn from the pages of Geoffrey Grigson's feisty little magazine *New Verse* helped secure Faber's dominance in the market for serious modern poetry.

Poets who were rejected by Eliot, Laura Riding and Basil Bunting for instance, had their acceptance in London literary circles delayed by decades. By the 1940s, however, he had become less sure of his ability to discover new talent, often seeking a second opinion from his former secretary Anne Ridler. Shortly before becoming a Faber poet herself, she chose the poems in Faber's *A Little Book of Modern Verse* (1941), unassumingly prefaced by Eliot, and in 1951, following Roberts's premature death from leukaemia, she updated the *Faber Book of Modern Verse*. By this time, Eliot's initial enthusiasm for several Faber poets had cooled. In 1950 he reacted with extreme distaste to the exhibitionism of *The True Confession of George Barker*. It appeared instead from the Parton Press and was omitted from Barker's Faber *Collected Poems* of 1957. Another of his protégés, Henry Treece, was so wounded by the detachment evident in Eliot's blurb for *The Exiles* (1951) that the repentant publisher offered him an apology. Nevertheless, Faber continued to attract outstanding poets throughout the 1950s, including Thom Gunn and Ted Hughes. Charles Monteith wrote a somewhat non-committal report on Hughes's *The Hawk in the Rain*, but a handwritten addition by Eliot urged that he be snapped up immediately. Hughes's diary records that he was in awe of his studiously correct, impeccably dressed publisher; yet beneath the carapace of old-fashioned courtesy, he saw Eliot as 'a rather over-watchful, over-powerful father'.[13]

In addition to poetry, Eliot was responsible, as Peter du Sautoy recalled, for a 'very distinguished' list of books on theology, to which he sometimes contributed prefaces and essays.[14] He also frequently consulted Philip Mairet, a collaborator on the *New English Weekly*, on proposals relating to sociology, economics and philosophy. Mairet recalled:

Of the costly attention [Eliot] has devoted to new or obscure authors I could a tale unfold; I mean, of his care that work in which he discerned value should not perish, though it might be quite unpublishable without onerous revision. Many people must have thought that the trouble he took in this direction was a work of supererogation, or even regrettable in a creative writer already heavily occupied in other ways; but I am sure he did not think so. The altogether rare kind of personality that he brought to publishing meant more than nursing the offspring of writers who are better thinkers than writers – though this can involve one in labours and in decisions that are harassing enough. A higher spiritual expense is liable to be incurred in deciding whether to sponsor the work of authors who may have undeniable competence of some kind, and are venturing into yet uncharted oceans of thought.

According to Mairet, 'a good part of Eliot's best influence on the younger intelligentsia was communicated personally through his ministrations as editor and publisher'.[15] Eliot took so much trouble over the submissions of young writers that Mairet was not alone in wondering if all these aspirants were worthy recipients of his rare critical intelligence. It should also be said that there were days when his routine of publishing duties – dealing with authors and agents, answering business correspondence, reading manuscripts, writing book reports, composing book-jacket blurbs – could feel like wasted labour.

After joining Faber, Eliot read the lion's share of unsolicited manuscripts in French and German. He also read a significant quantity of fiction and detective fiction, but he made it clear that his judgements on a genre he did not practice were fallible. Inevitably he made mistakes. He wrote on behalf of Faber to decline George Orwell's *Animal Farm*: it certainly wasn't prudent for his firm to be seen criticising the Soviet Union, then Britain's wartime ally.[16] Still, Eliot's rejection letters were always carefully worded and contained a personal touch. His habitual refrain was that since his areas of publishing expertise did not make the firm money, he was obliged to ensure that he didn't lose too much. (Not that his young poets were likely to grow rich on 10 per cent royalties on sales over 500 copies – which is probably why he declared that 'poetry is not a career, but a mug's game' [*UPUC*, 154].) Eliot's stated aim 'to lose as little [money] as possible' could sound a little disingenuous once his name had become synonymous with Faber's success as a publisher of modern literature.[17] He tended to overplay the occasions when his poetry recommendations were shot down in the boardroom. On the other hand, his infrequent recommendations designed to increase the effectiveness of the sales and marketing side of the business were far from compelling to his colleagues (in the late 1940s one suggestion regarding publicity sparked an apoplectic response from Geoffrey Faber).[18] From the 1950s onwards, Eliot scaled back his publishing duties. He was permitted the luxury of tackling *The Times* crossword during the longueurs of the weekly afternoon book committee, until a special 'Mr Eliot's list' was drawn up to concentrate the aged eagle's publishing eye. Excessive demands were no longer placed on this elder statesman of letters, Nobel laureate and OM, whose health, which had never been robust, was beginning to fail.

In his affectionate 1961 memorial address for Geoffrey Faber, Eliot remarked that his chairman could not have foreseen how the risky recruitment of an obscure avant-garde poet back in 1925 had altered his life. (In fact, Faber told A. L. Rowse he had 'rescued Eliot for poetry'.)[19] It is worth recalling the unhappiness of Eliot's private life in the years after he joined the firm; how the Fabers and the Morleys propped him up following his separation from Vivien Eliot in 1933, and how his loyal secretaries handled his distraught wife on her unscheduled appearances at Russell Square, keeping her in the waiting room until he could slip out of the building. The abiding memory of Eliot, recalled by Geoffrey Faber's secretary in the mid 1930s, was of 'an unhappy man, smoking innumerable Gauloise cigarettes, crouched over his desk in an attic in Russell Square'.[20] Yet in many ways, Eliot's office, decorated with cherished personal mementos, became his home from home. A poem addressed to Morgan, the company cat, whimsically depicted him sharing Eliot's wartime fire-watching duties at Russell Square and is indicative of the way Faber became his family: little Tom Faber, among other godchildren (the children of colleagues), was the inspiration for *Old Possum's Book of Practical Cats* (1939), lyrics which appeared posthumously in the musical *Cats*, swelling the coffers of the firm where he had worked for forty years. Faber had been a rock to Eliot in the years following his separation from his first wife and it is fitting that he should propose to his second wife in his office. Eliot's marriage in January 1957 to his devoted secretary of seven years, Valerie Fletcher, might be viewed – in respect of his connection with the publishing house he did so much to lend world renown – to have set a crown upon a lifetime's achievement.

NOTES

1. 'Short Notices', *Egoist* (August 1918), 99.
2. F. V. Morley, 'T. S. Eliot as a Publisher', *T. S. Eliot: A Symposium*, ed. Richard March and Tambimuttu (London: Editions Poetry London, 1948), p. 67.
3. Virginia Woolf suggested that Eliot had 'poached' Read. See Hermione Lee, *Virginia Woolf* (London: Vintage, 1997), p. 447.
4. The first UK edition of *Ulysses* was published by Bodley Head in 1936.
5. Quoted in Ronald Schuchard, 'T. S. Eliot at Fabers: Book Reports, Blurbs, Young Poets', *Areté* (summer/autumn 2007), 76.
6. F. R. Leavis, 'This Poetical Renascence', *Scrutiny* (June 1933), 70.
7. 'Mr Louis MacNiece', *The Times* (5 September 1963), 14.
8. In a 1956 report for the Faber book committee, Eliot remarked: '[Roy Campbell] has the inconvenient habit ... of satirising in his rough clownish way, Faber poets'. Quoted in Schuchard, 'T. S. Eliot at Fabers', 80.
9. 'The Publishing of Poetry', *Bookseller* (6 December 1952), 1568.
10. Quoted in *Selected Letters of William Empson*, ed. John Haffenden (Oxford University Press, 2006), p. 159.
11. 'Conversation with James Reeves', *Review* (1964), 69.
12. T. S. Eliot to George Barker, 26 September 1937: 'I believe in your genius, so far as one is ever justified in believing in genius except in retrospect, and I believe that it is genius if anything and not talent.' Quoted in Robert Fraser, *The Chameleon Poet: A Life of George Barker* (London: Jonathan Cape, 2001), p. 101.

13. Ted Hughes journal entry, 5 January 1965, quoted in *Guardian* (2 September 2009).

14. Peter du Sautoy, 'T. S. Eliot: Personal Reminiscences', *Southern Review* (autumn 1985), 954.

15. Philip Mairet, *T. S. Eliot: A Symposium for his Seventieth Birthday*, ed. Neville Braybrooke (London: Rupert Hart-Davis, 1958), p. 43.

16. T. S. Eliot to George Orwell, 13 July 1944: 'I am very sorry because whoever publishes this [*Animal Farm*] will naturally have the opportunity of publishing your future work: and I have a regard for your work, because it is good writing of fundamental integrity.' Quoted in Bernard Crick, *George Orwell: A Life* (Harmondsworth: Penguin, 1980), p. 458.

17. 'Publishing of Poetry', 1569.

18. Details from the Faber archive related by Matthew Evans in *Guardian Review* (6 June 2009), 20.

19. Quoted in Peter Ackroyd, *T. S. Eliot* (London: Hamish Hamilton, 1984), p. 328.

20. Erica Schumacher (née Wright), letter to Jason Harding, 1 February 1999.

CHAPTER 9

Censorship

Rachel Potter

T. S. Eliot worked in a context of heavy literary censorship. The conflict between literature and the law reached its peak in 1921, when a New York court decided to prevent the American public from reading James Joyce's *Ulysses*. Alongside the famous obscenity trials of D. H. Lawrence's *The Rainbow* in 1915, *Ulysses* in 1921, and Radclyffe Hall's *The Well of Loneliness* in 1928, there were also less famous and institutionalised kinds of censorship, which worked to control the dissemination of texts. Alfred Kreymborg's rather mild short story about a prostitute, *Edna: The Girl of the Street*, was seized by the New York police in 1916.[1] The same year, Ezra Pound was told by the British publisher Elkin Mathews to omit four poems from *Lustra* because the printer objected to their salacious content.[2] Copies of the magazine the *Little Review* containing Wyndham Lewis's short story 'Cantleman's Spring Mate' were stopped by a New York postman in 1917. Djuna Barnes was forced by her American publisher Horace Liveright to alter the text of *Ryder* in 1928. In 1937, Boots's circulating library refused a book by Wyndham Lewis simply because the title, *False Bottoms*, was considered too vulgar. The hard-up Lewis dutifully changed the title to *The Revenge for Love*.

In addition to these British and American policemen, printers, post-men, customs officers, publishers and circulating libraries, authors also had to contend with the censoring sensibilities of private individuals. Nelly Morrison, typing up the manuscript of *Lady Chatterley's Lover*, only managed to get as far as chapter 6 before she declared herself unable to continue. On another occasion it was the typist's husband who interfered. When a British embassy official found his wife typing the 'Circe' section from Joyce's *Ulysses*, he famously threw it on the fire.[3] Not only is it the case that there was barely a modernist writer who was not censored in one way or another, it is noticeable that the agents of censorship were not simply judges, lawyers and anti-vice crusaders, but also those involved in the production and dissemination of texts. For a period of time, these individuals had the responsibility and the power to decide the fate of some of the most important works of twentieth-century literature.

This complex and fragmented structure of censorship had been arrived at haphazardly. Lord Campbell's Obscene Publications Act of 1857 had been designed to control the circulation of pornography in Britain. In the original debate over Campbell's bill, Lord Lyndhurst asked whether its powers might be extended to what he called literary works. Campbell rejected the idea that his proposal would effect the publication of novels and poems. He produced a copy of Alexandre Dumas's *La Dame aux camélias* (1848) and announced that even though he disliked this kind of novel, his bill would not effect such publications. He was wrong. By the late nineteenth century the distinction between literature and obscenity had become culturally unstable. The interpretation of Campbell's act in 1867 by Lord Chief Justice Cockburn, known as the 'Hicklin Ruling', had laid down an extremely broad definition of written obscenity: a work was to be considered obscene if 'the tendency of the matter charged as obscenity is to deprave and corrupt those whose minds are open to immoral influences and into whose hands a publication of this sort may fall'.[4] Prosecuting lawyers merely had to prove that an isolated passage of the book under examination could corrupt the mind of a child in order to justify suppression. When the London publisher Ernest Vizetelly was thrown into jail in 1888 for publishing English-language translations of Émile Zola's novels, it signalled a shift in the target of censorship prosecutions. From this point onwards, works that were considered to be at the forefront of literary innovation would be hauled before the courts.

Campbell's act also put in place a particular structure of censorship, one which specifically encouraged and enfranchised individuals to instigate censorship proceedings. It paved the way for the impressive power of pressure groups in both Britain and the United States to initiative and direct censorship actions. The notorious New York Society for the Suppression of Vice, formed in 1873 and run by Anthony Comstock, not only introduced legislation that empowered customs officials and postmen to seize obscene publications, but also instigated censorship proceedings. In Britain, the National Vigilance Society, formed in 1885, and the National Social Purity Crusade, formed in 1901, also pursued and prosecuted authors, publishers, distributors and consumers of obscene works. One of the consequences of such scattered networks of censorship, which presided over the dissemination of texts during the interwar period, was that it was hard to pin down 'the censor' as an object of attack. There was not a single person or piece of legislation which could be openly challenged. The figures of Anthony Comstock and his successor, John Sumner, were angrily associated with censorship laws in the United States. In Britain, the anti-libertarian journalist James Douglas, editor of the *Sunday Express*, and Sir William Joynson-Hicks, Conservative home secretary from 1924 to 1929, were often reviled by authors. In reality, however, these individuals were only one part of a complex and wide-ranging structure of censorship.

Censorship changed significantly during T. S. Eliot's lifetime, but these shifts must be traced not only in the activities and the statements made in the law courts, but also in particular cases and publishing decisions, which were themselves manifestations of wider cultural changes. Books written by many of Eliot's close contemporaries were banned. Throughout his career as an author, editor and publisher, he defended the rights of writers to freedom of speech. In the *Egoist* in 1918, he publicly supported the editors of the *Little Review* for publishing Wyndham Lewis's short story 'Cantleman's Spring Mate'; he signed petitions and wrote a number of essays in support of *Ulysses*; and in his editorial for the *Criterion* in September 1928 he deplored the suppression of Radclyffe Hall's lesbian novel *The Well of Loneliness*. In 1929 he protested against the censorship of D. H. Lawrence's paintings and as a consequence was instrumental in publishing Lawrence's pamphlet *Pornography and Obscenity* in the Criterion Miscellany series.[5] He was even prepared to appear as an expert witness for the defence at the trial in 1960 of Penguin Books for their publication of an unexpurgated edition of *Lady Chatterley's Lover*, although in the end he was not called to the witness box.

Yet as the above description of the networks of censorship makes clear, the role of the publisher was complex. At Faber & Faber, Eliot performed a precarious balancing act between supporting authorial freedom, exercising his own aesthetic and moral judgement, and protecting his firm from possible prosecution (see Chapter 8 above). It is not always easy to identify the boundary between these last two categories. For example, while Eliot embraced the difficult project of publishing Djuna Barnes's *Nightwood* and supported her work in his important 1937 introduction to the first American edition of the book, he also exercised a fairly heavy editorial hand with her manuscript, particularly with regard to her references to homosexual sex. He asked Barnes to change the word 'bugger' to 'boys' and to remove a reference to 'pubic hair' from one of Doctor O'Connor's monologues. While it is probably the case that in recommending these changes Eliot had one eye on the possibility of prosecution, Barnes herself saw them as originating from his own aesthetic and moral judgements.[6] Other instances of editorial interference seem to be in tension with the aesthetic principles at work in his poetry. Despite complaining when in 1916 the editor of *Poetry* magazine, Harriet Monroe, removed a line containing the word 'foetus' from 'Mr Apollinax' without asking for his permission, as a publisher at Faber he sometimes recommended similar changes. He asked W. H. Auden, for instance, to remove the phrase 'the fucked hen' from the first Faber edition of *The Orators* (1932).[7]

Other conflicts between Eliot's editorial and aesthetic judgements are more clearly the product of strategic decisions at Faber. He reported to the Faber board in 1937, for instance, that Lawrence Durrell's novel *The Black Book* was 'unprintable'. Rather than giving specific reasons why this was the case, he invoked Henry Miller's name as a shorthand signalling issues about the book's obscenity: 'One can see why Henry Miller thinks so highly of him, and all the wrong reasons'. A similar use of Miller's name informs his damning Faber book committee report on the *Diary of Anaïs Nin*: 'The stuff has appealed to giants like ... Henry Miller'.[8] Yet, surprisingly, he also wrote very positive blurbs for the Paris-based Obelisk editions of Miller's and Durrell's books. He recommended Miller's *Tropic of Cancer* (1938) as 'A very remarkable book, with passages of writing as good as any I have seen for a long time', and described Durrell's *The Black Book* (1938) as 'the first piece of work by a new English writer to give me any hope for the future of prose fiction'.[9]

Eliot's support for texts such as *Nightwood* and *Tropic of Cancer* testify to a lifelong interest in literary obscenity. The word 'obscene' is originally derived from the Latin *obscenus* meaning 'ill-omened', but it had come to signify that which should be left off stage or unrepresented. Keeping this definition in mind, Eliot was not only an interested reader of literary obscenity, he was also a committed writer of obscene verse. His bawdy King Bolo poems – which circulated privately among a group of male writers including Clive Bell, James Joyce, Wyndham Lewis and Ezra Pound – feature scenes of sodomy and rape. Not only did Eliot write such verses from his time as an undergraduate at Harvard up until his death, he also actively contemplated publishing them – first in the 1915 issue of the avant-garde magazine *Blast* and then, in 1921, he wondered whether a private edition of the poems could be brought out from Sylvia Beach's Paris bookshop (see *L1*, 562). The references to 'pleasant rapes' and Fresca's 'needful stool' (*WLF*, 39) in the drafts of *The Waste Land* also explore the obscene boundaries of the human body. Eliot's public and private engagement with the limits of the obscene fuelled a number of significant interventions into questions of censorship and freedom of speech in his editorials for the *Criterion*, particularly in the late 1920s. The remainder of this chapter will focus on two aspects of this engagement: first, on Eliot's specific arguments against censorship; secondly, on the impact of the legal instability of the relationship between literature and pornography, a crucial issue for writers after the successful prosecution of Vizetelly in 1888.

Clive Bell, in his 1923 book *On British Freedom*, attacks the various kinds of prohibitions, both literary and personal, that have made British life (as he puts it) 'uncivilised':

Censors of plays and of the press, licensing justices and the prohibitionists behind you, licensers of theatres, music halls, and films, with your gang attendant and instigating busybodies, anti-gamblers, anti-smokers, watch and vigilance committee men and women, informers, district-visitors, policewomen, writers of letters denouncing kissing in the parks or on the river, all you who are incessantly interfering in our lives, telling us what we must do and not do, how we must spend our leisure and our money, what we may eat and drink ... you are bit by the lust of power.[10]

Bell's description of the fragmented and ubiquitous censors who hover over British life, whether in the committee room or at the park, seeps into a more general argument about the enemies of freedom in the 1920s. He accounts for the existence and extent of these anti-libertarian busybodies by focusing on their invisibility. The censor is a bureaucratic tyrant, he argues, who is difficult to pinpoint or visualise: 'our modern tyrants sit, not in palaces, but in committee rooms'.[11] This focus on the committee taps into wider debates of the period about the transfer of power from recognisable sources of authority to nameless bureaucrats. For Bell, Britain is uncivilised because of the tyrannical and unaccountable form and the anti-libertarian content of this censoring power.

Eliot referred to Bell's book in his *Criterion* editorial of September 1928, in which he engaged with the 'withdrawal from circulation' of *The Well of Loneliness*. The trial is disturbing, he claims, because of a 'solemn hysteria which, as Mr Clive Bell would say, is uncivilized'.[12] Eliot invokes Bell's concept of the uncivilised as a way of grounding his arguments against the anti-libertarian, fragmented and hidden British censors. The image of uncivilised and solemn hysteria captures Eliot's general perspective in his discussions of the hypocrisy and the obscure, contradictory values that fuel censorship. In a letter of 1918 to the New York lawyer John Quinn, who had defended the *Little Review* against charges of obscenity, Eliot bemoans the censorship of his 'Mr Apollinax' and Lewis's

'Cantleman's Spring Mate' and complains of the hypocrisy of 'American Liberal Varnish' exemplified by literary editors such as Harriet Monroe and Amy Lowell, who are 'always decrying abstract Puritanism' but capitulate when faced with 'some particular work of art offensive to Puritan taste' (*L1*, 254).

While Eliot indicated the double standards and hidden Puritanism of liberal American editors, by the 1920s he had turned his attention to a more powerful vehicle for such cultural contradictions – the mainstream press. In his discussion of *The Well of Loneliness* trial, Eliot criticised the role of the *Sunday Express* in pressurising Radclyffe Hall to withdraw her book from circulation. In his subsequent discussions of censorship, he repeatedly returned to the power and hypocritical values of the press. In his account of the censorship of Lawrence's paintings the following year, Eliot provides a neat description of these double standards: 'We have lately seen in the daily press, which offers to its readers a small amount of news and an extensive space of bathing beauties, direct its readers to "obscene" books and "obscene" picture shows, and then exult in their condemnation.'[13] In these editorial commentaries, Eliot tries to bring into the open a more nebulous and contradictory set of beliefs than the American Puritanism described in his letter to Quinn. In his view, the obsession of the popular press with condemning obscene books grows in conjunction with the increasing focus of the wider culture on sexuality. This produces a dynamic in which newspapers such as the *Daily Express* condemn the very thing they not only expose and advertise, but also embody. To many authors of the time, such as Eliot, Bell, Lawrence, Pound and Joyce, this is classic busybody thinking. The sexual double standards that informed the censorship of books had long been a preoccupation of writers. Ezra Pound, for example, in his poem 'L'Homme moyen sensuel' (1917) satirised the agents of the New York Society for the Suppression of Vice by suggesting that they censored obscene literature by day and then visited prostitutes by night. The legal theorists Morris Ernst and William Seagle, in their seminal work *To the Pure . . . A Study of Obscenity and the Censor* (1929), focused attention on the way that jurists would prohibit texts that they enjoyed reading because of a stated concern for the moral health of others.

Eliot also attacked the censoring busybody in his editorials on *The Well of Loneliness* and on Lawrence's paintings. Where Bell pictured a committee room filled with faceless bureaucrats, Eliot envisioned a more scattered kind of interfering individual. Thus the Home Secretary Joynson-Hicks is a busybody who fails to 'think independently' and who hides behind his role as a protector of 'public morals'. His actions are directed by the prompting of journalists and letter-writers: Joynson-Hicks 'takes the opinion of the penny press, or of any busybody who chooses to protest'.[14] The censoring busybody is, by definition, individual and fragmented: it is hard to pin him or her to a specific ideological or religious position. Eliot, aware of the power of this surreptitious assertion of opinion, attempts to make it cohere into something that could be named and therefore criticised. In his references to the 'tyranny of morality' and the 'shouting of the mob', he combines ideas about the bullying and censorious sensibility of public opinion in order to bring into the open the negative power of those 'public morals' which politicians and lawyers claim need protecting.[15] By so doing, he takes up a particular intellectual line on censorship. Eliot believed that censorship embodied the problems facing literary texts in the context of an expanding reading public. He was not alone. The expansion of the reading public in the late nineteenth century was one of the key stated reasons for the introduction of tighter censorship laws. Legislators and anti-vice crusaders were specifically worried about the corrupting effects on the public of cheap, mass-produced obscene writing. This anxiety continued to be a feature of censorship debates up until the *Lady Chatterley's Lover* trial in 1960. Throughout this trial, much was made by the prosecuting counsel of the fact that the book was sold at 3s 6d and was therefore affordable to a mass readership.

Many of the key polemics against censorship in the 1910s and 1920s argued within the parameters of liberal claims about safeguarding the freedom of speech. In 1911 an American legal scholar and leader of the American Free Speech League, Theodore Schroeder, argued that the rights of authors should be defended with reference to the First Amendment. Ernst and Seagle suggested, 'the obscenity laws set the whole tone of our society, and in all their ramifications represent a myopic counteragent to democracy'.[16] There were a number of writers, however, including Eliot, who argued against censorship from a different vantage point. Eliot claimed that modern censorship was an integral part of the democratisation of culture and the demise of literary-cultural authority. Focusing specifically on the complex censorship networks outlined above, he insisted it was the power and the moral values of a sex-obsessed public that were curtailing the freedoms of writers and artists.

These different points of view form part of the wider debate about the proper balance between freedom of speech and the controlling power of popular public opinion. In 1859, John Stuart Mill argued that with the rise of democratic accountability, censorship could be dangerously imposed by public opinion. In the interwar period the censoring public constituted an important framework for modernist discussion of the autonomy of a literary text: the importance of this context has been increasingly linked to discussions of modernist elitism. As early as 1918, Eliot defended 'contemporary work of the finest literary quality' against the censor, specifically attempting to differentiate its fate from the judgements of mass public opinion.[17] His arguments on behalf of *Ulysses* in 1923 also focused on the artistic integrity and literary authority of the text. When he came to defend Radclyffe Hall's novel in 1928 the issue was more complex, because he had a low opinion of the novel's quality. Hall's novel should not be withdrawn from circulation, Eliot insists, not on the grounds that it is a fine work of art, but because she is a 'cultivated person with literary standards and ambitions' and because her intentions are 'sincere'.[18] This strategic definition represented a significant shift in the nature of his argument against censorship and allowed him to broaden the range of texts that could be protected under the banner of public liberties.

Eliot's focus on literary sincerity echoes Virginia Woolf's claim in 'Modern Fiction' that despite the fact that *Ulysses* is indecent, Joyce's artistic intentions are 'of the utmost sincerity'.[19] The word 'sincere' is originally from the Latin *sincerus* meaning 'clean', but it obviously ties in with broader ideas of integrity deployed by Eliot's and Woolf's arguments, and acts as an oppositional term to perceptions of cultural hypocrisy. Above all, however, sincerity is a key means by which both writers try to separate what they consider to be obscene literature from pornography. Although Eliot considers *The Well of Loneliness* to be 'dull, badly written' even 'hysterical', he nevertheless believes it should be allowed to circulate in the name of 'public liberties'. At the same time, he insists that what he calls 'admittedly pornographic productions', or in a later editorial 'genuine pornography', should be suppressed.[20] It is in their attempts to differentiate between pornography and literature that arguments against censorship in this period can seem at their weakest. Writers who had experienced censorship – Lawrence, Lewis and George Bernard Shaw – as well as those who had not – Arnold Bennett and Woolf – insisted that there were clear differences between obscene literature and pornography. If this was true in the case of *Ulysses* and *The Well of Loneliness*, some of the texts published in the 1930s trouble such easy distinctions. Eliot's insistence that some kinds of writing are genuinely pornographic begs the question of how one can distinguish between these texts and, for instance, Miller's *Tropic of Cancer*?

Eliot's focus on authorial intention would not have been permitted in legal discussions of obscenity in the 1920s. The law was solely concerned with the text, and the intentions of the publishers and author were excluded from legal proceedings. Attempts to distinguish between artistic obscenity and pornography would also have been dismissed, and yet Eliot was right to argue that a robust conception of the literary work would alter the debate about artistic freedom. In 1933, New York judge John Woolsey made the groundbreaking decision to free *Ulysses* from censorship by shifting the parameters of the obscenity debate in precisely this direction: he refuted the idea that Joyce intended to write a pornographic book. He argued that literature and obscenity were mutually exclusive.

Eliot's interventions in the censorship debates of the late 1920s attempted to transfer the charge of obscenity away from literature and towards sexualised popular culture and the pornographic text. In effect, he wanted to unmask the hidden censors who, as Michel Foucault argued in *The History of Sexuality* (1976–84), had internalised the structures of power which defined the modern secular liberal state. Eliot's line on censorship was connected to his arguments about democracy and literary authority in the twentieth century. While his editorials in the *Criterion* polemically defended authors against censorious public opinion, his actions as a publisher and writer involved an awareness of those structures of censorship that both controlled the dissemination of books and the assertion of his own aesthetic judgements about the boundaries of literature. In this sense, the contradictions in his position were a product of particular historical circumstances and were to change significantly during his lifetime. He was a witness to the publication, suppression and rerelease of *Ulysses*. His own religious and moral beliefs also underwent change – after he joined the Church of England, Eliot suggested censorship in the UK should issue from Lambeth Palace – but, interestingly, he extended rather than curtailed his defence of literary freedom, taking an even stronger line against censorship.

NOTES

1. See Felice Flanery Lewis, *Literature, Obscenity and the Law* (Carbondale: Southern Illinois University Press, 1976), p. 63.
2. Elkin Mathews printed 200 copies of *Lustra* (excluding 'The Temperaments', 'Ancient Music', 'The Lake Isle' and 'Pagani's'), which he would sell to anyone requesting an unexpurgated edition. Nine more poems were omitted from a second edition (and the title 'Coitus' was changed to 'Pervigilium'). Alfred Knopf published an uncensored American edition of *Lustra* in 1917.

3. Richard Ellmann recounts that Joyce had employed a 'Mrs Harrison, whose husband had a post at the British Embassy. She made good progress until on April 8 her husband glanced at the manuscript, and, scandalised, threw it into the fire.' See *James Joyce* (Oxford University Press, 1959), p. 335.

4. Quoted in Donald Thomas, *A Long Time Burning: The History of Literary Censorship in England* (London: Routledge & Kegan Paul, 1969), p. 264.

5. D. H. Lawrence's *Pornography and Obscenity* was followed in the Criterion Miscellany series by William Joynson-Hicks's *Do We Need a Censor?* Faber published both pamphlets in 1929.

6. See Cheryl J. Plumb, 'Introduction', *Djuna Barnes 'Nightwood': The Original Version and Related Drafts* (Normal, IL: Dalkey Archive Press, 1995), p. xxii.

7. The original line, 'Three kinds of enemy face – the fucked hen – the favourite puss – the stone in the rain' was restored to later editions. See *The English Auden: Poems, Essays and Dramatic Writings*, ed. Edward Mendelson (London: Faber & Faber, 1977), p. 81.

8. Quoted in Ronald Schuchard, 'T. S. Eliot at Fabers: Book Reports, Blurbs, Young Poets', *Areté* (summer/autumn 2007), 76, 77 and 83.

9. See the dust jackets of *Tropic of Cancer* and *The Black Book* (Paris: Obelisk Press, 1938).

10. Clive Bell, *On British Freedom* (London: Chatto & Windus, 1923), p. 58.

11. Ibid., p. 53.

12. 'A Commentary', *Criterion* (September 1928), 3.

13. 'A Commentary', *Criterion* (October 1929), 5.

14. Ibid., 3.

15. See 'A Commentary', *Criterion* (December 1928), 187 and (January 1937), 292.

16. Morris L. Ernst and William Seagle, *To the Pure . . . A Study of Obscenity and the Censor* (London: Jonathan Cape, 1929), p. 8.

17. 'Literature and the American Courts', *Egoist* (March 1918), 39.

18. 'A Commentary', *Criterion* (September 1928), 2.

19. Virginia Woolf, 'Modern Fiction', *The Common Reader: First Series*, ed. Andrew McNeillie (London: Hogarth Press, 1984), p. 151.

20. See 'A Commentary', *Criterion* (October 1929), 2 and (October 1930), 382–3.

CHAPTER 10

Literary journalism

Peter White

A significant but sometimes overlooked part of T. S. Eliot's sizable contribution to the literary and intellectual life of his time was made through journalism. Periodicals of different kinds were an important focus of his activities for almost sixty years, during which period he authored a prodigious and varied array of articles, book reviews, editorial commentaries, correspondence and other occasional writings. Donald Gallup's list of Eliot's published works in his *T. S. Eliot: A Bibliography* (1969) identifies more than 740 contributions to over 160 different periodicals and newspapers, a tally that has grown steadily over the years as additional items have been brought to light. Only a very small proportion of this material was reprinted in the volumes of literary and social criticism published by Eliot during his lifetime.

The earliest products of Eliot's involvement with the periodical press are to be found among his juvenilia. In 1905, when he was a 16-year-old day boy at Smith Academy in St Louis, his short stories and poems were printed in the school magazine the *Smith Academy Record*. During his undergraduate years at Harvard University he contributed verse to the *Harvard Advocate*, and in January 1909, in his third year, joined its editorial board. His contributions to the *Advocate* during his tenure as one of its editors include a handful of pieces in prose that show him exploiting some of the journalistic forms – editorial commentary, article, book review – to which he would return hundreds of times over the ensuing decades. The last of these prose pieces, a short review of James Huneker's *Egoists* (1909), is a particularly assured performance. Serious, exacting, even faintly pontifical in tone, it is recognisably akin to his journalism from the beginning of the interwar period, the period of his critical maturity.

Eliot's introduction to journalistic networks in England came by way of his association with the philosopher Bertrand Russell, whom he had met early in 1914, when the latter was a visiting professor of philosophy at

Harvard. Their acquaintance was renewed by a chance encounter on New Oxford Street in October 1914. Towards the end of the following year, Russell provided his former student with an introduction to Sydney Waterlow, one of the editors of the *International Journal of Ethics*. It was through Waterlow's connections that Eliot came to be involved with the *Manchester Guardian*, the *Westminster Gazette*, and the *New Statesman*. Early in 1916, Russell also introduced Eliot to Philip Jourdain, the British correspondent of the *Monist*, a journal of philosophy and science. For the *International Journal of Ethics* and the *Monist* Eliot reviewed new publications in metaphysics, ethics, anthropology, sociology and religion, drawing upon the training he had received during the previous four years as a graduate student of philosophy at the universities of Harvard and Oxford. One of the books he discussed in the *Monist* – J. W. Swain's 1915 English translation of Émile Durkheim's *The Elementary Forms of the Religious Life* – also formed the subject of his sole contribution to the *Westminster Gazette*. Although Eliot took this work as a reviewer of philosophical books very seriously, it is clear that at this time he felt the pull of a literary career and was actively exploring opportunities in the realm of literary journalism. One indication of this comes in the form of three short literary reviews printed in the *Manchester Guardian* in 1916, in which he appraised new volumes of poetry by Charles Doughty and Edgar Lee Masters and a rather undistinguished study of Thomas Hardy's novels. These reviews are couched in a style that is brisker and more self-consciously journalistic, more throwaway, than the one he uses in the learned journals to which Russell had introduced him. Eliot's desire to launch a career as a literary journalist is also clear from his contributions to the *New Statesman*, which began appearing from June 1916. His association with this paper would turn out to be an especially significant and productive one, bringing him into contact with one of the most influential men of letters in wartime London.

Founded in 1913 by Sidney and Beatrice Webb with the aim of promoting Fabian socialism, the *New Statesman* boasted from its inception a lively and engaging literary section. The success of the latter was largely due to the paper's literary editor and leading literary contributor, J. C. Squire, who is remembered today, if at all, as a second-rank poet and as the leader of the forces of retrograde Georgianism – the so-called 'Squirearchy' – in interwar London (see Chapter 22 below). In fact, Eliot seems initially to have warmed to Squire, and he certainly enjoyed writing for the *New Statesman*. The evidence for this enthusiasm is explicit enough in his correspondence ('The *New Statesman* is rather the best fun to review for' [*L1*, 157]) but it is implicit too in the ebullience of much of his writing for the paper. In addition to providing the *New Statesman* with short reviews on a wide array of books – literary, philosophical, American, French – Eliot approached Squire with two unsolicited contributions for the paper's high-profile 'Miscellany' section. The first of these, published in March 1917 as 'Reflections on *vers libre*', is an ambitious, attention-grabbing feature on the vogue for free verse among contemporary poets and their readers. Contributions to the *New Statesman*'s 'Miscellany' pages were usually printed with a signature, so 'Reflections on *vers libre*' and its companion piece 'The Borderline of Prose' can be seen as an attempt on Eliot's part to announce his arrival on the literary scene. 'Reflections on *vers libre*' also shows that at this stage of his career he was prepared to align his pronouncements on contemporary verse with the views of his editor. Squire had lampooned free verse poets in a short parody entitled 'Very Libre' printed in the 'Miscellany' section in August 1916, just at the time Eliot began planning his article. Squire also later denounced the free verse of the American poet Edgar Lee Masters as a 'stunt', an attempt to disguise the 'essential commonplaceness' of Masters's work. 'It remains to be realised', Squire fulminated, 'that all that is free is not verse.'[1] These interventions by Squire supply a suggestive context for 'Reflections on *vers libre*', in which Eliot exposes *vers libre* as a 'preposterous fiction' and states categorically that 'there is no freedom in art' (*SP*, 31, 32). Squire's attack on Masters may also explain why Eliot, in his article, appreciably moderates his enthusiasm for Masters's poetry, on which he had bestowed qualified praise in his earlier piece for the *Manchester Guardian*.

The tautness, allusiveness and showmanship of 'Reflections on *vers libre*' certainly bespeak an effort to impress Squire, but may also have reflected a sense on Eliot's part that he was addressing a public accustomed to analytical journalism. The *New Statesman* was a sixpenny weekly, one of a group of influential periodicals sharing a similar format and price and alike in offering independent, critical commentary on political, economic, literary and artistic current affairs. Other notable sixpenny weeklies of the period included the *Spectator*, the *Saturday Review*, the *Nation* and the *New Age*. The *Athenaeum*, which at this time was a shilling monthly, would be relaunched as a sixpenny literary weekly in April 1919. These were comparatively expensive papers, sober and restrained both in appearance and general tone, and evidently a minority taste. Certainly their circulations seem small, given their high standing and influence. The *New Statesman* was said to have a weekly sale of 'something over 3,000 copies' at the end of July 1915 and at this time 'was second in circulation only to *The Spectator* among the sixpenny weeklies'. By the end of 1916, when Eliot was planning 'Reflections on *vers libre*', its circulation had reached 6,000 copies.[2]

The audience for the *Egoist*, of which Eliot became the assistant editor in May 1917, was on an altogether different scale. This periodical's account book, preserved among the papers of Harriet Shaw Weaver in the British Library, records that the print run had fallen to 500 monthly copies at the time Eliot joined the editorial staff. This number fell further to 400 copies by the time of the September 1919 issue containing the first instalment of what is widely recognised as Eliot's most important essay 'Tradition and the Individual Talent'.[3] Actual circulation figures were smaller still. According to one account, in mid 1915 the *Egoist* had a 'nucleus of circulation' of only about 160 copies per issue, rising to 200 copies around the time when Eliot joined as an editor.[4] Although this was insufficient to cover the magazine's costs, Eliot appears to have found the experience of writing for the select readership of this paper liberating and enabling.

In previous incarnations the *Egoist* had been a feminist review, the *Freewoman* (1911–12), subsequently the *New Freewoman* (1913–14). Relaunched in 1914 as the *Egoist*, it became a predominantly literary paper, serving in particular as a vehicle for the Imagist poets associated with Ezra Pound. It was Pound who secured for Eliot the post of assistant editor, which became vacant when Richard Aldington was called up for military service. In fact, the *Egoist* was the only London periodical in which Pound exercised the necessary degree of control to influence an appointment of this kind; his sway over the periodicals in which Eliot would eventually achieve fame as a critic was negligible or non-existent.

The provincialism of English writing, the need for internationalism in art and what Eliot called 'cross-breeding' with the best verse in other languages – these are recurrent preoccupations of his contributions to the *Egoist*. Throughout his time as a columnist in the paper, he sought to lay bare what he saw as the insular 'Wordsworthian strain' in the anthologies of *Georgian Poetry* and in contemporary English verse more generally. But while Eliot's point of view in these pieces remains relatively consistent, the tone of his contributions to the *Egoist* developed considerably over the course of the two and a half years he wrote for the paper. The early instalments of his 'Reflections on Contemporary Poetry' series deal with their subjects in a manner that seems pointedly even-handed, urbane, detached. Even as late as March 1918, in his review of *Georgian Poetry 1916–1917*, his dismissal of Georgian verse is tempered with occasional praise – Squire's poem 'Lily of Malud' is called 'an original and rather impressive poem which deserves better company'.[5] In later *Egoist* contributions, Eliot's voice takes on a new edge, a new cut-and-thrust trenchancy, and his phrasing is more resonant (one piece entitled 'Observations' refers to the 'annual scourge of the Georgian Anthology').[6] It is also in his *Egoist* work that readers first encounter a strain of Eliotic portentousness, a feeling for the disturbing and unsettling qualities of modern literature, which is also a distinctive element in his collected prose writings. In 'Contemporanea', published in the summer of 1918, he asserts that the 'test of a new work of art' is that it should be 'terrifying' in the way that Wyndham Lewis's *Tarr* and James Joyce's *Ulysses* (which were both serialised in the *Egoist*) 'are terrifying'.[7] 'In Memory of Henry James' suggests there is 'something terrible, as disconcerting as a quicksand' in the Jamesian focus on situation and atmosphere.[8] The words 'terrible' and 'terrifying' would become two of his favourites during this part of his career, imparting gravitas to a number of key passages in his contributions to the *Athenaeum* and the *Times Literary Supplement*.

Writing for the *Egoist* may have allowed Eliot to develop considerably as a prose stylist, as a critical voice, but it was not a lucrative occupation. The *Egoist* account book records that his salary as assistant editor was £9 per quarter (£5 was donated by Pound without Eliot's knowledge). To put this figure into perspective, Eliot's starting salary at Lloyds Bank in 1917 was £120. His contributions to the *Athenaeum* and the *Times Literary Supplement* in the years immediately following the First World War were rather more generously rewarded, but did not in themselves provide an income comparable to his salary at Lloyds Bank. The marked contributors copy of the *Athenaeum*, preserved among the archives of City University in London, reveals that Eliot was paid £4 4s for his first contribution to the paper, an unsigned review article entitled 'The New Elizabethans and the Old'. For 'Hamlet and His Problems', which launched the phrase 'objective correlative' (*SE*, 145) upon the world, Eliot earned £4 2s 6d. His twenty-two reviews for the *Athenaeum* in 1919 brought him only £74 8s 9d. The marked contributors copy of the *Times Literary Supplement*, held in the archives of News International Limited, does not record the payment for his first contribution, a leading article entitled 'Ben Jonson', but it does reveal that 'Philip Massinger' brought him £12 12s, 'Andrew Marvell' £13 17s 6d, and 'The Metaphysical Poets' – which outlines his theory of the 'dissociation of sensibility' (*SE*, 288) – £11 10s.

Fees for both papers varied according to the length of the contribution; the higher rate of payment in the *TLS* was probably a reflection of the larger circulation of that paper (the issue containing 'Ben Jonson' sold 32,055 copies according to the figure quoted on the front page of the following week's issue).

Although at this stage of his career Eliot seems to have been dependent upon the income he derived from occasional writing, it is clear that ready payment was far from being the only stimulus for his journalism at this time. In associating himself with the rejuvenated weekly *Athenaeum*, Eliot was allying himself with an extremely influential group of writers, one that had at its core most of the leading figures of the Bloomsbury Group (see Chapter 23 below). Other notable contributors included Aldous Huxley and Katherine Mansfield. Eliot's attitudes towards these writers, many of whom were already known to him before John Middleton Murry invited him to write for the paper, remained ambivalent. All the same, the brilliance of the *Athenaeum* led to its contributors being identified as a distinct 'set', and a rather glittering one at that. Eliot's association with the paper brought him prestige and increased celebrity; it also implicated him in the literary politicking of the day. In aligning himself with the *Athenaeum*, Eliot was setting himself against Murry's bitter rival Squire, his former associate on the *New Statesman*, who in November 1919 had become the editor of his own literary magazine, the *London Mercury*. Squire evidently hoped to enlist the author of 'Reflections on *vers libre*' in the ranks of the contributors to the *London Mercury*, since 'T. S. Eliot' was included among the names of other literary notables in a full-page advertisement which appeared in various periodicals before the publication of the first issue.[9] It is conceivable that Eliot had agreed to contribute to Squire's monthly but changed his mind as a result of Murry's invitation to write for the *Athenaeum*.

The *Times Literary Supplement*, to which Eliot began contributing leading articles on sixteenth-century and seventeenth-century poets and dramatists at the end of 1919, stood aloof from the rivalries of the post-war London literary scene. A policy of anonymity was maintained, ostensibly as an indication and guarantee of the impartiality of the paper's reviews, but also, perhaps, as a convenient way of disguising its heavy reliance upon staff writers. Either way, the absence of signed articles imparted an Olympian quality to the *TLS*, and added considerably to its mystique. For contributors, the policy of anonymity was also more than a mere convention, since all submissions were subject to amendment by Bruce Richmond, the paper's editor. In 1958, Eliot recalled how 'the occasional deletion of a phrase' in his work for the *TLS* 'taught me to temper my prejudices and control my crotchets and whimsies'.[10]

The timbre of Eliot's critical prose in his contributions to the *Athenaeum* and the *Times Literary Supplement* is so perfectly accommodated to the high tone of these periodicals that it is tempting to conclude – as some commentators have concluded – his writing for them incorporates parodic and subversive elements. As a contributor to the marginal *Egoist*, Eliot had repeatedly mocked the grandiosity of the *TLS*, so it is perhaps natural to suppose that in joining the literary establishment of his day he must have sought to subvert its forms of expression from within. On occasion Eliot certainly enjoyed mixing gravity and waggery in his journalism, as the parodic opening to his *Athenaeum* piece 'War-Paint and Feathers' amply demonstrates.[11] But it is also evident from his correspondence of this period that he valued highly the social prestige afforded by his association with the *Athenaeum* and *TLS*, and this concern for status seems a clear indication of his identification with these papers as institutions. Pound was well placed to detect subversive elements in the writings of the man he dubbed 'Old Possum', but it is notable that he failed to find any such subversive glimmer in Eliot's work for the *Athenaeum*.

Two more points about Eliot's association with these journals should be made. The first is that Eliot's articles for the *Athenaeum* and their reception appear gradually and subtly to have shaped the way he conceived of himself as a critic. The focus on contemporary poetic innovation (*vers libre*, prose poems) evident in his work for the *New Statesman* and the *Egoist* gradually gives way in his *Athenaeum* pieces to a more persistent emphasis on sixteenth-century and seventeenth-century writing. This reorientation of critical interests was very much reflected in and reinforced by his work as a contributor to the *TLS*. The second point is that Eliot's reading of the *Athenaeum* and the *TLS* and his participation in the social scene that formed itself around the *Athenaeum* may well have played a role in his development as a literary theorist at this time. The mode of theoretical speculation characteristic of his critical prose in the post-war period was by no means alien to the journals in which his work was printed, and a number of elements of his critical thought can be shown to have been part of a shared critical currency among his fellow contributors. For instance, there is an intriguing resemblance between the theory of tradition elaborated by Eliot in his famous *Egoist* essay and one put forward by Clive Bell in his article 'Tradition and Movements' published in the *Athenaeum* several months earlier (although Eliot would have baulked at the suggestion of any direct influence).

As Eliot came to associate himself with the more prestigious London journals, it seems that he also became increasingly disenchanted with literary journalism as an occupation. This disenchantment can be glimpsed in some of his contributions to the *Athenaeum* (in his essay on William Blake he writes about the corrupting effects of a 'journalistic-social career' [*SW*, 152]), but it found its fullest expression in Harold Monro's monthly miscellany the *Chapbook*. In an essay entitled 'A Brief Treatise on the Criticism of Poetry', Eliot inveighs against the practice of reviewing as 'a barbarous practice of a half-civilised age'.[12] One source of this preoccupation with the corrupting effects of the culture of reviewing was probably the dismay he felt at the success of the *London Mercury* and the power Squire wielded over a number of London periodicals. His correspondence of the period is filled with denunciations of the *Mercury*; in one letter he remarks that Squire 'knows nothing about poetry; but he is the cleverest journalist in London' (*L1*, 435). The same animus informed Eliot's first prose collection, *The Sacred Wood* (1920), which he assembled in the months following the publication of his *Chapbook* essay from articles and reviews published in the *Athenaeum*, the *TLS*, the *Egoist* and *Art and Letters* (one of the most significant of the little magazines he wrote for in the immediate post-war period). The opening movement of this collection is devoted to an unflinching attack on the doyen of the *London Mercury* group, Sir Edmund Gosse, though in its opening essay, 'The Perfect Critic', Eliot identifies his target only as 'a distinguished critic' (*SW*, 1).

Eliot's development in the period following the publication of *The Sacred Wood* is exhaustively chronicled in the eighteen volumes of the *Criterion*, the provocative and sometimes highly polemical review he founded in 1922 and edited for more than sixteen years. At first a straightforwardly literary periodical, the *Criterion* printed creative work of undoubted significance and quality. Many of Eliot's poems made their first outings there ('The Waste Land' was printed in the first issue), and throughout its run the review featured new work by writers in the vanguard of modernism, including Joyce, Pound, Woolf, Stein, Moore, Auden, Spender and MacNeice. During the second half of the 1920s the *Criterion* gradually metamorphosed into a forum for social and political commentary and debate, much of it with an explicit theological dimension. It was a transformation that was at once both a reflection of Eliot's increasing preoccupation with problems of a social and spiritual nature, and a response to the feverish political climate of the time. It is fair to say that the polemical content of the *Criterion* has found fewer receptive readers than the literary contributions, and that for some commentators the literary lustre of the review was tarnished by its association and alignment with rightist thinkers such as Charles Maurras (see Chapter 26 below). However, as recent studies have shown, the *Criterion* remained to the end a forum in which divergent points of view could be expressed and evaluated.

The story of the *Criterion* begins during the summer of 1921, when Eliot became involved in negotiations with Viscountess Rothermere, the estranged wife of the owner of the *Daily Mail,* about the possibility of establishing a new literary quarterly. Lady Rothermere apparently wished to fund the creation of 'a more chic and brilliant' (*L2,* 513) successor to the magazine *Art and Letters,* which had ceased publication in 1920. *Art and Letters* had devoted a large proportion of its space to fiction and verse, and was generously illustrated with woodcuts, photo-mechanical prints and other illustrations. But this was not a model Eliot was inclined to follow. In fact, even before he settled upon a title for the new review, he had a very strong sense of the pared-down visual style he wanted, and in his correspondence with potential contributors he wrote that his 'modest' new quarterly would be 'simple and severe in appearance, without illus-trations' (*L1,* 655); it was to be 'neat but [with] no extravagance and not arty' (*L1,* 642). At the end of June 1922 he informed his publisher Richard Cobden-Sanderson that the new quarterly would be called *The Criterion,* an imposing title that is immediately suggestive of an emphasis on criticism and the maintenance of critical standards.

The *Criterion* was initially conducted on a very modest scale. Eliot was still a full-time employee of Lloyds Bank at the time of the review's launch, and carried out his editorial duties – which included everything from soliciting contributions to calculating payments to contributors – in his spare time. From May 1923 he was assisted in this work by Richard Aldington, but this arrangement was not a successful or happy one and Aldington resigned his position in December that same year. Eliot's review was entirely dependent on Lady Rothermere's subsidy (which started at £600 a year), and would continue to be so even after 1925, when the running of the *Criterion* was taken over by the publishing company Faber & Gwyer (later Faber & Faber), which Eliot joined in the role of director and literary adviser. Following this takeover, the *Criterion* was relaunched, first (in January 1926) as the *New Criterion,* then (in May 1927) as the *Monthly Criterion.* It reverted to its original title and less ambitious quarterly schedule in June 1928, largely as a result of Lady Rothermere's withdrawal of her subsidy at the end of 1927. For a time the future of the review was highly uncertain, but was eventually secured by guarantees from a group of private individuals including the scholar Charles Whibley, Bruce Richmond, and *Criterion* contributor May Sinclair. By this time the *Criterion* was something of an institution, and Eliot had attracted a group of dedicated collaborators – notably Herbert Read and Bonamy Dobrée – who assisted with the production of each issue and met regularly to discuss editorial matters.

One of the most notable features of the *Criterion* during the 1920s was its cosmopolitanism, its promotion of new writing from abroad. This emphasis was clear in the first issue, which included an appraisal of James Joyce's *Ulysses* by the French novelist Valery Larbaud and a survey entitled 'Recent German Poetry' by the German novelist and poet Hermann Hesse. The *Criterion* was the first periodical in England to print the work of a number of important European writers, including Marcel Proust, Paul Valéry, Jacques Rivière, Jean Cocteau, Ramon Fernandez, Jacques Maritain and Wilhelm Worringer. In the political turbulence of the 1930s it became harder for Eliot to maintain these links with the Continent, more difficult to discover the work of up and coming writers and commentators from abroad; but to begin with at least, the *Criterion* was extremely successful in looking beyond a largely insular English literary scene and setting international standards.

This internationalism was an aspect of the review's inclination towards what Eliot and his contemporaries termed 'classicism' (sometimes 'Classicism'), which was in part a recognition of and commitment to pan-European Latin-Christian culture and the 'European mind' (see Chapter 6 above). For Eliot, the modern, classical tendency was towards 'a higher and clearer conception of Reason, and a more severe and serene control of the emotions by Reason'.[13] Readers of the *Criterion* learned more about this tendency towards classicism through Eliot's editorial 'Commentaries', which were a regular feature of the review from the April 1924 issue onwards. To begin with, these commentaries were printed over the pseudonym 'Crites' (perhaps because as an employee of Lloyds Bank he was reluctant to be openly identified as the editor of the review) and were prompted for the most part by topical literary, artistic and cultural questions. Eliot wrote about the Russian ballet; the difficulty of obtaining cheap reprints of seventeenth-century texts; the demise of the Egoist Press (which had published his first book, *Prufrock*); and the threatened destruction of the City churches (including St Magnus Martyr, which figures in 'The Waste Land'). There were also brief reviews of performances by the Phoenix Society (which revived Renaissance and Restoration plays) and obituary notices, for example on the novelist Joseph Conrad and the philosopher F. H. Bradley (the subject of Eliot's doctoral thesis). In the late 1920s and in the 1930s, Eliot's commentaries dwelt more on social and political questions – the rise of Fascism and Communism, the clearance of slum areas, censorship, the meaning of the phrase 'the standard of living', and so on. Eliot's point of view was a reactionary, classicist one, favouring authority over democracy and dogmatism over tolerance. In his commentaries, he often revealed himself to be a formidable controversialist, adept at exposing the pseudo-religions of his time; to some readers he also appeared to be out of touch with events. Eliot's critics have accused him of petulance, pomposity and condescension; even by his own admission, his commentaries in the 1930s betrayed a mind that was 'obscure and confused'.[14]

Eliot's termination of his editorship of the *Criterion* in 1939 was far from being the end of his career in journalism, despite the fact that in his 'Last Words' as editor of the review he commented that he no longer felt 'the enthusiasm necessary to make a literary review what it should be'.[15] During the sixteen years of his editorship, he had remained active as a contributor to other periodicals, notably the *TLS* and the *Nation and Athenaeum* (formed from the union of the *Nation* and Murry's *Athenaeum* in 1921); as the *Criterion* closed its doors, he maintained many existing associations and forged new ones. Particularly important in his post-*Criterion* period was the *New English Weekly*, in which he published the essays later revised to form the opening of *Notes Towards the Definition of Culture* (1948) as well as the three wartime poems collected in *Four Quartets* (1943). During the war he guest-edited five issues of the *Christian News-Letter* and made numerous contributions to a wide array of other periodicals throughout the 1940s and 1950s. Even towards the end of his life, during the 1960s, Eliot continued to make frequent appearances in the correspondence columns of *The Times* and other newspapers, writing to editors on such topics as the New English Bible and independent television. The last of these letters, headed 'Split Infinitive', was published in the *Daily Telegraph* only seven months before his death.

NOTES

1. J. C. Squire, 'Books in General', *New Statesman* (23 September 1916), 593.
2. See Edward Hyams, *The New Statesman: The History of the First Fifty Years, 1913–1963* (London: Longmans, 1963), pp. 46, 74.

3. Harriet Shaw Weaver Papers, British Library, Add. MS 57362.

4. See Jane Lidderdale and Mary Nicholson, *Dear Miss Weaver: Harriet Shaw Weaver 1876–1961* (London: Faber & Faber, 1970), pp. 106, 121.

5. 'Verse Pleasant and Unpleasant', *Egoist* (March 1918), 43.

6. 'Observations', *Egoist* (May 1918), 69.

7. 'Contemporanea', *Egoist* (June/July 1918), 84. *Tarr* was serialised in the *Egoist* from April 1916 to November 1917, while chapters 2, 3, 6 and 10 of *Ulysses* appeared there in 1919.

8. 'In Memory of Henry James', *Egoist* (January 1918), 2.

9. See, for example, 'The London Mercury edited by J. C. Squire', *New Statesman* (11 October 1919), 48.

10. 'The Disembodied Voice', *Times Literary Supplement* (17 January 1958), 31.

11. See 'War-Paint and Feathers', *Athenaeum* (17 October 1919), 1036.

12. 'A Brief Treatise on the Criticism of Poetry', *Chapbook* (March 1920), 9.

13. 'The Idea of a Literary Review', *Criterion* (January 1926), 5.

14. 'Last Words', *Criterion* (January 1939), 273.

15. Ibid., 274.

CHAPTER 11

Visual art

Charles Altieri

Now I am back in London, the town of cubist teas, and find it more
delightful and beautiful than ever

(*L1*, 100)

I enjoyed the article on the Vortex (please tell me who Kandinsky is)

(*L1*, 94)

As is evident from my epigraphs, it would not be easy to use T. S. Eliot's
various remarks on painters as an incisive measure of how the visual
functions in his poetry. Nor will it help much if we want to supplement
what David Trotter calls 'parallel histories' between literature and various
aspects of visual art.[1] We get a better picture of his relation to the visual
arts if we concentrate on the pains and difficulties that Eliot's work
displays when it renders visual experience. Such comparisons allow us to
trace analogies between his own discomfort before images that seem to be
vying for his attention and modernist visual artists' own alienation from
claims that description or representation provided the most stable means
of characterising knowledge and so clarifying values. Eliot's own actual
relation to the visual arts seems, then, an outgrowth of his wariness before
all visual experience, because that experience seemed so insistently bound
to objective surfaces that it could not display the density of relations that,
for Eliot, constituted a livable reality.

It is clear from Eliot's letters that what most interested him in the visual
arts were images of St Sebastian.[2] Perhaps intense visual experience put
Eliot in an analogous position to Sebastian, condemned to a passivity that
registers wounds but cannot actively address the infinite longings they
awaken. Consider an example from Eliot's early poetry of an incredible
bleakness evoked by the demands of sheer visuality. I quote from the
middle of 'First Debate Between the Body and Soul':

> The eye retains the images,
> The sluggish brain will not react

> Nor distils
> The dull precipitates of fact
> ...
> The cosmic smudge of an enormous thumb
> Posting bills
> On the soul.   (*IMH*, 64)

This passage does not require critical commentary, aside from recognising how in his first book of poetry Eliot typically emphasises visual surfaces painfully refusing any symbolic or even aesthetic dimension that might engage the alienated spirit. One might be

> moved by fancies that are curled
> Around these images, and cling:
> The notion of some infinitely gentle
> Infinitely suffering thing.

but sight can only ally with the mind eager to resume its self-protective ironies:

> Wipe your hand across your mouth, and laugh;
> The worlds revolve like ancient women
> Gathering fuel in vacant lots.   (*CPP*, 23)

Yet none of these poems submits entirely to visuality. Sound and pronounced structural patterns promise to sustain openings to a world from which sight withdraws by reinforcing third-person rather than first-person perspectives. So it seems that Eliot wants elaborate structure to establish a locus of values beyond vision, although it cannot assure that this locus will do anything more than intensify frustration and suffering.

The basic irony of my story is that the parallels Eliot develops with modernist painting occur because that painting also relies on structural effects to combat the primacy of objective vision and liberates an eye capable of resisting empiricist values. In other words, the affective context Eliot evokes for the visual helps indicate why both modernist art and modernist writing were reluctant to insist on the purely visual features of the image. Ezra Pound, for example, shared the fear of modernist painters from Paul Cézanne to Piet Mondrian that Impressionist opticality was of a piece with the project of cultivating the senses and minimising the powers of mind to resist empiricist values and claim access to more fundamental realities. Modernist writers and artists had to find means of showing how the art of painting could offer an embodied thinking: the more intense the thinking, the more elemental the bodies could become. The task of painting becomes overcoming the alienation produced by satisfaction with visual modes of objectivity, so that visual art could establish events making active the elemental features grounding appearances in dynamic structures. To establish an alternative to this, painters had to drastically alter the manifest role of the composing force establishing the fields of relatedness within the work. They rejected the kind of authority traditional painters might seek by displaying an overall mastery of a definable scene in favour of a sense that the art-making took place as a negotiation of tensions that were not resolvable except by recognising how various forces were intensified by the oppositions refusing synthesis. And that refusal of synthesis was to have major consequences for how artists thought about their relations to social authority, since they had to reject prevailing distinctions among what Meyer Abrams defined as the four basic topoi of western aesthetics – author, work, audience and universe.[3] Both artists and poets seemed devoted to giving a substance to the inner sensuousness that G. W. F. Hegel posited as the essential trait of the Romantic mode of art.

I can outline the story by developing some implications of what Cézanne expressed in 1881 when he painted a scene that Camille Pissarro rendered in 1873 as *The Railway Bridge at Pontoise*. Pissarro's is a brilliant painting in its dealing with contrasting details and in modulating those contrasts to create an overarching sense of a comprehensive painterly unity. The work elaborates careful contrasts like the relation between trees in shadow and in full sunlight as well as the more abstract contrast between the pull of that horizontal relation against the powerful recession that pulls the containing sky virtually beyond the vanishing point. This stretching of the image becomes the painterly point. Pissarro wants to give the eye a feeling for its capacity to negotiate capacious contrasts within a scene and still recognise how the composition manages to unify the scene and offer it for the contemplation of an audience.

Cézanne makes stunning changes in the scene, whose primary effect is to repudiate the generous and capacious Impressionist eye. Now the painting offers a slightly different angle of access than Pissarro's rendering that enables it to include houses on the left and to eliminate the road's continuity establishing depth of field. What depth there is comes from emphasising a hill in the background, so that the painting produces a continuous sense of recession as also a journey upward for the eye. That journey frees the sky to do something other than constitute a vertical force capable of containing all the horizontal diversity. This change opens up the trees on both sides and makes them more dramatic presences. There is still something of Pissarro's contrast between degrees of shadow. But

Cézanne is insistent on these contrasts being primarily a result of the weight and breadth of the brush strokes. Cézanne is less concerned with how light affects our sense of substance than how differences in brush stroke compose another kind of art substance that in turn suggests a somewhat different way of seeing. Because the trees become more active as markers of painterly energy, they also complicate the bridging and stretching roles played in Pissarro's painting. These trees extend towards the top of the painting and so emphasise a leafy vertical force barely mobilised in Pissarro. The effect of that vertical force is to lead away momentarily from the central path upward from the foreground foliage to the hill and to the strange striated sky. The trees do not want to be reduced to a co-operative structural horizontality (hence the lack of protracted shadows), and in their resistance they continue the colours of the water in permutations that reinforce a circular motion made possible by the partial erasure of the roads through the painting.

All this energy ultimately derives from how the painting establishes structural tensions that the painter can intensify and balance but not interpret or master. The painter's insistent presence has to work from the inside out, finding visual force less in the composition of the whole than in the pressure that the parts put on one another. Therefore the painting offers a drama of contending, or what William Carlos Williams called the figure of a 'composing –/antagonist'.[4] Notice, for example, how the foliage in the frontal plane and the striated sky both create a sense of the local that refuses to yield the feeling of generous capaciousness. More important, the tensions extend to the painting's demand that we situate ourselves within it in accord with two competing overall perspectives or modes of visual habitation. These contrasting perspectives simply refuse to allow hegemony to one painterly stance. One perspective enters the painting at its lowest point, has to struggle to get beyond the foreground foliage, and travels up to the hills and the flat sky so unlike Pissarro's containing dome. A second perspective organises those horizontal and circular forces that seem incompatible with the first. This perspective looks down from above and honours the anchoring force of the water. The horizontal line of the trees becomes a force mediating between depth and flatness. And as the water gains power it recedes sharply into its own spatial depth while pulling against the flattening effects of the striated sky without vanishing point. To honour the painting's achievement, we have to see these tensions not as a failure to provide a more inclusive view but as the redirecting of all the energies classical painting puts into unity so that they seek mutual adjustment rather than inclusion in a sense of the whole. Cézanne here becomes what the Russian painter and art theoretician Kazimir Malevich sees as his inspiration – the painter who makes intricate balance and various rhythms of emergence and dissolution the mark of painting's peculiar spirituality. Such painting does not master flesh but intensifies the relations by which the elemental forces make visible their own powers to gather being.

There are at least two levels to this play of mutually dependent forces that seem, to me, distinctively modernist and that afford a clear path back to Eliot's priorities as an artist. The first, the simplest, is the insistence on the constant co-presence of subject and object as each requiring the activity of the other. The world within the work is not seen; it is 'rendered' or 'realised' (to cite quite different but related ideals – one named by Joseph Conrad, the other by Cézanne). Such rendering or realising stages the object as visibly apprehended by a subject whose traces it cannot escape. And the subject lives only to the extent that it modifies the objects that come into its ken. In art at least, there is no sheer objectivity and no radical inwardness; there are only degrees of mutual modification.

Self-consciousness about this level leads some artists to a second level of reflection where they ask what this interpenetration involves for their understanding of the artwork as a whole. Such questioning leads to the recasting of Abrams's topoi mentioned earlier, which in turn leads to reconsidering the ideal of autonomy projected by most aesthetic theory in the nineteenth century. Rather than treat the work as an analogue for what Immanuel Kant called moral agency, the work becomes a site where individuality is constituted by how the particular qualities of the work establish distinctive interdependency. All the ladders to this new modernist artwork begin with the negative experience of having to resist models for art that focus on renderings of nature derived from studio traditions or that submit to the culture's demands for edifying narrative and melodramatic scenes. Then we can look positively at the resources found in works of art like Cézanne's *Bridge and Dam, Pontoise* (1881) that might flesh out a powerful set of claims on society. At the most elemental level, autonomy becomes the artist's trust that the intensity of those constructed internal relationships constitutes a complex engagement with experience that cannot be distinguished from a position beyond the tensions with which it engages. Eliot's doctoral thesis on the philosophy of F. H. Bradley can show the way here:

There is no reason, so long as the one feeling lasts and pervades consciousness, why I should cut off part of the total content and call it the object, reserving the rest to myself under the name of feeling. It is only in social behaviour, in the conflict and readjustment of finite centres, that feelings and things are torn apart. (*KEPB*, 24)

Just as impersonality fuses artist and audience, so the work tries to capture a fundamental sense of the world as suffused by feeling. Feelings are not added to objects as interpretations to events. Rather, feelings are inseparable from the objects as the work is from the aspects of the world it renders.

This is a very different sense of the world than that offered by Pissarro in his paintings of the 1870s. Pissarro does share Eliot's sense of the fusion of feeling and seeing. But he ignores the philosophical challenges Eliot poses to traditional modes of understanding. Pissarro's work depends on discrete understandings of each of Abrams's topoi. For him, a distinctive artistic purpose deploys the labour of craft to produce a fresh and capacious visual sense of the world for an audience that wants to contemplate what nature can become. For Cézanne, though, the situation is quite different, because his work does not honour such obligations. Cézanne's emphatic brushwork emphasises the mutual dependency between how the painting foregrounds technical accomplishments and the kind of world it makes possible. The mutual dependency determines not just the details one sees, but the qualities that one attributes to the event of seeing.

Cézanne's breaking down and reconstituting the author–audience distinction may be even more significant. It is clear from his letters and the paintings themselves that Cézanne imagined success in painting as the capacity to fully give his personality up to the space defined by the work. For he understood that holding on to empirical personality becomes a defence against the full intensity that one can experience as one enters the various forces that comprise a painted scene – as work and world become fused. So the authorial agency becomes inseparable from a kind of will to be other, to be defined solely by the painting's mode of access to the world. And that otherness is precisely the site where author and audience join. For it is the sharing in the audience function that is crucial in freeing the author from mere charm of personality into the intensities offered by the work. Author and audience and work and world need not become identical with each other, but these concepts become unthinkable without recognising how each component is profoundly modified by the roles the other topoi play in our making sense of the work. The claim I am making about Cézanne can be extrapolated to other modernist painters, especially to the non-iconic ones whose force depends most emphatically on redefining the elemental features of painterly experience as events where making and participating become one.

I will conclude by returning to Eliot – this time to *The Waste Land* – to suggest the difference it makes if we see this poem as stressing the mutual interdependency inviting redefinitions of author, audience, work and world. Several features of Eliot's thinking will support this point of view, including his distrust of personality,[5] his philosophical claims that degrees of reality are a matter of the thickness of relationships, his sense of how it is reductive to claim ownership of feelings by an individual subject, and his insistence on how what is objective as the work defines the possibilities for its intersecting with experience in the world. But for now I will elaborate how *The Waste Land* can be experienced if one emphasises its parallels with modernist painting, focusing on his manifest refusal to allow the self's empirical expectations to block us from the more direct and fluid experience of how something like spirit is unhappily meshed within particular social conditions. One might see Eliot's poem as mobilising and connecting a flow of feelings that open into more abstract worlds than the empirical personality is comfortable with: these abstract worlds are also concrete, but they are concrete in elemental ways that do not fit our habitual categories for psychological dramas.

Consider, for example, Eliot's use of 'you' as an audience term in both 'The Love Song of J. Alfred Prufrock' and *The Waste Land*. 'You' here is certainly concrete, at least in the sense that it designates both a clear function and a clear need to communicate. But there is no empirical 'you' who could quite fit the bill. This is because no empirical 'you' can quite satisfy the imaginary need eliciting the address. This need in turn foregrounds how much the 'you' is inseparable from the needs and desires and activities of the speaking voices. 'I' and 'you' become a desperately insubstantial pair, each continually collapsing into the other. And this mutual collapsing might be fundamental for the cross between a principle and a character made of the feeling for this lack that becomes *The Waste Land*'s 'third who walks always beside you' (*CPP*, 73). This projected 'third' provides a central figure enabling Eliot to transform and reactivate the most fundamental features of traditional lyricism.[6]

On one level, the poem does not stray much from tradition because we can see it as a return to an allegorical plot that builds to a climactic moment when the thunder utters its commands; then there is a tragic fall into disintegrated voices because of the paralysis manifest as the presiding consciousness tries to act on the values it wants to affirm.[7] Yet this is not conventional allegory, because the meanings for the poem derive less from what the symbols stand for than from two performative aspects of the impersonal and transpersonal authorial presence. First, the poem uses the interdependence of author and audience to present society in a distinctive way. Society is not primarily something referred to, but something that takes on presence because of the multiple voices that at once constitute it and express its modes of suffering. The presence of these voices affords a concrete level which serves to problematise the very allegory giving the voices significance. For the voices lack the energy and direction to make use of the allegorical level. At the same time their pain and confusion presents a human presence very much in excess of any meaningfulness the allegory can control. Eliot uses the mutual dependency of work and world not to establish a dynamism in nature but to make present forces and needs that so suffuse the world that they deprive it of determinable significance. Second, Eliot has to invent an authorial stance that can grapple with this massive limiting condition. He does this by correlating the problematic effort to secure the totalising figures of allegory with an authorial commitment to participate intimately in what these voices feel. Then the voices might elicit a sense that they embody directly what it means to feel oneself in a waste land. While the poem offers no specific hope, it does open a domain where sympathy itself takes on something approaching spiritual density. Impersonality provides a means of listening that is at once sympathetic and diagnostic, at once self-implicating and offering the possibility of self-transcendence.

The power of Eliot's impersonality is most pronounced at the point where work and world prove most inextricably related. I refer to uses of rhythm that are quite at odds from the regularities that critics have stressed in the analytic moments of 'The Burial of the Dead' and 'A Game of Chess'. Rhythm in 'What the Thunder Said' becomes the aspect of materiality that grounds these voices in something deeper than their social conditions and makes their emotional burden available for those who can shed the more analytic languages about society that for Eliot are part of the problem rather than forces working towards resolution. So both maker and audience have to be defined more by their capacity to respond to those rhythms than by any traditional cognitive power. There is taking place a spiritual struggle for cognition, but its instrument is a tearing away of reason so that there might be a more immediate and capacious way of responding to what these voices display. Yet that capaciousness remains utterly ineffective in a world where action depends upon the very modes of cognition the poem cannot trust.

For Eliot, modernist principles of composition fail to relieve the conditions making his world a waste land. But that failure is not total. Precisely because the work constructs such dense interrelationships on every level, it demonstrates something like a counter-reality won by products of the imagination. Minimally, the poem composes a substance for collective pity that can define a site of imaginative power painfully aware also of its impotence in the practical domain. And maximally the poem establishes for imagination a domain so free of the claims for personality that it offers a strange, almost physical space where work and world join. There is no possibility for action that internalises the Sanskrit wisdom of the poem's closing line 'Shantih shantih shantih' (*CPP*, 75). But there is the possibility of the imagination inhabiting an unreal space where we enter a communal life formed by attention to collective suffering. There is even the wistful promise that we could change our lives if we learned fully to inhabit this otherworldly space. Given what the visual had become, this possibility may well be still worth pursuing.

NOTES

1. See David Trotter, 'T. S. Eliot and Cinema', *Modernism/Modernity* (April 2006), 237–65.
2. Eliot informed Conrad Aiken, 19 July 1914: 'There are *three* great *St Sebastians* (so far as I know): 1) Mantegna (Ca d'Oro)[;] 2) Antonello of Messina (Bergamo)[;] 3) Memling (Brussels)' (*L1*, 46). In fact, the *St Sebastian* in Bergamo is by Raphael.
3. See Meyer Abrams, *The Mirror and the Lamp* (Oxford University Press, 1953), p. 6.
4. William Carlos Williams, *Imaginations* (New York: New Directions, 1970), pp. 98–9.
5. See Sharon Cameron *Impersonality: Seven Essays* (University of Chicago Press, 2007) for a superb account of the various kinds of mobility and relationality generated by Eliot's fascination with impersonality.
6. Criticism for the most part has not gone in this direction, especially in relation to *The Waste Land*. Marjorie Perloff's *21st-Century Modernism* (Oxford: Blackwell, 2002) finds *The Waste Land*'s version of impersonality a substantial falling off from the intricate instabilities of the earlier poetry. I think Perloff provides a powerful picture of the pressures Eliot had to confront in *The Waste Land* without sufficiently regarding the force that his innovations give to the poem's content.
7. For the best succinct version of a plot for *The Waste Land*, see Charles Tung, 'Modernist Contemporaneity: Rethinking Time in Eliot Studies and *The Waste Land*', *Soundings* (fall/winter 2006), 379–404.

CHAPTER 12

Dance

Terri Mester

Dance and poetry may seem like odd bedfellows. One exists only at the ephemeral vanishing point, while the other produces timeless, unchanging artefacts. One is the silent art of the body, the other a verbal art of the mind. Yet in the first quarter of the twentieth century, dance creatively fertilised the works of several of the leading literary modernists – W. B. Yeats, D. H. Lawrence, William Carlos Williams, Hart Crane and especially T. S. Eliot. For all his reserve, Eliot was a connoisseur of dance. Revealingly, there are no beautiful female dancers adorning Eliot's poetry as figures of a unified sensibility as there are in Yeats, nor women dancing alone as an expression of psychic imbalance as there are in Lawrence's novels, nor the lusty, dancing satyrs found in Williams's poetry. Moreover, Eliot had no use for the American dancer Isadora Duncan's liberation of the female body. In his poetry, moths dance ('The Burnt Dancer'), bears dance ('Portrait of a Lady') and cats dance (*Old Possum's Book of Practical Cats*), but when a woman dancer appears in 'Whispers of Immortality' she is disparagingly likened to a 'Brazilian jaguar' with 'so rank a feline smell' (*CPP*, 52, 53).[1]

Yet Eliot, like many of his acquaintances in the Bloomsbury Group, was enthralled with the Russian ballet that the impresario Sergei Diaghilev brought to Europe – and for good reason. Amy Koritz notes that 'major tenets of literary modernism, as expressed in Eliot's criticism of the late teens and early twenties, are cut from the same conceptual cloth as many of the aesthetic values informing the dance modernism of the Russian ballet'.[2] In particular, Eliot was influenced by two of the new ballet's leading male stars: Vaslav Nijinsky, whom he saw in Paris in 1911, and Léonide Massine, whom he saw in London from 1919 to 1924. Nijinsky was an inspiration behind several of Eliot's poems, just as Massine was a catalyst for many of his aesthetic speculations. In both performers, Eliot perceived a refinement, control and transcendence of the body which amounted to a triumph over the limitations of the self. Nijinsky haunts the early poem 'The Death of

Figure 4   Vaslav Nijinsky in *Petrouchka*.

Saint Narcissus', in which a martyr performs a *danse macabre* in the desert while burning arrows pierce his flesh. Although Eliot did not witness Nijinsky's choreographic score for *The Rite of Spring* in Paris, there is an uncanny resemblance between the ballet's atavistic, dehumanised masses

Figure 5   Léonide Massine in *The Three-Cornered Hat.*

and *The Waste Land*'s hordes of wandering automatons. In addition, key images in 'The Hollow Men', 'Burnt Norton' and 'Little Gidding' derive from ballets – *Petrouchka, Narcisse* and *Le Spectre de la rose* – that have become synonymous with this great dancer.

In articles for the *Dial* and the *Criterion* in the early 1920s, Eliot singled out Massine as exemplifying the virtues of the new ballet. The primary quality was the impersonality of the dancer in performance. Massine's impersonality was the result of self-sacrifice to a 400-year-old tradition in which the past and present existed simultaneously. Eliot was also influenced by the way Massine's choreography appropriated popular forms and transformed them into an elite art. From watching Massine, he observed how the ritualistic and rhythmical elements of dance tapped unconsciously into the spiritual springs of art. As a consequence, ballet became one of his ideal models for a new poetic drama.

Eliot loved to dance himself and frequently attended London dance halls. In 1919 he invited Mary Hutchinson, a Bloomsbury hostess and close friend, to join him at a dance hall near Baker Street: 'They teach the new dances and steps, which I don't know and want to learn' (*L1*, 326). Before their marriage, Eliot frequented these dance halls with Vivien Haigh-Wood, who had some training in ballet. He admitted to his cousin Eleanor Hinkley that he was attracted to Vivien because she appeared 'charmingly sophisticated', smoked and was a 'very good' dancer (*L1*, 105). Another London literary hostess, Brigit Patmore, recalled an incident which suggests that, in the early years of their marriage, Eliot took Vivien's dancing seriously. They were in a drug store when Vivien suddenly decided to imitate the prima ballerina Tamara Karsavina. She rose on one leg, extended the other in arabesque and held out her arm for her husband to support her. Overcoming his natural embarrassment, Eliot 'watched Vivien's feet with ardent interest whilst he supported her with real tenderness'.[3] Unfortunately, because he identified Vivien with dancing, his subsequent marital disillusionment may also have contributed to the derogatory portrayal, already evident in the brief appearance of female dancers in 'The Love Song of J. Alfred Prufrock' and 'Cousin Nancy', of the dancer 'Grishkin' in 'Whispers of Immortality'. As these poems make clear, Eliot harboured a strong distaste for the erotic connotations of dance. His female dancers are mistresses of deceit and artifice and their dancing is sterile. They fit into Lyndall Gordon's classification of Eliot's treatment of women in his early poetry as either butts of 'ironic dismissal' or of 'a sense of sin'.[4]

On the other hand, the male dancer in 'The Death of Saint Narcissus' (written in 1915), although morbidly self-absorbed, is treated sympathetically. A self-tormenting religious martyr, the saint is also an aspiring prophet who turns his narcissism into a virtue. He is 'struck down' by the knowledge of his own beauty and 'could not live men's ways', so he becomes instead a 'dancer before God' (*CPP*, 605). Secluded in the desert, he escapes from humanity and dances for the sensual pleasure–pain of God's arrows penetrating his bleeding flesh. The poem ends ambiguously with the suggestion that the saint may have been deluded: he turns 'green, dry and stained / With the shadow in his mouth' ultimately becoming a 'dancer to God' (*CPP*, 606) rather than before God.

Curiously, in his diary Nijinsky referred to himself as a 'dancer to God' and one critic has argued that Eliot modelled his martyred saint on the tragic life of the Russian dancer.[5] According to David Bernstein, the germ of the poem was planted when Eliot saw Nijinsky in the title role of *Narcisse* during his stay in Paris in 1911. Bernstein links the 'pointed corners' (*CPP*, 605) of Narcissus's eyes with Nijinsky's strikingly almond-shaped, oriental eyes. He draws a parallel between Narcissus's metamorphosis into a young girl who is raped by an old man and the young Nijinsky's stormy homosexual liaison with the older impresario Sergei Diaghilev. Nijinsky's religious fanaticism is also connected to that of Eliot's saint. Bernstein links the last two lines of the poem, which refer to Narcissus as a vegetable-like corpse – 'green, dry and stained' – who 'could not live men's ways' with Nijinsky's catatonic withdrawal from society and his subsequent institutionalisation in a Swiss sanatorium until his death in 1950. Since Eliot also spent time in a Swiss sanatorium while undergoing treatment for a nervous breakdown by the psychiatrist Dr Roger Vittoz, it is possible he was privy to gossip about the great dancer.

When Eliot saw the Russian ballet in London in 1919, Massine had replaced Nijinsky as Diaghilev's principal dancer, choreographer and lover. Eliot repeatedly expressed his admiration for Massine in his correspondence. In the first half of 1919, Eliot saw Massine perform his choreography for *The Three-Cornered Hat*, *La Boutique fantasque*, *The Good-Humoured Ladies* and later probably *Parade*. In the summer of 1921, before Eliot left for Lausanne to complete *The Waste Land*, he saw Massine's restaging of Nijinsky's choreography for *The Rite of Spring*. In April 1922 he wrote to Mary Hutchinson to say that he thought Massine 'more brilliant and beautiful than ever', adding: '[I] quite fell in love with him. I want to meet him more than ever, and he is a genius' (*L1*, 666–7). Two months later, after Hutchinson had arranged a meeting, Eliot wrote again to express his gratitude: 'I liked Massine very much indeed … Do you think Massine liked me? and would he come and see me, do you think?' (*L1*, 680–1). Even after Massine broke with Diaghilev to form his own company, Eliot continued to extol the dancer's virtues. Chief among these was what Eliot called Massine's impersonality, the same quality Stéphane Mallarmé had singled out in the ballerinas of the Paris Opéra and in his tributes to the abstract shapes of the American precursor of modern dance, Loïe Fuller.[6] Ballet demands the submergence of the performer's own personality to the choreography and to a four-hundred year-old tradition. As Eliot put it in 'A Dialogue on Dramatic Poetry' (1928): 'The ballet is valuable because it has, unconsciously, concerned itself with a permanent form' (*SE*, 47).

This interpenetration of past and present appealed to his conception of literary tradition, in which 'the poet has, not a "personality" to express, but a particular medium' (*SE*, 19–20). In the *Criterion* in 1923, Eliot called Massine the 'greatest actor whom we have in London … the most completely unhuman [*sic*], impersonal and abstract'. He added: 'the difference between the conventional gesture of the ordinary stage, which is supposed to *express* emotion, and the abstract gesture of Massine, which *symbolises* emotion, is enormous'.[7]

In his 1924 preface to an unwritten book on four Elizabethan dramatists, Eliot must have been thinking of Massine when he remarked:

Anyone who has observed one of the great dancers of the Russian school will have observed that the man or the woman whom we admire is a being who exists only during the performances, that it is a personality, a vital flame which appears from nowhere, disappears into nothing and is complete and sufficient in its appearance … The differences between a great dancer and a merely competent dancer is in the vital flame, that impersonal, and, if you like, inhuman force which transpires between each of the great dancer's movements. (*SE*, 113)

Along with Massine's impersonality, Eliot found in the dancer's choreography a paradigm for his desire to transform popular cultural forms into a new elite art that might still appeal to a broad public. According to Koritz, Massine's choreography 'illustrates the means by which ballet continued its assimilation into a realm of art defined by its autonomy, impersonality, and lack of commercial appeal'.[8] Yet Massine's choreography in his works for Diaghilev, partly because of his limitations as a classical dancer and partly because the ballet had to be a box-office success, transformed those characteristics that would usually be associated with this fine art. Massine appropriated popular culture by combining ethnic forms with classical ballet. In *The Three-Cornered Hat*, with syncopated music by Manuel de Falla and Cubist sets and costumes designed by Pablo Picasso, Massine danced the role of the Miller in an intense version of the Spanish folk dance the *farucca*. Cyril Beaumont recalled Massine as dancing like 'someone possessed':

[Few] will have forgotten the colour and bravura with which he invested his Farucca, the slow snap of the fingers followed by the pulsating thump of his feet, then the flickering movement of his hands held horizontally before him, palms facing and almost touching his breast. All at once this gave place to a new movement in which his feet chopped the ground faster and faster until he suddenly dropped to the ground on his hands, and as quickly leapt to his feet and stopped dead, his efforts greeted with thunderous applause.[9]

In *La Boutique fantasque*, Massine once again dropped to the ground during the performance while the ballerina Lydia Lopokova, dressed in a froth of petticoats, whirled her leg high over his head before landing in the splits in the choreography of the cancan. Beaumont, who was steeped in classical ballet, was shocked by these risqué gestures, even if other members of the audience were delighted by them. Ronald Schuchard has claimed: 'such ungainly gestures and unorthodox turns in the ballet were grist for Eliot's theatrical mill; they opened the way ... for Sweeney and his crude companions to inhabit poetic drama'. During this period, when he was frequenting both music halls and dance concerts, Schuchard asserts that Eliot must have been 'electrified to see the artistic fusion of the two in Massine's role of the Chinese Conjurer in Jean Cocteau's one-act ballet *Parade*'.[10] With Cocteau's acrobatic scenario, Picasso's set design and music by Erik Satie accompanying his choreography, Massine recalled:

Parade was not so much a satire on popular art as an attempt to translate it into a totally new form. It is true that we utilised certain elements of contemporary show-business – ragtime music, jazz, the cinema, billboard advertising, and circus and music-hall techniques – but we took only their salient features, adapting them to our own ends.[11]

Aside from their modernist sensibility, Massine's works influenced Eliot's admiration for the discipline of dance, which in 'The Death of Saint Narcissus' he equated with religious asceticism. Like the Christian Church, the ballet's authoritarian and hierarchical structure sanctioned and directed the individual performer's extinction of personality. In 'A Dialogue on Dramatic Poetry' one speaker asserts that the strength of ballet lies in 'a tradition, a training, an askesis ... which ascends for several centuries ... any efficient dancer has undergone a training which is like a moral training', to which another speaker agrees that ballet is 'a system of physical training, of traditional, symbolical and highly skilled movements. It is a liturgy of very wide adaptability' (*SE*, 47). Ballet was important to Eliot for other reasons besides its impersonality and moral discipline. He perceived a spiritual dimension similar to Mallarmé's view of dance as a sacred ritual: a mysterious and holy interpretation of our innermost being. Eliot tried to account for the sense of awe and intensity that ballet evoked in an audience, its defamiliarisation of everyday life, by reference to anthropological studies of the relationship between dance, art and ritual. As a result, he was convinced that primitive ritual was not only the source of ballet; it was the origin of all art and religion.

This anthropological view of dance was integral to Eliot's conception of a primitivist consciousness still operative in the modern mind. Although no Freudian, he derived from his studies in philosophy a theory of the unconscious connected to the physiological, psychological and metaphysical elements of dance. In an article entitled 'The Ballet' published in the *Criterion* in 1925, Eliot synthesised his thoughts on dance rhythms and ritual. Here he argues that anyone who wishes to understand the 'spirit' of dance must start by examining it in primitive tribes or amongst peoples like the Tibetans or the Javanese. One must also consider 'the evolution of Christian and other liturgy. (For is not the High Mass – as performed, for instance, at the Madeleine in Paris – one of the highest developments of dancing?) And finally, he should be able to track down the secrets of rhythm in the (still undeveloped) science of neurology.'[12] That is to say, critics should not give purely rational explanations of the sacred origins of dance.

Eliot criticised W. O. E. Osterley's study of primitive religious dances because the author fell into 'the common trap of interpretation, by formulating intelligible reasons for the primitive dancer's dancing'. Osterley claimed 'the origin of the sacred dance was the desire of early man to imitate what he conceived to be the characteristics of supernatural powers', but Eliot contended:

It is equally possible to assert that primitive man acted in a certain way and then found a reason for it. An unoccupied person, finding a drum, may be seized with a desire to beat it; but unless he is an imbecile he will be unable to continue beating it, and thereby satisfying a need (rather than a 'desire'), without finding a reason for so doing.

Eliot implies that the origins of ritual dance cannot be interpreted as a rational or practical need; 'primitive' man beat his drum and danced because of a pre-rational desire to do so. Primitive peoples respond bodily to rhythm by participating in a collective religious ritual. Furthermore, 'it is the rhythm, so utterly absent from modern drama, either verse or prose, and which interpreters of Shakespeare do their best to suppress, which makes Massine and Charlie Chaplin the great actors that they are'.[13] Eliot called this instinct for 'syllable and rhythm, penetrating far below the conscious levels of thought and feeling' the 'auditory imagination' (*UPUC*, 118–19). He thought that since artists are 'more primitive, as well as more civilized'[14] than their contemporaries, they could reintegrate dance rhythms and ritual in a modern art form stimulating dormant religious impulses.

These dance-inspired theories of the interrelation of rhythm and ritual make their presence felt in *The Waste Land* (1922) and 'The Hollow Men' (1925), which contain instances of *danse macabre* or anti-dance imagery – for example, 'crowds of people, walking round in a ring' (*CPP*, 62), 'hooded hordes swarming / Over endless plains' (*CPP*, 73), '*Here we go round the prickly pear*' (*CPP*, 85). These poems are the kindred spirits of two famous productions by the Russian ballet. Nijinsky's *The Rite of Spring* (1913), with its sacrifice of the Chosen Maiden and evocation of prehistoric Russia, was a radical, modernist anthropological fiction. It was typical of a new dance genre, portraying primitive myths, rituals and archetypes, that proliferated during this period. Contemporary reports indicate that the movement of the dancers resembled the involuntary condition of trance: performers shook, trembled, shivered and stamped convulsively. Lincoln Kirstein likened this ballet to an 'apocalyptic epilepsy hypnotizing a community of ecstatic spastics'.[15] In *La Nouvelle Revue Française*, Eliot's friend Jacques Rivière described the horror evoked by Nijinsky's depersonalised choreography: 'We find ourselves in the presence of man's movements at a time when he did not yet exist as an individual. Living beings still cling to each other; they exist in groups, in colonies, in shoals; they are lost among the horrible indifference of society.'[16] Although there is no evidence that Eliot saw this version of *The Rite of Spring*, he would have read approvingly Rivière's description of Nijinsky's anti-romantic choreography, its rejection of individualism and its transcendent idealism. He was disappointed by Massine's romantic restaging of the ballet in 1921. But in Igor Stravinsky's score, with its dissonance and abrupt juxtapositions of neoclassical and folk music, Eliot found a paradigm of the way the complexities and banalities of modern life could be rendered in a new art. In a similar way *The Waste Land* juxtaposes a fertility myth and the 'unreal' city of London, extending the time span to the beginnings of western civilisation and transforming 'current life into something rich and strange'.[17]

Another Russian ballet with music by Stravinsky, *Petrouchka*, informs 'The Hollow Men'. Valerie Eliot claims that the 'hollow' or 'stuffed men' (*CPP*, 83) were inspired by the marionette performed in this ballet by Nijinsky, which Eliot had seen in Paris in 1911 (Southam, 119). Petrouchka's soul is imprisoned in a sawdust body and his impossible 'human' love for the Ballerina is a correlative of the hollow men's impotent desire and psychological disintegration. The inhabitants of this dead land, for all their emptiness, are 'Trembling with tenderness' and possess 'Lips that would kiss' (*CPP*, 84). It is entirely possible that when Eliot described the condition of the hollow men as 'Paralysed force, gesture without motion' (*CPP*, 83), he was thinking of Petrouchka's disjointed, mechanical gestures. In 'The Hollow Men', Eliot followed the dictum: 'take a form of entertainment, and subject it to the process which would leave it a form of art' (*SW*, 70).

The spectres of both Nijinsky and Massine return in *Four Quartets* (1943), where the image of dance conveys an elusive, ineffable experience that words alone are incapable of expressing. The dance image also recapitulates and unifies Eliot's thoughts and feelings about dance. In section 2 of 'Burnt Norton', conjectures about the innate appeal of rhythm to the physiological and psychological unconscious are illustrated in the 'trilling' singing of the blood and the 'dance along the artery' (*CPP*, 172). In the same section, the mystical experience of the timeless moment, which Eliot had equated with F. H. Bradley's 'immediate experience', is figured as the dance 'At the still point of the turning world' (*CPP*, 173). Later, in the fifth section, Narcissus's dance of religious purification in the desert is abstracted into the impersonal image of 'The crying shadow in the funeral dance' (*CPP*, 175). 'East Coker' transforms the empty, vacant rituals of *The Waste Land* and 'The Hollow Men' into the more purposeful (though still imperfect) marriage rites of sixteenth-century peasants: 'In daunsinge, signifying matrimonie – / A dignified and commodious sacrament' (*CPP*, 178). While in 'Little Gidding' earthly dance is apotheosised and fused to the 'refining fire' purging the 'exasperated spirit': 'Where you must move in measure, like a dancer' (*CPP*, 195). Instead of a phoenix rising from the ashes, Eliot conjures 'the spectre of a Rose' (*CPP*, 196) and the ballet *Le Spectre de la rose* in which Nijinsky made his famous leap from the stage through a bedroom window.[18] The impersonality and asceticism Eliot saw in Massine and Nijinsky's art underlines not only the divine pattern – 'The complete consort dancing together' (*CPP*, 197) – but also the purgatorial dance of *Four Quartets*.

NOTES

1. 'Grishkin' was modelled on Serafima Astafieva, a Russian dancer who had opened a ballet school in London. 'Pound recollected that "I took Parson Elyot [*sic*] to see the Prima Ballerina and it evoked "Grushkin" [*sic*]' (Southam, 70).
2. Amy Koritz, *Gendering Bodies/Performing Art* (Ann Arbor: University of Michigan Press, 1995), p. 138.
3. Brigit Patmore, *My Friends When Young* (London: Heinemann, 1968), pp. 85–6.
4. Quoted in Ronald Bush, *T. S. Eliot: The Modernist in History* (Cambridge University Press, 1991), p. 14.

5. See David Bernstein, 'The Story of Vaslav Nijinsky as a Source for T. S. Eliot's "The Death of Saint Narcissus"', *Hebrew University Studies in Literature* (1976), 71–104.

6. Stéphane Mallarmé: 'the ballerina was not a woman dancing, because she was not a woman and did not dance. The ballerina was an otherworldly creature who wrote poems with her body and who appeared before us as a totally impersonal vessel teeming with abstract, preliterate suggestions.' Quoted in *What is Dance?: Readings in Theory and Criticism*, ed. Roger Copeland and Marshall Cohen (Oxford University Press, 1983), p. 112.

7. 'Dramatis Personae', *Criterion* (April 1923), 305.

8. Koritz, *Gendering Bodies/Performing Art*, p. 157.

9. Cyril Beaumont, *The Diaghilev Ballet in London: A Personal Record* (London: A. & C. Black, 1951), p. 144.

10. Ronald Schuchard, *Eliot's Dark Angel* (Oxford University Press, 1999), p. 111.

11. Léonide Massine, *My Life in Ballet* (New York: St Martin's Press, 1968), pp. 137–8.

12. 'The Ballet', *Criterion* (April 1925), 441–2.

13. 'The Beating of a Drum', *Nation and Athenaeum* (6 October 1923), 12.

14. 'Tarr', *Egoist* (September 1918), 106.

15. Lincoln Kirstein, *Nijinsky Dancing* (New York: Alfred Knopf, 1975), p. 144.

16. Quoted ibid., p. 168.

17. 'London Letter', *Dial* (August 1921), 214.

18. In response to John Hayward's query about the line, Eliot remarked: 'I was thinking of the Ballet' (*CFQ*, 202).

CHAPTER 13

Drama

Richard Badenhausen

Imagine for a moment that a chatty, drawing-room comedy written in verse and based loosely upon Euripides'*Alcestis*, which took as its subject matter the pressures of marriage and the difficulties of redemption, climbed to number 3 on the *New York Times* bestseller list; that a press conference preceding the play's opening at the Edinburgh Festival was attended by more than a hundred members of the press from around the world; and that once staged in London and New York, it would be seen by over a million people. These, in fact, were the very circumstances that attended T. S. Eliot's third completed drama *The Cocktail Party* in 1949 and 1950, a situation that would be very hard to envision today. How did Eliot find himself in this position, and why were middle-class theatregoers flocking to a verse play in which a character doing missionary work and trying to 'avoid the final desolation / Of solitude in the phantasmal world / Of imagination' (*CPP*, 419) ends up being crucified by natives?

The answer is complicated, but as good a starting place as any is Eliot's lifelong habit of cultivating a persona of withdrawn reserve while at the same time attracting publicity to help advance his career. Eliot adopted the opposite approach of his friend Ezra Pound, who was renowned for his promotional schemes and for his extravagant dress and behaviour. Eliot depended instead on a quiet, coy manner that forced both public and private audiences to lean forward and pay careful attention. In his enagaging memoir, Eliot's producer Henry Sherek relates the anger of one *Time* employee who seemed to have caught on to Eliot's strategy when he complained: 'That guy's a male Greta Garbo. By pretending that he hates publicity he gets more in the papers than anybody else I know. We ought not to fall for his clever tricks.'[1] In the case of *The Cocktail Party*, the frenzy surrounding Eliot was enflamed by the recent award of the Nobel Prize for Literature in 1948.

Eliot's position in 1950 as the toast of Broadway and the subject of a cover story in the decidedly middlebrow *Time* magazine would have been hard to predict at the start of his career, when he was publishing in little modernist magazines for coterie audiences ready to appreciate the experimentation and obscurity of *The Waste Land* or the scathing social critique contained in the poems collected in *Prufrock and Other Observations*. And yet if we pay close attention to Eliot's early meditations on drama, there are many signs pointing in this later direction, especially given his desire to reach out to a broader audience and his interest in collaboration as a theory and practice of art. These tendencies surface in Eliot's important obituary essay on the music hall performer Marie Lloyd, first published in the *Dial* in December 1922. In that piece, Eliot positions Lloyd as a performer who achieves both artistic success and popularity, a thought that must have been on his mind at this time as he started processing the confused responses to *The Waste Land*. Eliot idealises Lloyd as a performer who is able to control her audiences by maintaining 'sympathy' with them while still retaining a 'moral superiority'. She created an environment in which a 'working man who went to the music-hall and saw Marie Lloyd and joined in the chorus was himself performing part of the act; he was engaged in that collaboration of the audience with the artist which is necessary in all art and most obviously in dramatic art' (*SE*, 458). In this model, drama (particularly its ability to facilitate collaboration) became the ideal form in which an artist could interact with his audience, and not only audiences that might catch an allusion to Dante, but those who might appreciate the power of the poetry on a more emotional level. All that remained was to put this theory into practice. During the last three decades of his life, Eliot's creative output (with the exception of *Four Quartets*) consisted almost entirely of drama, a fact that many readers forget or choose to ignore.

Perhaps best known today by the general public as the author of the lyrics for Andrew Lloyd Webber's hugely successful musical *Cats* (based on poems he had written to entertain the children of his publishing colleagues), Eliot completed five poetic dramas between 1935 and 1958, as well as the choral odes for the religious drama *The Rock* (1934) and an incomplete experimental play entitled *Sweeney Agonistes*, whose two 'fragments' were published separately in 1926 and 1927 but not staged for another seven years. Yet those first halting steps taken in the *Sweeney Agonistes* fragments demonstrate his dilemma as he tried to integrate popular culture and high art. *Sweeney Agonistes* draws from a wide range of popular forms, including the music hall, vaudeville, burlesque, detective fiction, melodrama and jazz. These sources have been discussed by David Chinitz in *T. S. Eliot and the Cultural Divide* (2003), a study that charts Eliot's attempt to reconcile popular with high art. And yet despite those roots in decidedly non-highbrow art forms, after its initial brief staging at Vassar College in 1933, the play was performed in 1934 by Rupert Doone's avant-garde Group Theatre, which had been founded two years earlier as an alternative to what its members saw as London's debased commercial theatre. Instead, the Group Theatre hoped to return to the communal roots of drama and unite the different elements of the form – dance, speech and song – and through the power of this ensemble to re-envision the possibilities of a non-commercial theatre. In the case of *Sweeney Agonistes*, the non-naturalistic style of the performance was reinforced by Eliot's desire (stated in a letter to the director of the Vassar production) that the actors should wear masks, that drumming should accompany the lines, and that the production should adopt the highly stylised form of the Japanese Noh drama that had so interested Pound and W. B. Yeats.

Eliot himself had written about the power of rhythm in the theatre, locating the origins of drama in the repeated, ritualistic movements of dance (see above, Chapter 12). He found such rhythms entirely absent in the prose drama of Henrik Ibsen, the playwright who embodied how contemporary dramatists have 'lost the drum'. The emphasis on ritual, Eliot wrote, is what 'makes [Léonide] Massine and Charlie Chaplin the great actors that they are, and which makes the juggling of [Oreste] Rastelli more cathartic than a performance of *A Doll's House*'.[2] Ibsen came to represent for Eliot what he saw as the limitations inherent in naturalistic prose drama. In a lecture entitled 'Poetry and Drama' (1951), Eliot suggested that even 'great prose dramatists – such as Ibsen and [Anton] Chekhov ... have been hampered in expression by writing in prose' (*OPP*, 86–7): their plays expressed a more limited emotional intensity than poetic drama. In 'A Dialogue on Dramatic Poetry' (1928), one speaker attacked prose drama for its inability to get beyond the superficial, unlike verse, which emphasised the 'permanent and universal' (*SE*, 46), and for ultimately being incapable of providing the structure and control of verse drama.

Doone's training as a dancer in Sergei Diaghilev's Russian ballet enabled him to incorporate dance and movement into the productions of the Group Theatre in a meaningful way, attracting writers of the standing of Jean Cocteau, W. H. Auden, Christopher Isherwood, Louis MacNeice and Stephen Spender, who all had plays produced by the company. In December 1934, Yeats and Bertolt Brecht attended a performance of *Sweeney Agonistes* and in the following autumn the play moved to the Westminster Theatre for a double bill with Auden's *The Dance of Death*. These details illustrate that Eliot was operating in a climate far removed from London's commercialised West End theatre. The experimentalism (albeit incomplete) of *Sweeney Agonistes* was highly influential, although it charted a course that Eliot ultimately did not follow. As E. Martin Browne, the director of religious drama at Chichester Cathedral, pointed out: 'To the theatre-folk of the day, dominated by naturalism, such a work was incomprehensible ... and for my church audiences, just emerging from a puritan night, it would have been an unbearable shock.'[3]

These 'church audiences' would be far more comforted by Eliot's next foray into drama. In 1934 he was commissioned to write the choral odes and a small amount of prose dialogue for a pageant scheduled for a brief run at Sadler's Wells Theatre, in order to raise money for forty-five new churches in the London diocese. *The Rock* follows the attempt of workers to build a modern church against the backdrop of a contemporary society uninterested in these efforts and focused instead on more mundane tasks, such as 'devising the perfect refrigerator' (*CPP*, 155). The most ambitious feature of his choruses for *The Rock* is the attempt to successfully juxtapose contemporary dialogue with various historical and biblical episodes. The experience of writing for this pageant was important in at least four respects. First of all, it allowed Eliot to continue to devote his poetic talent to the religious subject matter that played an increasing role in his life after his baptism into the Church of England in 1927. Second, it demonstrated to Eliot the satisfaction of working with a wide variety of people on a theatrical production whose shared mission was so different from the solitary toil of poetic composition. *The Rock* had a cast of approximately three hundred actors (mostly amateurs from local parishes), a choir and forty musicians. In a letter to the composer Martin Shaw, Eliot complimented him on his music for the pageant, writing as 'a collaborator' who wished for future 'collaboration as workmen',[4] that last term recalling one of the play's themes of men constructing a vibrant church. Third, it provided him with the opportunity to work with the director Martin Browne for the first time. Browne was already a successful director and producer and would become director of the British Drama League. He remained Eliot's most important collaborator in the theatre for three decades and ended up directing all five of Eliot's full-length plays. Finally, this commission allowed Eliot to experiment with the chorus, which he saw as a key to restoring verse drama to the contemporary stage by returning the form to its roots. This experimentation would culminate in perhaps the most successful and powerful of his dramatic creations, the chorus of the Women of Canterbury in *Murder in the Cathedral*.

Murder in the Cathedral resulted directly from Eliot's work on *The Rock*. George Bell, the bishop of Chichester, attended a performance of the pageant and was pleased enough by what he saw to ask Eliot to write a drama for the 1935 Canterbury Festival of Music and Drama. Instead of providing only a part of the play text, as he did for *The Rock*, Eliot created this play from scratch and worked with Browne on all facets of the production. It took the martyrdom of Archbishop Thomas Becket for its subject matter, but it is most significant for the poetry of the choral odes. The Women of Canterbury play an important role in *Murder in the Cathedral*, for they respond to Thomas Becket's spiritual struggles in a raw, emotional manner that helps to enlarge the somewhat dry, didactic consideration of his temptations and political challenges. They experience a spiritual growth throughout the play and, in spite of their collective nature, seem the most alive of the dramatic personae. The chorus also serves a number of other key functions. It gave Eliot a poetic mouthpiece to articulate some of his most powerful lines without having to worry too much about the development of character, a challenge for him in his first full-length play. Manuscript drafts demonstrate that he was most comfortable with the chorus, for he wrote these lines first and then built the rest of the play around the odes. The chorus grew out of Eliot's interest in Greek drama and his belief that restoring the ritualistic, communal features of drama might help usher in a more powerful contemporary theatre, one which would have a public relevance as it did in ancient Athens. Such was his interest in these antecedents that particular Greek plays provided the 'point of departure' (*OPP*, 85) – a phrase he used on several occasions – for his four subsequent plays: the *Oresteia* in *The Family Reunion*, *Alcestis* in *The Cocktail Party*, *Ion* in *The Confidential Clerk*, and *Oedipus at Colonus* in *The Elder Statesman*. Interest in the dramatic possibilities of choral verse had increased in the first decade of the twentieth century as a result of Gilbert Murray's verse translations of Euripides, which had been successfully staged. (Eliot criticised Murray's translations as crude, inaccurate and verbose.) Furthermore, the popularity of choral verse gained ground in the 1930s due to a new emphasis in educational curricula on the study of speech and elocution. For example, Gwynneth Thurburn and Elsie Fogerty, who trained the amateur choruses for both *The Rock* and *Murder in the Cathedral*, taught at the Central School of Speech and Drama, which had as part of its course of study, the recitation of Greek choral odes.

Murder in the Cathedral opened in June 1935 at the Canterbury Festival, where it was staged seven times in the chapter house (an environment hardly conducive to drama), just yards from where Becket had been murdered. In attendance was the playwright, critic and producer Ashley Dukes, who in 1932 had opened the small Mercury Theatre in London as a forum for serious poetic drama. He had collaborated with Doone during the summer of 1934 in the hope of running a season of plays by Eliot and Yeats at the Mercury. Although those plans never came to fruition, Dukes was successful in bringing *Murder in the Cathedral* to the Mercury for an extended run in 1935/6, which was interrupted by tours in the provinces before eventually moving to the Duchess Theatre in the West End in the autumn of 1936. Four days before Christmas, the play was staged at the Duchess for a live television performance on the BBC. The play was seen by Queen Mary in 1937 and had a limited run in the summer of 1937 at the Old Vic. What is remarkable about this staging history is that Eliot had once again found himself with one foot planted firmly in the camp of experimental drama and one in the commercial West End theatre, still trying to advance his cause of popularising verse drama but uniting what seemed to many observers as two incompatible forces. Writing about the experimentation of independent London theatres in the 1930s, Maggie B. Gale points out that 'poetic drama was unattractive to the management monopolies, for whom it presented a potential financial loss; equally the West End theatre managements had little political sympathy with the ideological basis of much of the poetic drama'.[5] In these respects, Eliot was swimming against the commercial tide. This was a period when the economics of the theatre presented a variety of challenges to producers – including a rise in production costs, a reduction in the number of theatres and increased competition from radio and cinema – thus making the staging of poetic drama even riskier and more unlikely. (Radio would eventually become the medium for a number of important British verse dramas in the 1940s and 1950s.)

Although, according to Martin Browne, most commercial theatre producers 'regarded verse with the gravest suspicion',[6] Eliot celebrated verse as the answer to some of the problems he saw plaguing prose drama and, more importantly, as the medium that would bridge the gap between high and low culture, between popular and experimental theatre. Of course, the model for the transcendence of such categories was Shakespeare, although Eliot was always very careful never to compare himself to that poet/dramatist and instead simply held him up in many published and unpublished essays as an unattainable ideal. In 'Poetry and Drama', Eliot claimed that poetic drama operated below the level of conscious thought and thus had a more powerful emotional effect than prose; it was able to duplicate the rhythms of contemporary speech; and it worked in concert with dramatic movement in such a way as to almost do the acting for the actor.

Ironically, these aspirations for poetic drama ended up not being entirely realised by Eliot in his subsequent plays. In fact, those plays seem to adopt many of the trappings of naturalism that he had originally resisted, a quality noted by the reviewer of *The Family Reunion* (1939) in the *Times Literary Supplement*. The *TLS* reviewer observed that the dramatist 'clings in the text to naturalism of surface and the naturalistic time. For all the versification, he may be said to have hardly broken with the main tenets of Shaftesbury Avenue' (Brooker, 379). Further exacerbating this sense that Eliot's plays represented a return to a thoroughly conventional drama was the fact that the plots were built around the conventions of drawing-room comedy and the detective story. Nevertheless, his next play, *The Cocktail Party*, opened in New York before London because of the complications in securing a suitable West End venue: Sherek relates that commercial producers were somewhat wary of a play in verse that had first been performed at the Edinburgh Festival. The play did eventually find a home in London (at the New Theatre) and was a smash hit on both sides of the Atlantic. The opening paragraph of the 1950 *Time* magazine article on Eliot wrestles with the contradiction between his reputation as the highbrow author of an incomprehensible poem (*The Waste Land*) and audiences who were anything but highbrow turning up in droves in New York to watch *The Cocktail Party*. Yet it seems certain that the poetry itself was not the attraction for these theatregoers, especially since Eliot himself wondered in retrospect 'whether there is any poetry in the play at all' (*OPP*, 85). In his next play, *The Confidential Clerk* (1953), the versification was so muted that one reviewer encouraged potential members of the audience not to be scared off by the play's poetry, 'for the simple reason that they will not notice it'.[7] Part of the issue resulted from Eliot designing a poetic line organised around stresses rather than line length, but the power of the choral odes in *Murder in the Cathedral* (in my opinion, Eliot's greatest play) has largely disappeared. His last play, *The Elder Statesman* (1958), was a conventional melodramatic social comedy that takes marital love as its central subject. Compared to John Osborne's *Look Back in Anger* (1956), Samuel Beckett's experimental anti-naturalist dramas *Waiting for Godot* (premiered in Britain in 1955) and *Endgame* (1957), and Harold Pinter's early unsettling dramas, such as *The Birthday Party* (1958) and *The Dumb Waiter* (1960), Eliot's drama represented a dead end.

The trajectory of Eliot's career in the theatre can be understood in various ways. Randy Malamud, for example, breaks it into three stages: the experimental 'vintage modernism' of *Sweeney Agonistes*; the 'mystical spiritual incantation' of *The Rock* and *Murder in the Cathedral*; and finally the 'poetry of concord and consort' in the formulaic late comedies, *The Confidential Clerk* and *The Elder Statesman*.[8] As for *The Family Reunion* and *The Cocktail Party*, Malamud sees them straddling the second and third stages. However one chooses to understand the course of Eliot's drama, at the core of his programme was an attempt to bridge the various cultural divides that he had delineated in his early criticism, in the belief that drama offered the best medium for transcending those divisions. Ultimately, his aspirations were not fully realised, despite the commercial success of *The Cocktail Party*.

A brief survey of Eliot's dramatic output helps us to recast some commonly held conceptions. First, it reminds us of the importance of drama to Eliot's career, in spite of the fact that he is typically associated with his early modernist poetry, *Four Quartets*, and his literary criticism. More importantly, his work in the theatre challenges the commonly accepted view of Eliot as an isolated poet, the inscrutable genius working in isolation, an image that he himself helped to cultivate. Although he famously collaborated with Pound on *The Waste Land* and corresponded regularly with John Hayward (later his flatmate) during the composition of *Four Quartets*, Eliot's most extensive collaboration occurred in the theatre, where he worked with many different individuals who helped to put on his plays, not the least of whom was Martin Browne, who documented his collaboration with Eliot in his own book-length study and whose work on the drafts of Eliot's plays I have written about extensively elsewhere.[9] Drama allowed Eliot to test his idealised aspirations for literature as a collaborative exercise that ultimately turned on the ability of the audience to participate in shaping the meaning of the work. In that respect, he is still very much our vital contemporary, even if his theory of poetic drama was not always realised in practice.

NOTES

1. Henry Sherek, *Not in Front of the Children* (London: Heinemann, 1959), p. 146.
2. 'The Beating of a Drum', *Nation and Athenaeum* (6 October 1923), 12.
3. E. Martin Browne, 'T. S. Eliot in the Theatre: The Director's Memories', *T. S. Eliot: The Man and his Work*, ed. Allen Tate (New York: Delacorte Press, 1966), p. 118.

4. Quoted in E. Martin Browne, *The Making of T. S. Eliot's Plays* (Cambridge University Press, 1969), p. 13.
5. Maggie B. Gale, 'Theatre and Drama between the Wars', *The Cambridge History of Twentieth-Century English Literature*, ed. Laura Marcus and Peter Nicholls (Cambridge University Press, 2004), p. 330.
6. Browne, *Making of Eliot's Plays*, p. 1.
7. Quoted ibid., p. 288.
8. Randy Malamud, *T. S. Eliot's Drama: A Research and Production Sourcebook* (New York: Greenwood Press, 1992), pp. 23–4.
9. See Richard Badenhausen, *T. S. Eliot and the Art of Collaboration* (Cambridge University Press, 2004).

CHAPTER 14

Music

David Fuller

De la musique avant toute chose [music above everything]
(Paul Verlaine, 'Art Poétique')

Beethoven, Wagner, Stravinsky: these are the composers most obviously in, behind and around T. S. Eliot's poetry. Beethoven, the apogee of Classicism; Wagner, the epitome, zenith and in embryo the decadence of Romanticism; Stravinsky, a Proteus of modernism, myth-and-motors, pastiche, jazz and neoclassicism: Beethoven, behind *Four Quartets*; Wagner, in *The Waste Land*; Stravinsky, a contemporary with whom Eliot was in dialogue. Together they are an index of Classical and Romantic legacies in modernist eclecticism. But music is more to Eliot than three composers, however broadly representative. The Wagnerian backgrounds of French Symbolism mean that music is fundamental to Eliot's aesthetics. And although he had no technical training, music was the art that personally affected Eliot most deeply.

Stravinsky commented on their connection from his own point of view:

Were Eliot and myself merely trying to refit old ships while the other side – Joyce, Schoenberg – sought new forms of travel? I believe that this distinction, much traded on a generation ago, has disappeared. (An era is shaped only by hindsight, of course, and hindsight reduces to convenient unities, but all artists know that they are part of the same thing.) Of course we seemed, Eliot and myself, to have exploited an apparent discontinuity, to have made art out of the *disjecta membra*, the quotations from other poets and composers, the references to earlier styles ('hints of earlier and other creation'), the detritus that betokened a wreck. But we used it, and anything that came to hand, to rebuild, and we did not pretend to have invented new conveyors or new means of travel. But the true business of the artist *is* to refit old ships. He can say again, in his way, only what has already been said.[1]

Leaving aside the justness of associating James Joyce with Arnold Schoenberg, and the question of whether in art a new way of saying does not rather constitute a new thing said, Stravinsky identifies real correspondences: quotation from others (there is more of this in Eliot than Stravinsky) and reference to earlier styles (there is more of this in Stravinsky than Eliot). But as for refitting old ships, Eliot's 1923 review of *Ulysses* indicates that he saw Joyce as doing this, and in ways that others might imitate. Stravinsky would agree that, however revolutionary some of Schoenberg's methods, he continued to compose preludes, songs and string quartets – to write, that is, in musical forms that Eliot imitated. It is, of course, Stravinsky's point that beneath the distinctions created by hindsight poets and composers working as contemporaries in broadly similar cultural conditions face some common problems, and in his own work and in Eliot's these gave rise to some common solutions. Stravinsky's rewritings – pastiche of Giovanni Battista Pergolesi in the ballet *Pulcinella*, reworking of Carlo Gesualdo's *Tres sacrae cantiones*, reconstitution of an eighteenth-century opera in *The Rake's Progress* or the *concerto grosso* in *Dumbarton Oaks* – may differ from Eliot's – highly varied reworkings of Ovid, Shakespeare, Goldsmith and others in *The Waste Land*, or (again variously) of Dante in *Ash-Wednesday* and 'Little Gidding' (see Chapter 18 below). But there are common elements, from simple pastiche to a more profound novelty derived from a thorough-going contemporary reconstitution of earlier methods and materials – refitting old ships.

Stravinsky was looking back. Eliot's main comments on Stravinsky – on a production of *Le Sacre du printemps* in a 1921 'London Letter' for the *Dial* – come from a time when their artistic identities were being established. While Eliot registered some disappointment with *Le Sacre* as a whole, he praised Stravinsky's music as being truly modern: it gave 'the sense of the present ... it did seem to transform the rhythm of the steppes into the scream of the motor horn, the rattle of machinery ... and the other barbaric cries of modern life; and to transform these despairing noises into music'.[2] The effect of music and choreography together, however, Eliot compared to that of '*Ulysses* with illustrations by the best contemporary illustrator'[3] – who would fail, it is implied, adequately to match the modernity of the text. But Stravinsky is the Joyce of music, a true exemplar of modernity. Appearing in the *Dial* exactly a year before *The Waste Land* appeared there, this praise of music for a mythic subject made to resonate with the 'cries of modern life' may suggest more than Joycean analogies. The unexpressed hope that he might be the Stravinsky of poetry is the view of Eliot that Stravinsky formulated forty years later.

What Stravinsky might have added is that his work shared with Eliot's the incorporation of popular materials, especially jazz – the most obviously American element in the poetry of Eliot the adopted European, and a mark of Stravinsky's adopted American identity. Stravinsky may have judged that it indicated as much a difference as a similarity: Eliot's jazz is native to him. What Stravinsky learned from Jack Hilton, Woody Herman and Benny Goodman sounds in his *Ragtime, Preludium for Jazz Ensemble, Tango* or *Ebony Concerto* more hybrid and acquired. In *The Waste Land*, and above all in *Sweeney Agonistes*, the rhythms of ragtime came naturally to a native of St Louis (see Chapter 1).

Much that Eliot shared with Stravinsky – as Stravinsky's account implies – he shared with other contemporary composers. What Eliot described as the inevitable difficulty for the contemporary poet, the need 'to force, to dislocate if necessary, language into his meaning' (*SE*, 289), is reflected in the analogous difficulty of much contemporary music, which often employed radically new compositional techniques – dissolution of a sense of key and continuous use of unresolved dissonance; experiments (including the introduction of mechanically produced sounds) which challenged the whole idea of what constitutes music; an avant-garde consciously assaulting its audience; uncompromising address to an elite, implying that art can communicate only to a suitably educated intelligence; all kinds of elements that made music difficult to follow because traditional aids to listening, defined melodic structures, harmonic expectations, rhythmic patterns, formal procedures, were radically violated. These are all versions of the 'language' of music dislocated into meaning, equivalents of the situation thrust on poets, in Eliot's account, by the condition of their culture.

Quite different from this congruence of contemporaries is Eliot's creative struggle with Wagnerism. Wagner was the most important and controversial artist of late nineteenth-century Europe. He dominated music: a powerful influence on the most advanced forms on modernism in music and every composer who did not militantly resist him. In France and Germany he also dominated the arts more generally. In France, from the admiration of Charles Baudelaire's 1861 essay on *Tannhäuser* and the cult of Wagner that flowed from it, to the *Revue Wagneriénne* (1885–7), a home for poetic manifestos and the poetry of Jules Laforgue[4] and Stéphane Mallarmé; in Germany, from the admiration and later excoriations of Friedrich Nietzsche (see *Der Fall Wagner*, 1888) to the numerous writings (both for and against Wagner) of Thomas Mann. Amongst many other things, Wagner showed how myth could be used in modern art, and he brought together all the arts in his concept of the *Gesamtkunstwerk* [total work of art].

Eliot's attitude was divided: the Classicist deplored, the Romantic resonated. 'A Dialogue on Dramatic Poetry' (1928) encapsulates this ambivalence: speaker B (the nearest to Eliot) is said to have railed against Wagner as 'pernicious' (*SE*, 54), but he would not willingly resign his experiences of Wagner. The draft poem 'Opera' (1909) is congruent with Eliot's critique of Romanticism: Wagner's *Tristan und Isolde* shows music 'Flinging itself at the last / Limits of self-expression' (*IMH*, 17). But at their first meeting in 1956, Stravinsky thought 'Eliot's Wagner nostalgia ... apparent' and recalled Eliot as implying that '*Tristan* must have been one of the most passionate experiences in his life'.[5] Nor can Eliot have been wholly out of tune with the dedicatee of *Prufrock and Other Observations*, Jean Verdenal, who in 1911 described to him the close of *Götterdämmerung* as 'un des points les plus hauts où l'homme se soit élevé' ['one of the highest points ever reached by man'] (*L1*, 24).

The subjects of *Tristan und Isolde* and *Götterdämmerung* are both relevant to *The Waste Land*: *Tristan* – Romantic passion as a channel of the deepest knowledge and at odds with the world; *Götterdämmerung* – an epic of redemptive love and apocalypse. No contextual limits can be set to how much of these dramas the fragments in *The Waste Land* evoke. For somebody for whom – as for Eliot – *Tristan* was an overwhelming experience, any part of the poem will be resonant with the fundamental feelings of the whole. A reader may be reminded of the precise dramatic situations of the two fragments (although these can be construed quite differently: the first leads directly to Isolde's rage, indirectly to the release of passion; the second directly to Tristan's waking to loss, indirectly to fulfilment in death). Or a reader may feel the fragments as keynotes from acts 1 and 3, framing the act of romantic fulfilment and disaster. '*Frisch weht der Wind*' ['Fresh blows the wind'] (*CPP*, 61): Tristan has behaved like this mocking seducer, but another Tristan will soon be released by Isolde's magic. '*Oed' und leer das Meer*' ['Desolate and empty the sea'] (*CPP*, 62): the sea is empty at that moment, but the healing beloved will soon appear there. Between these moments Wagner depicts 'blood shaking [the] heart / The awful daring of a moment's surrender' (*CPP*, 74) with a force never before heard in music, and in terms so beautiful as to render the cataclysm compellingly attractive. 'I knew nothing, / Looking into the heart of light' (*CPP*, 62): Wagner's imagery is not of light but of Night, but this Night is the light – the world made so new that all previous knowledge is superseded. Knowing 'nothing' may mean not that the lovers are spiritually null, but that, as a result of their overwhelming experience, they have to begin again from deeper levels of being. It is an interruption from the world of daylight morality that checks the progress of Tristan and Isolde into their Night of knowledge. Which stage of this experience the reader encounters in *The Waste Land*, not the hyacinth girl episode itself, nor the framing quotations from *Tristan*, nor any view of Wagner that Eliot expressed outside the poem decides.

This is also the case with the song of the Rhine maidens, nature spirits whose ululations ('Weialala' [*CPP*, 70]) suggest the first shimmering flow of their great river. In citing their song from *Götterdämmerung*, Eliot points to the episode preceding apocalypse. There is a contrast: far from being, like Eliot's Thames daughters, passive victims undone by men, Wagner's Rhine maidens are undoers. They began the struggle between love and power of *Der Ring des Nibelungen* by rejecting the Nibelung, Alberich. Now they warn the hero, Siegfried, of the death that will generate the apocalypse of Wagner's title of the final part of the cycle – 'Dusk Falls on the Gods', as George Bernard Shaw rendered it. But Wagner's apocalypse is an end that is a beginning: as the Rhine obliterates the old world of corruption, the leitmotif of redemption through love shows the tone of the world renewed (one of Verdenal's 'highest points'). More affirmative than a gathering of fragments or any purely personal setting in order, *Götterdämmerung*'s final bars are congruent with at least part of what the thunder says: 'Datta' (*CPP*, 74), give. How much of this is made present, and in what ways, by the song of the Rhine maidens is once again left to the reader to decide.

With the allusions to Wagner and to Verlaine's poem 'Parsifal', some have felt that Eliot would like the reader to hear Wagner's *Parsifal* in *The Waste Land*. With its Fisher King, Grail chalice and spear, and Waste Land it is obviously the work by Wagner most relevant to Eliot's theme. There have been ingenuous and imaginative attempts to read it in, but Eliot left it out.

'Burnt Norton' (1936) articulated analogies between music and poetry, but the overall musical title of the sequence 'quartet' appeared first in a letter of September 1942 – that is, when *Four Quartets* was all but completed. After expressing a doubt about the application of vague musical analogies, and rejecting 'sonata' as too musical, Eliot explained that he meant 'quartet' to indicate that the poems were in a particular set form, which he had elaborated, and to suggest a poem 'weaving in together three or four superficially unrelated themes: the "poem" being the degree of success in making a new whole out of them' (*CFQ*, 26). The title, that is, indicated elements of both form and method.

Although Eliot's comments on *Four Quartets* give no direct warrant for this, it has often been supposed that he had specifically in mind the late quartets of Beethoven. Few artists have modelled better than Beethoven the injunction of 'East Coker', 'Old men ought to be explorers' (*CPP*, 182): in terms of harmony and counterpoint, the techniques of writing for string quartet as these were then conceived, and formal organisation within individual movements and overall, these acknowledged summits of the quartet repertoire are some of the most experimental works ever written. Some facts support the conjecture that Eliot had these quartets particularly in mind. In 1931, in a letter to Stephen Spender, he remarked of Beethoven's A minor quartet (opus 132): 'I find it quite inexhaustible to study. There is a sort of heavenly or at least more than human gaiety about some of his later things which one imagines might come to oneself as the fruit of reconciliation and relief after immense suffering. I should like to get something of that into verse before I die'.[6] Eliot apparently aimed to get something of Beethoven into verse at this time in the unfinished 'Coriolan' (1931) – though without the title this would scarcely be obvious.[7] Beethoven's *Coriolan* overture is made up of three elements – a dramatic chordal sequence, minor, heroic (evocative of Coriolanus), and two contrasting themes, the first minor, non-heroic (the Roman populace), the second major, noble and warmly human (Volumnia, Virgilia). The relation of this to Eliot's poem is at most a broad analogy: the wakeful life of the ego and other perspectives from which the demands of a public world appear empty (first theme) contrast with the personal perspectives of the second theme ('O mother') and the eternal ones of the prophet's 'What shall I cry?' (*CPP*, 130), the chordal sequence. But however the title is construed 'Coriolan' is a poem related to Beethoven. Then, in a 1933 lecture Eliot described his aim 'to write poetry which should be essentially poetry, with nothing poetic about it ... poetry so transparent that in reading it we are intent on what the poem *points at*, and not on the poetry ... To get *beyond poetry*, as Beethoven, in his later works, strove to get *beyond music*'.[8] He apparently sensed in Beethoven's late works some congruence with his fundamental aim of experiment that pressed against the limits of what had theretofore been conceivable, so as to constitute a radical new transparency of expression.

What this might mean is easier to see with poetry than with music. It may well reflect a view of Beethoven derived from J. W. N. Sullivan's *Beethoven: His Spiritual Development* (recommended by the music chronicler J. B. Trend to readers of the *Criterion* in 1928). Sullivan, who was known to Eliot, writes about 'Beethoven the explorer' ('Old men ought to be explorers'); he quotes as crucial paragraphs from Beethoven's journals on the need for 'strength and submission' ('submission' is a crucial term for Sullivan); and his whole focus is towards Beethoven's late quartets as the supreme exemplification of his genius. But what is most suggestive for understanding Eliot's comments on Beethoven is Sullivan's underlying thesis: Beethoven's music is a record of spiritual development, a mode of revelation and a form of wisdom – it points to extra-musical meanings, goes 'beyond music'. 'God the Companion' is Sullivan's introduction to the late work: writing in a Christian tradition, Beethoven also drew on eastern mystical literature and key personal experiences to embody his sense of the divine. All this may have influenced the way Eliot heard and thought about Beethoven, who on this view might plausibly seem a model *alter ego*.[9]

The presence of Beethoven in *Four Quartets* is not (as has sometimes been suggested) a matter of precise parallels: for example, that Beethoven's A minor quartet is in five movements, with a central third and a short fourth movement (a form Eliot had already discovered in *The Waste Land*); or that Beethoven's late quartets were the first to develop a fully equal conversation between the four instruments, which might be thought of as comparable to the interactions of Eliot's poetic 'voices' – prosaic, lyrical, didactic, visionary (in a religious or philosophical sense). Eliot's voices are far from self-contained – the lyric may be didactic or visionary; the prosaic may be didactic or philosophical; and within a single voice there are many shades (the prose of journalism, science, liturgy, the Bible; the lyric of rhyme and emphatic rhythm, of assonance and rhetorical parallels). The analogy with Beethoven is not precise; it is fundamental. Eliot expressed a desire to reproduce in poetry some of the states of experience he heard in Beethoven's music. To achieve this he needed to press against the boundaries of how words can be expressive in poetry, which includes a heightened feeling for the movement of verse and the structural patterns built up by that movement. Experiments with texture and structure in Beethoven's late quartets model in music congruent possibilities.

It has also been claimed that Eliot reported having in mind Béla Bartók's Quartets numbers 2–6,[10] although the sixth Quartet was not premiered until 1941 (in New York) and Eliot is unlikely to have heard it before *Four Quartets* was completed. However, the fifth Quartet (premiered in 1934) might have been drawn to his attention by the enthusiasm of Ezra Pound, who repeatedly praised it.[11] If Eliot followed up Pound's recommendation, he will have found a five-movement work, constructed in an arch shape, in which the first and fifth and second and fourth movements draw on related themes – weaving diverse materials into a whole in a novel way, analogous to Eliot's revisitings and transformations both within different sections of each quartet and between the separate poems. If Eliot heard it, he could have recognised a congruity with his own wrestling with form and pattern.

Eliot liked to stress that the very nature of poetry is in part music. This is most obvious in his use of musical titles – quartets, song, prelude, rhapsody, 'Words for Music', five-finger exercises, invention, suite, caprice, nocturne and humoresque. And there are many other songs embedded in the poetry – from the euphoniously hypnotic singing of the dry grass and the hermit-thrush in *The Waste Land* to the jazz croonings of *Sweeney Agonistes*.[12]

Poetry must avail itself of musical resources because 'the poet is occupied with frontiers of consciousness beyond which words fail, though meanings still exist' (*OPP*, 30); because poetry deals with 'feeling which we can only detect, so to speak, out of the corner of the eye and can never completely focus ... At such moments, we touch the border of those feelings which only music can express' (*OPP*, 86–7). Attempting to express the all but inexpressible, poetry aspires to the condition of music. To approach frontiers or borders of consciousness, the poet uses what Eliot calls the 'auditory imagination', that is, 'the feeling for syllable and rhythm, penetrating far below the conscious levels of thought and feeling' (*UPUC*, 118–19).

Eliot is most explicit about analogies between poetry and music in his writings about poetic drama. 'To work out a play in verse is to be working like a musician ... it is to see the whole thing as a musical pattern'. A verse play is like 'some musical form, like the sonata or fugue ... Underneath the action ... there should be a musical pattern which intensifies our excitement by reinforcing it with feeling from a deeper and less articulate level'.[13] In a later essay, Eliot wrote: 'I have before my eyes a kind of mirage of the perfection of verse drama, which would be a design of human action and of words, such as to present at once the two aspects of dramatic and of musical order' (*OPP*, 87). He wrote in similar terms about non-dramatic verse. Important as the music of rhyme, rhythm, assonance and alliteration may be, music is not only a matter of the local effects: in non-dramatic poetry too, music is structural. It is 'a question of the whole poem' (*OPP*, 36): 'a "musical poem" is a poem which has a musical pattern of sound and a musical pattern of the secondary meanings of the words which compose it, and that these two patterns are indissoluble and one' (*OPP*, 33). As he expressed it in 'Burnt Norton': 'Only by the form, the pattern, / Can words or music reach / The stillness' (*CPP*, 175). By 'secondary meanings' Eliot apparently means all the ways in which a word might signify apart from semantically – its sound qualities, the history of its meanings, the contextual flavours it carries, from its background in another language as well as from its characteristic uses in English, and how these elements interact with (to adopt a musical term) the overtones of other words in the line, the stanza, the paragraph, and ultimately the poem or group of poems as a whole. Alongside the more obvious elements of words considered as sounds, these are what, in Eliot's account, constitute a poem's 'music'.

One context of these views is transmuted Wagnerism, filtered to Eliot through late nineteenth-century French poets, intermediaries whose adoptive reactions incorporated scepticism and irony (see Chapter 21 below). Nevertheless, it is a view of poetry that emerged from, was engaged with and in reaction to actual music, and, in critical writings and in verse, Eliot continued to relate it to music proper. The analogy between poetry and music also has implications for the engagement of the reader in the act of reading: 'you are the music / While the music lasts' (*CPP*, 190) implies a totally absorbed reading of poetry analogous to that fully concentrated listening to music which means the mind is completely taken up with, even taken over by, the aesthetic experience. Only in this way can the structural music of a poem have its proper effect.

Being (in part) music, 'Good poetry ought to be read aloud'.[14] But how, and what does Eliot's own mode of reading poetry imply? He made recordings of all his major and many of his minor poems. The poems, that is, were published as sound structures to be heard as well as printed texts to be read. In doing this Eliot drew an analogy with music: the author's recorded reading is like the composer's recorded performance of a score – just one way of realising it, but a way that gives something the score alone cannot provide. With poetry it is 'a guide to the rhythms'.[15] Although Eliot often stressed the importance of the relation of the language of poetry to the spoken language, except in unusually colloquial fragments he did not read with inflections from spoken language. In *The Rock* (1934) he stressed 'the beauty of incantation' (*CPP*, 164), and he made the same point in an interview shortly after recording *Four Quartets*. Asked about his 'instinct to chant verse in a monotone', he replied: 'A great deal of the melodic arrangement is intuitive. As for chanting verse, for me the incantatory element is very important ... When I read poetry myself I put myself in a kind of trance and move in rhythm to the rhythm of the piece in question'.[16] It is a mode of reading more in keeping with traditions of French verse, and the quasi-singing style of French classical acting, than with the closeness of English poetry to the spoken language. The effect is that intonation emphasises formal structure (all aspects of euphony, but especially the structure of the line and patterns of rhyme), and does this at the expense of syntax. It adds to the intensity of effect by bringing out more strongly the rhythms, but it is also impersonal. Although Eliot's vocal tone is so sharply individual, his incantatory mode suppresses the inflections that are so important a part of what characterises the individual speaking voice. In a liturgical context chant is music's equivalent of the priest's robes: the individual is absorbed into the office, whether of priest or cantor. Incantation is the robe of the voice. For readers who are distracted by the surface difficulties of Eliot's poetry, allowing oneself to receive it in terms of its 'beauty of incantation' directs attention to the verbal music that was, for Eliot, so crucial an aspect of the poetry's meanings. As Paul Valéry puts it, if the reader approaches the meaning of a poem through its music, 'you will finally introduce [the meaning] as the supreme nuance which will transfigure your piece without altering it'.[17]

NOTES

1. Igor Stravinsky and Robert Craft, *Dialogues and a Diary* (New York: Doubleday, 1963), p. 30.
2. 'London Letter', *Dial* (October 1921), 453.
3. Ibid., 452.
4. Eliot compared Laforgue and Wagner as exemplars (albeit from different perspectives) of 'the philosophy of the unconscious and of annihilation' (*VMP*, 215).
5. Igor Stravinsky, 'Memories of Eliot', *Esquire* (August 1965), 92.
6. Quoted in Stephen Spender, 'Remembering Eliot', *T. S. Eliot: The Man and his Work*, ed. Allen Tate (New York: Delacorte Press, 1966), p. 54.
7. Eliot told G. Wilson Knight the poem was 'inspired by Beethoven'; quoted Tate, ed., *Eliot: Man and Work*, p. 247.
8. Quoted in F. O. Matthiessen, *The Achievement of T. S. Eliot* (Oxford University Press, 1947), p. 90.
9. See J. W. N. Sullivan, *Beethoven: His Spiritual Development* (London: Jonathan Cape, 1927).
10. See Hugh Kenner, *T. S. Eliot: The Invisible Poet* (London: Methuen, 1965), p. 261.
11. Pound described Bartók's 5th Quartet as 'the record of a personal struggle, possible only to a man born in the 1880s. It has the defects or disadvantages of my Cantos. It has the defects and disadvantages of Beethoven's music ... the defects inherent in a record of struggle.' *Guide to Kulchur* (London: Faber & Faber, 1938), p. 135.

12. Notable musical settings of Eliot's work include Alan Rawsthorne's *Practical Cats* (1954), Stravinsky's *The Dove Descending* (1962), John Dankworth's *Sweeney Agonistes* (1965), Benjamin Britten's *The Journey of the Magi* (1972) and *The Death of St Narcissus* (1977), and Thomas Adès's *Five Eliot Landscapes* (1990). Ildebrando Pizzetti's opera *Assassinio nella Cattedrale* (1958) is based on Alberto Castelli's authorised Italian translation of *Murder in the Cathedral*.

13. 'The Need for Poetic Drama', *Listener* (25 November 1936), 994.

14. Ibid., 995.

15. Author's note, HMV recording of *Four Quartets*, 1947.

16. Ranjee Shahani, 'T. S. Eliot Answers Questions', *John O'London's Weekly* (19 August 1949), 497.

17. Paul Valéry, *The Art of Poetry*, trans. Denise Folliot, intro. T. S. Eliot (New York: Pantheon, 1958), p. 165.

CHAPTER 15

Radio

Michael Coyle

T. S. Eliot's something-less-than-a-manifesto for the *Criterion*, 'The Idea of a Literary Review', modestly affirms that 'a review should be an organ of documentation'. But this documentation must extend beyond the 'narrowly literary', not least because of 'the impossibility of defining the frontiers, or limiting the context of "literature"'. Documenting something more than the tastes of the editor, in this extension the serious review reflects instead the relations among 'editor, collaborators, and occasional contributors'; these relations must issue in a ' "tendency" rather than a "programme" '.[1] The object of this documentary project is ultimately Arnoldian, aiming to reveal neither the vision of the editor nor the life of letters, but rather the relative health or disease of culture itself. The 'literary' review that Eliot imagined and planned could not, in other words, be strictly literary. Consider, then, the following segue – a segue at once as set up and as seemingly arbitrary as any between segments on a radio broadcast.

In the first of his *Criterion* 'Verse Chronicles' (April 1933), the Imagist poet F. S. Flint opened by discerning 'no reason why this review should have a verse chronicle … Verse is an obsolete or obsolescent, dead and moribund art, except for musical comedies and drawing-room ballads, and, mercifully, the "art" here is drowned out by the "music" '.[2] Flint's subsequent chronicles recurred to this posture often enough that it became a kind of refrain – and eventually material for something new. The following year, the first of Geoffrey Tandy's eighteen 'Broadcasting Chronicles' for the *Criterion* affirmed that 'we can say we have no literature, but it isn't possible to maintain that we have no broadcasting'. Parodying Flint's cheeky tone, Tandy turned Flint's complaint about the dire condition of literary culture on its head. Tandy believed in the work of the British Broadcasting Corporation (founded as the British Broadcasting Company in 1922); he was committed to defending its non-commercial character and was keenly interested in 'the differences between broadcasting and the other forms of communication upon which we relied until twelve years ago'.[3] Flint may have thought the only real poetry of his time was to be found in music halls but, defending the cultural newcomer radio, Tandy believed the BBC was already serving as the voice of the nation.

In this way, Tandy was following the lead of Sir John Reith, the director-general of the BBC, who championed an Arnoldianism as unembarrassed as it was resolute. Steadfast in his conviction that the purpose of art is soul-building – both for the individual and for the nation – he maintained that radio could and should be the ultimate 'instrument of power in the service of wisdom and beauty and peace'.[4] Reith argued that broadcasting should be 'an ally of immense potency in the campaign for a general intelligence and a higher culture', and culture, he added in an allusion to Matthew Arnold's *Culture and Anarchy* (1869), unacknowledged because he could assume none of his contemporaries would miss it, 'has been called the study of perfection'.[5] Reith's Arnoldianism wasn't merely an individual quirk. He was, like so many others in the early twentieth century, carrying the torch lit the previous century by Arnold, John Ruskin and other Victorian sages. Indeed, as I have argued in *Ezra Pound, Popular Genres and the Discourse of Culture* (1995), culture functioned, more than as a concept or an ideal, as a discourse; that is, as a way of conceiving social relations and understanding history – a way of urging unity rather than uniformity. As Todd Avery notes, 'Reith envisioned radio as an unparalleled means of bringing into being a new kind of public – an "imagined community", in Benedict Anderson's phrase, whose collective consciousness would be as listeners with a sure sense of national identity grounded in a shared moral understanding.'[6] In one of those coincidences of history with the potential to tease us out of thought, Reith applied for the job of general manager of the BBC in October 1922, the same month Eliot first published in the *Criterion* the poem that would establish him among the prophetic voices of his age – *The Waste Land*.

Eliot, like many BBC broadcasters, shared Reith's Arnoldian vision. Between 1929 and 1963 Eliot broadcast over a hundred times for the BBC.[7] Generally speaking, his broadcasting activity admits characterisation into five distinct periods:

1. 1929–32. From June 1929 through December 1931, Eliot's talks focused on English poetry; mostly of the seventeenth-century 'Metaphysical' poets, although including in 1931 five talks on John Dryden (the middle three comprise a distinct series).

2. 1932–6. In March 1932, Eliot gave four church-related talks. Thereafter he stayed away from radio work for nearly four years. His next recorded broadcast was for Radio Athlone (the Republic of Ireland's national broadcaster), an interview with the writer Maura Laverty about his new career as a dramatist, which took place in January 1936.

3. 1936–7. Between November 1936 and February 1937, Eliot resumed regular radio work, mixing four talks on seventeenth-century poets with two talks on church-related matters. Thereafter, he stayed away from the radio studio for almost three years, returning only with the outbreak of the Second World War.

4. 1940–6. In November 1940 a discussion with Desmond Hawkins on the topic of 'The Writer as Artist' opened the most conscientious period of Eliot's radio work. Less than a year later, in May 1941, he agreed to read his own work on air – something he had never before been willing to do – partly as a contribution to wartime morale. Between 1940 and 1947 he broadcast at least thirty-six times; eleven of these broadcasts were directed at European audiences and sixteen were made for the BBC Eastern Service, directed chiefly at India.

5. 1948–63. Between 1948 and 1963 Eliot spoke over the air another thirty-six times. In this final period he worked primarily for the BBC's highbrow *Third Programme.* The purpose of the *Third Programme* was, in the words of the BBC Director-General Sir William Haley, who launched it in 1946, to 'seek every evening to do something that is culturally satisfying and significant' and that would be 'directed to an audience that is not of one class but that is perceptive and intelligent'.[8]

Despite some variety of subject matter, there is an unmistakable arc to Eliot's broadcasting activity. The work of these last years in some ways represents the synthesis of what can be seen as a dialectical relation between strictly literary activity and orthodox Christian talks, for in this last period, whatever his particular topic, Eliot focused on the unity of culture. In retrospect, we can see that Eliot's radio performances observe both the principles of BBC policy and also his own convictions about cultural integrity. Reith's principles can help us to understand the form, manner and style of the broadcasts; as for Eliot's own convictions, we can look to them to explain both the content of those talks and also why he was moved to offer his services to the BBC in the first place.

Eliot's correspondence with Deputy Director of Programmes Charles A. Siepmann, now in the BBC archive at Caversham, makes it clear how anxious he was to make the most of this new technology. He was keenly alive to the genre differences between a public lecture and a broadcast talk, and worked hard to establish a suitable tone. But his sensitivity to the matter owed a lot to Siepmann's boss, Hilda Matheson, the BBC's Director of Talks from 1926 until 1931. Matheson's mission was to develop the radio talk as an effective means of communication, 'as a mediating agency between the state and people' and as a means of 'bridging the gap between expert and citizen'. From the beginning, she understood that 'by enabling a whole country or continent to listen to a disembodied voice, wireless concentrates attention upon it – flood-lights it, as it were – bringing out every little trick and peculiarity'.[9] Matheson was in many ways the right woman for the moment. She had an ear for language, was sensitive to nuance, and recognised from the first the damage that could be done by stuffy or snooty announcers:

Broadcasting is enabling complicated, difficult and novel ideas and experiences to be conveyed to people whose lack of literary education would ordinarily prevent or hinder them from getting in touch with those ideas and experiences direct from printed books. Readings of prose and poetry, plays, are giving them new life to many people who missed the sound and significance of them in print. (It is, of course, true that reading aloud means rendering in a spoken form what was designed as written language. That raises yet another problem, which is not easily solved.) But, in addition, broadcasting is redressing the balance in favour of the vernacular. Early experiments with broadcast talks showed that it was useless to address the microphone as if it were a public meeting, or even to read it essays or leading articles. The person sitting at the other end expected the reader to address him personally, simply, almost familiarly, as man to man.[10]

It was Matheson more than anyone else who forged the template for the modern radio talk. And it was her model to which Eliot initially applied himself. More than this, Eliot's very engagement with the BBC follows another pattern established by Matheson – even if it was to Siepmann that he first applied. As Briggs observes, Matheson 'introduced some of the country's best speakers and writers to the BBC and in the course of doing so performed an equally important task, that of introducing the BBC to them'.[11]

Given the suspicions that still attended the new medium of radio in 1929, one might have anticipated Eliot's initial interest to prove little more than curiosity, but as the years went on his attraction to radio grew stronger and what might have been infatuation grew into a serious and complex commitment. My suggestion is that the discourses on culture that Eliot produced in the 1940s and 1950s, and in particular his pronouncements on the BBC, reveal him to be the last of the Victorian sages – a Victorian sage who not only published his ideas but also intoned them over the airwaves. In fact, without the broad *readership* known to Arnold and Ruskin, Eliot's status as a sage was to an important degree made possible by the BBC. Eliot knew – what these Victorian sages could not have known – an *audience*. His correspondence with the BBC makes it clear that his connection with the listening audience was, for him, a matter of concern. In 1937, for example, he advised against further broadcasts of his 'Cats' poems until the BBC learned how they had been received. We know, too, that he was eager to learn the results of listener surveys done after his 1951 talk, 'Virgil and the Christian World', and his 1953 broadcast lecture, 'The Three Voices of Poetry'. For the first, he received an 'appreciation index' of 72, for the second, 77, which was 'well above the average (66) for all *Third Programme* talks reported during 1953'.[12]

This is not to say that Eliot ever pandered to popular taste. Neither did he seek celebrity. But he did hunger for community – and radio offered an opportunity to build one. As radio developed into a global industry and the BBC gradually assumed a global role, this early promise stayed with Eliot. That it did contradicts received notions of Eliot and modernism. Some theorists and promoters of high modernism, who followed the lead of Theodor Adorno and the Frankfurt School critique of mass culture, have long argued that modernist art was at once opposed to all things Victorian as well as to the formations of modern mass culture. Since the detail provided by David Chinitz's *T. S. Eliot and the Cultural Divide* (2003), such assumptions have looked increasingly untenable. Eliot was not consistently hostile to popular or mass culture: he enjoyed jazz and music hall, read detective stories and listened to radio; he sent flowers to the *chanteuse* Eartha Kitt and exchanged photos with the comedian Groucho Marx; and his poetry often alluded to or even included slang and 'pop culture'. Although disdain for mass culture does appear in Eliot's poetry and prose, it was neither dogmatic nor programmatic.

From a theoretical point of view, Eliot's abiding interest in popular culture makes sense in terms of his commitment to Arnoldian notions of cultural integrity – that is, to expectations that all aspects of a people's life are interrelated. This holistic way of thinking represented a reaction against Enlightenment conceptions that had come to be seen as overly rationalising and disintegrative. Arnold, like Coleridge and Ruskin, envisioned culture as a single shared life and ultimately a spiritual life. Consequently, what happens in the arts is related to what happens in commerce, in religion, in politics, and so on. Moreover, cultures, like plants, grow from the bottom up. The Victorians, as well as modern thinkers like Adorno, took serious art to be the flower of this plant, while mass or popular productions were viewed as little more than detritus. But in this regard as others, Eliot was exceptional. As early as his 1923 review of Marianne Moore's *Poems*, Eliot was refusing quasi-Marxist distinctions between 'proletariat', 'middle-class' and 'aristocratic' arts: 'fine art is the *refinement*, not the antithesis, of popular art'.[13] This is a vision of relatedness, not relativeness; it would stay with Eliot for the rest of his life and underlay the thirty-five years he worked for the BBC and other broadcasters.

Eliot's most immediate attraction to broadcasting seems to have come from his sense that it might enable a new relation with his audience, as well as the possibility of reaching an audience beyond regular readers of literature. His concern with audience is quite explicit in his first letter to Charles Siepmann on 24 February 1929. The letter appears to follow up an earlier conversation, since Siepmann's reply remembered Eliot 'raising the question of quotation'. In any case, Siepmann remarked that he was 'very much attracted' by Eliot's 'outline scheme' and had 'no material alterations to suggest'. He asked Eliot to 'remember that a standard of simplicity is essential in such talks' and invited him 'to come along and have your voice tested at the microphone'.[14] That invitation – a requirement really – exemplifies the trouble that Eliot took to involve himself in broadcasting. For the BBC, voice checks served to test the attractiveness of particular voices over the air, as well as to enable guest speakers to familiarise themselves with the tricks of speaking into a microphone. In 1929 there was little about the microphone that was actually 'micro': heavy and unidirectional, these microphones required the speaker to maintain a more or less physical attention – speaking into them was something of an acquired skill. That Eliot never wholly became comfortable with microphones might be surmised from reservations evident in objections he made to Ronald Boswell nearly twenty years after his first voice test. Boswell had arranged for Eliot's 1947 lecture on John Milton to the British Academy to be recorded for later broadcast. Sharing Matheson's concerns that the genres of public lecture and recorded broadcast were incompatible, Eliot warned that he did not want to find himself talking *to* a microphone rather than to the members of the British Academy who had come to hear him. Fifteen years later, Eliot positively refused to allow the broadcast of his 1961 Convocation Address at the University of Leeds. His objection in these instances was not to the obtrusive effects of technology, but to the presentation of one kind of performance as another: the presentation of a formal address as a radio talk.

Voice tests such as the one Eliot made at the Savoy Hill studio in March 1929 were only one step in the preparation of a broadcast; after the test, rehearsals of the actual talk would follow. Eliot took these rehearsals very seriously, especially in the early years of his broadcasts, or whenever he was anxious about the subject, or broadcasting in a language other than English. In March 1946, for instance, he spent five hours rehearsing the first part of his series 'Reflections of an English Poet on European Culture', which he gave in German. And, of course, before practising a talk, Eliot had to write it. At this stage, he also demonstrated particular conscientiousness, and not just because the BBC was contracted (in spite of Eliot's objections) to publish his scripts within twenty-eight days of their first broadcast.[15] Long after he had become an experienced broadcaster, Eliot continued to submit scripts to BBC producers. In March 1932 he corresponded closely with Siepmann while developing his four contributions to *The Modern Dilemma* series; ten years later he submitted to the Reverend Eric Fenn and to Philip Mairet several drafts of his contribution to Dorothy Sayers's series *The Church Looks Ahead*. Eliot's talk 'Towards a Christian Britain' (broadcast on 2 April 1941) caused him sustained concern. Trying to avoid making the issue sound either too easy or too difficult, he wrote to Fenn about the particular importance of both the rhythm and the tempo of his delivery.[16] There was, in other words, absolutely nothing casual about either Eliot's individual talks or his decision to undertake them.

As a citizen, Eliot wanted community; as a poet he wanted culture; as a sage he wanted audience. But in each instance, as he wrote in 'Tradition and the Individual Talent' (1919), tradition 'cannot be inherited' or taken for granted, it had to be earned with 'great labour' (*SE*, 14). In each case, the individual would paradoxically achieve individuality through conformity. With regard to BBC policy, conformity meant mastering the art of the radio talk and attempting to achieve a new intimacy with his audience.

In a 1940 retrospective on H. G. Wells, looking back over Wells's long and popular career, Eliot proposed that such success as Wells had known was no longer possible due to changes in the nature of the reading public and in its relations to authority. Implicitly, Eliot betrayed regret, perhaps envy, at the way in which 'through being a popular entertainer, [Wells] found an opening as a prophet':

There is, I believe, no place for a modern Wells to educate the public in more modern opinions. Our public is not yet in existence ... [Today] We can have very little hope of contributing to any immediate social change; and we are more disposed to see our hope in modest and local beginnings, than in transforming the whole world at once.[17]

In Eliot's career, radio became that 'no place' wherein he made his best effort not just to educate but to create that public whose existence he could not take for granted. Indeed, by presenting a disembodied voice that comes at once from everywhere and nowhere, radio is a 'no place' unprecedented in its ubiquity.

Of course, there is drift between Tandy's 'voice of the nation' and this later sense of 'no place'. The key is to see how 'no place' becomes everyplace. In the most ambitious period of his radio work from 1940 to 1946, Eliot devoted himself to the BBC's Eastern Service, addressing the audiences of the Asian subcontinent on English literature and giving the first ever broadcast readings of his own work. At the end of the Second World War he broadcast to a German audience on the unity of European culture, both reaffirming his remarkable broadcasts on the liberation of Rome in June 1944 and anticipating the arguments he would put forward in *Notes Towards the Definition of Culture* (1948). Eschewing any mention of the immediate political situation, these talks worked to build a community and also to ennoble that community with what Eliot understood as a deep and deepening sense of tradition. A paraphrase of Eliot's estimation of James Joyce's *Ulysses* offers a telling summary of his goals for radio: no one had built upon such a foundation before, it had never before been necessary, and yet such building was, Eliot seriously believed, a step towards making the modern world possible for art.

NOTES

1. 'The Idea of a Literary Review', *Criterion* (January 1926), 2–3.
2. F. S. Flint, 'Verse Chronicle', *Criterion* (April 1933), 474.
3. See Geoffrey Tandy, 'Broadcasting Chronicle', *Criterion* (October 1934), 104–13.
4. For a discussion of the darker side of Reith's vision, see Debra Rae Cohen, 'Annexing the Oracular Voice: Form, Ideology, and the BBC', *Broadcasting Modernism*, ed. Debra Rae Cohen, Michael Coyle and Jane Lewty (Gainesville: University of Florida Press, 2009), pp. 142–57.
5. Quoted in Todd Avery, *Radio Modernism: Literature, Ethics, and the BBC, 1922–1938* (Aldershot: Ashgate, 2006), p. 16.
6. Ibid., p. 15.
7. I listed 101 items in 'The Radio Broadcasts of T. S. Eliot, 1929–1963: A Checklist'; see *T. S. Eliot and our Turning World*, ed. Jewel Spears Brooker (London: Macmillan, 1997), pp. 203–13. This number does not include rebroadcasts, readings by other voices of Eliot's work or critical commentaries upon it. It is likely that additional items will be discovered in the archives of the BBC.

8. Quoted in Burton Paulu, *British Broadcasting: Radio and Television in the United Kingdom* (Minneapolis: University of Minnesota Press, 1956), pp. 152–3.
9. Hilda Matheson, *Broadcasting* (London: Thornton Butterworth, 1933), pp. 154, 161.
10. Ibid., p. 75.
11. Asa Briggs, *The Birth of Modern Broadcasting 1896–1927* (Oxford University Press, 1995), p. 117.
12. Details in the BBC Written Archives Centre, Caversham.
13. 'Marianne Moore', *Dial* (December 1923), 595.
14. C. A. Siepmann to T. S. Eliot, 25 February 1929, quoted by permission of the BBC Written Archives Centre, Caversham.
15. Contract details outlined by C. A. Siepmann to T. S. Eliot, 31 March 1931. BBC Written Archives Centre, Caversham.
16. Correspondence contained in the BBC Written Archives Centre, Caversham. Eliot Talks File II, 1938–42.
17. 'Views and Reviews: Journalists of Yesterday and Today', *New English Weekly* (8 February 1940), 238.

PART THREE

Literary Cross-Currents

CHAPTER 16

Allusion: the case of Shakespeare

Hugh Haughton

Walton Litz has spoken of T. S. Eliot's 'almost insatiable appetite for allusion', observing that 'one of the most striking aspects' of Eliot's poetic development between 1915 and 1920 was 'the thickening of conscious, orchestrated allusion'.[1] Litz draws attention to Eliot's 'A Note on Ezra Pound' published in 1918, which contrasts the 'deliberateness' and the 'positive coherence' of Pound's use of allusions to those of James Joyce, 'another very learned literary artist', who 'uses allusions suddenly and with great speed, part of the effect being the extent of the vista opened to the imagination by the very lightest touch'.[2] Desmond MacCarthy was one of the first reviewers to comment upon Eliot's allusiveness. In a 1921 notice of *Ara Vos Prec*, bracketing Eliot with Pound, MacCarthy observed that 'The allusions in their poems are learned, oblique, and obscure; the mottoes they choose for their poems are polyglot, the names that occur to them are symbolic ... known only to book-minded people' (Brooker, 31). Noting that Eliot's 'phrases are frequently echoes', MacCarthy claimed Eliot was 'the reverse of an imitative poet', his echoes were 'tuned to a new context which changes their subtlety. He does not steal phrases; he borrows their aroma.' Quoting the stanzas beginning 'Defunctive music under sea / Passed seaward with the passing bell' (*CPP*, 40) from 'Burbank with a Baedeker: Bleistein with a Cigar', MacCarthy comments:

Just as 'weeping, weeping multitudes' ... is an echo from Blake, so 'Defunctive music' comes from 'The Phoenix and the Turtle' and 'Her ... barge / Burned on the water', of course, from *Antony and Cleopatra*. But the point is that the poet means to draw a subtle whiff of Cleopatra and poetic passion across our minds, in order that we may feel a peculiar emotion towards the sordid little siren in the poem itself, just as he also uses later a broken phrase or two from *The Merchant of Venice* for the sake of reminding us of Shakespeare's Jew, compared with the 'Bleistein' of the poem. (Brooker, 33–4)

It is an exaggeration to say these allusions are 'known only to book-minded people', since most of them are references to well-known passages in Shakespeare. They are typical of Eliot's tactics in handling 'broken' material from the literary past, and of the way quoted words can be reactivated in new lyric forms.

MacCarthy's remark that Eliot does not 'steal phrases' recalls Eliot's own remarks in his 1920 essay on Philip Massinger: 'Immature poets imitate, mature poets steal'. The context of Eliot's oft-quoted aphorism about quotation tends to be forgotten:

> One of the surest of tests is the way in which a poet borrows. Immature poets imitate; mature poets steal; bad poets deface what they take, and good poets make it into something better, or at least something different. The good poet welds his theft into a whole of feeling which is unique, utterly different from that from which it was torn; the bad poet throws it into something which has no cohesion. A good poet will usually borrow from authors remote in time, or alien in language, or diverse in interest. Chapman borrowed from Seneca; Shakespeare and Webster from Montaigne. (*SE*, 206)

Eliot goes on to discuss the way Massinger borrows from Shakespeare, and his remarks have a bearing on the poems in *Ara Vos Prec*. Eliot generally preferred to 'borrow from authors remote in time, or alien in language', but we should remember that the Massinger essay not only confirms the overlap of Eliot as essayist and poet, it highlights something he and Massinger have in common: borrowing from Shakespeare. Eliot's claim that 'the good poet welds his theft into a whole of feeling which is unique, utterly different from that from which it was torn', is revealing in the light of his own systematic Shakespearean thefts, with their blend of violation ('torn') and creative unity ('welded' into 'a whole').

In a discussion of literary sources in 'Kubla Khan', Eliot said that the poem's imagery 'whatever its origins in Coleridge's reading, sank to the depths of Coleridge's feeling, was saturated, transformed there – "those are pearls that were his eyes" – and brought up into daylight again' (*UPUC*, 146). Discussing the poetic transformation of a poet's reading, Eliot notes that 'the re-creation of word and image which happens fitfully in the poetry of such a poet as Coleridge happens almost incessantly with Shakespeare'. Shakespeare gives a 'new meaning' or extracts a 'latent one' from familiar words: 'the right imagery, saturated while it lay in the depths of Shakespeare's memory, will rise like Anadyomene from the sea' (*UPUC*, 146–7). Talking of such 'reborn' words and images, Eliot discusses his own appropriation of an image from George Chapman, who borrowed it from Seneca, suggesting that 'what gives it such intensity as it has in each case is its saturation ... with feelings too obscure for the authors even to know quite what they were' (*UPUC*, 147–8). This suggests the study of allusion is not only about literary sources or influences, but about what Eliot called the 'auditory imagination': 'the feeling for syllable and rhythm, penetrating far below the conscious levels of thought and feeling ... sinking to the most primitive and forgotten, returning to the origin and bringing something back' (*UPUC*, 118–19). Literary borrowing, then, is not a display of conscious learning or cultural memory; it is more personal and opaque than that. In this discussion of the poet's transformation of literary sources, Eliot's quotation from Ariel's song in *The Tempest* – the same phrase he had used in *The Waste Land* – shows how crucial Shakespeare was to his own auditory imagination.

Although there have been many studies of Eliot and his sources, Eliot and quotation, his poetic borrowings from Shakespeare, although easily recognised, have not aroused sustained critical attention.[3] Eliot tended to play down the presence of Shakespeare in his work. With the exception of the 1919 *Hamlet* article and the 1927 piece on 'Shakespeare and the Stoicism of Seneca' – two revealing essays – Eliot published little exclusively on Shakespeare. In 1961 he observed that the critical essays of his own that he liked best were 'on the contemporaries of Shakespeare, not those on Shakespeare himself' (*TCC*, 18). Yet though Eliot generally steered clear of Shakespeare in published essays, it has been said that he 'virtually invented the twentieth-century Shakespeare in a collection of asides'.[4] Taken together, his dispersed comments amount to a substantial body of work. In 'Shakespeare and the Stoicism of Seneca', Eliot took sideswipes at the 'up-to-date Shakespeares' presented by Lytton Strachey, John Middleton Murry and Wyndham Lewis, offering instead a Senecan stoic writing in 'a period of dissolution and chaos' (*SE*, 132) and drawn to 'the attitude of self-dramatization' (*SE*, 129). Eliot's Shakespeare reminds us that his own early poetry, with its use of dramatic monologue and allusions to dramatic situations, displays comparable 'dissolution and chaos' as well as attitudes of 'self-dramatization'.

In essays and interviews, Eliot paid tribute to the influence of Dante and Laforgue, but Shakespearean allusion is also a crucial thread in his poetry from the outset. J. Alfred Prufrock appeals to Shakespeare's melancholy soliloquising prince – 'No! I am not Prince Hamlet, nor was meant to be' (*CPP*, 16). The negative allusion records Prufrock's refusal to cast himself as a contemporary counterpart to the famously indecisive Hamlet ('nor was meant to be' takes up *the* famous soliloquy 'To be or

not to be'), but it also intensifies our puzzlement about what Prufrock *is*
meant to be. Despite the disavowed comparison with Hamlet, he presents
himself in inherently theatrical terms as 'an attendant lord, one that will
do / To swell a progress, start a scene or two, / Advise the prince' (*CPP*, 16).
The lines, although not blank verse, recall Shakespeare's pentameters and
occasional couplets, and the idiom is fully Shakespearean (he is 'Full of
high sentence' like Polonius). 'Almost, at times, the Fool. / I grow old . . .
I grow old' (*CPP*, 16) invokes both 'the Fool' and king in *King Lear*. Even
the closing sea images recall the world of *Pericles* and *The Tempest*,
revealing Eliot's peculiarly aqueous sense of Shakespeare. If Prufrock talks
of composing a theatrical scene, then the speaker in 'Portrait of a Lady'
says 'You have the scene arrange itself', conjuring 'An atmosphere of
Juliet's tomb' (*CPP*, 18), thereby using the world of *Romeo and Juliet* as
an analogy for the stifling, would-be romantic room where the cultured
Bostonian lady serves him tea. Eliot is subtly recapitulating the mode of
his early Laforguean pastiche 'Nocturne', with its 'Romeo, *grand sérieux*,
to importune / Guitar and hat in hand, beside the gate / With Juliet'
(*CPP*, 601).

Ara Vos Prec (1920), laced with epigraphs, embedded quotations, polyglot phrases and recondite references, turned up the volume of allusion,
including Shakespearean allusion. 'Gerontion' takes its epigraph from
Measure for Measure – Shakespeare's play offering a 'measure' of the
protagonist stiffening in his rented house. The speaker's acrid psychic
world is full of half-throttled echoes and smothered memories of the
cadences and rhetoric of earlier drama.[5] If the bulk of these poems move
away from the dramatic monologue, they remain haunted by theatrical
echoes. 'Ode' takes its epigraph from *Coriolanus*, quoting the disaffected
hero's speech to Tullus Aufidius as he prepares to betray his country: 'To
you particularly, and to all the Volscians / Great hurt and mischief' (iv.v).
In the play Coriolanus speaks of the 'drops of blood' he has shed for his
'thankless country'; casting a strange light on the 'blood upon the bed' in
Eliot's nuptial poem about a 'Tortured' bridegroom (*IMH*, 383). The
same poem incorporates two other Shakespearean allusions relating to
'hurt and mischief': 'Indignant / At the cheap extinction of his taking-off'
mangles Macbeth's famous soliloquy before the assassination of Duncan,
while 'Now lies he there / Tip to tip washed beneath Charles' Wagon'
(*IMH*, 383) recalls Antony's powerful oration over the body of Caesar.
Such echoes give an eerie inflection to Eliot's bloody bridegroom, the
dragon-slaying Perseus of the poem: 'The fooled resentment of the
dragon' (*IMH*, 383) crosses back upon the hero of *Coriolanus* (who is

compared three times in the play to a dragon). Eliot's tortuously allusive poem, with its 'Subterrene laughter' and the Shakespearean equation between political murder and blood of the 'Succuba eviscerate' (*IMH*, 383), is disturbed and disturbing. It may turn upon Eliot's marriage to Vivien without his parents' approval (the allusion to Coriolanus suggesting a symbolic desertion of his family and his country). The bloody sheets of the marital bedchamber are stained with quotations from Shakespeare's violent dramatisations of civil strife, suggesting 'feelings too obscure for the author even to know quite what they were'.

According to Grover Smith, 'Burbank with a Baedeker: Bleistein with a Cigar' contains 'more quotations and functional allusions than any [Eliot poem] of comparable length'.[6] Among the collage of quotations resonant of Venice – the most allusive of cities – Eliot draws on Shakespeare's two Venetian plays, *The Merchant of Venice* and *Othello* (Othello's 'Goats and monkeys!' appears in the macaronic epigraph). 'Defunctive music under sea / Passed seaward with the passing bell' (*CPP*, 40) remembers 'That defunctive music can, / Be the death-divining swan, / Lest the requiem lack his right' from 'The Phoenix and the Turtle'. Eliot's poem is a mock-elegy, an excursion into venereal Venice, where love and constancy are dead. This theme coalesces with the comparable music 'under the earth' heard by soldiers in *Antony and Cleopatra*, which is interpreted in the play as 'the god Hercules, whom Antony lov'd, / Now leaves him' (iv.iv). Cleopatra is invoked in Eliot's poem by the reference to the barge that 'Burned on the water all the day' (*CPP*, 40), recalling Enorbarbus' description of Cleopatra: 'The barge she sat in, like a burnish'd throne, / Burned on the water' (ii.ii). The phrase 'On the Rialto once' (*CPP*, 41) recalls *The Merchant of Venice* where variants of 'on the Rialto' occur five times in the play, identifying 'Bleistein' – 'Chicago Semite Viennese' (*CPP*, 40) – as a modern Shylock. Opinions vary as to the degree of anti-Semitism in Eliot's poem, as in Shakespeare's play: the racist association of rats and Jews has a source in the metaphorical 'land-rats and water-rats' that Shylock has heard about 'on the Rialto' (i.iii). The 'Time's ruins' (*CPP*, 41) in the final line of Eliot's poem may allude to Antony's words in *Julius Caesar*: 'Thou art the ruins of the noblest man, / That ever lived in the tide of times' (iii.i). The allusive web in these quatrains requires a literary Baedeker to make sense of them. In its mixture of virtuosity, pastiche and collage, 'Burbank with a Baedeker: Blestein with a Cigar' resembles the contemporary paintings of Pablo Picasso, which raid past and present for their multi-plane compositions. They are responses to the post-war fracturing of communal certitudes. Allusion forges a mirage of cultural continuity even as it registers contemporary chaos, dissolution and disorder. The grotesque Shakespearean montages presented in *Ara Vos Prec* offer a disturbing 'objective correlative' of the poet's attempt – as Eliot thought Shakespeare struggled to do in *Hamlet* – to 'express the inexpressibly horrible' (*SE*, 146).

The Waste Land is famously (or notoriously) marinaded in allusion. Because of the paratextual references in Eliot's notes to *The Golden Bough* and *From Ritual to Romance*, and the textual allusions to among others Dante, Baudelaire and Wagner, the very familiarity of the Shakespearean allusions can prevent us from taking due notice of them. 'A Game of Chess' opens with another warped account of Cleopatra's barge from *Antony and Cleopatra* – 'The Chair she sat in, like a burnished throne' (*CPP*, 64). Enorbarbus had reported 'pretty dimpled boys, like smiling Cupids' (II.ii) standing on either side of her. Eliot's opening verse paragraphs draw upon this as well as Iachimo's description of Imogen's bedchamber in *Cymbeline* – 'The roof o'the chamber / With golden cherubins is fretted. Her andirons – / I had forgot them – were two winking Cupids' (II.iv). These two scenes are conflated in *The Waste Land*'s feminine bedchamber where 'a golden Cupidon peeped out' (*CPP*, 64). Iachimo also noted on a visit to Imogen's bedchamber that 'She hath been reading late / The tale of Tereus; here the leaf's turn'd down / Where Philomel gave up' (II.i). This 'sylvan scene / The change of Philomel, by the barbarous king / So rudely forced' (*CPP*, 64) is on display in *The Waste Land*.[7] Here Eliot's elaborate pastiche of Elizabethan Ovidian verse mutates after the conventional nightingale's 'Jug Jug' from a nightmare vision of 'other withered stumps of time' which 'were told upon the walls' (*CPP*, 64) into a modern domestic dialogue, dramatising the contrast and the continuities between the representation of a mythological scenario and this marital *scene*.

The section title 'A Game of Chess' recalls Miranda and Ferdinand who are discovered playing chess in *The Tempest*, the only play by Shakespeare to be directly quoted in *The Waste Land*. The question 'Do you remember / Nothing?' prompts the reply 'I remember / Those are pearls that were his eyes' (*CPP*, 65), which in turn prompts us to remember Madame Sosostris's earlier parenthetical aside '(Those are pearls that were his eyes. Look!)' (*CPP*, 62). The echo of Ariel's elegy for Prince Ferdinand's father, who is presumed drowned – 'Full fathom five thy father lies' (I.ii) – links it to Madame Sosostris's 'drowned Phoenician Sailor' and her warning about 'death by water' (*CPP*, 62), further anticipating section 4, entitled 'Death by Water', where Phlebas the Phoenician drowns. The interjection of 'Those are pearls that were his eyes' from Ariel's song – perhaps suggesting Eliot's grief for his own dead father – into the desultory, neurotic conversation of the unnamed couple in 'A Game of Chess' is eerie and unnerving.

The quotation from *Hamlet* at the end of 'A Game of Chess' is transferred to a London pub at closing time: 'good night, sweet ladies, good night, good night' (*CPP*, 66). It connects the speaker suffering from 'bad' nerves to mad Ophelia, another drowned figure. Earlier the question 'Are you alive, or not? Is there nothing in your head?' is the cue for the poem to launch weirdly into an allusion to a popular American vaudeville song 'O O O O that Shakespeherian Rag' (*CPP*, 65). The jazzy ragtime rhythms of Gene Buck and Herman Ruby's popular lyric, 'That Shakespearian Rag', mock and appropriates the 'high browed rhymes' of Shakespeare's 'syncopated lines': 'That Shakespearian rag / Most intelligent, very elegant / That old classical drag'.[8] Eliot's popular allusion is *about* allusion and plays upon the relationship between popular culture and the 'high-browed' culture of the past, which generates a new 'syncopated' music. The song's opening quotation from Mark Antony's funeral speech in *Julius Caesar* – 'Friends, Romans, Countrymen' – suggests that if you 'lend an ear' you can hear Shakespeare in ragtime. By tweaking the nominal form 'Shakespearean' to 'Shakespeherian', Eliot allows us, in Shakespeare's name, to lend an ear to the word 'hear' and to infer the rhythms of the American jazz song. *The Waste Land*'s 'O O O O', which might appear to add nothing, in fact opens out the nothings, reminding us of Lear's near final words ('Pray you, undo / This button. Thank you, sir, O, O, O, O!' [v.iii]) paving the way for the Os which sound and resound in the poem: 'O the moon shone bright on Mrs Porter', '*O ces voix d'enfants*', 'O City city', 'O you who turn the wheel', 'O swallow swallow' (*CPP*, 67, 69, 71, 75).

'The Fire Sermon' returns us to the world of *The Tempest,* as a voice speaks of 'fishing in the dull canal / On a winter evening round behind the gashouse / Musing upon the king my brother's wreck / And on the king my father's death before him' (*CPP*, 67). The effect of these transitions is neither mock-heroic nor satirical, but there is something uncanny, turning again upon the death of the father, in the transposition of Shakespeare's lines into Eliot's against the backdrop of the gasworks. In the next reference to *The Tempest* – 'This music crept by me upon the waters' (*CPP*, 69) – the words are in quotation marks, suggesting a different form of auditory allusion to Shakespeare's magical island. Later the Thames barges remind us of Cleopatra's barge, just as mention of Elizabeth and Leicester recalls Shakespeare's contemporaries, and the fragment 'To Carthage then I came' (*CPP*, 70) remembers not only Augustine's *Confessions* but also the courtiers of *The Tempest* shipwrecked on their way back from North Africa, prompting Gonzalo's remark that 'This Tunis, sir, was Carthage' (II.i). After 'Death by Water', associated with the deathly sea-change of Ariel's song (a grotesque anti-Semitic travesty of Ariel's song entitled 'Dirge' was cut, on Pound's recommendation, from the published poem), Shakespearean allusion effectively disappears from *The Waste Land*, although thunder figures in both *The Tempest* and 'What the Thunder Said' and the inverted 'Tolling reminiscent bells' (*CPP*, 73) are reminiscent of the sea-nymphs in *The Tempest* who 'hourly toll his knell' as well as Prospero's 'cloud-capped towers' (IV.i).

At the close, however, Shakespeare sponsors one of the most arresting allusive moments of the entire sequence: 'Only at nightfall, aethereal rumours / Revive for a moment a broken Coriolanus' (*CPP*, 74). Shakespeare's controversial Roman hero is one of only three literary figures (alongside Tiresias and Kyd's Hieronymo) named in the poem. Grover Smith sees Coriolanus, like Dante's Ugolino, as 'another traitor, who betrayed his country and those who loved him'.[9] And yet 'a broken Coriolanus' suggests not only *the* broken Coriolanus of Shakespeare's play but also a role with which many other persons might associate themselves. Is this baffling and oracular image alluding to the 'broken' hero in the later stages of the tragedy, or a reference to a fragmented memory of the play? After all, 'aethereal rumours' sound more at home in the world of *The Tempest* or *Pericles* than in this abrasively secular Roman tragedy. What is the broken Roman general doing amid the final fragments 'shored against my ruins' (*CPP*, 75) as the poem dissolves into a welter of broken quotations? 'My ruins' is architectural, reminding us of Roman ruins and Roman ruin. Comminius talks of Rome laid flat in 'heaps and piles of ruin' (III.i) while Volumnia (who uses the word 'ruin' three times) implores her son not to 'triumphantly tread upon thy country's ruin' (V.iii). If brokenness is a condition of Eliot's poem, so is a country's and a city's ruin. The 'awful daring of a moment's surrender' (*CPP*, 74) recalls the moment when Coriolanus (named after a conquered city) surrenders to the force of his mother's pleading, and breaks down. We remember that Eliot wrote this poem about breakage, ruin and fragmentation during his own 'breakdown' after his mother's visit to London. The allusion to *Coriolanus* leads on to the 'controlling hands' *(CPP*, 74) that follow. In her final showdown with her son, Volumnia says that Coriolanus has torn 'with thunder the wide cheeks of the air' (V.iii), but what the thunderous 'aethereal rumours' say to Eliot's Coriolanus intimates regenerative possibilities. These Shakespearean 'rumours' suggest the impact of sound (*Coriolanus* is a play full of noise, voices, clamour, trumpets, rumours), which, along with the 'music' of Ariel's song, confirm that allusion and the auditory imagination are scarcely distinguishable in the acoustic arena of *The Waste Land*.

Eliot's understanding of Shakespeare changed radically in the late 1920s when he wrote his two most overtly Shakespearean poems. Under the influence of G. Wilson Knight's interpretations of the patterns in Shakespearean drama, Eliot argued that 'The whole of Shakespeare's work is *one* poem ... united by one significant, consistent, and, developing personality' (*SE*, 203). 'Marina' and 'Coriolan', with their titles pointing towards *Pericles* and *Coriolanus*, mark this stage of Eliot's Shakespearean investment. Here allusions to Shakespeare are less invasive than pervasive. 'Marina' crosses the recognition scene from *Pericles*, described by Eliot as 'the speech of creatures who are more than human, or rather, seen in a light more than that of day',[10] with the New England coastline of his childhood; crossing them again with a Latin epigraph from Seneca's *Hercules Furens* with its tragic allusion to another coast where Hercules in his madness kills his wife and sons.[11] Through the epigraph, Eliot keeps Senecan paternal terror in play within the paternal awe of Shakespeare's triumphant reunion of Marina with her father Pericles. The poem offers a free-floating, fugal variation on Shakespeare's recognition scene. It opens:

> What seas what shores what grey rocks and what islands
> What water lapping the bow
> And scent of pine and the woodthrush singing through the fog
> What images return
> O my daughter. (*CPP*, 109)

'Shore' is a rich Shakespearean term, especially in the late romances. It appears twenty-one times in the plural ('shores'), five times in *Pericles*, once associated with Marina's apparent death and three times in association with her recovery and meeting with her father. In the main, however, the Shakespearean music of 'Marina' resigns itself to this influence without quotation. 'What images return' the poem says, and the allusions draw on a bank of Shakespearean imagery (the word 'image' itself returns over eighty times in his oeuvre) explicated by Wilson Knight's criticism. Eliot dedicated 'Marina' to Knight, who called the poem 'a perfect poetical commentary on those Shakespearean meanings which I had unveiled'.[12] But it is both more and less than commentary. Eliot's speaker, who longs to resign 'speech for that unspoken' (*CPP*, 110), may be recalling Pericles' grief-stricken silence before his reunion with his daughter, anticipating a mirage-like human meeting. The poem's hallucinatory participial present tells us that Pericles is still at sea, while the phrase 'the sty of contentment' (*CPP*, 109) calls up Marina in the brothel, who speaks of fortune having placed her 'in this sty' praying that the 'gods / Would set me free' (iv.iv). The speaker's question 'What is this face, less clear and clearer / The pulse in the arm, less strong and stronger – Given or lent?' (*CPP*, 109) has roots in Pericles' question to Marina: 'But are you flesh and blood? Have you a working pulse' (v.i), gratefully exhibiting the debt Eliot owes to Shakespeare within the 'working pulse' of his poetry.

Pericles allowed Eliot to tune into a father–daughter story. 'Coriolan' turns on the mother–son relationship dramatised in *Coriolanus*. Grover Smith has said that 'Triumphal March', the first part of 'Coriolan', 'competes with *The Waste Land*' in its allusiveness, such that its difficulty could have been 'moderated by the judicious insertion of quotation marks'.[13] The poem draws on Eliot's memories of London parades at the end of the First World War; an account in the *Daily Mail* of Benito Mussolini's march on Rome; extracts from Charles Maurras's *L'Avenir de l'intelligence* and the philosopher Edmund Husserl's *Ideas*; while the allusion in the title to Beethoven's *Coriolan* overture suggests a musically mediated relationship to Shakespeare (the overture was to Heinrich von Collin's 1802 play). Although it does not quote directly from *Coriolanus*, Eliot's dramatic collage incorporates some of the imagery and brazen music of Shakespeare's play, opening with a triumphal march in the streets of Rome:

> Stone, bronze, stone, steel, stone, oakleaves, horses' heels
> Over the paving.
> And the flags. And the trumpets. And so many eagles.
> How many? Count them. And such a press of people.
> We hardly knew ourselves that day, or knew the City.   (*CPP*, 127)

The poem is aligned with Wilson Knight's account of the play (which he sent to Eliot), emphasising a 'world of hard weapons, battle's clanging contacts, civic brawls', full of 'metallic' imagery and 'numerous weapons', through which 'Coriolanus strides gigantic, thunderously reverberating his aristocracy above the multitude'. Knight insists on the play's sounds and Eliot's poem, too, is sound conscious: its steel and trumpet flourishes recall the 'steel pikes' (v.vi) and funeral music at the end of the play. Further, 'Coriolan' reinforces Knight's claim that *Coriolanus* is 'not alone a play of iron, but of irony'.[14] Eliot's poem places a partly ironic, anachronistic world of martial public images in counterpoint with more

vulnerable ones associated with the hero's feelings for his mother. 'Difficulties of a Statesman', the second part of 'Coriolan', begins: 'CRY what
shall I cry?' (*CPP*, 129), and the word 'cry' recurs eight times in this poem
and fourteen times in *Coriolanus*. Again, the Shakespearean allusions
channel material that Eliot struggled with: not only his difficult relationship
with his demanding mother, but his dissatisfactions with the Versailles
Treaty, Fascist ideals of authority and the psycho-pathology of the political hero.[15] Like 'Marina', the unfinished 'Coriolan' involves familial
virtuosic re-castings of the Shakespearean drama it grew out of.

Ronald Bush has argued that in the two lectures on Shakespeare that
Eliot delivered in Edinburgh in 1937, he was feeling his way not only
towards a more visionary reading of Shakespeare's 'hidden music' but that
of *Four Quartets*.[16] The 'broken king' (*CPP*, 191) of 'Little Gidding' recalls
the 'broken Coriolanus' of *The Waste Land*, but also Willoughby's account
of King Richard II as 'a broken man' (II.i). The phrase 'History is now and
England' (*CPP*, 197) is permeated by the presence of Shakespeare's history
plays – notably Henry VI's 'now in England' (*3Henry VI* I.i) and Henry
V's 'gentlemen in England now a-bed' (IV.iii) from the field at Agincourt.
There is also a haunting allusion to Shakespeare in what Grover Smith
has called 'the astonishing phalanx of allusions and imitations' lurking in
the second movement of 'Little Gidding'.[17] The spectral meeting with the
'familiar compound ghost' (*CPP*, 193) is a literary haunting, acknowledging in 'com*pound*' a Dantean debt to Ezra Pound – 'il miglior fabbro'
(*CPP*, 59) from the dedication to *The Waste Land* and a key influence on
Eliot's allusive method. Grover Smith recognises 'that affable familiar ghost'
of Shakespeare's Sonnet 86, a poem that asks, 'Was it his spirit, by spirits
taught to write / Above a mortal pitch, that struck me dead?', reflecting on
the interconnection between literary competition and inspiration. Eliot's
allusion surely touches on his rivalry with and debt to Shakespeare.
The dawn parting of the compound ghost of 'Little Gidding' – 'And
faded on the blowing of the horn' (*CPP*, 195) – creates an inter-textual
rhyme with Marcellus' description of the disappearance of the ghost in
Hamlet: 'It faded on the crowing of the cock' (I.i). The metrical ghost of
'the crowing of the cock' reminds us that *Hamlet*, like this Dantean
episode, is concerned with the purgatorial. The ghost of Hamlet's father
says he is 'confined to fast in fires, / Till the foul crimes done in my days
of nature / Are burnt and purged away' (I.v), whereas the ghost in 'Little
Gidding' says: 'From wrong to wrong the exasperated spirit / Proceeds,
unless restored by that refining fire' (*CPP*, 195). The episode's final auditory
allusion compounds war-torn London with a reflex of Shakespeare's

haunted Denmark. The familiar (indeed insistently familial) ghost of Shakespeare is never far away in Eliot's poetry, moving, if not always to ragtime, then to the distinctive poetic rhythms of his twentieth-century individual talent.

NOTES

1. A. Walton Litz, 'The Allusive Poet: Eliot and his Sources', *T. S. Eliot: The Modernist in History*, ed. Ronald Bush (Cambridge University Press, 1991), p. 138.
2. 'A Note on Ezra Pound', *Today* (September 1918), 6.
3. Charles Warren's valuable survey of Eliot's critical writings on Shakespeare documents numerous articles discussing Eliot's 'reworking of Shakespeare in this or that poem'. See *T. S. Eliot on Shakespeare* (Ann Arbor: University of Michigan Press, 1987), p. 88.
4. G. K. Hunter, *Dramatic Identities and Cultural Tradition: Studies in Shakespeare and his Contemporaries* (Liverpool University Press, 1978), p. 299.
5. For example, compare Gerontion's 'Virtues / Are forced upon us by our impudent crimes' (*CPP*, 38) with 'Our means secure us, and our defects / prove our commodities' from *King Lear* (IV:i).
6. Grover Smith, *T. S. Eliot's Poetry and Plays* (University of Chicago Press, 1974), p. 51.
7. Shakespeare makes ten other references to the rape of Philomel in his oeuvre, notably in *Titus Andronicus*.
8. Quoted in Lawrence Rainey, *The Annotated Waste Land with Eliot's Contemporary Prose* (New Haven, CT: Yale University Press, 2005), p. 97.
9. Grover Smith, *Eliot's Poetry and Plays*, p. 96.
10. Cited in Elizabeth Drew, *T. S. Eliot: The Design of his Poetry* (New York: Scribner, 1949), p. 127.
11. The Latin lines are translated by Jasper Heywood as 'What place is this? What region? Or of the world, what coast? / Where am I?', *Seneca: His Tenne Tragedies*, ed. Thomas Newton, intro. T. S. Eliot (London: Constable, 1927), p. 46.
12. G. Wilson Knight, 'Some Literary Impressions', *T. S. Eliot: The Man and the Work* (Harmondsworth: Penguin, 1967), p. 247.
13. Grover Smith, *Eliot's Poetry and Plays*, p. 160.
14. See G. Wilson Knight, *The Imperial Theme* (Oxford University Press, 1931), pp. 154–98.
15. Ronald Bush suggests that the poem dramatises 'Eliot's horror of both conforming and rebelling from the self-contained in his mother's eyes'. *T. S. Eliot: A Study in Character and Style* (Oxford University Press, 1985), p. 155.
16. Ibid., pp. 168–9.
17. Grover Smith, *Eliot's Poetry and Plays*, p. 290.

CHAPTER 17

Classics

Hannah Sullivan

T. S. Eliot made repeated, polemical, and idiosyncratic use of the word 'classic' and its cognates 'classical' and 'classicism' in his prose writings. In the earlier part of his career, he tended to use the term not to refer to writing in Latin and Greek (the Classics) or even to canonical texts in a wider range of languages, but as a call to arms. In his critical lexicon of the 1910s and 1920s, 'classicism' meant writing that was intelligently organised, mature, well proportioned and impersonal rather than gushingly emotional, personal or vague; and the opposite of 'classicism' was 'romanticism'. Both terms are to be understood primarily as formal and stylistic rather than temporal distinctions. Andrew Marvell is a 'classic in a sense which [Thomas] Gray and [William] Collins are not' because of his sense of argumentative and aesthetic 'equipoise, a balance and proportion of tones' (*SE*, 302). Charles Baudelaire's poetry may superficially appear classical, but a subtle 'inner disorder' means that it has 'the external but not the internal form of classic art' (*SE*, 423–4).

In an essay on John Milton – the most classically educated and classicising of English poets – Eliot again withholds the label: his style is baroque, 'peculiar', and too divorced from common speech, 'it is a style of a language still in formation' (*OPP*, 58). The 1923 essay '*Ulysses*, Order, and Myth' may ostensibly be about James Joyce's use of Homeric myth to structure the chaos of modern life, but it is also a personal intervention in literary politics: 'I think that Mr Aldington and I are more or less agreed as to what we want in principle, and agreed to call it classicism' (*SP*, 176). Eliot admits in this essay that the question of how to achieve or even define classicism is more complex. By 1928, however, he was using his own term as part of a much broader statement of faith and belief, as if its meaning were transparent and historically stable. He declared in the preface to *For Lancelot Andrewes* that he was 'classicist in literature, royalist in politics, and anglo-catholic in religion' (*FLA*, ix). But not everyone was convinced that Eliot had a right to appropriate the term.

In 1926, John Middleton Murry reviewed Eliot alongside Virginia Woolf and decided that they were not really classicists: 'the classicism, if classicism there is, is of some novel and esoteric kind, and a classicism which is at once novel and esoteric would be a very queer classicism indeed'.[1]

Two honorary public lectures delivered during the 1940s gave Eliot the opportunity to reflect upon the gap between his own 'classicism' and the more conventional meanings of the word. What did his brand of classicism have to do with the Classics? He raised the question himself in the title of his 1944 presidential address to the Virgil Society, 'What is a Classic?' Speaking in front of an audience of Classical scholars, Eliot deftly promised to ignore the vexed 'literary politics' of the 'classic–romantic controversy' in order to focus on the literature of antiquity. He even picked out a Classical metaphor, asking Aeolus to keep the stormy winds of controversy 'in the bag' (OPP, 53–4). Two years earlier, Eliot had served as president of the Classical Association. In his less well-known address to that society, 'The Classics and the Man of Letters', he reflected more straightforwardly upon the relationship between classical studies and the contemporary 'man of letters'. But was Eliot a 'Classicist' in the conventional sense of the term, and if so, what kind of Classicist was he? His poetry and drama make extensive use of Latin and Greek texts, yet they rarely engage with the most canonical of ancient authors. Petronius, Seneca, the Palatine Anthology and the anonymous late Latin poem *The Vigil of Venus* figure as prominently in his early writings as Virgil or Homer.[2]

One might say that Eliot was an unclassical Classicist. He was certainly quick, in front of an audience of professional scholars, to confess that he was not a particularly good one: 'In my earlier years I obtained, partly by subtlety, partly by effrontery, and partly by accident, a reputation amongst the credulous for learning and scholarship, of which (having no further use for it) I have since tried to disembarrass myself' (TCC, 145). Eliot's awkwardness about parading 'learning and scholarship' in front of a gathering of academic Classicists is understandable, but this self-critique is also unduly harsh. Compared to many British men of his age and social class, his education in Latin and Greek had been relatively limited: he was not, like Leonard Woolf, a 'really first-class classical scholar'[3] when he left Milton Academy for Harvard at the age of 18. But that is only to say that Latin and Greek had never formed the main current of his extensive school and university education. His instruction had been more wide-ranging, and perhaps more pleasurable. He recalled: 'At school, I enjoyed very much reciting Homer or Virgil – in my own fashion. Perhaps I had some instinctive suspicion that nobody really knew how Greek ought to be pronounced, or what interweaving of Greek and native rhythms the Roman ear might appreciate in Virgil' (*OPP*, 27). As an undergraduate at Harvard, Eliot chose to take a wide range of courses in Latin and Greek, beginning with Greek prose composition and the 'Classics of Greek Literature' (including Aristophanes, Thucydides, Aeschylus and Sophocles) and finishing with more advanced courses on Latin poetry and 'The Roman Novel: Petronius and Apuleius'.

Eliot's graduate work in philosophy opened up a second, perhaps deeper engagement with Greek language and literature. In 1911 he took a course on Plato and other Greek philosophers at Harvard. He impressed Bertrand Russell in a course on symbolic logic by casually making a connection between the pre-Socratic philosopher Heraclitus and the medieval French poet François Villon. When he arrived at Oxford in 1914, he attended lectures on Aristotle's *De Anima* and *Ethics*, and studied the *Posterior Analytics* with Harold Joachim. His letters from the period give a sense of the intensity of this encounter; in fact, it was through his studies with Joachim that Eliot claimed that he learned to write clear English prose.

This study of ancient philosophy emerges in unexpected places in both Eliot's prose and poetry. In the 1920 essay 'The Perfect Critic', he begins by summoning the spirit of the two great poet-critics of the nineteenth century, Coleridge and Arnold, before proceeding to identify two flaws in contemporary criticism: it tends either to the *faux* scientific (Eliot cites Sir Edmund Gosse's observation that poetry 'is the most highly organized form of intellectual activity' [*SW*, 1]) or to a lax impressionism. It is the second part of the essay that makes an unexpected turn. Eliot invites us to compare the imprecision of contemporary writing with 'the opening phrases of the *Posterior Analytics*', holding up Aristotle's pure, disinterested intelligence as 'an eternal example – not of laws, or even of method, for there is no method except to be very intelligent, but of intelligence itself swiftly operating the analysis of sensation to the point of principle and definition' (*SW*, 10–11). Six years later, he was to compare reading Lancelot Andrewes's precise, elucidating sermons to 'listening to a great Hellenist expounding a text of the *Posterior Analytics*: altering the punctuation, inserting or removing a comma or a semi-colon to make an obscure passage suddenly luminous' (*SE*, 347).

As a prose writer, Eliot took Aristotle as an example, but his poetry is more deeply engaged with earlier Greek thinkers. Platonic Idealism and the long philosophical tradition it spawned can be heard in the disappointed repetitions of the word 'absolute' in Eliot's earliest poetry. The undated poem 'Afternoon', for example, shows us a group of modern women, preciously 'interested in Assyrian art', gathering in the hall of the British Museum and ends as they fade away beyond the Roman statuary 'Towards the unconscious, the ineffable, the absolute' (*IMH*, 53). The original draft of *The Waste Land* thickened the resonances of the 'Unreal City' with a reference to Plato's *Republic*. The line 'Not here, O Glaucon, but in another world' (*WLF*, 30–1), which Pound scored out, points to the disjunction between a swarming, breeding, temporal city and an ideal timeless city. Eliot returns in *Four Quartets* to the philosophically puzzling relationship between different temporal moments, citing Heraclitus' Greek in the epigraph to 'Burnt Norton'. The form of this epigraph acknowledges the fractured and piecemeal state of Heraclitus' text, referring us to Hermann Diels's *Die Fragmente der Vorsokratiker* [*Fragments of the Pre-Socratics*], first published in 1903. This epigraph might be read as an instance of the mock-scholarly 'subtlety or effrontery' that Eliot later confessed to in his lecture 'The Classics and the Man of Letters', but it is also an effective enactment of several key themes in the *Quartets*. In the first of the two fragments, Heraclitus complains: 'Although the word [*logos*] is common to all, most people live as if each of them had a private understanding of his own'. The second fragment is the gnomic statement: 'The way up and the way down are one and the same'.[4] In a poem centrally concerned with the shape of historical process – 'Neither movement from nor towards, / Neither ascent nor decline' (*CPP*, 173) – and with the failure of language adequately to represent that process – 'Words strain, / Crack and sometimes break, under the burden' (*CPP*, 175) – Heraclitus' words, broken into fragments, filtered through a German edition and yet still insisting on the unity underlying apparent opposites, serve as a dubious exemplum.

By the appearance of 'Burnt Norton' in 1936, Eliot's Greek epigraphs had become something of a poetic trademark. The sophistication of their use as a framing device had also increased over time. In 'Sweeney Among the Nightingales' (1919), the epigraph from Aeschylus' *Agamemnon* – translated literally as 'Alas, I am struck deep with a mortal blow' (Southam, 75) – functions primarily as a contrastive device and, as Vincent Sherry notes, 'the feeling of decline in the descent from the classical to the modern event is usual and conventional'.[5] In Aeschylus' play, Agamemnon returns victorious from the Trojan War to be murdered by his adulterous wife, Clytemnestra. Eliot's Sweeney, who appears not to have fought in the First World War, lounges like an ape in an urban dive. Only the nightingales, whose 'liquid siftings' (*CPP*, 57) break upon the night air at the end of the poem, provide a tenuous connection between the classical past and the sordid present. Other epigraphs in Eliot's *Poems* (1920) are drawn from equally remote sources. 'Burbank with a Baedeker: Bleistein with a Cigar' introduces an archaeological tour of Venice with an epigraph of astonishing density: quotations from Shakespeare, Théophile Gautier, Henry James, Robert Browning and John Marston are spliced together with an obscure Latin tag – '*nil nisi divinum stabile est; caetera fumus*' ['only the divine endures, the rest is smoke'] (*CPP*, 40) – discovered by Eliot in Venice on a painting of the martyrdom of St Sebastian by the fifteenth-century Italian master Andrea Mantegna.

For *The Waste Land*, Eliot originally chose the famous passage from Conrad's novel *Heart of Darkness* ending 'The horror! the horror!' and he relinquished it only reluctantly, at Pound's suggestion, before turning instead to a passage from the *Satyricon* by Petronius, a satire by a Roman writer from the first century AD.[6] In the epigraph from the *Satyricon*, the character Trimalchio reports in Greek the words spoken to the Sibyl hanging in a cage at Cumae – 'Sibyl, what do you want?' – and her reply – 'I want to die' (Southam, 84). The epigraph to 'Marina' (1930) juxtaposes a relatively familiar Shakespearean context with a perversely unfamiliar Classical reference. William Empson asked the poet Ronald Bottrall to identify the Latin epigraph: '*Quis hic locus, quae / regio, quae mundi plaga?*' ['What is this place, what country, what region of the world?'] (*CPP*, 109). He realised at once that 'if it's poetry it's very unclassical poetry' and was then able to suggest the source as Seneca's play *Hercules Furens*. The title of the poem and its last line, 'My daughter' (*CPP*, 110), allude to the joyful reuniting of father and lost daughter at the end of *Pericles*, but the Senecan allusion furnishes a hideous parallel: Hercules stumbles disorientated out of madness to discover that he has killed his wife and children. Eliot himself described the aesthetic pattern as 'a criss-cross between Pericles finding alive and Hercules finding dead – the two extremes of the recognition scene'.[7] Empson praised the balancing of comedy and tragedy, and commented: 'One could not grumble at the technique after seeing it achieve a success, though I think a modern edition should print *Hercules Furens* at the end of the Latin'.

The story of Hercules' madness was told and retold in antiquity, and Seneca's play is not the most obvious source. According to Empson, Eliot took some pleasure in the wilful obscurity of the quotation, informing him that 'Seneca isn't in the school syllabus, so all the classical men were caught out'.[8] Later, Eliot recalled that it was 'only an accident that I know Seneca better than I know Euripides',[9] implying, as he did in his 1942 presidential address to the Classical Association, that his own education in the Classics had been deficient. At the same time, Eliot's preference for Seneca over Euripides, or Ovidian over Homeric versions of myth in *The Waste Land*, might be understood as a consequence of his broader beliefs about literary tradition and inheritance. Seneca blends more delicately with the Shakespearean recognition scene because Shakespeare read Latin rather than Greek;[10] Hesiod told the story of Tiresias' sex change before Ovid, but Ovid was a far more important source for Medieval and Renaissance English writing.

In the first half of his career, Eliot's use of Latin and Greek texts in his own poetry can be viewed as consciously oppositional to nineteenth-century pieties about 'The Classics' as a repository of supreme value. Victorian and Edwardian scholars – even those, like A. E. Housman, who were fine poets themselves – saw a sharp disjunction between the literature of the past and present: a Classical education centred around a small number of texts of eternal value; modern literature was various, expanding, and ultimately ephemeral. In his early essays, Eliot argued for a more flexible, dialectic model of the relationship between 'tradition' and the 'individual talent'. He explained that a new work of art alters 'the *whole* existing order' and that a writer equipped with an 'historical sense' should be alert to the 'simultaneous existence' of 'the whole of the literature of Europe from Homer' (*SE*, 14) to the present day. He was not interested in Classical literature as unchangeable museum pieces, but as something that needed to be reinterpreted, retranslated and reordered by every subsequent generation. At the same time, he was aware that this argument depended for rhetorical effect on his own command of traditional linguistic skills. By making frequent, curt and even offhand reference to a wide range of Classical sources, Eliot's early poetry and prose suggest wide and deep reading, and casual facility with difficult linguistic material.

This synchronic historical sense animates Eliot's interest in translation, both as a past practice and as a contemporary one. In 'Euripides and Professor Murray' (1920), Eliot faulted Gilbert Murray's translations from the Greek, not for their inaccuracy but for their lazy archaism. The 'fluid haze' of nineteenth-century aestheticism in which Eliot felt Murray clothed his verse translations 'has simply interposed between Euripides and ourselves a barrier more impenetrable than the Greek language' (*SW*, 74–5). Echoing his reflections in 'Tradition and the Individual Talent'

(1919), Eliot warns that 'few persons realize that the Greek language and the Latin language, and, *therefore*, we say, the English language are within our lifetime passing through a critical period' (*SW*, 73). This was an opinion shared by other modernist writers, most notably Pound. His peculiar sequence 'Homage to Sextus Propertius' (1919) is a free adaptation, in a medley of styles, of selected passages from the Roman elegiac poet Sextus Propertius. The Chicago professor William Hale, who identified 'three-score errors', thought Pound 'incredibly ignorant of Latin' and begged him to 'lay aside the mask of erudition'.[11] In response, Pound accused Hale of being a 'perfect example of the spirit which keeps the classics "uninteresting"', adding that the mask of erudition 'is precisely what I have thrown on the dust heap'.[12]

By focusing on processes of translation, mediation and reception, Eliot and Pound simultaneously highlighted the gulf between antiquity and modernity, as well as some surprisingly immediate similarities. Their interest in the byways of classical literature – Propertius, Seneca, Petronius – served as a subtle corrective to the idealising Classicism of the nineteenth century. 'The Greek is no longer the awe-inspiring Belvedere of Winckelmann, Goethe, and Schopenhauer', wrote Eliot in his essay on Murray's translation of Euripides, 'and we realize better how different – not how much more Olympian – were the conditions of the Greek civilization from ours' (*SW*, 76). He was critical of contemporary writers who relied too unthinkingly on any one portion of the past, and, although he preferred H.D.'s translations of Euripides to Murray's, Eliot felt in her own poetry the Hellenism became monotonous and 'lacks vitality' (*L1*, 606). Changing political and social circumstances during and after the First World War helped to make these – initially aggressive and even eccentric arguments – canonical. The war itself had occasioned a flurry of poems written in a classically 'high' heroic vein, but the decidedly unheroic reality of trench warfare quickly exploded the language and sentiments of the classical past: Horace's martial tag 'Dulce et decorum est pro patria mori' ['It is sweet and honourable to die for your country'] was now, according to Wilfred Owen, 'The old Lie'.[13] After the war, education in Classics in schools and universities began the process of slow decline that has continued until the present day. In 1917, Cambridge University established a course of study in English literature – one in which Eliot's work was quickly to assume a central position – as an alternative to the study of literature in Greek and Latin. Sir Arthur Quiller-Couch, Professor of English at Cambridge, claimed the study of English literature would provide soldiers returning from the war with a 'language ready for the land they shall recreate and re-people'.[14]

To the extent that Eliot's early classicism was a strategic position, it was also a dispensable one. By the 1930s he was ready to discharge the term 'classicism' as the prime criterion of literary value and to engage more simply with Classical literature, particularly Greek drama. In the early 1920s he had praised the 'vital', popular, and collaborative music hall acts of Marie Lloyd, but found the audience for Murray's *Medea* 'serious and respectful and perhaps inclined to self-approval at having attended the performance of a Greek play' (*SE*, 59). As he began to compose his own poetic plays, Eliot wondered if Greek drama might provide a point of departure for a work that could function on two levels, appealing to 'members of the audience who "like poetry"', as well as to 'those who go for the play alone'. The unfinished and experimental drama *Sweeney Agonistes*, subtitled 'Fragments of an Aristophanic Melodrama' (*CPP*, 115) and prefaced with an epigraph from Aeschylus, develops the 'high'–'low' oscillation of the earlier poem 'Sweeney Among the Nightingales'. The framing of the play and its division into 'Fragment of a Prologue' and 'Fragment of an Agon' suggest a formal or structural link to Greek comedy, but the two parts might just as well have been titled 'I' and 'II'. In fact, an early draft of part I had an up-to-date American title 'Wanna Go Home Baby?'. The more important connection is to be found in Eliot's use of metre to suggest a ritual mythology. Intensive repetition and irregular stresses on simple words – 'Oh I *think* it's only a chill' (*CPP*, 116) – combined with abrupt stichomythia (dialogue in alternating lines of verse) and a quick background drumbeat, imply an archetypal pattern behind Sweeney's brutal story.

From the 1930s onwards, Eliot was fascinated by the possibility of a poetic drama that would be both serious and popular, and he experimented with various conventions and techniques drawn from Greek, Elizabethan and Jacobean theatre to achieve this aim (see Chapter 13 above). *Murder in the Cathedral*, performed at the Canterbury Festival in 1935, borrows from the ritual aspects of Athenian drama. The story of Thomas Becket's murder was so familiar to his audience that Eliot's presentation required little narrative explanation or creation of suspense; instead a chorus and groups of impersonal figures (the four tempters, the four knights) reflect on the great themes of Greek tragedy – the conflict between state and individual, civilisation and nature. *The Family Reunion* (1939) and *The Cocktail Party* (1949) take complete plot motifs as well as a structural and a ritual method from Greek drama. In 'Poetry and Drama'

(1951), Eliot explained the source of these borrowings and also reflected rather negatively on their dramatic potential. Indicative of a broader failure 'to adjust the ancient with the modern', the appearance of Aeschylus' Furies in *The Family Reunion* looked like 'a still out of a Walt Disney film' (*OPP*, 84). In *The Cocktail Party*, Eliot was 'still inclined to go to a Greek dramatist for my theme' (*OPP*, 85), but he hid the source from the *Alcestis* of Euripides so thoroughly that it went unrecognised.

Eliot had begun by pressing the Classics into the service of willed obscurity and difficulty – visible in his offhand references, curt footnotes, unexplained Greek epigraphs, and neologisms. In the second half of his career, after his reception into the Anglican Church, he became more interested in a direct line of descent between past and present; his focus was no longer on history's 'cunning passages' (*CPP*, 38) and on lines of broken and indirect mediation, but on the importance of preserving some central texts from a shared cultural past. In 'What is a Classic?' he modified the dialectical argument of 'Tradition and the Individual Talent' by placing Virgil – not those 'ruffians' Catullus and Propertius (*OPP*, 62) – 'at the centre of European civilization, in a position which no other poet can share or usurp' (*OPP*, 68). Following the argument of Theodor Haecker's *Virgil, Father of the West*, Eliot viewed Virgil, author of the messianic fourth *Eclogue* (taken by medieval commentators as a prophecy of the birth of Christ), as an *anima naturaliter Christiana* [naturally Christian soul] who smoothed the passage between the Roman Empire and the Holy Roman Empire.[15] In a 1951 BBC broadcast Eliot remarked of Virgil that, 'he makes a liaison between the old world and the new' (*OPP*, 123). Indeed, in *Four Quartets* he alluded more substantially to the *Aeneid* – passed through Dante and Tennyson – than he had in his earlier poetry. The haunting brevity of Eliot's description of Phlebas the Phoenician, 'a fortnight dead' (*CPP*, 71), in *The Waste Land* is indebted to the elliptical epigrams on dead sailors in the Palatine Anthology: death by water is something inexplicable and random. By contrast, his description in 'The Dry Salvages' of the 'ragged rock in the restless waters' (*CPP*, 187) is Virgilian in its calm acceptance of migration and dangerous voyages as historical necessities.

As the cultural prestige of what Eliot called 'our classical heritage' (*TCC*, 161) seemed on the wane, so he publicly championed the 'dependence of English literature upon the Latin and Greek literatures' (*TCC*, 159). His focus was now on the mainstream of Latin and Greek literature rather than on its Alexandrian or post-classical byways; the Classics became a model for a healthy future public culture rather than an elitist prod at complacent readers. In his social criticism of the 1940s, Eliot employed the Greek term *metoikos* [resident alien] as a nom-de-plume in response to a writer appearing under the Latin word *civis* [citizen], gesturing towards a small homogeneous society as a cultural ideal. The two public addresses he delivered during the Second World War – 'The Classics and the Man of Letters' and 'What is a Classic?' – are especially mournful in tone, pessimistic about the survival of the Classical tradition outside a small group of expert scholars. Without suggesting a purely reactionary return to the educational system of a previous generation, Eliot questions whether future readers, divorced from the literature of the Classical past, will have any 'common body of literary and historical knowledge' (*TCC*, 151). The very future of literature is at stake, for the old is necessary for clear-eyed discernment of the new, and experimental writing can quickly become 'eccentricity and even charlatanism' (*TCC*, 152) without a mooring in the classical. The dialectical argument of this essay is in some ways reminiscent of 'Tradition and the Individual Talent', but it lacks the earlier essay's confidence. By 1942 he had started to wonder how long it would be before 'the connection between the classics and our own literature is completely broken' (*TCC*, 150–1) and what new literary era might then dawn. By a temporal quirk that he might have appreciated, Eliot the revolutionary modernist was now crying 'après moi, le déluge'.

NOTES

1. See John Middleton Murry, 'The "Classical" Revival', *Adelphi* (February 1926), 585–95.
2. Eliot recalled as an obstacle to his schoolboy enjoyment of the *Iliad* the 'irresponsible' behaviour of the gods, who were as 'devoid of public spirit' as the heroes, above all, the 'ruffian' Achilles (*OPP*, 124).
3. Victoria Glendinning, *Leonard Woolf* (London: Simon & Schuster, 2006), p. 45.
4. *Heraclitus*, trans. Philip Wheelwright (Princeton University Press, 1959), pp. 19, 90.
5. Vincent Sherry, *The Great War and the Language of Modernism* (Oxford University Press, 2004), p. 194.
6. Cf. Eliot: 'we think more highly of Petronius than our grandfathers did' (*SW*, 77).
7. Quoted in Richard Abel, 'The Influence of St Jean Perse on T. S. Eliot', *Contemporary Literature* (spring 1973), 235.
8. See William Empson, 'Eliot and Politics', *T. S. Eliot Review* (fall 1975), 3–4.
9. Quoted in Abel, 'Influence of St Jean Perse', 235.

10. Eliot discusses Seneca's influence on Elizabethan tragedy in his introduction to *Seneca: His Tenne Tragedies*, ed. Thomas Newton (London: Constable, 1927), pp. v–liv.
11. William Gardner Hale, 'Correspondence', *Poetry* (April 1919), 52.
12. *Selected Letters of Ezra Pound, 1907–1941*, ed. D. D. Paige (London: Faber & Faber, 1950), p. 149.
13. Wilfred Owen, *Collected Poems*, ed. C. Day Lewis (London: Chatto, 1963), p. 55.
14. See Arthur Quiller-Couch, *On the Art of Reading* (Cambridge University Press, 1928).
15. Eliot praised Haecker's *Virgil, Father of the West* as 'an example of literary criticism given greater significance by theological interests' (*SE*, 388).

CHAPTER 18

Dante

Massimo Bacigalupo

Speaking of Dante in 1950 to the Italian Institute in London, T. S. Eliot said: 'I still, after forty years, regard his poetry as the most persistent and deepest influence upon my own verse' (*TCC*, 125). Poets' statements about their own work are not always to be trusted, but it is true that Eliot found in Dante a continuous source of inspiration, as probably only a non-Italian poet could. Inevitably, his reading developed over the decades, with his style and outlook, and within the context of contemporary culture and society. But certain passages remained 'touchstones' (as Matthew Arnold called them), to which he returned again and again.

The poet Arnaut Daniel, caught in the purgatorial fire and speaking in his arcane and melodious tongue, remained an Eliot persona, perhaps *the* Eliot persona. In *Purgatorio* XXVI another poet, Guido Guinizelli, tells Dante that 'questi ch'io ti cerno col dito ... fu miglior fabbro del parlar materno' ['he whom I point out ... was a better craftsman of the mother tongue'] and Eliot appropriated the sobriquet '*miglior fabbro*' in the generous dedication of *The Waste Land* to Ezra Pound. He used the final line of this canto, narrated by Dante, 'then he hid in the fire that refines them', among the fragments 'shored' at the end of his masterpiece, in the original Italian. But he had already borrowed from Arnaut's Provençal speech the title of his second poetry collection, *Ara Vos Prec* (1920), and was to return to it in the original section titles and the line '*sovegna vos*' ['remember'] of *Ash-Wednesday* (1930). The 'refining fire' was to appear again in *Four Quartets* (1943).

Arnaut describes himself in 'superb verses' (*SE*, 256) as 'Ieu sui Arnaut, que plor e vau cantan; / consiros vei la passada folor, / e vei jausen lo jorn, qu'esper, denan'. Eliot renders this as 'I am Arnold, who weeps and goes singing. I see in thought all the past folly. And I see with joy the day for which I hope, before me' (*SE*, 256). The image of the suffering poet who weeps and sings would be recognised by Eliot as a portrait of his own ordeals. The fact that Arnaut was punished among the lustful also played a role, since Eliot's sexuality was more than usually conflicted. The attention devoted by Eliot in his 1929 pamphlet on Dante to *La Vita Nuova*, the allegorised account of young Dante's meeting with and love for Beatrice, shows how interested he was in the varieties (adolescent and mature) of love and in the relation between private experience and literary form.

Eliot insisted that 'genuine poetry can communicate before it is understood' (*SE*, 238). He approached Dante 'with a prose translation beside the text' (*TCC*, 125) in the small Temple Classics volumes (translated 1909–10), which have ample commentary and marginal captions but no general critical introduction. They present the three canticles – *Inferno*, *Purgatorio* and *Paradiso* – unadorned, and were often reprinted. Eliot explained in 1950 that 'forty years ago', that is when he was a student at Harvard, 'I began to puzzle out the *Divine Comedy* in this way'. He would parse a favourite passage with the help of the Temple crib, then memorise it and repeat it 'lying in bed or on a railway journey' (*TCC*, 125). Thus he acquired some knowledge of Italian, a reading rather than a speaking knowledge, though paradoxically it was the sound of Dante's words that kept echoing in his mind.

Of the shock of recognition upon first encountering a fellow spirit like Laforgue or a master like Dante, Eliot wrote: 'There is a first, or an early moment which is unique, of shock and surprise, even of terror (*Ego dominus tuus*): a moment which can never be forgotten, but which is never repeated integrally' (*SE*, 250). The Latin quotation from *La Vita Nuova* is itself an example of the shock that Eliot is speaking of and of his use of a foreign language to suggest a revelation. This prose statement recalls the lines in *The Waste Land*, 'My friend, blood shaking my heart / The awful daring of a moment's surrender' (*CPP*, 74). Eliot's criticism is appealing because he brings his personal experience to bear, but always to illuminate what he generally believes to be the case. He shows more readiness to reveal his feelings than he is usually given credit for. An anthology of memorable aphorisms could easily be compiled from his remarkable prose output.

The first-hand encounter with Dante's text could not have occurred if Eliot had not been born into a book-loving family and into a late Victorian milieu where volumes such as the Temple Classics were available, sought after, studied and read for pleasure. F. O. Matthiessen pointed out that Eliot's Puritan background played a role in attracting him to Dante's stern moral vision and that at Harvard he found a flourishing school of Dante studies:

From Longfellow through Charles Eliot Norton, Santayana, and Charles Grandgent there was an unbroken line of Dante scholarship at Harvard. It may be that in the end Eliot gained a more challenging insight into the technical excellences of *The Divine Comedy* through conversations with Ezra Pound, but ... in the preface to his own introduction to Dante he lists as his principal aids all the names which I have just mentioned.[1]

George Santayana's *Three Philosophical Poets* (1910) was particularly important as an aid in Eliot's search for an explanation of the relation of poetry and philosophy, a question which recurs in all his essays on Dante. He agrees with Santayana that philosophy is central to the great poems of Lucretius and Dante, that it is integral to the poetry, or realised by the poetry, and that a clearly held philosophical vision enhances a poem. He is less sure whether the merits of a given philosophical system play a role in the valuation of poetry, but finally seems to decide that Dante's line 'E'n la sua voluntade è nostra pace' ['And in His will is our peace'] is more '*literally true*' than Shakespeare's line 'Ripeness is all' (*SE*, 270). Here, Eliot's growing conviction that man's lot was hopeless without an appeal to God played a central role. Instead, Shakespeare's line from *King Lear* suggests (and in a dramatic context) that the best one can do is to live fully and maturely (Eliot would have agreed with that, adding only that it is not *enough*).

Eliot took an active interest in Dante scholarship. Before composing his lectures and papers he read scholars such as Charles Grandgent and Mario Praz. He even deferred to Praz when deciding not to publish his 1926 Clark Lectures, some of whose generalisations Praz had questioned (see *VMP*, 19–21). But Eliot drew a distinction between criticism and scholarship. He made no pretence to the latter, asserting that his view of Dante was that of a poetic practitioner. However, he was formally educated in philosophy, and this gave his criticism a wider appeal, enabling it to approach general and personal questions that are of lasting interest. Add to this his brilliant, concise and powerful style and it will be seen why René Wellek called Eliot 'the most important critic of the twentieth century in the English-speaking world'.[2]

Although enamoured of the sounds of poetry and a master of rhyme, rhythm and language, Eliot is always concerned with the content of poetic statement. In the Clark Lectures it is easy for him to prove that the opening metaphors of John Donne's 'The Extasie' form 'one of the most hideous mixed figures of speech in the language' (*VMP*, 109), as against Dante's absolute appropriateness of image. On these occasions Eliot can sound pedantic, since you cannot really compare Dante's Gothic cathedral to Donne's baroque somersaults. This lack of historical perspective would have perplexed a scholar like Praz. But Eliot was searching for a true use of language beyond shifting movements and tastes. To him, poets are not like painters in a gallery, whom we can enjoy without enquiring if Giovanni Bellini is more or less true to life than Francis Bacon. They are to some extent moral guides (the Puritan tradition again), and we read them in our search for poetic knowledge and for a method that writers may still apply. When Eliot read James Joyce's *Ulysses* he found there 'a method which others must pursue' (*SP*, 177), and which he himself went on to pursue in *The Waste Land*, and more consistently but less successfully in his plays. When he read Laforgue and Dante ('*Ego Dominus Tuus*') he went on to write 'The Love Song of J. Alfred Prufrock', where the opening simile – the evening spread out 'Like a patient etherised upon a table' (*CPP*, 13) has a Dantesque immediacy, realism, clarity and unexpectedness. (In *Purgatorio* VI, Dante did compare, less fancifully, ailing Italy to a sick patient 'che non può trovar posa in su le piume, / ma con dar volta suo dolore scherma' ['who finds no rest on her bedding, / but by turning shields herself from pain'].)

To return to the moment of discovery. According to Mario Praz, Ezra Pound played an essential role in Eliot's approach to Dante: 'Arthur Symons revealed to him Laforgue; Ezra Pound, through his book on *The Spirit of Romance* (1910), and still more through his table-talk, made him aware of the greatness of Dante, gave him that shock of surprise that no recognised authority on the poet could have communicated'.[3] Praz proceeds to show how many of the points made by Eliot in his 1929 study *Dante* are anticipated by Pound's enthusiastic account of the poet in *The Spirit of Romance*. Speaking of Arnaut's lines, Praz notes with his usual gusto and acumen:

One may doubt whether, without the stimulus of the actual delivery of those lines on the part of such a gourmet of pure sounds as Pound, Eliot's imagination would ever have crystallized round them. For, I think, one may trace to Pound that aspect of Eliot which consists in investing a quotation in a foreign language with a significance infinitely more potent than its verbal import, a significance which in Eliot achieves an emblematic pregnancy.[4]

Never a great admirer of Pound (as the final qualification 'in Eliot' makes clear), Praz may be right in seeing Pound's fingerprints on such passages as the final shoring of fragments in *The Waste Land* and even in the more chastened use of foreign tags in *Four Quartets*. This may be an instance of Eliot's maxim: 'Immature poets imitate; mature poets steal' (*SE*, 206).

It may safely be concluded that Pound's passionate advocacy of Dante and his love for certain passages, such as the Glaucus simile in *Paradiso* XXXIII, confirmed Eliot's youthful admiration, though he carefully pointed out in one of his last lectures, 'To Criticize the Critic' (delivered in 1961), that Dante 'impressed me profoundly when I was twenty-two and with only a rudimentary acquaintance with his language', and added that 'Dante's astonishing economy and directness of language … provided for me a wholesome corrective to the extravagances of the Elizabethan, Jacobean and Caroline authors in whom I also delighted' (*TCC*, 23). Thus in 1910, when *The Spirit of Romance* was published in London, Eliot was reading Dante alongside the Elizabethans and the French Symbolists. These are the three areas of poetry to which he returned again and again, claiming that they amounted to three manifestations of 'metaphysical poetry'. Possibly the age of modernism constituted a fourth manifestation. Eliot moved from his personal taste for poets whom he found essential to his own development, to a generalisation that he presented as his version of literary history. Such was his persuasiveness and the acuteness of his taste, that this version gained ascendancy, so much so that these periods and writers are still more popular and widely studied than others. The opening essay in *The Sacred Wood* (1920), entitled 'The Perfect Critic', has an epigraph from Remy de Gourmont that suggests precisely and perhaps ironically Eliot's progress from the personal to the general: 'Eriger en lois ses impressions personnelles, c'est le grand effort d'un homme s'il est sincère' (*SW*, 1). The critic's personal impressions are to be transformed into objective laws. Though it should be added that Eliot was at pains to suggest that his critical statements should not be taken too literally or too seriously, being occasional, and in any case subordinate to his main artistic effort.

Eliot's poetry and prose are framed by Dante. His first collection *Prufrock and Other Observations* (1917) is dedicated to his late friend Jean Verdenal with an epigraph from *Purgatorio* about a love so strong as to overcome death, taking '*l'ombre come cosa salda*' ['shadows for solid things'] (*CPP*, 11). The closing line of *Four Quartets*, and of a lifetime's poetic effort, 'And the fire and the rose are one' (*CPP*, 198), evokes the White Rose which in *Paradiso* gathers as in an amphitheatre all the souls of the blessed, now at last united with Arnaut's penitential fire that Eliot never really escaped. Likewise, the title of Eliot's first collection of critical prose, *The Sacred Wood*, alludes to Dante's forests – *Inferno*'s dark wood and the divine forest at the end of the *Purgatorio*, described in cantos that Eliot loved and mined in *Ash-Wednesday*. His final prose volume, *To Criticize the Critic* (1965), includes 'What Dante Means to Me' as well as the statement (in the title essay) about his discovery of Dante at the age of 22. Within this comprehensive relation to Dante, which informs Eliot's oeuvre, it is possible to distinguish at least three phases, roughly corresponding to the three canticles of the *Divine Comedy*.

Eliot and Pound were unusual in emphasising the greatness of *Purgatorio* and *Paradiso*, with their more philosophical and less corporeal poetry, since for many lay readers Dante is primarily the author of *Inferno*. Both poets, however, had been brought up on the Romantics and the Victorians and had imbibed a Pre-Raphaelite vision of the Middle Ages as an unsullied time of great art, poetry and theology. Eliot reacted against Dante Gabriel Rossetti's *The Blessed Damozel* and even more strongly against the cheerfulness of Robert Browning, which he detested. 'We have', he said, presenting as usual his view as that of an informed majority, 'a prejudice against beatitude as material for poetry' (*SE*, 264). In his case, however, the attraction for suffering as a subject was connected with the main thrust of his personality and his art, which is the story of a quest starting with the abject and the sordid. The concluding essay of *The Sacred Wood*, 'Dante' (polemically titled 'Dante as a "Spiritual Leader"' when it first appeared in the *Athenaeum*), is already concerned with the vexed relation of poetry and philosophy, and stresses the necessity of Dante's theoretical 'scaffold', taking issue with Paul Valéry's dismissal of philosophical poetry. But the central point of this brilliant discursive essay is taken from a statement made in an imaginary dialogue by Walter Savage Landor: 'Dante is the great master of the disgusting'. 'That is true', Eliot says, though he adds: 'The contemplation of the horrid or sordid or disgusting, by an artist, is the necessary and negative impulse toward the pursuit of beauty. But not all succeed as did Dante in expressing the complete scale from negative to positive. The negative is the more importunate' (*SW*, 169). When writing this, Eliot was himself a 'great master of the disgusting', having just published *Poems* (1920), with its vignettes of Sweeney and company, and the dark musings of Gerontion. He was composing his Inferno, which begins with the observations of Prufrock and was to continue in the symphonic *The Waste Land*, a trip through a modern hell with a glimpse of Purgatory at the end ('*Poi s'ascose nel foco che gli affina*' [*CPP*, 75]). Eliot's hell is not, however, a place 'for the *other people*' (*ASG*, 43), as Eliot astutely remarked of Pound's Hell

Cantos, but populated by figures with whom he feels a bond. Between the silly blessed damozel and the vulgarian narrator of 'Portrait of a Lady', he would possibly prefer the latter. Degradation attracts the fastidious and puritanical Eliot like the haunted characters in Sherwood Anderson's *Winesburg, Ohio* (1919). Hence the puzzling (and rather Byronic) statement in his 1930 essay on Baudelaire (whom Eliot continually compares with Dante), that 'it is better, in a paradoxical way, to do evil than to do nothing: at least, we exist' (*SE*, 429).

It is possible to think of Eliot's early poetry as a journey through hell in which he meets ghosts who tell their sorry stories (Prufrock, Gerontion or the Hollow Men, who are incapable of good or evil). He describes the journey, landscape and its inhabitants. In the widely admired study *Dante* (1929), published in Faber's 'The Poets on the Poets' series, Eliot moved on, as a Christian convert, to a more Purgatorial phase.[5] The poetic version of this can be found in *Ash-Wednesday*, which is heavily indebted to the final cantos of *Purgatorio*, with their pageantry and the apparition of Matilda gathering flowers. Here, Eliot the convert invokes a Lady who partakes of aspects of both Beatrice and Mary. It is ironic that *Ash-Wednesday* was originally dedicated to Vivien Eliot, his first wife, who had little of Beatrice, which would lead a psychologist to question the motives behind Eliot's conversion. However, *Ash-Wednesday* is a moving religious poem in which Dante's example is again evident in the use of clear visual images and diction ('Lady, three white leopards sat under a juniper-tree . . .' [*CPP*, 91]).

The year 1929 was when the lackadaisical mood of the 1920s gave way to the Wall Street Crash and then the Great Depression. Artists and writers became politicised in the following decade, which would see first the Spanish Civil War and then the Second World War. Eliot, in turn, became more concerned with order and government, and his 1929 *Dante* should be read in the context of the general movement known as the Call to Order or *Rappel à l'ordre*.[6] *Dante* bore a telltale dedication to the reactionary political activist and thinker Charles Maurras of the Action Française, an anti-Dreyfusard disgraced in old age because of his support of Marshal Pétain's Vichy government. For an epigraph, Eliot quoted from Maurras's lengthy introduction to a French translation of the *Inferno*: 'La sensibilité, sauvée d'elle-même et conduite dans l'ordre, est devenue un principe de perfection' ['Sensibility, saved from itself and submitted to order, has become a principle of perfection'].[7] This indicated Eliot's desire for order or submission to a larger order (the Church) as a refuge from the errors of unguided sensibility. In 1920, Eliot had stressed that 'Dante's is the most comprehensive, and the most *ordered* presentation of emotions that has ever been made' (*SW*, 168). The dedication to Maurras is preceded by an Italian epigraph, the opening statement of *La Vita Nuova*: 'Early on in the book of my memory – almost before anything else can be read there – is a rubric which says: "The New Life begins"'. This anticipates the hopeful conclusion in *Dante*: 'There is almost a definite moment of acceptance at which the New Life begins' (*SE*, 277). Eliot believed he had found a new life of austerity and acceptance, thus actually reprising in another key his Arnaut persona. When Faber published a new edition of *Dante* in 1965, the dedication, epigraphs and the preface (containing Eliot's confession of a lack of scholarly credentials) were not reprinted, thus removing the essay from its topical context. This was only right, since Eliot had by now moved into his third, 'classic' phase.

Before turning to this I would draw attention to the discussion in *Dante* (1929) of allegory and vision, as conducive to clear visual images (the 'three leopards'). This material 'belongs to the world of what I call the *high dream*, and the modern world seems capable only of the *low dream*' (*SE*, 262). One of the plangent lines of *Ash-Wednesday* reads: 'Redeem the time, redeem the dream' (*CPP*, 95). While the denunciation of modernity, anticipated by Santayana and Grandgent, fits in with Maurras's reactionary creed, the '*high dream*' is a good definition of Eliot's attempt in *Ash-Wednesday*, though the unsympathetic might say that his use of striking images, tortuous wordplay (especially in part 5), Catholic pageantry, biblical snippets and Dantesque visions is a sublimation of the tradition of Rossetti and Edgar Allan Poe, from which he took such care to distance himself.

In the years leading up to the Second World War, Eliot pursued a less visionary poetry. The results were the prosaic and meditative *Four Quartets*. Here the diction is mostly straightforward and the music is a subtle series of phrases and themes recurring at intervals. As his later prose writings show, Eliot was seeking a classic voice. He wished to interpret European culture as Virgil and Dante had before him, especially in a period of crisis, without animosity, but with goodwill to all. In 'What Dante Means to Me' he placed himself among Dante's English followers and quoted from Shelley's 'The Triumph of Life', commenting: 'this is better than I could do' (*TCC*, 132). He was referring to his own rewriting of *Inferno* xv – Dante's meeting with Brunetto Latini – in 'Little Gidding', where patrolling the London streets during the Blitz, Eliot imagines an encounter with a 'familiar compound ghost' (*CPP*, 193), the ghost of several masters, but chiefly of W. B. Yeats, who had recently died. The episode is also meant to recall Hamlet's encounter with his father's spirit at Elsinore. A striking feature of this stately and quietly eloquent passage is that the conversation with the ghost (reverting to *the* typical Dantesque situation) wholly ignores the war. Instead, the ghost tells Eliot about the sorrows and regrets of old age. There is no hope 'unless restored by that refining fire' (*CPP*, 195). The poets take a very long view of human history and while London Bridge might be literally falling down (during the Blitz), consider (as did Dante and Brunetto Latini) 'come l'uom s'etterna' ['how man becomes eternal'].

It is instructive to compare this episode in 'Little Gidding' with two cantos Ezra Pound wrote in Italian at about the same time from the other side of the front. Here Pound imagines meeting the ghosts of Guido Cavalcanti, of his old ally and adversary F. T. Marinetti (recently dead like Yeats, but mentioned here by name), and of Ezzelino da Romano, a truculent figure straight out of Dante, just as Pound's language is a free imitation (in Italian) of Dante's *terza rima*. All the spirits encountered by Pound speak with passionate intensity of the current war and denounce 'Churchill's bankers', the Pope and other wrong-doers who have betrayed Mussolini's 'effort'.[8] If Pound used Dante to present to an imaginary Italian audience his partisan politics, and produced a wild old man's Yeatsian invective, Eliot erred, if anything, by not taking sides. This is not to question his wartime loyalty to England, only to point out his detachment from current events while describing the present-day tragedy. In this respect Pound was more Dantesque, for the *Divine Comedy* is full of political passion. Eliot shared the philosophy that he detected in the *Vita Nuova* – 'the Catholic philosophy of disillusion' (*SE*, 275). It is strange that he should characterise this as Catholic. However, Eliot's disillusion did not keep him from strenuously supporting, after the war, his vision of literature and society. Enough of the Puritan spirit remained in the self-declared Anglo-Catholic.

Eliot did not reach a Paradiso, though it would be tempting to say this about his last phase. There was perhaps a decrease of passion, unlike Dante, whose last cantos of the *Divine Comedy* are, as Eliot said, the most passionate. Instead, *Four Quartets* offer their solemn and slow ruminations, and a sequence of visions and similes that are nothing if not Dantesque: 'As, in a theatre, / The lights are extinguished, for the scene to be changed' (*CPP*, 180). They present the sober wisdom of age in a language that aspires to the universality of Dante's Italian. Only an American, like Henry James and himself, said Eliot, can become that admirable thing, a true European.[9] Eliot's last phase was a process of identifying and coalescing England and America in a larger European culture, which he hoped to transmit to us, his grateful readers.

NOTES

1. F. O. Matthiessen, *The Achievement of T. S. Eliot* (Oxford University Press, 1959), p. 10.
2. René Wellek, *A History of Modern Criticism, 1750–1950*, vol. v (New Haven, CT: Yale University Press, 1986), p. 176.
3. Mario Praz, 'T. S. Eliot and Dante' (1937), *The Flaming Heart* (New York: Doubleday, 1956), p. 349. Praz refers to a letter from Eliot as his authority for this statement.
4. Ibid., p. 350.
5. However, Samuel Beckett, another follower of Dante and tireless visitor of infernos, found Eliot's *Dante* (1929) to be 'insufferably condescending'. *The Letters of Samuel Beckett*, vol. 1 (Cambridge University Press, 2008), p. 531.
6. Eliot published an English translation of Jean Cocteau's *Le Rappel à l'ordre* in Faber's spring 1926 list as *A Call to Order*.
7. Quoted in James Torrens, 'Charles Maurras and Eliot's "New Life"', *PMLA* (March 1974), 315.
8. See Ezra Pound, *Cantos* (London: Faber & Faber, 1987), pp. 425–41.
9. See 'In Memory of Henry James', *Egoist* (January 1918), 1.

CHAPTER 19

Seventeenth-century literature

Jennifer Formichelli

William Empson, an independent mind if such a thing ever existed, did not begrudge Eliot an odd honour. 'I do not propose', he wrote in 1948,

> to try to judge or define the achievement of Eliot; indeed I feel, like most other verse writers of my generation, that I do not know for certain how much of my own mind he invented, let alone how much of it is a reaction against him or indeed a consequence of misreading him. He has a very penetrating influence, perhaps not unlike an east wind.[1]

Eliot himself was occasionally tossed by the wind of his own intellectual influence. In 1956 he acknowledged obliquely 'a few notorious phrases which have had a truly embarrassing success in the world' (*OPP*, 106) and in 1961 he disavowed with more aplomb his 'generalizations, and the phrases which have flourished, such as "dissociation of sensibility" and "objective correlative"':

> They have been accepted, they have been rejected, they may soon go out of fashion completely: but they have served their turn as stimuli to the critical thinking of others. And literary criticism, as I hinted at the beginning, is an instinctive activity of the civilized mind. But I prophesy that if my phrases are given consideration, a century hence, it will be only in their historical context, by scholars interested in the mind of my generation. (*TCC*, 19)

Of this mind, Eliot might fairly be said (though he did not claim) to have invented quite a bit, being not only the greatest poet but also the finest critic of his generation. Empson hits the mark here: Eliot's influence is very like an east wind; it tends to be especially germinating. It also comes from a distinctive direction. For much of Eliot's influence on his own generation is due to the influence of another generation upon him. A good part of Eliot's thought, and the better part of his thinking, in poetry and prose, is rooted in the age stretching from the late sixteenth to the late seventeenth centuries.

Eliot immersed himself in the writers of the seventeenth century, those authors of drama, poetry and prose about whom he wrote some of his finest essays: Christopher Marlowe (1564–93); Ben Jonson (1572–1637); Shakespeare (1564–1616); Thomas Middleton (1580–1627); Cyril Tourneur (?–1626); Philip Massinger (1583–1640); John Ford (1586–1639?); John Webster (1578?–1638?); John Donne (1572–1631); Andrew Marvell (1621–78); Abraham Cowley (1618–67); Richard Crashaw (1612–48); Lancelot Andrewes (1555–1626); Henry King (1592–1669) and John Bramhall (1594–1663).

Of this age Eliot was an expert, and his interest abiding. When John Middleton Murry proposed his name for the Clark Lectures at Trinity College, Cambridge, Eliot suggested the subject of the metaphysical poetry of the seventeenth century. In 1926, Eliot delivered eight lectures – one on the definition of metaphysical poetry, four on Donne, one each on Crashaw and Cowley, and a final lecture on the influence of metaphysical poetry on the nineteenth century – to a large and daunting audience, including Alfred North Whitehead, G. E. Moore, Sir James Frazer and A. E. Housman. (He delivered a condensed variation of these lectures at Johns Hopkins University in Maryland in 1933.) From their inception, Eliot had planned to turn the lectures into a book on 'The School of Donne', but having failed in 1926 to win a research fellowship at All Souls College, Oxford, and never finding sufficient time to revise the lectures, he finally declined – perhaps put off by the reservations of the scholar Mario Praz – to publish them.[2] Nevertheless, Eliot's desire to publish a book on Donne and the metaphysical poets persisted for the next thirty years, and he continued to find occasion to write and publish on the subject. In 1930, for instance, when asked to deliver a series of BBC radio talks (later printed in the *Listener*), Eliot again chose as his subject seventeenth-century poetry.

Stretching from roughly 1919 to 1934, Eliot's most intense period of engagement with the literature of the seventeenth century also marks a period of his life when his criticism and creation flourished. Besides a series of brilliant essays, radio talks and lectures, numerous poems – including 'Gerontion', *The Waste Land*, 'The Hollow Men', *Sweeney Agonistes*, 'Coriolan', the Ariel Poems and *Ash-Wednesday* – emerged out of the influence of seventeenth-century literature. Eliot was particularly attentive to the minor writers of this time, being ever cautious to distinguish between influence that 'can fecundate' and imitation, 'especially unconscious imitation', that 'can only sterilize' (*TCC*, 18). This caveat accounts, in part, for Eliot's relatively minimal critical attention to the largest figure of the period, Shakespeare. A great writer like Shakespeare was, he postulated, more likely to be a source of imitation than influence. From minor writers, however, who now and then scaled small walls of perfection or made little innovations, or who impressed their age without dominating it, something could be gained by a later and greater writer such as Eliot. It is a testament to Eliot's rare gifts of judgement, genius and humility that he knew just what to take and exactly how to use it. Hence it was his distinctive bent towards the lesser and sometimes even little-known poets of this age that stirred him most. In 1961, Eliot remarked of Shakespeare's contemporaries that 'it was from these minor dramatists that I, in my own poetic formation, had learned my lessons' (*TCC*, 18).

Eliot's praise of seventeenth-century literature had a particular value bestowed by the fact that he was himself a practitioner, not a critic only but a 'poet who had praised' (*TCC*, 22). His praise was therefore both critical and creative. The great poet-critic of his own time, Eliot observed of these two casts of his mind that they were coterminous neighbours. 'The best of my *literary* criticism', he observed,

consists of essays on poets and poetic dramatists who had influenced me. It is a by-product of my private poetry-workshop; or a prolongation of the thinking that went into the formation of my own verse. In retrospect, I see that I wrote best about poets whose work had influenced my own, and with whose poetry I had become thoroughly familiar, long before I desired to write about them, or had found the occasion to do so. (*OPP*, 106)

A debt is owed to the perspicuity of Bruce Richmond, editor of the *Times Literary Supplement* from 1902 to 1937, for offering Eliot such occasions to turn his appreciation to criticism. Richmond invited Eliot to lunch on 29 September 1919, at the suggestion of Richard Aldington, a fellow poet and a regular contributor to the *TLS* who admired Eliot's essays in the *Egoist* and the *Athenaeum* (see Chapter 10 above). After the meeting, Eliot was invited to contribute an occasional leading article. Writing to his mother to give her the news, Eliot remarked that Richmond's invitation was 'the highest honour possible in the critical world of literature' (*L1*, 404).

Richmond's first assignment for Eliot was a leading review of G. Gregory Smith's *Ben Jonson*. The article, entitled 'Ben Jonson', was published anonymously (the practice of the periodical at the time) on the front page of the *TLS* on 13 November 1919. It was combined with another piece on Jonson in *The Sacred Wood* (1920) and included with further alterations in *Selected Essays* (1932), where it remains one of Eliot's central statements on poetic drama, addressing the relations of criticism to creation and erudition in poetry.[3] Eliot begins the essay: 'The reputation of Jonson has been of the most deadly kind that can be compelled upon the memory of a great poet' (*SE*, 147). However, far from being stifled by the erudition attributed to him, Jonson 'behaved as the great creative mind that he was: he created his own world', a unique world that is not superficial but in which 'the superficies *is* the world' (*SE*, 156).

The *TLS* provided a rich soil, and this but the first flower. In a 1961 tribute to Richmond, Eliot remarked that 'nearly all of my essays on the drama of that period – perhaps all of my best ones – started as a suggestion by Richmond'. Eliot was grateful to Richmond for giving him occasions to extend the range of his knowledge of the literature of the late sixteenth and early seventeenth centuries. Though books in a particular field were initially allotted to a designated contributor in order that he might become an expert, Richmond would afterwards endeavour to expand a reviewer's breadth. Eliot recalled:

once a writer was established among his reviewers and leader-writers, Richmond was ready to let him make excursions outside of the original area. Thus, a chance remark in conversation revealed that I was an ardent admirer of Bishop Lancelot Andrewes, and I was at once commissioned to write the leader which appears among my collected essays.[4]

The 1926 essay on Andrewes – a seminal figure in the Anglican Church and a principal translator of the King James Bible – has an especial biographical interest, appearing shortly before Eliot's conversion to the Church of England in 1927. A year later, it opened the collection *For Lancelot Andrewes: Essays on Style and Order*. The essay also has an especial critical curiosity, containing quotations from Andrewes's 1622 Nativity Sermon, which Eliot had earlier borrowed from in 'Gerontion' (1920)[5] and from which he later 'lifted several lines' (*TCC*, 20) in 'Journey of the Magi' (1927), the first of his Ariel Poems.

This essay is evidence that Eliot's book reviewing – especially for the *TLS*, under the eagle eye of Richmond – contributed substantially to the development of his poetry as well as his criticism, sending him to peer into places he might not otherwise have looked. Between 1919 and 1934, Eliot contributed pieces to the *TLS* on early English satire, early English novels, John Lyly (1554–1606), Shakespeare and Montaigne, George Chapman (1559?–1634), Richard Edwards (1525–66), Robert Southwell (1561–95), Thomas Dekker (1572–1632), Richard Hooker (1554–1600) and Thomas Hobbes (1588–1679). Along with this extensive book reviewing, Eliot, whose attraction to Renaissance drama was already much in evidence in the epigraphs to his early poems – 'Portrait of a Lady' (taken from Marlowe's *The Jew of Malta*), 'Sweeney Erect' (taken from Beaumont and Fletcher's *The Maid's Tragedy*) and 'Gerontion' (taken from Shakespeare's *Measure for Measure*) – also reviewed a number of stage productions of Elizabethan and Jacobean dramas performed in London between 1919 and 1922. Moreover, though his admiration of modern actors was less than robust, he paid (despite scant personal funds) to support such performances. Most notably, he belonged to the Phoenix Society, a London subscription theatre group devoted to performing minor or rarely staged verse dramas. On behalf of the Phoenix Society, Eliot sent a stern letter to the *Athenaeum* in 1920 appealing for additional subscribers.[6]

Although this voluminous reviewing contributed significantly to Eliot's scholarship on the minor poetic dramatists and metaphysical poets of the seventeenth century, his acquaintance with the figure of Donne had occurred much earlier, during his first year as an undergraduate at Harvard. Eliot remembered that 'Professor Briggs used to read, with great persuasiveness and charm, verses of Donne to the Freshmen at Harvard'.[7] It is apt that Eliot's early impressions of Donne, whom he credited with enlarging 'the possibilities of lyric verse as no other English poet has done',[8] were auditory, since this long-standing affinity inclines to the sound of Donne's verse, especially what he called its 'conversational tone', which 'makes one feel that Donne is himself speaking to you personally and familiarly, although speaking great poetry'.[9] This speaking tone is audible in several of Donne's openings; for instance, in 'The Relique' (a poem Eliot quoted often):

> When my grave is broke up againe
>   Some second ghest to entertaine,
>   (For graves have learn'd that woman-head
>   To be to more then one a Bed)
>   And he that digs it, spies
> A bracelet of bright haire about the bone,
>   Will he not let'us alone,
> And thinke that there a loving couple lies . . .[10]

In 1917, Eliot remarked of these lines that 'the feeling and the material symbol preserve exactly their proper proportions'.[11] By 1926 he had had some change of mind. Though continuing to admire the 'famous line' – 'A bracelet of bright haire about the bone' – as an 'example of those things said by Donne which could not have been put equally well otherwise', Eliot went on to rebuke the poem:

> But the notion of the violation of the grave for 'entertaining' a 'second guest', and still more the analogy of the fickleness of graves with the fickleness of women, are of very doubtful value in this place. Still more, the reference to female wantonness, of doubtful taste in itself, is particularly out of place in a poem intended to celebrate an instance of reciprocal fidelity ... (*VMP*, 125)

Eliot gradually came to pepper his admiration for Donne with censure, his criticism becoming more severe as time went on. This slow semi-repudiation is already evident in the Clark Lectures, where Eliot dismantles Donne's poetry in his attempt to find out that hidden mystery, the source of sudden felicities that capture for a moment 'the pure instinctive clinging to any contact or memory of contact' (*VMP*, 126). Here one catches snatches of Eliot's verse commemoration of Donne, 'Who found no substitute for sense', in 'Whispers of Immortality':

> He knew the anguish of the marrow
> The ague of the skeleton;
> No contact possible to flesh
> Allayed the fever of the bone.   (*CPP*, 52)

This clutches at the ear with its faint rhymes that make for a clinging contact between the lines, a contact whose tenuous grip belies a separation of expert from experience, the loss of a sense that once brought flesh and bone immediately to mind. A fissure that began in the seventeenth century and expanded into the Romantic period of the nineteenth century, this disjunction finally broke into a 'sadness' which, Eliot feelingly observed in 1930, 'is due to the exploitation of the fact that no human relations are adequate to human desires, but also to the disbelief in any further object for human desires than that which, being human, fails to satisfy them' (*SE*, 428).

   The seventeenth century initiates this transition. Eliot sometimes finds in Donne a 'disappointed romanticism, the vexation of resignation at finding the world other than one wanted it to be' (*VMP*, 128). Hovering between the passionate and the reflective, Donne, Eliot asserted, is 'the great ruler of that borderland of fading and change' (*VMP*, 127). He was 'capable of experiencing and setting down many super-sensuous feelings, only these feelings are of a mind in chaos, not of a mind in order' (*VMP*, 133). Donne had sensual unity, but mental chaos; he could feel with his mind, but groped his way; he is 'imprisoned in the embrace of his own feelings', but first made it possible to think in lyric verse; his 'immediate experience passes into thought', but it is 'far from attaining *belief*' (*VMP*, 133). No matter how Eliot tries to pin him down, Donne is always wriggling away.

However strange, Donne was not unique in his capabilities. Eliot found him, rather, in good company. Reflecting on Herbert Grierson's 1921 anthology *Metaphysical Lyrics and Poems of the Seventeenth Century*, one of the most influential books he was ever assigned to review, Eliot was struck by a sixth sense that seemed to possess the mind of Donne's generation. This perception sparked his formulation of one of his most influential – though later disavowed – principles, the 'dissociation of sensibility'. Comparing Tennyson's 'The Two Voices' (1842) to a poem collected in Grierson's anthology, Lord Herbert of Cherbury's 'An Ode upon a Question moved, whether Love should continue for ever?' (1665), Eliot remarked:

> The difference is not a simple difference of degree between poets. It is something which had happened to the mind of England between the time of Donne or Lord Herbert of Cherbury and the time of Tennyson and Browning; it is the difference between the intellectual poet and the reflective poet. Tennyson and Browning are poets, and they think; but they do not feel their thought as immediately as the odour of a rose. A thought to Donne was an experience; it modified his sensibility. When a poet's mind is perfectly equipped for its work, it is constantly amalgamating disparate experience; the ordinary man's experience is chaotic, irregular, fragmentary. The latter falls in love, or reads Spinoza, and these two experiences have nothing to do with each other, or with the noise of the typewriter or the smell of cooking; in the mind of the poet these experiences are always forming new wholes.
>
> We may express the difference by the following theory: The poets of the seventeenth century, the successors of the dramatists of the sixteenth, possessed a mechanism of sensibility which could devour any kind of experience. (*SE*, 287)

The 'dissociation of sensibility', the occurrence of which Eliot locates in the mid seventeenth century, was, he claims, a schism aggravated by the achievements of two of the century's giants, John Milton and John Dryden, who 'performed certain poetic functions so magnificently well that the magnitude of the effect concealed the absence of others' (*SE*, 288). Beneath this superficial brilliance lay a substratum of decay. So, Eliot notes that 'while the language became more refined, the feeling became more crude' (*SE*, 288). The division Eliot describes is partly between ratiocination and reflection, between turning one's interests into poetry and meditating 'on them poetically' (*SE*, 288), as he accused both

Tennyson and Browning of doing. But it is also something else and other; it is the loss of a kind of sense he succeeds only in adumbrating, a sense whose presence is often felt in his poems, and even in the fumes of this formulation, where the intellect and the 'odour of a rose' mingle with the 'smell of cooking'. It is a faculty found in Donne at his best, an 'emotional power' that 'sees the thing as it is'.[12]

Likewise, Eliot's poems often operate on the tips of their senses, full (and sometimes consciously empty) of poignant smells and sounds and tastes, replete with physical and mental feelings. 'Gerontion', for instance, a poem infused with the seventeenth century, giveth sense even as it is taken away:

> I that was near your heart was removed therefrom
> To lose beauty in terror, terror in inquisition.
> I have lost my passion: why should I need to keep it
> Since what is kept must be adulterated?
> I have lost my sight, smell, hearing, taste and touch:
> How should I use them for your closer contact?   (*CPP*, 38)

The first line alludes to Middleton's play *The Changeling*, where the villainous heroine Beatrice evokes the 'common sewer' and reminds us that through our senses once came another and equally pungent kind of thing, the common sense. Transforming with this deft allusion Beatrice's confession of decrepitude into Gerontion's accusation of decay, Eliot reminds us that the 'isolation of thought as an object of sense could hardly have been possible before the seventeenth century' (*VMP*, 133).

Eliot's perceptive recreation in the twentieth century of tactile mental sensings is perhaps his most important contribution to modern poetic practice and criticism: a subtle evocation of that penetrating intelligence which 'is the discernment of exactly what, and how much, we feel in any given situation'.[13] Eliot sought to recover this sensibility from the dissociation that had destroyed it, first by dividing thought from feeling, and later through an exaltation of feeling that had its origins in Jean-Jacques Rousseau and spread widely throughout the eighteenth and nineteenth centuries. Eliot claimed that 'the two great currents of the nineteenth century – vague emotionality and apotheosis of science (realism) alike spring from Rousseau'.[14] Eschewing these currents of Romanticism, Eliot was led back to the seventeenth century in a search for feeling minds, those which cogitated and amalgamated rather than ruminated and divided. This was not because he had failed to find such minds among the nineteenth-century poets he grew up reading; but he found them less sensual and engrossing than the dazzling, devouring and absorbing mind of the seventeenth century. Eliot conceded that Tennyson 'had a brain (a large dull brain like a farmhouse clock) which saved him from triviality'.[15] And in a sporting jab, he praised Henry James for carefully fencing off his civilised mind from the herds of ideas which 'run wild and pasture on the emotions'. According to Eliot, 'James's critical genius comes out most tellingly in his mastery over, his baffling escape from, Ideas; a mastery and an escape which are perhaps the last test of a superior intelligence. He had a mind so fine that no idea could violate it.'[16] Tennyson was saved by a dull brain; James escaped by a fine mind. But neither quite possessed the quality of 'thinking with our feelings' with which Eliot credited the writers of the seventeenth century,[17] who could 'devour any kind of experience' with their 'wit', a quality that Eliot described in his 1921 essay on Andrew Marvell as 'a recognition, implicit in the expression of every experience, of other kinds of experience which are possible, which we find as clearly in the greatest as in poets like Marvell' (SE, 303). Eliot noted: 'The seventeenth century sometimes seems for more than a moment to gather up and to digest into its art all the experience of the human mind which (from the same point of view) the later centuries seem to have been partly engaged in repudiating' (SE, 293).

Eliot therefore sought to reclaim in his own age a modern association of sensibility, one which recognised that 'there are some pretty complicated feelings in life, which are worth a little pains to express'.[18] Such pains, as Eliot found in his study of seventeenth-century literature, were larger than little; they involved a great effort, in which the 'poet must become more and more comprehensive, more allusive, more indirect, in order to force, to dislocate if necessary, language into his meaning' (SE, 289). This vigorous allusiveness is an aspect of Eliot's genius evident everywhere and evident equally in his criticism and his poetry. No one excelled Eliot in his felicitous choice of quotations, a gift that shows his own considerable powers of mind devouring all kinds of experience, including the expression of others' experience: Eliot's whole work is an impressive meeting of minds across the ages. It is also, equally impressively, a meeting of minds of the ages. For, occasioned by a concentration on the writers of the seventeenth century, Eliot achieved a remarkable reciprocity across time. The thoughts, feelings, senses, sights, smells and sounds that he inbreathed from that age, especially from its minor writers, inspired his invention of his own. The result is a marvellous, and true, recovery.

NOTES

1. William Empson, 'The Style of the Master', *T. S. Eliot: A Symposium*, ed. Richard March and Tambimuttu (London: Editions Poetry London, 1948), p. 35.
2. Eliot admired Praz, who initially criticised Eliot's Clark Lectures but subsequently encouraged him to publish them. They were posthumously published as *The Varieties of Metaphysical Poetry*, ed. Ronald Schuchard (London: Faber & Faber, 1993).
3. On the revisions to 'Ben Jonson', see Christopher Ricks, *Decisions and Revisions in T. S. Eliot: The Panizzi Lectures 2002* (London: British Library and Faber & Faber, 2003), pp. 42–3.
4. 'Bruce Lyttelton Richmond', *Times Literary Supplement* (13 January 1961), 1. In the preface to the first edition of *Selected Essays*, Eliot thanked Richmond, 'without whose suggestions and encouragement the essays on Elizabethan dramatists would not have been written' (*SE*, 7).
5. 'Gerontion' also borrowed from Andrewes's 1618 Nativity Sermon (see Southam, 52–3).
6. See 'The Phoenix Society', *Athenaeum* (27 February 1920), 285.
7. 'Donne in our Time', *A Garland for John Donne*, ed. Theodore Spencer (Cambridge, MA: Harvard University Press, 1931), p. 1.
8. Ibid., p. 14.
9. 'Rhyme and Reason: The Poetry of John Donne', *Listener* (19 March 1930), 503.
10. 'The Relique', *Metaphysical Lyrics and Poems of the Seventeenth Century*, ed. Herbert Grierson (Oxford: Clarendon Press, 1921), p. 21.
11. 'Reflections on Contemporary Poetry [I]', *Egoist* (September 1917), 118.
12. Ibid.
13. 'Reflections on Contemporary Poetry [III]', *Egoist* (November 1917), 151.
14. From Eliot's notes for a lecture entitled 'What is Romanticism?' in his Oxford University extension lectures on modern French literature. Quoted in Ronald Schuchard, *Eliot's Dark Angel* (Oxford University Press, 1999), p. 27.
15. 'Verse Pleasant and Unpleasant', *Egoist* (March 1918), 43.
16. 'In Memory of Henry James', *Egoist* (January 1918), 2.
17. Ibid., 2.
18. 'The Post-Georgians', *Athenaeum* (11 April 1919), 171.

CHAPTER 20

Romantic and Victorian poetry

Michael O'Neill

In 'Baudelaire' (1930), Eliot describes the French poet as 'Inevitably the offspring of romanticism, and by his nature the first counter-romantic in poetry'. Half-intimating that Baudelaire's cultural predicament was one shared by himself, Eliot continues: 'It must not be forgotten that a poet in a romantic age cannot be a "classical" poet except in tendency' (*SE*, 424). Eliot may have sometimes sounded as though he regarded literary history from Dante onwards as a long fall into a sundering apart of thought and feeling. But it might be claimed that, in doing so, he reprises in his own terms a major motif from William Blake's Prophetic Books, a reprise that typifies the strange meetings of apparent extremes in Eliot. For Eliot, ostensibly in revolt against nineteenth-century poetry, especially the work of the major Romantics (which receives the lion's share of attention in this chapter), is recognisably its heir.

THE ROMANTICS

In June 1918, Eliot wrote to his mother that, for the sake of their health, he and his wife Vivien were staying in Marlow, 'a charming old little town, in the street where Shelley used to live' (*LI*, 266). Eliot's poetry constructs and deplores modernist waste lands, and fiddles a post-symbolist whisper music, but it dwells among metaphorical places 'where Shelley used to live'. And not just Shelley: roads leading into the Eliotic metropolis come from Blake, William Wordsworth, Samuel Taylor Coleridge, John Keats, Lord Byron and Thomas Lovell Beddoes. Nor is this simply a matter of stray phrases blowing in from the Romantic storm. The major British Romantics are powerfully significant presences in the poetry.

In 'William Blake' (1920), Eliot praises the great short poems as 'the poems of a man with a profound interest in human emotions, and a profound knowledge of them': praise that might be extended to the author of lines such as 'I was neither / Living nor dead' (*CPP*, 62) or

'Teach us to care and not to care' (*CPP*, 90). As those condensed formulations might indicate, as they juggle their way across a line ending or between cognate words, Eliot admires the fact that, in Blake's short poems, 'The emotions are presented in an extremely simplified, abstract form', one illustrative of 'the eternal struggle of art against education' (*SE*, 319). Blake's ability to break away from educated opinion strikes a chord with Eliot, whose own poetry can move between the allusively erudite and the quasi-primitive, between polite conversation about art and ragged claws. Thus, it is wrong to see Eliot as only patronisingly dismissive of Blake's 'philosophy' when he speaks of it as 'an ingenious piece of home-made furniture' (*SE*, 321). Rather, Blake compels his absorbed if dissenting response as an exemplar of ultra-Protestant, imaginative individuality.

Blake manifests himself in the poetry as a primary force. In 'Gerontion' (1920), the Romantic poet's best-known symbol inspires the narrator's half-awed, almost rueful, quickly ironised vision of a spiritual rejuven-ation: 'In the juvescence of the year / Came Christ the tiger'. Recalling Blake's 'Tyger, burning bright, / In the forests of the night',[1] Eliot's Christ is a dramatically enjambed power at once rebuking the modern world and corruptly tamed 'In depraved May', his divinity travestied in a parody of the Eucharist as he is 'eaten', 'divided' and 'drunk / Among whispers' (*CPP*, 37). But, to the degree that 'Gerontion' imagines a state, a 'new year', beyond fracturing and desiccation, it is Blake who is its sponsor: 'The tiger springs in the new year. Us he devours' (*CPP*, 38). Even 'devours', a retort to the earlier depraved eating, recalls the Blakean category of 'the Devouring', a term used in *The Marriage of Heaven and Hell* where it is set in a dialectical interplay with 'the Prolific'.[2] There is a side of Eliot drawn to Blake's fascination with contraries, to his diagnosis of spiritual sickness and his concern for spiritual recovery. When, in 'Burnt Norton', Eliot speaks of 'the torpid / Driven on the wind that sweeps the gloomy hills of London' (*CPP*, 174), the 'wind' may blow in from Dante's *Inferno*, but the 'gloomy hills of London' rise out of Blake's *Jerusalem*, a work which, in its determination to sustain a redeeming vision in a dark time, has real if surprising affinities with *Four Quartets* (1943). Eliot's moment of homage signals itself through a brief use of the long line typical of Blake's prophecies.

Wordsworth's importance for Eliot is manifest in 'Animula' (1929). In that poem, Eliot provides a complex, ambivalent rewriting of 'Ode: Intimations of Immortality', as 'the simple soul / Irresolute and selfish' (*CPP*, 107) replaces Wordsworth's pre-existent soul, which enters the world 'trailing clouds of glory',[3] only to learn of suffering, loss and thoughts that lie beyond tears. More generally, Eliot grew to see the connection between his attempt to modernise poetic diction and the Romantic poet's own endeavours in this direction, most famously theorised in the 1802 preface to *Lyrical Ballads*. In 'The Music of Poetry' (1942) Eliot writes: 'Every revolution in poetry is apt to be, and sometimes to announce itself to be a return to common speech. That is the revolution which Wordsworth announced in his prefaces, and he was right: but the same revolution had been carried out a century before ... and the same revolution was due again something over a century later' (*OPP*, 31). This is not an unqualified tribute, but it implies a sense of kinship, also suggested in his 1932 Norton Lecture, 'Wordsworth and Coleridge', where Eliot argues: 'Any radical change in poetic form is likely to be the symptom of some very much deeper change in society and in the individual' (*UPUC*, 75). The implications of this statement include Eliot's historicising awareness of the parallels and differences between Wordsworth's innovations and his and Pound's attempts to 'make it new'.

Again, Eliot's treatment of memory, which, mixed with desire, leads to the labyrinth of *The Waste Land*, has a Wordsworthian dimension. Haunting the Hyacinth Girl episode is the example of Wordsworth's use of freeze-frame effects, as when, at the close of 'The Two April Mornings', the Romantic poet writes:

> Matthew is in his grave, yet now
> Methinks I see him stand,
> As at that moment, with his bough
> Of wilding in his hand.[4]

'As at that moment'; poetry for Eliot, as for Wordsworth, is often a moment's monument (in Dante Gabriel Rossetti's phrase), capturing 'The awful daring of a moment's surrender' (*CPP*, 74) or 'the moment in the rose-garden' (*CPP*, 173), moments ablaze with meaning. The pathos of the lost, somehow abandoned girl in 'She dwelt among th'untrodden ways' who made such a 'difference to me'[5] attaches itself in Wordsworth to the figure of Lucy; a comparable figure, for all the veils of irony, reappears in Eliot, notably in 'La Figlia Che Piange'. Nor is Eliot's self-consciousness about emotion without precedent in Wordsworth, whose poems often brood on their meanings.

In *Four Quartets*, Eliot risks competing with Wordsworth as he offers equivalents to the Romantic poet's 'spots of time'. In 'The Prelude' (1805), the spots of time provide memory with a locatable spacialisation of fundamentally unlocatable feelings that require 'Colours and words that are unknown to man'.[6] Solving the problem of how to express the inexpressible, Wordsworth fuses tenacious evocativeness and recognition of mystery to recreate a sense of near numinous experience. Eliot, with more religious explicitness than Wordsworth, believes with the older poet that 'Only through time time is conquered' (*CPP*, 173). Eliot fashions a language closer to Symbolist suggestion than to Romantic evocation, but when, in 'Burnt Norton', 'The surface glittered out of heart of light, / And they were behind us, reflected in the pool' (*CPP*, 172), he takes his reader, by way of his verbs and the potent absences between them, close to the kinds of poetic events typified by times when, for instance, the young Wordsworth heard 'Low breathings coming after me' or 'saw / A naked Pool that lay beneath the hills', charged, for some not wholly explicable cause, with 'visionary dreariness'.[7]

If Eliot and Wordsworth meet as visionary poets, Coleridge impresses the younger poet as a critic, though Eliot is moved to dispute the distinction in *Biographia Literaria* between Fancy and Imagination to this degree: he cannot accept a theory of imagination that downgrades the importance of memory and revises Coleridge to say that 'if you are to distinguish between imagination and fancy in Coleridge's way you must define the difference between memory in imagination and memory in fancy' (*UPUC*, 79). The passage, with its reference to 'a small boy peering through sea-water in a rock-pool, and finding a sea-anemone for the first time' (*UPUC*, 78–9), clearly enters sacred territory for Eliot as a poet; and one senses that Coleridge has lured him into this territory, just as it is the 'sad ghost of Coleridge' who 'beckons' to Eliot 'from the shadows' at the close of his final Norton Lecture, warning the younger writer of the risks of 'theorising about poetry' (*UPUC*, 156).

Eliot found in Coleridge, then, a near double, and thought of his 'Dejection: An Ode' as containing in its sixth stanza 'one of the saddest of confessions that I have ever read' (*UPUC*, 68). Eliot marked the following lines in his copy of Coleridge's *Poetical Works*:

> For not to think of what I needs must feel,
>   But to be still and patient, all I can;
> And haply by abstruse research to steal
>   From my own nature all the natural man –[8]

Eliot seems circumspectly but intensely to identify with Coleridge when he writes that it was Coleridge's fate to have 'been visited by the Muse (I know of no poet to whom this hackneyed metaphor is better applicable) and thenceforth was a haunted man'. He glosses the last phrase thus, as though out of a deeply personal experience: 'for anyone who has ever been visited by the Muse is thenceforth haunted' (*UPUC*, 69). Eliot might have been thinking of passages in *The Waste Land* that read like hallucinatory gifts bequeathed by a tragic or intermittently ecstatic muse, such as the longing for water in 'What the Thunder said', which recalls the cursed predicament of the Ancient Mariner, or, suggestive of Xanadu in 'Kubla Khan', the 'Inexplicable splendour of Ionian white and gold' (*CPP*, 69) in 'The Fire Sermon'.

   Byron receives a scolding in Eliot's 1937 essay on him for his 'imperceptiveness . . . to the English word', shown in the way in which he writes 'a dead or dying language' (*OPP*, 201). Eliot seizes on vulnerable phrasing from the third canto of *Childe Harold's Pilgrimage*, quoting the lines 'And all went merry as a marriage bell' and 'On with the dance! let joy be unconfined' (*OPP*, 200). Disappointingly, he ignores the poem's heights and depths. But aspects of Eliot's response are original and positive; he is among the first to 'suggest considering Byron as a Scottish poet' in explaining his 'peculiar diabolism', which he argues is 'very different from anything that the Romantic Agony (as Mr Praz calls it) produced in Catholic countries' (*OPP*, 194). Eliot appears to have found a covert chime between Byron's ancestral Calvinism and his own Puritan ancestors. Moreover, he praises the Romantic poet's 'genius for digression', most in evidence in *Don Juan*, where, in Eliot's words, 'The continual banter and mockery, which his stanza and his Italian model serve to keep constantly in his mind, serve as an admirable antacid to the high-falutin which in the earlier romances tends to upset the reader's stomach' (*OPP*, 202). The Byronic 'antacid' is prominent in early Eliot. The second poem in his 'Suite Clownesque' engages in what might be called poker-faced tomfoolery (if the pun can be excused), as it speaks of being 'perplexed' and 'vexed':

>   In trying to construe this text:
>   'Where shall we go to next?'   (*IMH*, 34)

an echo, as Christopher Ricks remarks, of canto 9 of *Don Juan*:

>   Men should know why
>   They write, and for what end; but, note or text,
>   I never know the word which will come next.[9]

Wittily sliding forward with droll post-Byronic aplomb, via the risky chances and serendipities of rhyme (such as the boomingly ironic mismatch between 'go' and 'Michelangelo'), is one way of describing the formal and emotional procedures of *Prufrock and Other Observations* (1917).

Of the major Romantic poets, it is, arguably, with Shelley that Eliot has his most fraught and productive relationship. Eliot's poetry and prose are almost at schizoid loggerheads, the latter losing few opportunities to find fault (though there are notable exceptions), the former, from the poems in *Inventions of the March Hare*, through to *The Triumph of Life*-inspired encounter with the 'familiar compound ghost' (*CPP*, 193) in 'Little Gidding' (1942), showing a responsive engagement with Shelley. Ideological hostility is at the forefront of Eliot's critical reservations. In his 1933 Norton Lecture 'Shelley and Keats', he argues that 'the reason why I was intoxicated by Shelley's poetry at the age of fifteen, and now find it almost unreadable' was that at age 15 'the question of belief or disbelief did not arise' (*UPUC*, 96–7). Once such Edenic innocence vanished, Eliot was left to 'regret that Shelley did not live to put his poetic gifts, which were certainly of the first order, at the service of more tenable beliefs – which need not have been, for my purposes, beliefs more acceptable to me' (*UPUC*, 97). That final clause allows some breathing space, but Shelley is among the most significant writers to be caught up in Eliot's obsession with poetry and belief. His most trenchant criticism of Shelley's writing focuses on the fact that it contains 'good lines amongst bad', though Eliot's critical touch seems less than sure in singling out supposedly 'bad' lines from Shelley, which look, in the case of the passage from *Epipsychidion* beginning 'True love in this differs from gold and clay' (*UPUC*, 92), suspiciously like lines that provoke the moralist as much as the poet.

Eliot's poetry itself tells a different story. 'Oh little voices of the throats of men', among his major minor poems, explores 'dialectic ways' of thinking about a world of 'Appearances, appearances'. It executes sardonic variations on Shelley's own theme, itself not without irony, of what is, in Eliot's words, 'unreal, and yet true; / Untrue, yet real' (*IMH*, 75). The Romantic poet who sought to create 'Forms more real than living man' was also the poet for whom this world was a place 'Where nothing is, but all things seem'.[10] Eliot responds to passages in Shelley where spaces open up, even as links suggest themselves, between a world of seeming and some more vivid if elusive world of being. So, highly suggestive lines from the first act of *Prometheus Unbound* play a prominent role towards the close of *The Cocktail Party* (1949). There, Reilly, to shed light on his intuition of Celia's violent death, quotes from the passage in which Earth tells Prometheus that '*The magus Zoroaster . . . / Met his own image walking in the garden*' and that '*there are two worlds of life and death*' (*CPP*, 437; Eliot's italics).

The double haunts Shelley and Eliot as an image of incomplete selfhood and of connections with other destinies and possibilities, reappearing in the 'familiar compound ghost' passage from 'Little Gidding'. Although he vies in Eliot's conception with Yeats, Dante's Brunetto Latini (see Chapter 18 above), and others, Shelley's Jean-Jacques Rousseau is a central element in the 'compound' figure met 'In the uncertain hour before the morning'. Eliot's syntax, with its 'uncertain' movements towards resolution, enacts the sense of being 'At the recurrent end of the unending' (*CPP*, 193), as it reworks the line 'In their recurrence with recurrent changes' from the post-Shelleyan James Thomson's *The City of Dreadful Night*.[11] Such a state of recurrence is one in which Shelley's *The Triumph of Life* endlessly places its personae, especially Rousseau. Eliot quotes Rousseau's meeting with the poet in a 1950 talk entitled 'What Dante Means to Me' as a 'passage which made an indelible impression upon me over forty-five years ago' and as 'better than I could do' (*TCC*, 130, 132). Dante's influence on Shelley is the subject in this talk of a brief, subtle commentary; Eliot describes the wording of 'like ghosts from an enchanter fleeing'[12] in 'Ode to the West Wind' as 'impossible but for the Inferno', the canticle most concerned with 'the various manifest-ations of *wind*' (*TCC*, 130). In fact, Eliot misquotes Shelley's line, inserting 'stricken' before 'ghosts', a striking addition that rewrites Shelley so as to make the Romantic poet more preoccupied by affliction, more 'Struck to the heart'[13] (to quote the opening of *The Triumph of Life* passage recounted in Eliot's talk). It illustrates, in miniature, how Shelley presented Eliot with opportunities for imaginative adaptation.

Keats impressed Eliot as a far more 'attractive' (*UPUC*, 89) man than Shelley, as 'a great poet', especially in the Odes, and as the author of the 'most notable and the most important' (*UPUC*, 100) letters produced by an English poet. Eliot quotes admiringly Keats's remark that 'Men of Genius are great as certain ethereal chemicals operating on the Mass of neutral intellect – but they have not any individuality, any determined character' (*UPUC*, 101), possibly detecting a covert link between Keats's image and his own account in 'Tradition and the Individual Talent' (1919) of 'The mind of the poet' as a catalytic 'shred of platinum' (*SE*, 18) that allows creative transformations of experience. Keats as a presence in the poetry is decidedly sparse, partly because Eliot recognised that words such as '"Easeful" will never be of any use until Keats's trademark has worn off',[14] though in the 'familiar compound ghost' passage, the use of 'loitering' (*CPP*, 193) recalls 'La Belle Dame Sans Merci' to resourceful effect.

THE VICTORIANS

Eliot's formal innovations in 'The Love Song of J. Alfred Prufrock', 'Portrait of a Lady' and 'Gerontion' remodel the Victorian dramatic monologue, especially as practised by Robert Browning. In 'The Three Voices of Poetry' (1953), Eliot discusses the difference between the 'dramatic monologue' and 'drama', and argues that the former does not require the creation of character. Rather, it allows us to hear 'the voice of the poet ... speaking in the role of an historical personage'. For Eliot, Pound, who liked to speak through a 'persona', was 'Browning's greatest disciple' (*OPP*, 95). Eliot's own experimentation with the dramatic monologue would, however, be impossible without Browning's example. His monologues manage cunningly, in the terms used by 'The Three Voices of Poetry', to be poems both of 'the first voice' and of the 'second voice' (*OPP*, 96): poems, that is, in which the poet both does not and does seek to communicate with others. The J. Alfred Prufrock who finds it 'impossible to say just what I mean' (*CPP*, 16), for example, blurs into some version of the voice of Eliot himself, and this blended voice at once self-communes with unprecedented interiority and struggles to speak with an imagined audience. Major differences in Eliot's monologues compared with Browning's include a post-Freudian mistrust of the old stable ego, along with sudden juxtapositions that disrupt narrative coherence. Besides, Eliot's voices are not just individual voices; they speak for and out of a culture, and out of that culture's id as much as its ego. Still, when the speaker of 'Portrait of a Lady' half-laments, 'And I must borrow every changing shape / To find expression' (*CPP*, 21), he might be conceding his debt to the Browningesque dramatic monologue, even as the Victorian form undergoes 'change'.

Alfred Tennyson's symphonies of word-music, mimicked in 'The Love Song of J. Alfred Prufrock' in the lines beginning 'I have seen them riding', belong among 'the chambers of the [poetic] sea' in which 'We' are said to 'have lingered' (*CPP*, 17). In addition, the neurotic despair of *Maud* leaves its trace on the poem. When Prufrock speaks of the need 'To prepare a face to meet the faces that you meet' (*CPP*, 14), he recalls the speaker in *Maud* appalled by 'the faces that one meets, / Hearts with no love for me'.[15] Eliot disciplines Tennysonian anguish into an urbane twitch of irony at the near necessary falsity of social relations. Eliot's 1936 introduction to *In Memoriam* contains some of his best criticism of another poet, as in his praise for section 7, opening 'Dark house, by which once more I stand',[16] described as 'great poetry, economical of words, a universal emotion related to a particular place' (*SE*, 333). In its own way, Eliot's poetry searches for 'universal emotion related to a particular place'. Eliot admired *In Memoriam* less for the 'quality of its faith' than for 'the quality of its doubt' (*SE*, 336), admiration which is of some force from the author of *Ash-Wednesday* (1930). No doubt it was the quality of the doubt, not to say despair, evident in Thomson's *The City of Dreadful Night*, as well as that poem's terrifying metropolitan simulacrum of Hades, which appealed to the younger Eliot.[17] *The Waste Land* reshapes its own desolate response to a nightmarishly post-Christian cityscape, and the Thomson who 'sat forlornly by the river-side'[18] anticipates the Eliotic figure 'fishing in the dull canal' (*CPP*, 67).

Matthew Arnold earns harsh judgements from Eliot, notably in his 1933 Norton Lecture 'Matthew Arnold', in which his view of poetry as something which 'supersedes both religion and philosophy' is dismissed as 'a conjuring trick' (*UPUC*, 113), his account of poetry as a criticism of life is haughtily caricatured, and his supposed (and disputable) lack of '"the auditory imagination"' (*UPUC*, 118) inspires Eliot's memorable definition of such a thing. One senses that the relationship was more complex than Eliot will allow, that he saw lineaments of his own culture-shaping ambitions in his forebear's features, and that the figure of Marguerite left more of an impression than the younger poet was prepared to acknowledge. In 'Portrait of a Lady', Eliot alludes to Arnold's obsessive preoccupation with 'The Buried Life' (to quote the title of one of the Victorian poet's poems), when the lady speaks of 'these April sunsets, that somehow recall / My buried life' (*CPP*, 19), her 'somehow' mannered yet affecting. Arnold bequeaths to Eliot's work more generally the sense of 'an unspeakable desire / After the knowledge of our buried life'.[19]

Eliot deplored William Morris's 'day-dreamy feeling' (*SE*, 300) and its fake suggestiveness, but he was impressed by, even as he criticised, Algernon Swinburne's virtuosic substitution of 'the hallucination of meaning' for 'meaning' (*SE*, 327). For a poet as intent on the music of poetry as Eliot was, Swinburne represented a cul-de-sac but also a point of departure; without Eliot's readiness to experiment with 'the hallucination of meaning', it is doubtful whether he would have composed the opening of 'What the Thunder said', a passage propelled by its own 'independent life of atmospheric nourishment' (*SE*, 327). It is clear from Christopher Ricks's annotations to *Inventions of the March Hare* that Arthur Symons and Ernest Dowson nourished the young Eliot's self-conscious pursuit of a conversationally nuanced pathos, as when in 'Do I know how I feel? Do I know what I think?' the thought of 'beauty spilled' (*IMH*, 80) redeploys lines from Symons's 'Wasted Beauty'.

Eliot spoke of poets who were of 'capital importance' for him, such as Dante and Baudelaire. He also spoke of 'other debts, innumerable debts, to poets, of another kind' (*TCC*, 127). Such debts include the possibilities suggested by John Davidson's use of a challengingly demotic idiom in his searing 'Thirty Bob a Week', which underpins the pub scene in 'A Game of Chess'. Eliot's critical smokescreens have not helped; but it is evident that nineteenth-century poetry should be at the fore of thinking about the engrossing, multiple ways in which his work shapes itself out of its poetic debts.

NOTES

1. William Blake, *The Complete Poems*, ed. Alicia Ostriker (Harmondsworth: Penguin, 1977), p. 125.
2. Ibid., p. 189.
3. William Wordsworth, *The Major Works*, ed. Stephen Gill (Oxford University Press, 1984), p. 299.
4. Ibid., p. 142.
5. Ibid., p. 148.
6. 'The Prelude (1805)', ibid., p. 566.
7. Ibid., pp. 383, 566.
8. Samuel Taylor Coleridge, *Poetical Works*, ed. Ernest Hartley Coleridge (Oxford University Press, 1912), p. 367.
9. Lord Byron, *The Major Works*, ed. Jerome McGann (Oxford University Press, 1986), p. 688.
10. Percy Bysshe Shelley, *The Major Works*, ed. Zachary Leader and Michael O'Neill (Oxford University Press, 2003), pp. 266, 460.
11. James Thomson, *The City of Dreadful Night and Other Poems* (London: Dobell, 1899), p. 4.
12. Shelley, *Major Works*, p. 412.
13. Ibid., p. 609.
14. Quoted in Helen Gardner, *The Composition of 'Four Quartets'* (London: Faber & Faber, 1978), p. 191.
15. Alfred Tennyson, *A Critical Edition of the Major Works*, ed. Adam Roberts (Oxford University Press, 2000), p. 341.

16. Ibid., p. 208.

17. Eliot remarked that Thomson's *City of Dreadful Night* 'impressed me deeply in my formative years' (*IMH*, 398), although he later came to think it was a 'small work compared to *In Memoriam*' (*SE*, 336).

18. Thomson, *City of Dreadful Night*, p. 15.

19. Matthew Arnold, *The Complete Poems*, ed. Kenneth Allott (London: Longman, 1965), p. 289.

CHAPTER 21

French poetry

Stephen Romer

Among the many tributes that Eliot paid to the Baudelairean tradition in French poetry throughout his career, there is none more eloquent than the one he gave in 1933, in his third and final Turnbull Lecture. Speaking in particular of Jules Laforgue and Tristan Corbière, he extends his acknowledgements to other poets:

> I know that when I first came across these French poets, some twenty-three years ago, it was a personal enlightenment such as I can hardly communicate. I felt for the first time in contact with a tradition, for the first time, that I had, so to speak, some backing by the dead, and at the same time that I had something to say that might be new and relevant. I doubt whether, without the men I have mentioned – Baudelaire, Corbière, Verlaine, Laforgue, Mallarmé, Rimbaud – I should have been able to write poetry at all. (*VMP*, 287)

Shortly afterwards he declares roundly: 'The ultimate purpose, the ultimate value, of the poet's work is religious' (*VMP*, 288). It is no accident that this declaration should follow so close upon the naming of his different French masters. True, the wider context is philosophical and/or metaphysical poetry, and the overarching figure is Dante, but it is in reference to the French (and to something he often referred to as the 'French mind')[1] that Eliot so often, implicitly or explicitly, came to define his own choices on moral and aesthetic matters. Beyond the technical accomplishments he took from them is a particular idea of civilisation, and a state of mind – in a word, a *self-consciousness* – that fascinated him, in its different applications, his whole life. When we try to describe the French context for Eliot, we find ourselves coming close to the very quick of his life and art. For it was a French poet who first changed him, as he testified in 1919: 'from a bundle of second-hand sentiments into a person' (*IMH*, 399). In his 'romantic' Parisian year of 1910/11, Eliot was nourished by different intellectual currents, and, equally importantly, by a close friendship with a young French poet, Jean Verdenal, who shared his passion for

Laforgue and his interest in Henri Bergson (see Chapter 3 above). But if French thought as such became subsumed in other currents, his interest in French poetry and poetics remained with him always; it was the context that provided the most astringent intellectual and spiritual forum for advanced debate about the nature of his art. The lessons of Stéphane Mallarmé and Paul Valéry in particular, whether they commanded his assent, or, equally crucial, his disagreement, provided the set of propositions that stimulated him or piqued him into the creative responses that are central to his later poetry.

It is Charles Baudelaire (1821–67) who stands at the wellhead – he who, as Eliot remarked in 1930, 'gave to French poets as generously as he borrowed from English and American poets' (*SE*, 425). But he gave also to English and American poets – and to European ones. The shock of recognition that rippled outward from the lines 'Fourmillante cité, cité pleine de rêves / Où le spectre en plein jour raccroche le passant' ['Swarming city, city full of dreams, where ghosts in broad daylight accost the passer-by'] caught Eliot, who remarked in 1950: 'I knew what *that* meant, because I had lived it before I knew that I wanted to turn it into verse on my own account' (*IMH*, 390). The same lines are behind the haunted opening pages of Rainer Maria Rilke's young man arriving in Paris, as recorded in *The Notebooks of Malte Laurids Brigge*. But in his 1930 introduction to a translation of the *Journaux intimes*, with Eliot a recent convert to Christianity, it is once more matters of faith and belief that concern him. It comes as no surprise that he alights upon Baudelaire's great curse on nineteenth-century progress, quoting almost triumphantly his definition of civilisation as 'la diminution des traces du péché originel' ['diminution of the traces of original sin'] (*SE*, 430) as his clinching argument at the end of the essay. As so often, he is using his model to refine his own position, and Baudelaire here shores up his own beliefs. What counts for Eliot is no longer the Baudelaire of 'Les Litanies de Satan', but the less ostentatious, more deeply disturbing poet of 'L'Ennemi', with its apprehension of *fallenness*, of 'Le Rançon', with its evocation of a terrible day of judgement, of the death wish in 'Brumes et Pluies', and, at the other end of the scale, something that resembles the feeling of Dante's *Vita Nuova*, in the great idealising poems to Mme Sabatier, 'Le Flambeau vivant' and 'L'Aube spirituelle'.

Eliot, so keen on literary genealogy, recognised that Baudelaire begat Laforgue. It is worthwhile retracing Eliot's first encounter with Arthur Symons's study *The Symbolist Movement in Literature* (1899) as an undergraduate at Harvard University in 1908. There is the chapter on Paul

Verlaine – the unbuttoned, torrid, lachrymose, childlike musical genius – and there is the chapter on Mallarmé, the priestly theorist of exquisite refinement. Between them comes the chapter on Laforgue, the pale, perfectly composed, impeccably detached, ironic young man – a spectator at the *comédie humaine* – yet, sickly and under sentence of death, valetudinarian almost, controlled, disciplined, despairing. Laforgue, who defers to the German metaphysician Eduard von Hartmann's *Philosophy of the Unconscious*, would have been happy with Sigmund Freud's vocabulary of the nature of love. He would have approved of the sentence 'It is generally much harder to convince an idealist that his libido is inappropriately located than it is to convince the uncomplicated sort who has remained modest in his expectations'; or this, which puts the matter succinctly: 'sexual over-valuation of an object constitutes an idealisation of that object'.[2] Laforgue, like Freud, was a keen student of 'libidinal drives'.

As for Eliot, whose memory was prodigious – his friends dubbed him 'the elephant' – he never seems to have forgotten a phrase. In this case, Symons's description of Laforgue – 'He composes love-poems hat in hand'[3] – burned its way into his consciousness. That hat reappears in 'Portrait of a Lady': 'I take my hat: how can I make a cowardly amends / For what she has said to me?' (*CPP*, 20). Everywhere his poems bear the trace marks of his reading. For example, 'Spleen' (written as an undergraduate before his year in Paris), is as much Laforgue as Symons's portrait of Laforgue:

> And Life, a little bald and gray,
> Languid, fastidious, and bland,
> Waits, hat and gloves in hand,
> Punctilious of tie and suit
> (Somewhat impatient of delay)
> On the doorstep of the Absolute.   (*CPP*, 603)

Where Symons is waylaid, in his account, by the sulphurous decor of Satanism, the suggestive veils and the twilights, Eliot sees more clearly. In his 1926 Clark Lectures, he diagnoses Laforgue's malady and suggests a cure, in terms so richly suggestive they are worth pausing over. The remarks reveal both the drama of identification he feels for this French 'elder brother' (the shock of recognition) and the need (by this time) to leave him behind. His appreciation of Laforgue, Eliot seems to be saying, must finally be understood in the light of his appreciation of Dante:

Only Laforgue is in revolt, not in acceptance; he is at once the sentimentalist day-dreaming over the *jeune fille* at the piano with her geraniums, and the behaviourist inspecting her reflexes. What he wants, you see, is either a *Vita Nuova* to justify, dignify and integrate his sentiments toward the *jeune fille* in a system of the universe, or else some system of thought which shall keep a place [for and] even enhance these feelings and at the same time enable him to *feel* as intensely the abstract world. On the one hand he was fascinated by Miss Leah Lee, the English governess, and on the other hand by the Kantian pseudo-Buddhism of Schopenhauer and Hartmann. (*VMP*, 216)

This is extraordinary criticism, of the kind poets write best, because Eliot feels his subject as keenly as he feels his own life – the drama of identification is patent. Informed by an urgent need to understand, Eliot appears to know Laforgue and his needs better than Laforgue himself. When in 1883 the young French poet, bored with the constant *politesse* required of him as Reader to the Empress Augusta in Berlin, breaks out into the completely new vein of *Les Complaintes*, he explained in a letter to his sister Marie that he had abandoned the inflated eloquence of his philosophical poems in favour of a new style, 'more fantastic and "clownesque"' with only one end in view: 'faire de l'original à tout prix' ['to make something new at all cost'].[4] The early poems, collected under the lachrymose title *Le Sanglot de la terre*, are decidedly less original exercises in sub-Baudelairean spleen, an almost comic litany of anguish, insomnia, nostalgia, desolation and infinite resignation. We do not need to share Laforgue's own deferential view of his newfangled *Complaintes*, and as Eliot well saw, the desolation in them is, if anything, more piquant, because disguised.

The French poet's fondness for abstraction; the existence of the flesh and blood *jeune fille* and the chaos of feeling she provokes; the need for a system of the universe; this was also the young Eliot's predicament during his year in Paris, and indeed before that, in Boston, where he had the experience that found its synthesis (thanks to Laforgue) in 'Portrait of a Lady'. There are instants of existential anguish in the early draft poems, later published posthumously in *Inventions of the March Hare*, quite as tortured by the sterilities of philosophical categories as anything in Laforgue:

> Appearances appearances he said,
> I have searched the world through dialectic ways;
> I have questioned restless nights and torpid days,
> And followed every by-way where it lead;
> And always find the same unvaried
> Intolerable interminable maze.   (*IMH*, 75)

Or take the acutely distressed, solipsistic piece, beginning 'Do I know how I feel? Do I know what I think?', which articulates a disabling, neurasthenic self-consciousness, similar to one of Laforgue's early unpublished poems entitled simply 'Suis-je?'. Here, the poet makes a frenzied appeal to the 'sereine Loi' ['serene Law'] to indicate to him that he exists: 'Il faut pourtant presser ce mot! Oui, suis-je, suis-je? / Ce corps renouvelé chaque jour est-il mien?' ['It is necessary nevertheless to press this word! Yes, am I? am I? Is this body renewed everyday mine?']. In Eliot's poem, significantly, there is the sense of something beyond, ungraspable, 'which should be firm but slips, just at my finger tips' (*IMH*, 80).

These drafts were too vulnerable, too subjective, and knowing this Eliot never published them. It becomes clear that the great successes of the early period, notably 'The Love Song of J. Alfred Prufrock' and 'Portrait of a Lady', depend on the brilliantly prolonged amalgam of satire – delivered with a Laforguean *politesse* – and queasy subjective unease. But in the end Laforgue's banter is shriller, lighter in touch than Eliot's, his performance briefer and smarter. Eliot's approach is prowlingly catlike, his moral and philosophical insinuations are more drawn out and worried at; like the Prufrockian fog, they envelope and they suffocate. But the admiringly percipient comment of Symons, 'It is an art of the nerves, this art of Laforgue', fingers exactly the quality that unites him with Eliot.[5]

The other major French influence that Eliot underwent at this crucially receptive stage was that of Tristan Corbière, the tortured, tubercular, diminutive Breton poet. Verlaine paid him the signal honour of including him among *Les Poètes maudits* ['accursed poets'] and Ezra Pound, too, treasured him as one of the 'hard' in French poetry: 'since Gautier, Corbière has been hard, not with a glaze or parian finish, but hard like weather-bit granite'.[6] But Eliot prized him less for his seascapes or his major poems such as 'La Rapsode foraine' – which he quotes approvingly for its startling imagery – than for his love poems. Like Laforgue, Corbière was chiefly a love poet of a very acerbic, perverse kind. Woman, Laforgue's 'mammifère à chignon' ['mammal with hair in a bun'] is hailed in *Les Amours jaunes* as 'la Bête féroce' ['the ferocious beast'], and Corbière is snide about 'l'odeur de femme' which Eliot imported into the 'female smells' (*CPP*, 25) of 'Rhapsody on a Windy Night' and the deleted misogynistic Popean pastiche of *The Waste Land* manuscript. Eliot shared these violently divided feelings: sexual unease is the taproot of his early work. Trying for the umpteenth time to define his particular notion of 'metaphysical poetry', Eliot says it comes about 'when you have a philosophy exerting its influence, not directly through belief, but indirectly through feeling and behaviour, upon the minute particulars of a poet's daily life, his quotidian mind, *primarily perhaps his way of love-making*, but also any activity' (*VMP* 294; my emphasis). Quite as much as

Laforgue, Corbière is a poet of the nerves, of attack and parry, of dramatisation and staccato wit. It is Corbière who is behind the most important of Eliot's own poems in French – the astonishing 'Dans le restaurant'. But in this poem Eliot goes beyond either Laforgue or Corbière, for hidden within it – it is easy to miss – is a moment of vision, something resembling ecstasy, that occurred in the waiter's childhood:

> Je la chatouillais, pour la faire rire.
> J'éprouvais un instant de puissance et de délire.
>
> [I was tickling her, to make her laugh.
> I experienced a moment of power and delirium.]   (*CPP*, 51)

This is the moment that is picked up, and magnified, in the 'hyacinth garden' (*CPP*, 62) interlude in *The Waste Land* – the blessed, irrecoverable moment from which that poem exfoliates.

Eliot worked hard to shed the pervasive influence of Laforgue, and he did so by turning deliberately to two other French poets – Corbière, as we have seen, and Théophile Gautier, whose *Émaux et Camées*, which came with a glowing recommendation from Pound, was the inspiration for the 'hard' quatrain poems in *Poems* (1920). These quatrain poems, though clear in outline, by no means deliver a clear semantic content – the ambiguities and dislocations go far beyond Gautier, and indeed threaten to overflow the vehicle. Gautier was not perhaps the happiest of influences – there is evidence of forcing, and an unmistakable frigidity about these poems. Earlier, in 1917, Eliot was actually writing poems in French, almost exclusively, including an accomplished sonnet in homage, entitled 'Tristan Corbière'. Pound reported to James Joyce that Eliot 'has burst out into scurrilous french [*sic*] during the past few weeks'.[7] In a 1959 interview with the *Paris Review*, Eliot himself explained the phenomenon deferentially:

I hadn't written anything for some time and was rather desperate. I started writing a few things in French and found I *could*, at that period. I think it was that when I was writing in French, I didn't take the poems so seriously ... I wasn't so worried about not being able to write ... I think it was just something that helped me get started again. (*IMH*, 291)

Along with Baudelaire, the two French geniuses to preside over Eliot's early 'art of the nerves' – Laforgue and Corbière – liberated him both in terms of form and content. Gautier and minor figures such as Laurent Tailhade helped focus his satire in (deceptively) clear-cut form. Other figures crowd to the fore, and an exhaustive account of Eliot's French influences in poetry, especially early on, would have to include the cosmopolitan sophistications of Guillaume Apollinaire, Blaise Cendrars and Valery Larbaud, Paul Claudel's mighty verse and his theological passion, and also Saint John Perse, whose long poem *Anabase* Eliot translated in 1930. But the second major engagement for Eliot with the French tradition, and the Symbolist movement in particular, occurs in the latter part of his career. The presiding geniuses here are Stéphane Mallarmé and his disciple Paul Valéry. And in this process of contextualisation, we cannot but mention the *grands absents*: Eliot was almost wholly indifferent to the overwhelmingly dominant movement of the interwar period in France, Surrealism. Instead, he sided with Valéry, who was also baffled by the apparent arbitrariness and lack of literary constraint or formal discipline (as he conceived it) of André Breton's avant-garde movement. Eliot's sideswipes were offered at the time of his religious conversion, and the highly moral nature of his enquiry meant he had little time for experimentation such as automatic writing. For Eliot at this time, this was a pursuit 'after strange gods', and one that opened a veritable Pandora's Box of unconscious horrors of the type he had struggled with but in an attempt not merely to entertain them, but (to recall the words of his 1926 Clark Lectures) to 'dignify' and 'justify' them 'in a system of the universe'.

It was *self-consciousness*, not unconsciousness, that Eliot came to prize, and in particular, the self-consciousness that Mallarmé, supremely, embodied in his life as well as his art, and that Valéry expounded more discursively. Self-consciousness in the composition of a poem means essentially a 'knowledge of what one is doing', the process of reflexivity by which the poem itself bears the trace of that knowledge. While the more pressing ontological questions had been, so to speak, settled by Eliot's formal adherence to Christian mysteries, the status of language, the role of the word in relation to the Word, became burning issues. Eliot's encounter with Symbolist and post-Symbolist poetics led him to confront (and debate) major questions, like the means and ends of the poem, the role of the writing subject, the nature of poetic language and its relation to speech, the place of abstract thought in poetry, the effects of syntax and structure on propositional meaning, and in what way exactly does poetry aspire to the condition of music?

The 'French context' here is actually complicated by that displaced European, Edgar Allan Poe, whose extraordinary 'career' in France is one of literature's curiosities. Eliot's 1948 lecture at Washington's Library of Congress, 'From Poe to Valéry', may help us to focus upon this tradition.

It is chiefly Poe's essay 'The Philosophy of Composition' that riveted the attention of the young Valéry. The quality or otherwise of Poe's piece on his poem 'The Raven' is less important. As Eliot sees it, it is Valéry's response that fascinates, and how he himself came to adopt an attitude of extreme self-consciousness, combined with an exacerbated scepticism, in his poetry and in his poetics. Always a debunker of the mysterious, or the miraculous, whether in theology, philosophy or poetry, Valéry liked to scandalise by saying that he would prefer to write a second-rate poem, while remaining conscious of every linguistic and formal choice, than write a masterpiece 'dictated' by some external power. Of inspiration, he also remarked, deflatingly, that the spirit blows not precisely where it will, but *what* it can to *whom* it can. A poem is a 'machine' that sets up the poetic emotion in the reader; or else it is a mechanism to elicit the larynx of the reader, and so on. These are provocative quips and *trouvailles* from a writer who wrote 'la bêtise n'est pas mon fort' ['stupidity is not my strong point'] in the opening sentence of his text about a man who is all head, *Monsieur Teste*.

Valéry also disappointed believers in the absolute form of a poem, by publishing different versions of the same sonnet and apparently according them equal status. This raises the question of the importance of subject matter, which is the one that most engaged Eliot. 'We must be careful', he writes, 'to avoid saying that the subject matter becomes "less important". It has rather a different kind of importance: it is important as *means*: the *end* is the poem. The subject exists for the poem, not the poem for the subject' (*TCC*, 39). A little earlier, Eliot explores the question of *la poésie pure*, which was a wraith raised by Valéry's comment about 'poésie à l'état pur' ['poetry in the pure state'] and magnified by a poetry-loving cleric, the Abbé Henri Bremond, into a full-blown if wrong-headed theory. In fact, the abbé's contention, not very controversial, was that a current passed through certain lines of poetry that galvanised the reader, in a way that could not be explained semantically or rationally. This notion, and Valéry's later comments, represent the tail end of *l'art pour l'art* [art for art's sake], the movement largely promulgated in France by Gautier and Baudelaire, both of whom agreed that poetry should have only collateral relations with 'truth' as conceived in any religious, philosophical or moral mode. Poetry was no longer to be historical or didactic. Mallarmé implied much the same thing when he wrote in *Crise de vers* that 'narrer, enseigner, meme décrire' ['to narrate, to instruct, even to describe'] was no longer part of the poet's brief. The poet was to serve 'l'intellectuelle parole à son apogée' ['intellectual language at its peak'] and to *suggest* rather than to describe in any naturalistic, novelistic fashion. Syntactic ambiguity was axiomatic. Mallarmé idealised language itself, and his celebrated flower, understood as a phonetic sign, with no physical attributes and to be found in no bouquet, was itself the heart of the mystery, for it is conjured out of nothing in our minds by the simple utterance of the word.

In a later refinement, Valéry gave a fresh definition of *la poésie pure*, assimilating it to music, which is pure *expressiveness*, rather than expression, since music has no fixed semantic lexicon (see Chapter 14 above). He imagined a poetry that would have no prose content, in which the relation between meanings would be like a system of harmonics in music, a poetry in which 'la transmutation des pensées les unes dans les autres paraîtrait plus important que toute pensée, où le jeu des figures contiendrait la réalité du sujet' ['the transmutation of thoughts into other ones would seem to be more important than any thought, where the interplay of tropes contains the reality of the subject'].[8] It may be that Wallace Stevens's 'Sea Surface Full of Clouds' is the closest we have in English to a poem of this kind, a virtuoso, purely tonal exercise, in which the content is negligible and merely the means. Eliot, predictably, had serious reservations about these wilder shores of French theorising. Yet responding to the implications of *la poésie pure*, Eliot arbitrates between two extreme positions thus: 'An aesthetic which merely contradicted it would not do. To insist on the all-importance of subject-matter, to insist that the poet should be spontaneous and irreflective, that he should depend upon inspiration and neglect technique, would be a lapse from what is in any case a highly civilised attitude to a barbarous one' (*TCC*, 41).

The poetics of Valéry, and in particular Mallarmé, have momentous implications that have suffused philosophical enquiry into language and continue to do so in the age of postmodernism. To say that Eliot took the measure of at least some of these implications is already to say a good deal. It was Mallarmé who refocused the analogy of poetry with music, turning attention away from the superficial level of phonetic 'muscicality' to questions of structure or leitmotif. Eliot's *Four Quartets* (1943) uses parataxis, modulation of tonal register and recurrent image clusters that accrue semantic richness at each repetition, much in the manner of chamber music. Mallarmé's attempt to 'transcribe a constellation' – Valéry's description of his master's radically experimental poem 'Un coup de dés' – finds no immediate echo in Eliot, although the whole tenor of the passage 'Words move, music moves / Only in time' (*CPP*, 175) needs to be read in terms of the division Symbolist theorists set up between speech (as a tool of everyday communication) and the incantatory poetic *parole* that continually resuscitates in our memory and on our tongue. Valéry went so far as to suggest that poetry was a language *within* a language. Eliot again corrects him by insisting that the language of poetry must remain rooted and take as its reference the way a poet's contemporaries speak. Even more far-reaching is the passage in 'East Coker' when Eliot, after writing a passage of Mallarméan opacity, demeans it:

> That was a way of putting it – not very satisfactory:
> A periphrastic study in a worn-out poetical fashion,
> Leaving one still with the intolerable wrestle
> With words and meanings. The poetry does not matter.   (*CPP*, 179)

Those last five words constitute the moment when Eliot takes his leave of Mallarméan poetics: for Mallarmé, it is inconceivable that the poetry should not matter, since to an atheist like himself there *is* no salvation outside of the word. Eliot, however, had to leave his French masters at this point. They had given him a voice, they had given him a poetic technique to borrow and a poetic theory to ponder. In the end it was only Dante, the poet of the word and the Word, who could take him further.

NOTES

1. See, for example, 'The Lesson of Baudelaire', *Tyro* (spring 1921), 4.
2. Sigmund Freud, *Beyond the Pleasure Principle and Other Writings* (Harmondsworth: Penguin, 2003), pp. 23–4.
3. Arthur Symons, *The Symbolist Movement in Literature* (1908) (New York: Haskell House, 1971), p. 304.
4. Jules Laforgue, *Oeuvres complètes*, vol. 1, ed. J-L. Debauve et al. (Paris: L'Age d'Homme, 1986), p. 821.
5. Symons, *Symbolist Movement in Literature*, p. 303.
6. Ezra Pound, *Literary Essays*, ed. T. S. Eliot (London: Faber & Faber, 1954), p. 288.
7. *Pound/Joyce*, ed. Forrest Read (London: Faber & Faber, 1968), p. 112.
8. Paul Valéry, *Oeuvres complètes*, vol. 1, ed. Jean Hytier (Paris: Gallimard, 1957), p. 146.

CHAPTER 22

Georgian poetry

Peter Howarth

Eliot's reviews of his contemporaries and rivals, the Georgian poets, look like a thorough hatchet job. Written between 1917 and 1922 as Eliot began to establish his place in the London literary world, they leave the reader in little doubt that modern English poetry is morally, poetically and culturally bankrupt. According to Eliot, the Georgians are sentimentalists who substitute 'Georgian emotions for human ones'.[1] They produce 'a style quite remote from life'.[2] With their complete ignorance of foreign poetry, their verse is technically complacent and morally lightweight. It offers no real culture to its smug middle-class readership, only decoration of what its audience are already proud of feeling. Contented in their own littleness and humility, the emotional self-satisfaction of the Georgians is the correlative of both a provincial insularity and an aversion to taking risks of any sort.

Unfortunately, if one turns the pages of the later Georgian anthologies, Eliot's verdict seems depressingly just. The first of the five volumes of *Georgian Poetry* had created a stir when it appeared in 1912, because it allowed readers to sample work from younger poets with a new ethos of uninhibited writing, and – by the standards of the time – direct emotions in plain language. D. H. Lawrence summed up the aims of the contributors – who included Rupert Brooke, W. H. Davies and Walter de la Mare – as a fearless 'exultation in the vast freedom' from restrictive nineteenth-century ideals of verse writing.[3] An unexpected success with the Christmas public that year, the Georgian anthologies had become a popular series by the time Eliot began to diagnose a fatal sentimentality in his review of the third volume, *Georgian Poetry 1916–1917*. This volume contained war poems by the young Robert Graves and Siegfried Sassoon, but although their work is clearly in a different class from John Freeman's 'Happy is England Now' ('happy is England in the brave that die') or John Drinkwater's praise of cider, Eliot thought that even the bitter satire of Graves and Sassoon had a pose to it. In 1922 he caustically remarked that certain war poets owed their popularity to the fact that 'they appeared to represent a revolt against something that was very unpleasant and really paid a tribute to all the nicest feelings of the upper-middle class British public schoolboy'.[4] And with the steady decimation of that class during the war and the collapse of its cultural self-confidence, the Georgians' fresh-air wholesomeness began to feel ever more implausible. In the final volume of *Georgian Poetry* published in 1922, Wilfrid Gibson and Robert Nichols strain to be simple, while J. C. Squire's hymn to dewy April and John Drinkwater's to misty September are equally watery-eyed about their own feelings. Even the poets who went on to do better things, like Graves and Edmund Blunden, were then still too close to the war to write about it with any gravity. D. H. Lawrence's free-verse poem 'Snake' alone feels modern, although, of course, it was Eliot who partly defined what 'modern' poetry should feel like. The first generation of Eliot's academic advocates concluded, sensibly enough, that only Eliot's kind of poetry had the emotional honesty, the relevance to contemporary life, and technical daring to count as *modernist* poetry.

Thanks to the revisionary accounts offered by Philip Larkin and Donald Davie after the Second World War, however, Eliot's condemnations came to seem an unfair way to characterise all the Georgians, especially in the wider sense of the term 'Georgian' that could include Wilfred Owen or Edward Thomas. Although their verse is more formally and syntactically patterned than that of the modernists, these poets were using patterns to resist emotional complacency or moral self-satisfaction. But the claim of Larkin and Davie that the Georgians were part of an 'English tradition' of accessible speech-based poetry was in turn attacked in the late 1970s by the late modernists of the 'British Poetry Revival'. This 'English tradition', they felt, was a spurious justification for a revival of the insular, market-driven verse that Eliot had originally criticised in the Georgians. In this sense, Eliot's attacks on the little-Englandism of the Georgian anthologies established arguments still being used eighty years later.[5]

Eliot's relations with individual 'Georgian' poets, on the other hand, tell a rather different story. Thanks to his familiarity with the way Pound had constructed a collective 'Imagism', he recognised more quickly than anyone else that 'Georgian' was also a flag of convenience for poets of diverse interests and talents. In fact, both groups had initially shared a publisher in Harold Monro's Poetry Bookshop, and Pound had modelled the format of *Des Imagistes* on the success of Edward Marsh's first

Georgian Poetry. Knowing how different he was from other poets collected in Pound's *Catholic Anthology* (1915), Eliot then used the example of the Georgians to warn other modernists against the belief that anthologies exhibited a collective artistic goal. Poets who forget that anthologies are for advertisement purposes and who believe they really possess a common aim are in danger of losing touch with their individuality: 'They come to resemble each other more and more, and, like members of a family in old age, they become simply instances of a type. All that is now left of the Georgian Poets is what we may call the family features.'[6] This looks at first like an insult. It was certainly aimed at a close-knit coterie of second-generation Georgian poets whose publicity was guaranteed by their leader, J. C. Squire, editor of the *London Mercury* (see Chapter 10 above). But in criticising the formulae that give anthologies a brand identity, as well as the group politics of rival anthologies, Eliot's comments actually provided covert justification for maintaining rather better relations with many individual Georgian poets.

In 1927, when he was a director of Faber & Gwyer, one of Eliot's innovations was the Ariel Poems series of single poems published in limited-edition illustrated pamphlets (Eliot's own Ariel poems are now the best known of them). They were an adaptation of the Poetry Bookshop's illustrated Rhyme Sheets – cheap posters with poems that could be hung as a decoration. Eliot's choice of companions for the Ariel series was also a continuation of the Poetry Bookshop series: he published Davies, de la Mare, Monro, Sassoon, Blunden and Gibson, whose appearance as Georgian poets he had previously attacked. Indeed, it was not long before Sassoon, de la Mare and Blunden became Faber stalwarts. Sassoon's *Poems Newly Selected* (1940), published by Faber, contained some of the same poems that Eliot had dismissed on their first appearance in anthologies of *Georgian Poetry.* Eliot also maintained a lifelong friendship with the Georgians' publisher, Monro. He contributed articles to Monro's *Chapbook* magazine and regularly published Monro's poetry in the *Criterion,* along with, most surprisingly of all, poetry by ex-Georgians Gibson and Gordon Bottomley. The only tribute poem he ever wrote was dedicated to de la Mare. Nor did Eliot's criticism always fix a great gulf between modernists and Georgians. Though he never cared much for the naivety of the tramp-poet W. H. Davies, his 1926 Clark Lectures made a striking connection between Davies's deliberate refusal to think or moralise in his poetry and the Surrealist procedures of Jean Cocteau and André Breton (see *VMP,* 211). And Eliot would later remark, in a 1935

Criterion editorial, that the 'Hebraic' rhythms of Isaac Rosenberg – whose free verse poem 'Ah Koelue' he had read in *Georgian Poetry 1916–1917* – had had a 'fertilizing effect upon *English* [poetry]: and fertilization, either from its own relations or from foreign languages, is what it perpetually needs'.[7]

Taken in context, then, Eliot's ruthless attacks on the Georgian 'family features' were aimed not at all Georgians, but (as he put it in a memorial to Monro) at 'the poetry of writers not unfairly representable in anthologies'. He admitted that 'in those days I was interested only in the sort of thing I wanted to do myself, and took no interest in what diverged from my own directions'.[8] In other words, Eliot's reviews of Georgian poetry represent a series of object lessons on how *not* to write the poetry which Eliot wanted to write. But those lessons do not always give consistent advice, and it is revealing to examine their differences in detail. For Eliot's demands for honesty, technical daring and individuality were the same qualities that other critics had discovered in the first anthology of *Georgian Poetry*, which suggests that these virtues are less the sole property of modernist verse than general demands for poetry engaged with modernity, demands which that modernity also makes it difficult for the poet to fulfil. Escaping rhetoric, for instance, means knowing your own meaning perfectly and not writing for the sake of being merely impressive: but how is this possible in a public language, in a genre which has conventions, to a modern audience more diverse than the poet can ever know? Rather than seeing the Georgians as Eliot's polar opposites, and concluding that there must be a life or death struggle between them, it makes more sense to see them as figures whose cultural position he needed to take over, but whose cultural problems his own verse also inherited.

Between 1917 and 1920, Eliot's attacks on the Georgians focused on their supposed insincerity. In the first of his 'Reflections on Contemporary Poetry' series in the *Egoist*, he complained that the Georgian appetite for English rural themes adopts Wordsworthian emotions about nature, but without taking on board the moral philosophy that supports them. In Georgian poetry

The emotion is derived from the object, and such emotions must either be vague (as in Wordsworth) or, if more definite, pleasing. Thus, it is not unworthy of notice how often the word 'little' occurs; and how this word is used, not merely as a necessary piece of information, but with a caress, a conscious delight.[9]

Caressing what one touches, of course, involves a self-conscious pleasure in one's own simplicity that is impossible to reconcile with the 'concrete and immediate realization of life' which the Georgians profess. In a review of an anthology containing both Imagist and Georgian poets, Eliot argued that the Georgians, lacking even the inchoate philosophy of Wordsworth, end up using a particular vocabulary to convince themselves they are more simple than they really are. By narrating simple tales of simple folk, the Georgians John Masefield and Wilfrid Gibson attempt to rid themselves of rhetoric, a feat the Imagists were attempting by other means. Eliot was doubtful, though, whether either group was successful:

> as for the escape from rhetoric – there is a great push at the door, and some cases of suffocation. But what is rhetoric? . . . There is rhetoric even among the new poets . . . I am inclined to believe that Tennyson's verse is a 'cry from the heart' – only it is the heart of Tennyson, Latitudinarian, Whig, Laureate.[10]

Quoting Yeats's aspiration to bypass rhetoric with 'a style like speech . . . like a cry from the heart', Eliot argued that the modern poet's direct address to the reader can become a kind of rhetoric, if it means deluding oneself into believing that one's actual feelings are simple. The cure for poetic rhetoric is not an especially direct vocabulary or verse form, since these can become a formula like anything else, but rather 'the discernment of exactly what, and how much, we feel in any given situation'.[11] As Eliot summarised the following year, Georgian poetry was 'wholly corrupted by simplicity' because it allowed these poets to flatter themselves: 'Simplicity is merely a means, a means of direct contact. It is a virtue of expression. Simplicity was not hard worn by the Georgians, it was given them by the fairy, and so, securely simple in their hearts, they neglected the more pharisaical virtue of simplicity in expression.'[12] How, though, is the poet to know himself? Eliot's answer was counter-intuitive: 'The serious writer of verse must be prepared to cross himself with the best verse of other languages and the best prose of all languages. In Georgian poetry there is almost no crossing visible; it is inbred. It has developed a technique and a set of emotions all of its own.'[13] This is Eliot's second line of attack on Georgian poetry; that it refuses either 'to recognise foreign competition' or to learn from it.[14] Simplicity and self-knowledge is found not merely through wider reading, but by absorbing and being transformed by what one reads, and the echo of religious commitment in the genetics metaphor of 'crossing oneself' is not an accident. This openness to foreign influences is picked up in 'Tradition and the Individual Talent' (1919), where the individual author, in order to be really individual, must now surrender himself 'as he is at the moment to something which is more valuable', the tradition of the 'mind of Europe' (*SE*, 16–17). The Georgians, on the other hand, think they have a tradition, but it is dead:

The Englishman, completely untrained in critical judgement, looks complacently back over the nineteenth century as an accumulation of Great Writers. England puts her Great Writers away securely in a Safe Deposit Vault, and curls to sleep like Fafner. There they go rotten; for if our predecessors cannot teach us to write better than themselves, they will surely teach us to write worse; because we have never learned to criticize Keats, Shelley, and Wordsworth (poets of assured though modest merit), Keats, Shelley, and Wordsworth punish us from their graves with the annual scourge of the Georgian Anthology.[15]

That banking metaphor inaugurates Eliot's third line of attack; namely, that Georgian poetry's 'lack of curiosity in technical matters . . . is only an indication of their lack of curiosity in moral matters'.[16] This moral complacency reveals a fatal indifference to art in contemporary culture. In a review of Harold Monro's *Some Contemporary Poets* (1921), Eliot refined his previous judgements of the Georgians:

I cannot see in the Georgian Anthology any such influence as Wordsworth, Keats, and Shelley had upon Arnold, Tennyson, and Browning. The dulness of the Georgian Anthology is original, unique; we shall find its cause in something much more profound than the influence of a few predecessors. The subtle spirit inspiring the ouija-board of Mr J. C. Squire's patient prestidigitators is not the shattered Keats but the solid and eternal Podsnap himself. This party represents, in fact, the insurgent middle class, Mr Monro's General Reading Public.[17]

Secure in these standards of taste and 'able to respect no other standards than its own', this General Reading Public 'rejects with contumely the independent man, the free man, all the individuals who do not conform to a world of mass-production': it finds 'safety in Regular Hours, Regular Wages, Regular Pensions, and Regular Ideas'. In a single swoop, Eliot has condensed his previous condemnations of insincerity, insularity and class conformity, so that the Georgians' fault is now to manifest too perfectly a desire to please the wrong kind of audience: 'The Georgian public is a smallish but important public, it is that offensive part of the middle class which believes itself superior to the rest of the middle class; and superior for precisely this reason that it believes itself to possess culture.'[18] At this point, however, some of the inconsistencies in such arguments begin to intrude themselves more insistently. For who would buy Eliot's own poetry if not that part of the middle class which thought itself superior to the rest of the middle class by virtue of possessing true culture? Why couldn't Eliot be accused of providing a section of the upper-middle-class reading public with exactly the means to make itself feel superior? He could reply that such a public would not be a class, since they would be independent nonconformists. But if that were the case, how could they belong to a tradition that required a 'self-sacrifice' to the 'mind of Europe'? And if the 'only thing which gives a work pretending to literary art its justification' is 'a truly independent way of looking at things, a point of view which cannot be sorted under any known religious or political title',[19] how could the independent artist also incarnate the 'traditional habit of life' to be found in 'European, that is to say, Latin, culture' (*SE*, 293)?

The problem occurs in another way when Eliot declares that a truly independent art would always be detested by the public. For in many of the same articles in which he was consigning the Georgians to oblivion, he contrasted them unfavourably with the happier relationship between music-hall artistes and their working-class audience. The music-hall comedians did not merely engage with their public; they incorporated them into their art. Creating a symbolic or mythic character, the music-hall performer would engage the spectator in songs and repartee to leave him 'purged of unsatisfied desire' so that he 'transcends himself, and unconsciously lives the myth'.[20] The workman who 'joined in the chorus' with Marie Lloyd saw 'himself performing part of the act; he was engaged in that collaboration of the audience with the artist which is necessary in all art and most obviously in dramatic art' (*SE*, 458). But Eliot regretted that the middle classes have no such expressive figure to dignify them – except, precisely, *Georgian Poetry*. In other words, Eliot's reviews of the 1920s argue both that Georgian poetry is the perfect expression of the middle class, but that this class has no art to express it; that true art works like a transformative collaborative ritual and yet requires a truly independent way of looking at things.

These rapid switches between individuality and collectivity also matter for Eliot's previous arguments about poetic rhetoric. Georgian poets are rhetorical, he argued, when they are not sure what they feel. But the poet of 'Tradition and Individual Talent' learns what he feels by sacrificing himself to tradition: 'All the ideas, beliefs, modes of feeling and behaviour which we have not time or inclination to investigate for ourselves we take second-hand and sometimes call Tradition'.[21] That is to say, the tradition cannot be wholly turned into the service of self-knowledge because it is too big: it offers the chance for the poet to become a 'medium' for 'emotions which he has never experienced' (*SE*, 21). But in that case, it will be difficult to distinguish when the poet is being rhetorical and when he is possessed by tradition, for in both cases he will speak with a voice that is not his own. The effect of one of Rupert Brooke's poems was 'completely spoilt', Eliot complained, by the adjective 'scattering-bright'.[22] But since it is taken from Donne's 'Aire and Angels', why couldn't this quotation work not as a pretentious borrowing but as tacit recognition of how much Brooke's own emotions want to sound metaphysical? It is not a coincidence that the same metaphor of the poet-as-medium under-lies the ideal situation both of 'Tradition and the Individual Talent' and of Eliot's complaint that Squire's coterie of poets are unconsciously animated by the 'subtle spirit' of Charles Dickens's complacent business-man Mr Podsnap, for tradition eliminates the rhetorical by attacking 'the metaphysical theory of the substantial unity of the soul' (*SE*, 19). The mystery is how loss of self makes the poet more truly original.

What these contradictions underline is the difficulty of the task Eliot set himself in seeking to replace the Georgians. The ideal artist is to be both original and yet part of tradition. He will be impossible to classify and technically innovative, and yet capable of giving an audience characters they recognise so intimately that they are in the work of art itself. But Eliot could not put these demands this openly, for it would have revealed the similarities between his cultural position and that of the Romantic poets who stood behind the Georgian anthologies (see Chapter 20 above). Wordsworth's claim in the preface to *Lyrical Ballads* that the poet is both hostile to mere custom and yet manifests the real heart of the community, and Shelley's idea that the poet's ordinary self is consumed like a coal in the fire of artistic inspiration that unites reader and poem; these are the precursors of Eliot's ideal fusion of uncompro-mised individuality and communal belonging, achieved through the depersonalisation necessary to connect to tradition. All of these writers want a poetry whose unique nature will resist social homogenisation while at the same time cutting across social divisions to attain the 'simplified, universal' appeal Eliot missed in Henrik Ibsen's drama but which he found in the poetry of William Blake (*SW*, 69). But the difficulty of writing this poetry perhaps explains why Eliot's reviews of the Georgians uncannily resemble criticism of his own alienated mod-ernist poetry. For when he complains that they have a 'style quite remote from life'[23] or that they flatter 'that offensive part of the middle class which believes itself superior ... for precisely this reason that it believes itself to possess culture',[24] these accusations would become standard criticisms of modernism itself. In truth, Eliot's problems with the Georgians are really every poet's problem with the complex social position modern society allots to art; a position at once uniquely original but democratically available to everyone.

Yet perhaps one moment in Eliot's own poetry recognises a common interest with the Georgians at some deep level. In the third section of *Ash-Wednesday* (1930), Eliot's spiritual protagonist climbs a staircase in the manner recalling Dante the pilgrim ascending Mount Purgatory. Eliot apparently told Penelope Fitzgerald the staircase he had in mind was based on the one in Harold Monro's Poetry Bookshop, in which case the staircase leads not only away from the deceitful 'twisting, turning' of the lower levels of literary publicity, or past the temptations of the 'pasture scene' (*CPP*, 93) higher up, but also towards the unknown heaven of the Bookshop's poetic attic, whose erstwhile denizens had included Wilfred Owen, Robert Frost and T. E. Hulme.[25] It would be nice to think that Eliot's poetic heaven could include all of them.

NOTES

1. 'Verse Pleasant and Unpleasant', *Egoist* (March 1918), 43.
2. 'Prose and Verse', *Chapbook* (April 1921), 10.
3. *D. H. Lawrence: Introductions and Reviews*, ed. John Worthen and N. H. Reeve (Cambridge University Press, 2005), p. 201.
4. 'London Letter', *Dial* (May 1922), 511.
5. For an account of these controversies, see Randall Stevenson, *The Last of England? Oxford English Literary History*, vol. xii (Oxford University Press, 2004), pp. 173–237.
6. 'The Post-Georgians', *Athenaeum* (11 April 1919), 171.
7. 'A Commentary', *Criterion* (April 1935), 611.
8. 'Critical', *The Collected Poems of Harold Monro*, ed. Alida Monro (London: Cobden-Sanderson, 1933), pp. xiii–xiv.
9. 'Reflections on Contemporary Poetry [i]', *Egoist* (September 1917), 118.
10. 'Reflections on Contemporary Poetry [iii]', *Egoist* (November 1917), 151.
11. Ibid.
12. 'Post-Georgians', 171.
13. 'Verse Pleasant and Unpleasant', 43.
14. 'London Letter', *Dial* (May 1922), 510.
15. 'Observations', *Egoist* (May 1918), 69.
16. 'The Lesson of Baudelaire', *Tyro* (spring 1921), 4.
17. 'London Letter', *Dial* (April 1921), 450–1.
18. Ibid., 451–2.
19. 'London Letter', *Dial* (May 1922), 511.
20. 'The Romantic Englishman', *Tyro* (spring 1921), 4.

21. 'Reflections on Contemporary Poetry [III]', 151.
22. 'Reflections on Contemporary Poetry [I]', 119.
23. 'Prose and Verse', 10.
24. 'London Letter', *Dial* (April 1921), 452.
25. *So Have I Thought of You: The Letters of Penelope Fitzgerald* (London: Fourth Estate, 2008), p. 244.

CHAPTER 23

Bloomsbury

Mark Hussey

'Bloomsbury Group' is convenient shorthand with which to identify the disparate individuals associated with the term, but there is no 'Bloomsbury' context for Eliot. Despite the fears of Wyndham Lewis that he was 'under the poor and ridiculous uterine influence' of being 'too fundamentally at house with Bloomsburies',[1] and despite John Middleton Murry's pronouncement 'Wherever "The Waste Land" is, it is not situated in Bloomsbury',[2] Eliot's relations with those whom Leonard and Virginia Woolf termed 'Old Bloomsbury' were singular, not collective. In addition to themselves, the Woolfs regarded Clive and Vanessa Bell, Adrian Stephen, E. M. Forster, Roger Fry, Duncan Grant, J. M. Keynes, Desmond and Molly MacCarthy, Saxon Sydney-Turner and Lytton Strachey as members of 'Old Bloomsbury'.[3] As Quentin Bell remarked, the Bloomsbury Group 'can hardly be said to have had any common ideas about art, literature or politics'.[4] It had 'no body of doctrine, no code of conduct, no masters'.[5] Both Leonard and Virginia Woolf held that 'Bloomsbury' was a creation of journalists and rivals, a term of abuse. Yet even those who, like the Woolfs, denied the existence of the Bloomsbury Group also acknowledged the central importance in their lives of those friends identified as belonging to it.

For John Maynard Keynes as a student at Cambridge at the turn of the twentieth century, the moral philosopher G. E. Moore's *Principia Ethica* (1903) was the bible of a new religion. Eliot's own scepticism about philosophical idealism, expressed in his Ph.D. thesis on F. H. Bradley, aligned him with the dedication to the primacy of subjective knowledge characteristic of the young Cambridge men who formed the nucleus of Bloomsbury. When Eliot arrived in England in 1914, Bertrand Russell (with whom Eliot had studied for a term at Harvard) had recently abandoned Moore's ethics under the influence of another of Eliot's Harvard professors, George Santayana. In his incarnation as a philosopher, Eliot contributed reviews to the *International Journal of Ethics* through the good offices of Sydney Waterlow, a friend of Clive Bell's and an early suitor of Virginia Woolf. In March 1915, Eliot wrote to J. H. Woods at Harvard to say that he was working on a 'paper I am to read before the Moral Science Club at Cambridge. As I have chosen an ethical topic I feel some fear of rough treatment at the hands of Moore and his disciples' (*L1*, 97–8). Eliot's sights were set, however, on the sources of London literary power. Russell introduced him to Lady Ottoline Morrell's gatherings at Garsington Manor, a country estate near Oxford. At Garsington, where the Morrells created a haven for conscientious objectors during the First World War, Eliot came into contact with Clive Bell, Lytton Strachey, Duncan Grant and others, whose Bloomsbury credentials provided him with valuable connections in the London literary world.

When Eliot arrived in England, those associated with Bloomsbury were already well established in the careers that would make them famous. Desmond MacCarthy had been editor of the *New Quarterly* since 1907, where he had published Roger Fry's important 'An Essay in Aesthetics' in 1909; Keynes and Strachey both wrote regularly for the *Spectator*; Clive Bell, whose influential study *Art* was published in 1914, reviewed frequently for the *Athenaeum*, moving from literature to art criticism following his role in organising, with Fry and MacCarthy, a 1910 exhibition of post-Impressionist paintings; Leonard Woolf, who after seven years as a colonial administrator in Ceylon had married Virginia, acted as secretary to the second exhibition of post-Impressionist paintings, which took place in 1912, and published his first novel, *The Wise Virgins*, in 1914; Virginia Woolf had been publishing essays in a variety of publications, including frequent contributions to the *Times Literary Supplement* since 1905. Eliot soon formed relationships with the core of Bloomsbury. He recalled that of these relations only his friendship with the Woolfs was of lasting significance, yet throughout his writing career he would continue to publish, correspond with, gossip about, review (and be reviewed by) the 'Bloomsberries'.

Clive Bell claimed to have been one of the first people to sing Eliot's praises, bringing with him to Garsington in 1917 copies of *Prufrock and Other Observations*, from which Katherine Mansfield read aloud. Bell introduced Eliot to his mistress Mary Hutchinson, with whom Eliot struck up a friendship that was close enough to evoke Bell's jealousy, and to Roger Fry. It was Fry who told Leonard Woolf that Eliot sought a publisher for a collection of poems. In October 1918, Leonard wrote to Eliot inviting him to send them for consideration by the fledgling

Hogarth Press. The following month Eliot met the Woolfs, inaugurating relations which were accompanied by wariness on both sides but which became intimate and mutually satisfying. Eliot's *Poems* was published by the Hogarth Press in May 1919, although Bloomsbury gossip almost derailed Eliot's relations with Woolf before they had begun. In the spring of 1919, while *Poems* was still in production, Bell apparently let slip to Virginia Woolf that Eliot had made disparaging remarks about her to Mary Hutchinson: a series of letters and telephone calls ensued. The situation was exacerbated by Vivien Eliot stirring the pot with Mary Hutchinson. Vivien distrusted Bloomsbury from the outset, even fearing that her husband's book was in doubt because of Woolf's spite. In a letter to Virginia (which she forwarded to her sister Vanessa for her opinion), John Middleton Murry wrote to insist that Eliot had nothing but praise for her distinguished mind. For her part, Virginia suspected Mary was being unfairly blamed and confided to her diary that this imbroglio made Eliot more interesting. Eliot, disguising names in an alphabetical code of the kind familiar among Bloomsbury members, sought to explain all the intrigue in a letter to his cousin Eleanor Hinkley (see *L1*, 363–4).

Eliot tolerated Clive Bell. In 1921 he told Robert McAlmon that Bell was 'a most agreeable person, if you don't take him seriously, but a great waster of time if you do, or if you expect to get any profound knowledge or original thought out of him' (*L1*, 563). Nevertheless, they would have recognised each other as, to some extent, kindred spirits. Bell's 1919 article 'Tradition and Movements' and his series of articles on 'Order and Authority' published in the *Athenaeum* might have appealed to Eliot, who was seeking to establish a similar sense of tradition and order in his own critical writings. Furthermore, Bell's notion of 'significant form', described in *Art* as 'lines and colours combined in a particular way, certain forms and relations of forms' which evoke an 'aesthetic emotion',[6] has affinities with Eliot's definition in the *Athenaeum* of the 'objective correlative': 'a set of objects, a situation, a chain of events which shall be the formula of that *particular* emotion; such that when the external facts, which must terminate in sensory experience, are given, the emotion is immediately evoked' (*SE*, 145).

In March 1920, Bell railed in the *Athenaeum* against an exhibition entitled 'Imperial War Pictures' at Burlington House. As examples of 'Wilcoxism' (Virginia Woolf had earlier reviewed Ella Wheeler Wilcox's *The Worlds and I* under the title 'Wilcoxiana'), Bell adduced the (to him) absurd comparisons that an art critic had made between the paintings of Wyndham Lewis and those of Henri Matisse and André Derain.[7]

The next issue of the *Athenaeum* carried Lewis's angry *ad hominem* reply, which cited as an example that the 'Pot is calling the kettle Black', Bell's exaggerated praise of the Bloomsbury painter Duncan Grant. Lewis called Bell 'one of the most ridiculous figures we possess'.[8] The following week Bell replied, also *ad hominem*, explaining that his charge of 'Wilcoxism' was not directed at Lewis but at those critics who failed to see the absurdity of comparing inferior English artists with French artists. Bell cautioned Lewis against losing his temper whenever someone admired him less than he appeared to admire himself. Lewis brought the correspondence to a close in the next issue. The 'Lewis–Bell controversy', as Eliot described it in a letter to Ottoline Morrell, is a salient example of how Eliot's broad connections among the London intelligentsia could lead to mixed allegiances and frayed friendships. To Morrell, Eliot expressed outrage at 'Bell's prostitution of art criticism to vulgar spite' (*L1*, 453). Writing to Lewis, he made it clear that Lewis's attack on Bell 'gave several people considerable pleasure' (*L1*, 452), urging Lewis not to let Bell have the last word. In 1924, Eliot published in the *Criterion* extracts of what would become Lewis's book-length attack on the Bloomsbury Group, *The Apes of God* (1930). He was quick to defend himself by writing to Virginia Woolf to remind her that she, her husband and Clive Bell had advised him 'that it was in pursuance of "the best tradition of British journalism" to let one contributor say what he likes about another' (*L2*, 412–13).

In a *New Republic* article of 1921 entitled 'Plus de Jazz', Bell identified Eliot as a Jazz Age poet. By 1923, however, while continuing to claim credit for his early championing of Eliot, Bell complained in the *Nation and Athenaeum* that the poet had 'little imagination' and had been 'repeating himself'. Bell went on to argue that Eliot's critical writing was simultaneously interesting and silly: 'His conclusions are worthless; the argument and analysis by which he arrives at them are extraordinarily valuable' (Brooker, 113–14). Eliot, who had referred to Bell in the *Egoist* in 1918 as 'the Matthew Arnold of his time',[9] later published an article on nineteenth-century painting by him in the *Criterion* and reviewed Bell's *Civilization* there himself in 1928. It was a coy review. Eliot remarked: 'Having chosen one of those subjects which are the food of interesting and lively conversation, Mr Bell has wisely avoided the profundity of treatment which would have destroyed it'. (After reading this book, which was dedicated to her, Virginia Woolf said that Bell's idea of civilisation turned out to be little more than a lunch party at his house in Gordon Square.) Eliot's review identified Bell as a humanist in the mould of Irving Babbitt, whom Eliot believed was seeking converts to his 'private form of humanistic civilization'.[10]

The general tenor of Eliot's editorship of the *Criterion* ran counter to Bloomsbury aesthetics. Reviewing Fry's Hogarth Essay *The Artist and Psycho-Analysis* there in 1925, Herbert Read adopted the editorial *we* to opine: 'Mr Roger Fry has a theory of art which we believe to be wrong'.[11] The *Criterion* also published several articles hostile to Lytton Strachey. The Reverend Charles Smyth drew attention to the mutual admiration voiced publicly by Bloomsbury members that appeared to boost their popularity. In 1929, Smyth noted in the *Criterion* that Strachey's *Elizabeth and Essex* had been hailed by 'the Bright Young Men', notably Desmond MacCarthy. The problem for Smyth was that Strachey's mode of argument was to 'snigger' rather than actually engage in historical analysis and that this is 'the real issue between the historians and Mr Lytton Strachey'.[12] According to Strachey's biographer, his first meeting with Eliot did not go well. Vivien Eliot told Mary Hutchinson that her husband very much wanted to become friends with Strachey. They met again at Garsington and got on better. Although Strachey's 'overtures to a closer relationship' were welcomed by Eliot, 'some hindrance to its further development persisted'.[13] In 1927, Eliot cast doubt on Strachey's representation of Shakespeare, since it bore a 'remarkable resemblance' to Strachey himself (*SE*, 128). Drawing on an unpublished memoir of Eliot written by Mary Trevelyan, Lyndall Gordon noted that in the 1940s Eliot identified both Fry and Strachey as heretics, and she points out that by the late 1940s he had begun to distance himself from Desmond MacCarthy. Although there were similarities of outlook that might have made leading figures in the Bloomsbury Group congenial acquaintances – aside from their usefulness to him in penetrating the inner circle of literary London – Eliot explained to his brother Henry that most of his beliefs were anathema to the Bloomsbury Group.[14] Most significant was Eliot's religious faith, which baffled the Woolfs and made him the subject of ridicule in Bloomsbury. In 1948, Clive Bell recalled: 'Between Virginia and myself somehow the poet became a sort of "family joke"'.[15]

E. M. Forster remained throughout his life somewhat distant from Eliot. They met at Garsington in 1922 and Forster contributed a short story, 'Pan', passed on translations of the Greek poet C. P. Cavafy, and wrote an article entitled 'The Novels of Virginia Woolf' for the *Criterion*. In an essay on Eliot, published in *Life and Letters* in 1929 and reprinted several times, Forster described *The Waste Land* as a poem imbued with the horror of the First World War. Eliot acknowledged the 'horror' in a letter to Forster, but told him: 'you exaggerate the importance of the War in this context. The War crippled me as it did everyone else ... but the Waste Land might have been just the same without the War'.[16] Forster stressed Eliot's importance to the younger generation but complained of his 'love of the cryptogrammatic': 'Why, if he believes in it, can he not say it straight out and face the consequences?'[17] They joined forces against the prosecution of Radclyffe Hall's novel *The Well of Loneliness* (see Chapter 9 above), yet Forster was repelled by the emotional reserve of Eliot's doctrine of impersonality and by his 1941 obituary of Virginia Woolf in *Horizon*.[18] They had a public spat in 1930 following Forster's letter to the *Nation and Athenaeum* which described D. H. Lawrence 'straight out' as 'the greatest imaginative novelist of our time'. Many obituaries of Lawrence had been harsh in tone and Forster's letter reinforced a lauda- tory memorial written by Ottoline Morrell. The following week, Eliot wrote to the *Nation and Athenaeum* to demand an explanation of Forster's praise, in terms that are strongly reminiscent of G. E. Moore's philosophical method: 'the virtue of speaking straight out is somewhat diminished if what one speaks is not sense. And unless we know exactly what Mr Forster means by *greatest, imaginative*, and *novelist*, I submit that this judgment is meaningless.'[19] In 'My Early Beliefs', Keynes described Moore's method of asking 'What *exactly* do you mean?' as 'a kind of combat in which strength of character was really much more valuable than subtlety of mind'.[20] Forster did not rise to the bait, replying that on this occasion he was content to be a fly caught in Eliot's web.[21]

The Lawrence affair was a storm in a teacup. During the years follow- ing the Second World War, Eliot's connections with the Bloomsbury Group became tenuous to the point of vanishing. MacCarthy and Forster reviewed his plays, praising their diction but not their conception and content, and Bell continued to tell the story of how he had immediately recognised Eliot's significance as a poet. Leonard Woolf and Eliot kept up an affectionate correspondence until Eliot's death. In his autobiography, Leonard called the publication of Eliot's *Poems* 'a red letter day for the Press and for us' and expressed his pride in having published *The Waste Land*.[22] In a 1919 *Athenaeum* review of Eliot's *Poems*, Leonard had com- mented that 'Eliot is certainly damned by his newness and strangeness', adding, 'the poetry of the dead is in his bones at the tips of his fingers' (Brooker, 21–2). In addition to publishing Eliot's poetry at the Hogarth Press, Leonard also collected three of Eliot's influential *TLS* articles together in a book, *Homage to John Dryden* (1924). Not only did Leonard support Eliot as a publisher, but in the spring of 1925 he offered confidential advice on how to cope with the increasing strain of Vivien's illnesses, recommending doctors (Leonard passed on the names of doctors he had consulted about Virginia) as well as his opinion about whether Vivien should be encouraged to write or not. It seems likely that Virginia and Leonard Woolf were drawn to Eliot by the way his marriage, in some ways, hauntingly refracted aspects of their own.

By the mid 1920s Virginia had proved herself a tireless campaigner on behalf of the American émigré. She assisted Ottoline Morrell in efforts to raise money for the 'Eliot Fellowship Fund' with the aim of releasing him from his work at Lloyds Bank (eliciting in the process an hilariously sarcastic response from Lytton Strachey pledging a large sum). When the scheme came to nothing, Virginia became involved in an effort to secure Eliot a position as literary editor of the *Nation* after the journal had been bought by a consortium headed by Keynes. Woolf wrote to Keynes to say that Eliot would bring with him the enthusiasm of the younger generation. She also wrote to Strachey to ask if she could tell Keynes that Strachey – a literary celebrity – would contribute to the *Nation* were Eliot appointed as literary editor: '[Keynes's] hand would be immensely strengthened, he says, if he could say that Tom is well thought of by writers of the highest importance, like Mr Lytton Strachey'.[23] Eliot, however, wanted a guarantee that the editorship would last at least five years. Virginia asked Keynes if he could be guaranteed at least two. As it turned out, Eliot remained at the bank and Leonard Woolf became the *Nation*'s literary editor.

Virginia Woolf's efforts on behalf of Eliot, pressing the goodwill of old friends, were remarkable. From their first meeting, Eliot fascinated her. In 1919 she remarked: 'Eliot I liked on the strength of one visit & shall probably see more of, owing to his poems which we began today to set up'.[24] She was troubled by his apparent lack of interest in her own writing and she disagreed with his high estimation of Joyce, Wyndham Lewis and Pound. She recognised, too, Eliot's ardent desire to dominate literary London – 'The Underworld', as she termed it – inhabited by 'bad men' like Murry and enemies like Lewis. Eliot hurt the Woolfs by joining, without warning, the rival publisher Faber & Gwyer in 1925. Virginia reflected in her diary that Eliot 'intends to get on by the methods of that world; & my world is really not the underworld. However, there is a kind of fun in unravelling the twists & obliquities of this remarkable man'.[25] Woolf recognised Eliot as a peer with whom she could sharpen her wits, in spite of their profound disagreements. In 1921, after reading an article by Eliot in the *Chapbook*, she told Sydney Waterlow that she was 'shocked

as usual, when I read Eliot, to find out how wrong I am, and how right
he is'. Yet she was 'sure he's wrong' in admiring Edgar Allan Poe and
disliking Thomas Browne.[26] Later that year, she expressed genuine delight
when Eliot praised her short stories *Monday or Tuesday* in his 'London
Letter' for the New York *Dial* and began to feel less intimidated by him.
In 1924, Woolf sent her manifesto 'Character in Fiction' to Eliot for
publication in the *Criterion*. Eliot wrote to say that her essay expressed his
own thoughts about their generation; that they were burdened by the
necessity of forging new forms rather than building on what had preceded
them: 'I feel myself that everything I have done consists simply of
tentative sketches and rough experiments' (*L2*, 430). Virginia echoed these
sentiments in her essay 'How it Strikes a Contemporary' in *The Common
Reader* (1925) and had written in almost identical terms to Gerald Brenan
in 1922: 'nothing is going to be achieved by us. Fragments – paragraphs –
a page perhaps: but no more'.[27]

Woolf and Eliot shared a concern for distinctions between thought and
emotion and a strong sense of the continuing presence of the past,
indicating that they laboured in the same field whatever their differences.
For example, Eliot's remarks in a 1932 lecture at Harvard describing the
way a poet's mind is 'magnetised' by language, strikingly recalls the
opening pages of Woolf's *Jacob's Room*: 'There might be the experience
of a child of ten, a small boy peering through sea-water in a rock-pool,
and finding a sea-anemone for the first time: the simple experience ...
might lie dormant in his mind for twenty years, and re-appear transformed in some verse-context charged with great imaginative pressure'
(*UPUC*, 78–9). There are also significant resonances between *Four Quartets* and Woolf's posthumously published *Between the Acts* that remain
unexplored. In truth, the intimacy between Eliot and Woolf was similar
to that she shared – sometimes limited by patriarchy and misogyny – with
male members of the Bloomsbury Group. At a dinner party in 1940,
Woolf discussed with Eliot, Clive Bell and others the war's likely effect on
civilisation. She recorded in her diary: 'All the gents. against me'.[28] Later
that year, she reflected again on her difference from her male peers:

These queer little sand castles, I was thinking ... Little boys making sand castles.
This refers to H. Read; Tom Eliot; Santayana; Wells ... But I am the sea which
demolishes these castles ... man is no longer God. My position, ceasing to accept
the religion, is quite unlike Read's, Wells', Tom's, or Santayana's.[29]

Eliot's religious faith did not, as might have been expected, divide him
from Woolf or from the Bloomsbury Group at large. Virginia told

Vanessa in 1936 that she 'could have loved' Eliot had they been younger, asking her 'how necessary do you think copulation is to friendship? At what point does "love" become sexual?'[30] Their intimacy was not founded on shared beliefs; it weathered profound differences.

NOTES

1. Wyndham Lewis to Sydney Schiff, 3 October 1922, quoted in Bonnie Kime Scott, *Refiguring Modernism: The Women of 1928* (Bloomington: Indiana University Press, 1996), p. 115.
2. John Middleton Murry, 'The "Classical" Revival', *Adelphi* (March 1926), 653.
3. See Mark Hussey, 'Bloomsbury Group', in *Virginia Woolf A to Z* (Oxford University Press, 1996).
4. Quentin Bell, *Bloomsbury* (London: Weidenfeld & Nicolson, 1986), p. 12.
5. See *The Bloomsbury Group*, ed. S. P. Rosenbaum (University of Toronto Press, 1975), p. x.
6. Clive Bell, *Art* (1914) (New York: Perigee, 1981), p. 16.
7. Clive Bell, 'Wilcoxism', *Athenaeum* (5 March 1920), 311.
8. *The Letters of Wyndham Lewis*, ed. W. K. Rose (London: Methuen, 1963), pp. 117–18.
9. 'Shorter Notices', *Egoist* (June–July 1918), 87.
10. 'Books of the Quarter', *Criterion* (September 1928), 162.
11. 'Books of the Quarter', *Criterion* (April 1925), 471.
12. Charles Smyth, 'A Note on Historical Biography and Mr Strachey', *Criterion* (July 1929), 654, 660. Eliot said that his own anonymous review of *Elizabeth and Essex* in the *TLS* would have been more severe had he been writing in his own name. T. S. Eliot to Bonamy Dobrée, 11 December 1928. Brotherton Library, University of Leeds.
13. Michael Holroyd, *Lytton Strachey* (New York: Farrar, Straus & Giroux, 1994), p. 457.
14. T. S. Eliot to Henry Eliot, 1 January 1936. Houghton Library, Harvard University.
15. Clive Bell, 'How Pleasant to know Mr Eliot', *T. S. Eliot: A Symposium*, ed. Richard March and Tambimuttu (London: Editions Poetry London, 1948), p. 15.
16. Quoted in Ronald Schuchard, 'Burbank with a Baedeker, Eliot with a Cigar', *Modernism/Modernity* (January 2003), 6.
17. E. M. Forster, *Abinger Harvest* (London: Edward Arnold, 1936), p. 90.
18. Of the Woolf obituary, Forster remarked: 'I thought Eliot disgraced the human race'. E. M. Forster to William Plomer, 12 June 1941. Palace Green Library, University of Durham.
19. 'Letters', *Nation and Athenaeum* (5 April 1930), 11.
20. Quoted in Rosenbaum, ed., *Bloomsbury Group*, p. 56.

21. For an account of Eliot and Forster's relations, see P. N. Furbank 'Forster, Eliot and the Literary Life', *Twentieth-Century Literature* (summer/autumn 1985), 170–5.

22. Leonard Woolf, *An Autobiography*, vol. II (Oxford University Press, 1980), p. 175.

23. *The Letters of Virginia Woolf*, vol. III, *1923–1928*, ed. Nigel Nicolson (London: Hogarth Press, 1977), p. 14.

24. *The Diary of Virginia Woolf*, vol. I, *1915–1919*, ed. Anne Olivier Bell (London: Hogarth Press, 1977), p. 235.

25. *The Diary of Virginia Woolf*, vol. III, *1925–1930*, ed. Anne Olivier Bell with Andrew McNeillie (London: Hogarth Press, 1980), p. 41.

26. *The Letters of Virginia Woolf*, vol. II, *1911–1922*, ed. Nigel Nicolson (London: Hogarth Press, 1976), pp. 466–7.

27. Ibid., p. 598.

28. *The Diary of Virginia Woolf*, vol. V, *1936–1941*, ed. Anne Olivier Bell with Andrew McNeillie (London: Hogarth Press, 1984), p. 268.

29. Ibid., p. 340.

30. *The Letters of Virginia Woolf*, vol. VI, *1936–1941*, ed. Nigel Nicolson (London: Hogarth Press, 1980), p. 59.

CHAPTER 24

Ezra Pound

Anne Stillman

In 'Desolation Row' Bob Dylan sings:

> And everybody's shouting
> 'Which Side Are You On?'
> And Ezra Pound and T. S. Eliot
> Fighting in the captain's tower
> While calypso singers laugh at them
> And fisherman hold flowers
> Between the windows of the sea
> Where lovely mermaids flow
> And nobody has to think too much
> About Desolation Row[1]

Ezra Pound and T. S. Eliot turn up in a line where 'and' is sent in two syntactical directions: 'And Ezra Pound and T. S. Eliot'. Eliot's early poem 'Opera' begins with 'Tristan and Isolde / And the fatalistic horns' (*IMH*, 17), swerving from fusing two selves to point out structural distinctions. In Dylan's song the first 'and' spotlights how the next conjunction works differently, linking Pound and Eliot in an intimately antagonistic double act. The tuneful pairing of their names, like Bonnie and Clyde, Laurel and Hardy, Tristan and Isolde, might prompt us to wonder about the nature of the 'and' in pairs so famous, seeming to join two persons, elusively, as one. Our habituation to the cadences of pairing (after all, why not Clyde and Bonnie or Cleopatra and Antony?), registers how we become culturally accustomed to the sound of a composite identity, hailing from two persons but not exactly belonging to either of them. In the second act of Wagner's opera *Tristan und Isolde*, Isolde sings: 'How else could this small word "and" be destroyed but with Isolde's life?'[2] 'And' is the note of their togetherness, but they are still distinct, unlike Dr Jekyll and Mr Hyde.

Pairing of names can conjure atmospheres evoking both personation and indistinct identities, like 'Elizabeth and Leicester' (*CPP*, 70) in *The*

Waste Land, or 'Ben and la Clara' in Pound's *Pisan Cantos*, where the cross-contact of name with name sketches the notional possibility of a miniature scene.[3] Dylan's lines conjure a version of what Eliot found in Henry James, the 'curious precipitates and explosive gases which are suddenly formed by the contact of mind with mind'.[4] (And T. S. Eliot alone in the captain's tower would not be the same.) It is hard not to hear in the lines that follow a mock-composite of the 'mermaids singing' and 'chambers of the sea' (*CPP*, 16, 17) of 'The Love Song of J. Alfred Prufrock' with the 'window / with the sea beyond'[5] from *The Pisan Cantos*, and Pound's 'fishermen picnicking in the sun'[6] with the 'whining of a mandoline / . . . Where fishmen lounge at noon' (*CPP*, 69) from *The Waste Land*. Dylan's sinking pastoral shows the calypso singers laughing at Pound and Eliot, but part of what may be funny is that 'calypso' conjures up both Odysseus' sea voyage as it appears in Pound's *Cantos* and a style of Caribbean music, so this cameo appears something like *The Waste Land*'s 'Shakespeherian Rag' (*CPP*, 65). As one art talks or perhaps fights with another in this song, Dylan's lyrics incite an imaginative reach, showing us how registering the relations between creations involves listening in for echoes, impersonations and static, the textures of affiliation and development that make up a shared creative atmosphere and are present when the small word 'and' is placed between one artist and another.

Pairings raise searching questions about the penumbral edges of a self, but the sketch of Pound and Eliot in Dylan's song focuses some reasons for making an analogy between their collaboration and friendship and the creation of double acts and the creations made by double acts. The present volume intends to situate Eliot 'in context'. But what kind of 'context' is the impact of one person on another? We describe meeting someone 'out of context', or we situate sentences in different contexts to illustrate possible meanings, but if the interrelations between Pound and Eliot are described as a 'context', then the word is standing in for many situations with ragged edges. Documents record part of the history of their connection, but as Eliot writes, 'I cannot say what Pound's critical writing will mean to those who have not known the man, because to me it is inextricably woven with his conversation'[7] – and comic quick turns, gestural sympathies, flirtatious antagonisms are all ephemeral aspects of people talking. Imagining Pound and Eliot as a double act retains at least some of the playfulness of personal encounter depicted in Eliot's 1917 sketch of their conversation in 'Eeldrop and Appleplex': 'Both were endeavouring to escape not the commonplace, respectable, or even domestic, but the too well pigeonholed, too taken-for-granted, too highly systematized areas, and, – in the language of those whom they sought to avoid – they wished "to apprehend the human soul in its concrete individuality" ' (*E&A*, 2). In the spirit of 'Eeldrop and Appleplex', one way to misapprehend the individual nature of the relations between Pound and Eliot would be to present a highly systematised account: their relation, like many relations, resists easy classification. But it may be possible to listen in for several concrete particulars and apprehend Pound and Eliot as different individuals with singularity in common, while also recognising that by putting their names together in a book about contexts, you may well be speaking in the language of those whom Eeldrop and Appleplex sought to avoid.

The question 'What would Eliot be without Pound?' is whimsical and has no answer, but the speculation brings into focus the mutuality and contingency which Eliot stresses in his depiction of literary influence as analogous to 'personal intimacies in life': a 'cause of development' that 'may and probably will pass', but which 'will be ineffaceable'. For Eliot, literary influence is like love, leaving traces written in a curious kind of ink, indelible and invisible, sometimes rough and ready: 'the "influence" of James hardly matters, to be influenced by a writer is to have a chance inspiration from him; or to take what one wants; or to see things one has overlooked'.[8] Eliot perceived, not the influence of Hawthorne on Henry James, but the Hawthorne aspect of James. 'Aspect' allows for a semblance as vivid and as apparitional as the countenance of a face, suggesting how similarities between writers, like family resemblances between persons, are suddenly caught, then gone. Eliot writes of Pound: 'I avoid the word *influence*, for there are dangers in estimating a poet by his influence. It takes at least two to make an influence: the man who exerts it and the man who experiences it.'[9] The comic sidestep implies it takes (at least) two to tango while also imagining a serious creative reciprocity, where, like a double act, two persons may be at once clearly individuated and, at the same time, it can be hard to tell where one ends and the other begins.

Classic comic double acts contrast the personages of the poker-faced 'straight man' and the 'funny man'; although the roles can be interchangeable (it's not always the funny man who gets the laughs). Pound and Eliot self-consciously play up to this kind of dynamic with the forms of caricature they devise for each other. In 1922, Pound styled Eliot as 'Possum' – an animal playing dead – with emphatic mischief: '*supposed* to be PLAYIN' POSSUM' (*L1*, 772). The joke was more cutting in

1930: 'Mr Eliot is at times an excellent poet and who has arrived at the supreme Eminence among English critics largely through disguising himself as a corpse'.[10] Eliot coolly depicted Pound as furiously alive: 'He would cajole, and almost coerce, other men into writing well: so that he often presents the appearance of a man trying to convey to a very deaf person the fact that the house is on fire';[11] or, 'every room, even a big one, seemed too small for him'.[12] Eeldrop and Appleplex, like Eliot and Pound, are what Pound called an 'excellent pair of pincers':[13] Appleplex has 'the gift of extraordinary address', while Eeldrop 'preserved a more passive demeanour'; Appleplex industriously files the results of his inquiry 'from A (adultery) to Y (yeggmen)' as 'Eeldrop smoked reflectively' (*E&A*, 1–2); although it is often Appleplex who is the comic stooge:

> 'The artistic temperament –' began Appleplex.
> 'No, not that.' Eeldrop snatched away the opportunity.   (*E&A*, 9)

Like other creatively fertile relationships, it is hard to say whether these persons make the performance or the performance makes these persons. In their initial depictions of each other, when they first met in 1914, Pound comes across as the energetic campaigner Eliot later praised him for being: 'Prufrock is the best poem I have yet seen or had from an American ... [Eliot has] modernized himself on *his own*'.[14] Eliot is laconic, cautious: 'Pound is rather intelligent as a talker: his verse is well-meaning but touchingly incompetent; but his remarks are sometimes good' (*L1*, 63); 'he is not the sort of person whom I wish to be intimate with my affairs ... [he] has been and will be useful; but my acquaintance with him is primarily professional' (*L1*, 128). But there is nothing surprising about correspondence sounding different for different people about different people. A complex ventriloquism is mutually cultivated between the poet who ends a poem in 1925 '*Not with a bang but a whimper*' (*CPP*, 86) and the poet who says in the first Pisan canto, 'yet say this to the Possum: a bang, not a whimper'.[15] Cross-talk like this incorporates caricature, but also goes beyond any basic opposition. It should be hard to read the countenance on the face that turns back to see itself with and in others in the final section of *Four Quartets*: 'See, they return, and bring us with them' (*CPP*, 197). Half reaching for Pound's 1912 poem 'The Return', the allusion might speak to, of, or with a soul of blood from that poem, combining recognition, disappointment, perhaps loving admonishment; or, it may just be imagining faces and poems that are not there, rather as the dedication of *The Waste Land* – 'For Ezra Pound / *il miglior fabbro*' ['the better craftsman'] (*CPP*, 59) – is potentially double-edged:

the allusion to both Dante and Pound's *The Spirit of Romance* is a tribute printed sedately at the opening of the poem, and, at the same time, it is a comically disembodied ventriloquism of Dante's phrase to Arnaut Daniel, first handwritten in pen in a presentation copy, and now teasing us into imagining how the impersonated roles could be tinged with gratitude and competition, or perhaps all that's left of a shared, impromptu joke.

To portray Pound as emphatic, boldly impolitic, and Eliot as tentative, cautious, politic, would be to miss the shared scepticism of 'Eeldrop and Appleplex': 'Eeldrop was a sceptic, with a taste for mysticism, and Appleplex a materialist with a leaning toward scepticism' (*E&A*, 2). Pound's critique of *After Strange Gods* (1934) is shrewdly sceptical about Eliot's own excesses.[16] Eliot is 'doubtful about some of the *Cantos*', but this scepticism does not lessen the emphatic warmth of his praise: 'There is nobody living who can write like this: how many can be named, who can write half so well?'[17] The same person who makes the invective of cantos XIV and XV containing, among others, 'Profiteers drinking blood sweetened with sh-t'[18] is the person who ingenuously suggested the nightingales' 'droppings' (*IMH*, 381) at the end of 'Sweeney Among the Nightingales' be turned into 'siftings' (*CPP*, 57) and who can hear in the early draft of 'The Fire Sermon' that this is 'verse not interesting enough as verse to warrant so much of it', crossing out the lines 'And at the corner where the stable is, / Delays only to urinate, and spit', pencilling in the margin 'probaly [*sic*] over the mark' (*WLF*, 45–7).

In one of his first letters to Pound, Eliot writes: 'The closer one keeps to the Artist's discussion of his technique the better, I think, and the only kind of art worth talking about is the art one happens to like. There can be no contemplative or easychair aesthetics, I think; only the aesthetics of the person who is about to do something' (*L1*, 94). This is an early instance of a shared and lasting emphasis on workmanship and technique. In 1946, Eliot singled out as the 'most important principle of Pound's criticism' an explicit delineation of the relation between theory and practice: 'the man who formulates any forward reach of co-ordinating principle is the man who produces the demonstration'.[19] Merely saying that technique is important risks settling into its own easy chair, but their collaboration is a living demonstration of these principles, and this letter is its beginning. It ends, from a 'person who is about to do something':

Sincerely yours Thomas S. Eliot

I enclose one small verse. I know it is not good, but everything else I have done is worse. Besides, I am constipated and have a cold on the chest. Burn it. (*L1*, 94)

The postscript may be throwaway; still, 'Burn it' signals the inception of an exchange which seems, retrospectively, present in this early letter, not just because Eliot's willingness to put one small verse in Pound's hands seems to anticipate how he will, in some respects, put himself in Pound's hands, but also because, in the deadpan glumness, there is the possibility of rapport, as if the letter hears the comic potential, given the right listener, of self-dramatising your own self-deprecation and still being genuinely self-sceptical.

Eliot applauded Pound for giving practical advice and learned from him how to give it: 'Technique ... can only be learned, the more difficult parts of it, by absorption. Try to put into a sequence of simple quatrains the continuous syntactic variety of Gautier or Blake, or compare these two with A. E. Housman.'[20] The instruction to 'try' a verse experiment sounds like Pound and glances towards his suggestion in 1917 to read Théophile Gautier's *Émaux et Camées*, which prompted 'Hugh Selwyn Mauberley' and Eliot's quatrain poems: 'We studied Gautier's poems and then we thought, "Have I anything to say in which this form will be useful?" And we experimented. The form gave impetus to the content.'[21] Observing the family resemblances across these works is itself an instructive experiment. Compare 'Hugh Selwyn Mauberley' and 'Burbank with a Baedeker: Bleistein with a Cigar':

> 'Daphne with her thighs in bark
> Stretches toward me her leafy hands,' –
> Subjectively. In the stuffed-satin drawing-room
> I await The Lady Valentine's commands[22]
>
> Defunctive music under sea
>   Passed seaward with the passing bell
> Slowly: the God Hercules
>   Had left him, that had loved him well.   (*CPP*, 40)

As if plotted by the same choreographer, but performed by distinct bodies, the similar rhythmic pratfalls light up wider differences across the poems, such as Pound's fondness for slightly off-kilter rhymes against Eliot's adherence to the measure. Eliot's flickering reference to *Antony and Cleopatra* points to another lifelong distinction between them emphasised in Donald Gallup's account of their collaboration, which contrasts Pound in 1923 – 'I (personally) believe that "the theatre" in general is no good, that plays are no good ... Most plays are bad, even Greek plays' – with Eliot in 1933 – 'The ideal medium for poetry ... and the most direct means of social "usefulness" for poetry, is the theatre'.[23] The divergence

suggests a different sense of the word 'useful' to the 'usefulness' of
Gautier's quatrains. But when Eliot notes how Pound 'ignores consideration of dramatic verse', he describes this as 'a deliberate limitation' and
says this is precisely what gives Pound 'a wider range'.[24]

In 1946, Eliot wrote:

(It was in 1922 that I placed before him in Paris the manuscript of a sprawling,
chaotic poem called *The Waste Land* which left his hands, reduced to about half
its size, in the form in which it appears in print. I should like to think that the
manuscript, with the suppressed passages, had disappeared irrevocably: yet on the
other hand, I should wish the blue pencilling on it to be preserved as irrefutable
evidence of Pound's critical genius.)[25]

The brackets may seem coy, tantalising an audience with what Pound
later caricatured as '"The mystery of the missing manuscript"' which is
'pure Henry James' (*WLF*, vi), but in taking a parenthetical shape, Eliot
perhaps wishes to stress and to mute a genuine ambivalence concerning
the decisions and revisions of drafting, and does so in a stage whisper,
drawing us in to notice the special compositional history of this poem.
The title page of the published facsimile of *The Waste Land* drafts quotes
Pound pronouncing this mystery as 'solved', but the history of their
collaboration should be seen as retaining the mysterious, because it is
bound up with the rapport between two persons, a shared breath that can
seem both very fully and only partially documented by their correspondence and the surviving manuscripts. During the composition of *The Waste
Land* their exchanges witness the caricature of Pound as an energising life
force to 'Possum':

Caro mio:
MUCH improved. [. . .] The thing now runs from April . . . to shantih without
[a] break. That is 19 pages, and let us say the longest poem in the Englisch
langwidge. Don't try to bust all records by prolonging it three pages further. [. . .]
   Complimenti, you bitch. I am wracked by the seven jealousies, and cogitating
an excuse for always exuding my deformative secretions in my own stuff, and
never getting an outline. (*L1*, 625–6)

'Complimenti appreciated, as have been excessively depressed', Eliot
replied. His letter is made up mostly of questions: '1. Do you advise
printing Gerontion as prelude in book or pamphlet form? 2. Perhaps
better omit Phlebas also???' (*L1*, 629). 'Perhaps' neatly sketches a distinction between them: Eliot frequently gravitates to a hypothetical contingency ('Time present and time past / Are both perhaps present in time
future' [*CPP*, 171]). 'Perhaps be damned' (*WLF*, 45) is one of Pound's

memorable annotations on the drafts of 'The Fire Sermon'. But then it is
Pound who can help Eliot to hear the force of the rhythmic understate-
ment: 'Jug Jug, into the dirty ear of death; lust' (*WLF*, 11) is clipped to
'"Jug Jug" to dirty ears' (*CPP*, 64), an exciting short line to end a long
sentence, which perhaps suggests something dirty, but certainly doesn't
say that death has a dirty ear.

Together with Pound, Eliot made changes to 'A Game of Chess':

> where staring forms
> Leaned out, and hushed the room and closed it in.
> There were footsteps on the stair,
> Under the firelight, under the brush, her hair
> Spread out in little fiery points of will,
> Glowed into words, then would be savagely still.   (*WLF*, 11)

> staring forms
> Leaned out, leaning, hushing the room enclosed.
> Footsteps shuffled on the stair.
> Under the firelight, under the brush, her hair
> Spread out in fiery points
> Glowed into words, then would be savagely still.   (*CPP*, 64–5)

Pound may not pay much critical attention to the nature of the dramatic,
but by crossing out 'in' and both 'and's in one line, he prompts Eliot to
make changes that render the verse more dramatic, altering the passage
from a redescription locked in a narrative past towards the conditional
future: 'would be savagely still'. Replacing 'closed it in' with 'enclosed',
eerily hovering somewhere between an adjective and a verb, creates a
change of tense, suggesting a double take, sensation both experienced and
attended. Pound crossed out 'little' and 'will', writing beside these lines:
'dogmatic deduction but wobbly as well' (*WLF*, 11). The will/still rhyme
might be thought 'dogmatic' by deducing that the fire is metaphorically
within the person, ending the section with the pat conclusiveness of a
fulfilled predication, whereas the revision concisely smudges any such
firm psychological location: the fire may be within the person, or around
her, and where the person ends or begins is hard to say.

These instances show why Eliot depicts Pound's gift as a critic as related
to a vital aspect of the dramatic: being an audience, listening in on a voice,
while guarding against the temptation to rewrite it as you would. Eliot
describes this task as 'maieutic'.[26] The etymology is from the Greek, the
word is used figuratively by Socrates 'to act as midwife' and is defined by
the *OED* as 'relating to or designating the Socratic process, or other

similar method, of assisting a person to become fully conscious of ideas previously latent in the mind'. The definition outlines an ambiguous object of knowledge: if something is drawn out, was it there to begin with? To say 'I didn't realise I was thinking that until you showed me' is an ordinary experience, but it houses the metaphysical intricacies of shared minds and words. Collaborative drafts provide an intriguing record of this practice. Consider the changes Pound and Eliot made to these lines:

> She turns and looks a moment in the glass,
> Hardly aware of her departed lover;
> Across her brain one half-formed thought may pass:
> 'Well now that's done, and I am glad it's over'.   (*WLF*, 35)

> She turns and looks a moment in the glass,
> Hardly aware of her departed lover;
> Her brain allows one half-formed thought to pass:
> 'Well now that's done: and I'm glad it's over.'   (*CPP*, 69)

Pound crossed out 'may' – pencilling beside it 'make up yr. mind' (*WLF*, 47) – and, in another draft, changed 'I am' to 'I'm', inserting a dash after 'done' instead of a comma (*WLF*, 35). Eliot wrote in the changes, placing a colon after 'done'. In the first draft, 'may' has the uncertainty of 'perhaps a half-formed thought passes', more mealy-mouthed than concisely sceptical, especially as it sits awkwardly beside the stress in the next line, 'and I àm glad its over' (my emphasis), which risks sounding glibly histrionic, a self-congratulatory self-pity lacking the quick but piteous catch in the person's voice heard in the published version, which briskly and uniquely recognises this situation to be not all that unique. Pound prompted Eliot to overhear his own voice and listen for the voice he was trying to hear. The revised version is both more emphatic (her brain does do this) and more gently tentative, etching the chimerically half-formed in scripted pauses and elisions which sound spoken while retaining the ambiguity as to whether they are spoken aloud. This dialogue between Pound and Eliot shows what it might mean to become 'fully conscious' of that which was 'previously latent', and traces of this cognitive mystery are left across lines which themselves depict the dawning of a thought that is 'half-formed'.

The alteration from 'I am' to 'I'm' speaks of a connection between Pound and Eliot, arising from the rapport of two voices in sympathy to the extent that they can move freely between making jokes about sex and discussing possible alterations of syntax, a freedom that is not uncommon in Pound's letters to many people, but is unusual in

Eliot's letters: 'Sincerely yours Thomas S. Eliot' becomes 'Good fucking, brother. [unsigned]' (*L1*, 709). One running joke they share 'on each Occasion / Ezra performed the caesarean Operation' (*L1*, 626) registers collaboration to be creatively erotic, but what is more surprising is that they seriously considered publishing these squibs beside *The Waste Land*. 'Wish to use caesarean operation in italics in front' Eliot wrote (*L1*, 629), but Pound advised not to use them since they would hit the wrong note. The letters from this time show Pound and Eliot doing the poets in different voices for each other. This aspect of the compositional history of the poem meets with the allusion to Charles Dickens's *Our Mutual Friend* in Eliot's working title for the poem 'He Do the Police in Different Voices': '"You mightn't think it, but Sloppy is a beautiful reader of a newspaper. He do the Police in different voices"' (*WLF*, 125). Impersonation is an ordinary trick that is easy to enjoy but trickier to describe. Doing different voices can be entertaining or sinister, a way of disguising yourself or showing off; there are many possible feedback effects contained within the simple truth that a beautiful reader is made by an attentive listener; what we have in the letters of Pound and Eliot, as in the manuscript revisions of *The Waste Land*, is evidence that sharing a joke is not an adjunct to creativity but part of its fabric.

The 'and' connecting their names around the composition of *The Waste Land* can be imagined as fading ineffaceably, with something like the caprice and tenacity of personal intimacy: 'People change, and smile: but the agony abides' (*CPP*, 187). Pound's obituary note for Eliot in 1965 returns force and elusiveness to this conjunction with an acoustic playfulness acting the part, again, of the tireless campaigner '*for* T. S. E.', while, also, quietly, saying how death disfigures companionship, even if you cajole, or almost coerce, another person to come back, once he's gone:

Who is there now for me to share a joke with? Am I to write 'about' the poet Thomas Stearns Eliot? or my friend 'the Possum?' Let him rest in peace. I can only repeat, but with the urgency of 50 years ago: READ HIM.[27]

NOTES

1. 'Desolation Row', *Highway 61 Revisited* (New York: Columbia Records, 1965).
2. 'Doch dieses Wörtlein: *und,* / wär es zerstört, / wie anders als / mit Isoldes eignem Leben', *Tristan und Isolde*, ed. Nicholas John (London: John Calder, 1981), p. 73.

3. *The Cantos of Ezra Pound* (London: Faber & Faber, 1986), p. 439.
4. 'In Memory of Henry James', *Egoist* (January 1918), 2.
5. *Cantos of Pound*, p. 458.
6. Ezra Pound, 'Salutation', *Personae* (London: Faber & Faber, 2001), p. 86.
7. 'Ezra Pound', *Poetry* (September 1946), 331.
8. 'In Memory of Henry James', 1.
9. 'Ezra Pound', 336–7.
10. Ezra Pound, *Selected Prose 1909–1965*, ed. William Cookson (London: Faber & Faber, 1978), p. 53.
11. 'Introduction', *The Literary Essays of Ezra Pound* (London: Faber & Faber, 1954), p. xii.
12. 'Ezra Pound', 327.
13. Quoted in Donald Gallup, 'T. S. Eliot and Ezra Pound: Collaborators in Letters', *Atlantic Monthly* (January 1970), 52.
14. *Selected Letters of Ezra Pound 1907–1941*, ed. D. D. Paige (London: Faber & Faber, 1950), p. 80.
15. *Cantos of Pound*, p. 439.
16. For an account of Pound's critique, see Christina Stough 'The Skirmish of Pound and Eliot in *The New English Weekly*', *Journal of Modern Literature* (1983), 231–46.
17. 'Ezra Pound', 335–6.
18. *Cantos of Pound*, p. 61.
19. 'Ezra Pound', 333.
20. 'Professional, or . . .', *Egoist* (April 1918), 61.
21. 'T. S. Eliot Speaks', *Poetry Review* (October/December 1960), 209.
22. *Personae*, p. 193.
23. Gallup, 'T. S. Eliot and Ezra Pound: Collaborators in Letters', 55.
24. 'Introduction', p. xiii.
25. 'Ezra Pound', 330.
26. Ibid., 335.
27. Pound, *Selected Prose 1909–1965*, p. 434.

CHAPTER 25

The avant-garde

Marjorie Perloff

In October 1915, four months after Eliot's precipitous wedding to Vivien Haigh-Wood in a London registry office, Bertrand Russell wrote to the poet's mother, evidently trying to allay her fears about Eliot's marriage and career prospects:

> I have taken some pains to get to know his wife, who seems to me thoroughly nice, really anxious for his welfare ... The chief sign of her influence that I have seen is that he is no longer attracted by the people who call themselves 'vorticists', and in that I think her influence is wholly to be applauded. (*L1*, 129–30)

Russell's remark was more prescient than he could have known: the year 1915 did prove to be a turning point in Eliot's outlook on poetry and poetics. The 'vorticists' to whom Russell alludes were members of a short-lived avant-garde group of poets and visual artists, led by Wyndham Lewis and Ezra Pound: the latter coined the term 'vortex' as the 'point of maximum energy, the radiant node or cluster ... from which, and through which, and into which, ideas are constantly rushing'.[1] The Vorticist painters fused Cubist geometry with a Futurist emphasis on bodies and machines in motion: in the first issue of Lewis's *Blast* (July 1914), a 12-inch by 9-inch periodical whose texts were printed in oversize bold black type and bound in bright puce-coloured wrappers, England is 'blasted' for its allegiance to a stultified Victorian past, not to mention the country's cursed climate and other evils. *Blast* 1 contains Pound's 'Salutation the Third' ('Let us deride the smugness of the "Times": GUFFAW! ...'), Lewis's Futurist-inspired abstract painting *Portrait of an Englishwoman* and Henri Gaudier-Brzeska's elegantly curved, semi-abstract stone *Stags*.

Within two months of publication, the war intervened; indeed, the second number of *Blast* (July 1915) carried, under the headline 'MORT POUR LA PATRIE', the brief announcement of Gaudier-Brzeska's death, 'killed in a charge at Neuville St Vaast'. The sculptor was aged 23: his death came just a month after Eliot received the news of another friend 'mort pour la patrie', this time the French medical student Jean Verdenal, killed in action at Gallipoli. Ironically, the Eliot poems published in *Blast* 2 – 'Preludes' and 'Rhapsody on a Windy Night' – date from the poet's year in Paris, 1910/11, when he made the acquaintance of Verdenal at the Pension Casaubon on the rue St Jacques. The arrangement to publish these poems in *Blast*, evidently at Pound's behest, had been made before Eliot received word of Verdenal's death: in April he wrote to Isabella Stewart Gardner in Boston that the second number of 'a certain infamous soi-disant quarterly called *Blast*' will 'contain a few things of my own' that might 'amuse you' (*L1*, 102). The reference is made casually, but in fact the *Blast* publication of four 'Preludes' and 'Rhapsody' marks Eliot's first appearance in print in England, indeed his first appearance in print anywhere other than the *Harvard Advocate*, where seven of his short early poems had appeared between 1907 and 1910.[2]

'Preludes' and 'Rhapsody' – lyrics whose graphic urban imagery carries strong emotional resonance – have little in common with the vituperative scorn, hyperbole and exuberance of Vorticist Lewis and Pound, much less with the hard-edge black and white abstract art of Christopher Nevinson or Edward Wadsworth. Indeed, Eliot's link to Vorticism and its Cubist-Futurist antecedents was largely negative: he adamantly opposed, as did Lewis and Pound, the poetry of the Edwardian establishment and its American counterpart. Again and again, in his later prose, Eliot recalls how hard it was to be a poet in the first decade of the twentieth century, given 'the absence of any masters in the previous generation whose work one could carry on' (*IMH*, 387). 'The young American poets, who came to London about that time [1910]', Eliot remarks, 'had left a country in which the status of poetry had fallen still lower than in England' (*IMH*, 388). Indeed, in 1946 Eliot explained:

Whatever may have been the literary scene in America between the beginning of the century and the year 1914, it remains in my mind a complete blank. *I cannot remember the name of a single poet of that period whose work I read*: it was only in 1915, after I came to England, that I heard the name of Robert Frost. Undergraduates at Harvard in my time read the English poets of the '90s who were dead: that was as near as we could get to any living tradition. Certainly I cannot remember any English poet then alive who contributed to my own education. Yeats was well-known, of course; but to me, at least, Yeats did not appear, until after 1917, to be anything but a minor survivor of the '90s . . . The only recourse was to poetry of another age and to *poetry of another language*. (emphasis added)[3]

That language, of course, was French and the poetry in question is usually taken to be that of Jules Laforgue and Tristan Corbière, poets

Eliot himself regularly cites as having provided the initial impetus for his early poetry (see Chapter 21 above). The link has been well documented, as has Eliot's attendance, during his Paris period, at Henri Bergson's weekly philosophical lectures and his acquaintance with the writers Alain-Fournier and Jacques Rivière (see Chapter 3 above). Thus, when Eliot settled in London – or so the usual narrative has it – the newly forged relationship with the Imagist and Vorticist groups activated the French connection and led to Eliot's first contacts with such 'advanced' little magazines as Harriet Monroe's *Poetry*, Dora Marsden's *Egoist* and *Blast*. Pound, to whom *The Waste Land* was to be dedicated, acted as go-between.

Certainly, it was through Pound's ministry that the young Eliot came to find at least a simulacrum of Paris excitement in the London literary world. 'I have just been to a cubist tea', he writes to his cousin Eleanor Hinkley in January 1915. 'There were two cubist painters, a futurist novelist, a vorticist poet and his wife, a cubist lady black-and-white artist, another cubist lady, and a retired army officer who has been living in the east end and studying Japanese ... We discussed poetry, art, religion, and the war, all in quite an intelligent way, I thought' (*L1*, 84). Grateful to Pound for his support, Eliot tries to share his friend's interests, but his scepticism comes through:

I have been reading some of your work lately. I enjoyed the article on the Vortex (please tell me who Kandinsky is). I distrust and detest Aesthetics when it cuts loose from the Object, and vapours in the void, but you have not done that. The closer one keeps to the Artist's discussion of his technique the better ... There can be no contemplative or easychair aesthetics, I think; only the aesthetics of the person who is about to do something. (*L1*, 94)

This is a revealing statement about Eliot's relation to the programmatic *isms* of the pre-war avant-garde. For all his sophisticated chatter about Cubist teas and Futurist novels, Eliot knew nothing of the Russian painter and writer on art Wassily Kandinsky, much less of the German Expressionists or the Russian Futurists, then at a high point of activity, culminating in Kasimir Malevich's *0–10* exhibition in St Petersburg, which featured the famed *Black Square*. There is no mention of the scandal of Marcel Duchamp's *Nude Descending a Staircase* (1912), or the New York Armory Show of 1913. When, in April, Pound sends Eliot his first Vorticist manifesto, the latter objects, 'I think that a thing of [this] sort has to be written by one man, and cannot be made up like an Appropriation Bill to please the congressman from Louisiana and Dakotah' (*L1*, 103).

So much for what the founder of Italian Futurism, F. T. Marinetti, called 'l'arte di far manifesti', the art of making manifestos.

Indeed, if Eliot's brief and tenuous association with Vorticism were his only link to the avant-garde, that connection would hardly be worth mentioning. By the time of his marriage, as Russell noted, Eliot was becoming bored with Vorticism. Charlotte Eliot must have been relieved. 'I cannot read Pound', she wrote to Russell: 'His articles seem over-strained, unnatural. As for the *Blast*, Mr Eliot [Henry Ware, the poet's father] remarked when he saw a copy he did not know there were enough lunatics in the world to support such a magazine' (*LI*, 144). The irony in this situation is that, even as Eliot was pulling away from the world of Futurist/Vorticist manifestos and Poundian claims to 'make it new', he had already produced during his Paris year his own avant-garde poems – poems actually much more 'advanced' than Pound's early dramatic monologues and short Imagist lyrics. But Eliot's radicalism went largely unnoticed because there was nothing programmatic about his new poetic, and he was never a member of a group or purveyor of an *ism*.

Recalling this crucial year half a century later, Eliot said: 'I had at that time the idea of giving up English and trying to settle down and scrape along in Paris and gradually write French.'[4] No doubt, Paris marked an escape from the Puritanism of his St Louis and New England childhood (see Chapters 1 and 2 above). 'I cannot bear', his mother told him shortly before his departure, 'to think of you being alone in Paris ... I do not admire the French nation, and have less confidence in individuals of that race than in English' (*LI*, 12). Eliot obviously felt otherwise. His letters to his cousin Eleanor Hinkley are exuberant about the Paris spring, and he was evidently savouring Paris street life, theatres, outdoor festivals, with his new close friend Jean Verdenal. Most important, the new freedom provided new possibilities for the poetic enterprise. Consider what was actually being published in Britain and the United States in 1910. In London, a much admired poet was the Poet Laureate, William Watson:

> You in high places: you that drive the steeds
> Of Empire; you that say unto your hosts,
> 'Go thither', and they go; and from our coasts
> Bid sail the squadrons, and they sail, their deeds
> Shaking the world ...[5]

Generalising statement, stock phrase ('the steeds / Of Empire'), rhyming iambic pentameter stanzas, second-person address: this was the popular poetry of imperialism. Its more intimate counterpart, in 'genteel tradition' America, was a poem like Sara Teasdale's 'Central Park at Dusk':

> Buildings above the leafless trees
>   Loom high as castles in a dream,
> While one by one the lamps come out
>   To thread the twilight with a gleam.
>
> There is no sign of leaf or bud,
>   A hush is over everything –
> Silent as women wait for love,
>   The world is waiting for the spring.

Again, sing-song metre and rhyme structure ('dream' / 'gleam'; 'everything' / 'spring'); more importantly, a recycling of a familiar poetic diction that allowed for no deviation: lamps, predictably enough, 'thread the twilight with a gleam'. And even the most distinguished American poet of 1910, Edward Arlington Robinson, couched his ironies in conventionalised Pre-Raphaelite imagery and flowing tetrameter rhyming stanzas, as in 'For a Dead Lady':

> No more with overflowing light
> Shall fill the eyes that now are faded,
> Nor shall another's fringe with night
> Their woman-hidden world as they did.
>
> No more shall quiver down the days
> The flowing wonder of her ways,
> Whereof no language may requite
> The shifting and the many shaded.

Inversions ('No more shall'), archaisms ('Whereof'), vague description ('The flowing wonder of her ways'): these, it seems, were the staple of what was called 'poetry' in 1910. Even Pound's poems of this time resort, more often than not, to an archaic poetic diction.

Imagine what it must have been like, in this poetic environment, to come across a so-called 'Love Song' that begins:

> Let us go then, you and I,
> When the evening is spread out against the sky
> Like a patient etherised upon a table;
> Let us go, through certain half-deserted streets,
> The muttering retreats
> Of restless nights in one-night cheap hotels
> And sawdust restaurants with oyster shells ...   (*CPP*, 12)

The word 'avant-garde' is a military term: it refers to the front flank of the army, the daring foot soldiers that pave the way for the rest of the troops that follow. According to this definition, what anglophone poet is more avant-garde than the Eliot of 'The Love Song of J. Alfred Prufrock'? In France, it is true, Eliot had the example, not only of Laforgue and Corbière, but also of a much greater poet, Stéphane Mallarmé, whose lyric poetry and great visual experiment *Un Coup de dés* still look radical today. But Mallarmé made no attempt to be accessible to a wide audience, whereas the breakthrough of 'Prufrock' was – and remains – that it allows for colloquialism and popular culture as well as complex figures of speech and recondite allusion. The sound structure, moreover, enacts the poem's meaning. Take that opening line:

> Lét ûs gó then | yóu ând Í

where the seven monosyllables, each one demanding at least some degree of stress and with a caesura after 'then', create a note of torpor, an inability to move, that is further accented by its pairing, via rhyme, with a second line, this time eleven syllables long and carrying at least six primary stresses –

> Whên the évenîng is spréad oút agaínst the ský

the line dragging along in a catatonic torpor that extends into the third line, which is even longer (twelve syllables) and markedly ungainly, what with the awkward shift from falling to rising rhythm in the second half:

> Líke a pátient étherísed upón a táble

These delicate adjustments are not ones that Eliot could have derived from Laforgue, if for no other reason than French prosody, dependent as it is on quantity rather than stress, cannot produce such pronounced shifts in intensity and pitch. Note, for example, the way the fifth line – 'The muttering retreats' – provides an echo, as in a dark passageway, of the preceding representation of the 'half-deserted streets', an echo, incidentally, visual as well as aural, the fifth line providing a short response to its rhyming partner. And now the poem shifts ground and moves into a rhyming iambic pentameter couplet, whose dominant consonants are *s* (used twelve times) and *t* (used eight times), used in the most various combinations:

> Of res*t*less nigh*ts* in one-nigh*t* cheap ho*t*el*s*
> And *s*awdu*st* res*t*auran*ts* with oys*t*er *s*hells   (*CPP*, 12)

In this couplet not a single word could be altered: if, say, 'restless nights' were to be replaced by 'troubled evenings', the aural effect of these stunningly graphic lines would be wholly lost.

And this applies not only to aural effect but to semantic density. Gustave Flaubert's advocacy of *le mot juste* is the operative principle – a strong counterweight to such references as 'the flowing wonder of her ways'. Eliot's avant-garde invention – an invention that went much further than the precepts of Imagism or Futurism – was that the new poetry of the twentieth century, written on the typewriter to be both seen and heard, must pay attention to each and every word in a given poem. The oyster is an aphrodisiac; hence in Prufrock's etherised world there are only oyster *shells*; or again, 'rest' in the fifth line – with its pun on 'remainder' – finds an echo in the first syllable of '*rest*aurants' – an echo measuring the meaningless vacuum of Prufrock's daily round. And the 'sawdust' sets the stage for the 'soot that falls from chimneys' and the 'yellow smoke that slides along the street' (*CPP*, 13) in the second verse paragraph. Everything in this poem relates to everything else, even as the identity of the mono-logue's speaker is so fluid and evasive that it spills over into the external world, denying all demarcation between self and other. Indeed, the inde-terminate pronouns – 'is', 'you', 'I' – coupled with the poem's abrupt tense and mood shifts, its juxtaposition of ordinary speech rhythms with pas-sages in foreign languages, and the curiously contorted conceits like the comparison of evening sky to a 'patient etherised upon a table' make for an astonishingly dense verbal fabric. 'Etherised', for example, also connotes, as Stephen Spender noted, 'ethereal' – a more logical epithet for the evening sky, which is by definition, in motion, rather than 'etherised'.[6] Then again 'etherised' takes the reader right to Prufrock's final line: 'Till human voices wake us, and we drown' (*CPP*, 17).

How did the Eliot of 1910/11 write such an avant-garde poem – a poem that when it finally appeared in book form in *Prufrock and Other Obser-vations* (1917) was declared by the anonymous reviewer for the *Times Literary Supplement* to be 'untouched by any genuine rush of feeling' and 'frequently inarticulate'? 'His "poems"', predicated this reviewer, 'will hardly be read by many with enjoyment' (Brooker, 6). No doubt this was true: these poems were sufficiently advanced in conception, structure and in their use of graphic, even shocking, urban imagery, so as to turn off the literary establishment of 1917. Indeed, in later years Eliot would himself be hard put to explain what had produced his breakthrough. He only knew that Paris had something to do with it. Shortly after arriving in London in 1914, Eliot wrote to his old friend, the poet Conrad Aiken:

Pound has been *on n'est pas plus aimable* [kindness itself], and is going to print 'Prufrock' in *Poetry* and pay me for it. He wants me to bring out a vol. after the war. The devil of it is that *I have done nothing good since J. A[lfred] P[rufrock] and writhe in impotence* . . . Sometimes I think – if I could only get back to Paris. But I know I never will . . . I think now that all my good stuff was done before I had begun to worry – three years ago. (*L1*, 62–3; emphasis added)

Furthermore, he told Eleanor Hinkley: 'I don't think that I should ever feel at home in England, as I do for instance in France . . . I should always, I think, be aware of a certain sense of confinement in England, and repression' (*L1*, 66). The repression, it seems, has been dramatised in 'The Love Song of J. Alfred Prufrock', where the most ordinary action seems impossible to carry out: thus, 'Shall I part my hair behind? Do I dare to eat a peach?' (*CPP*, 16). In the 'Love Song', Prufrock's creator could at least stand back and treat the situation with irony; in his life, by contrast, there was little to smile about. As Eliot confided to Aiken in December 1914:

I have been going through one of those nervous sexual attacks which I suffer from when alone in a city . . . One walks about the street with one's desires, and one's refinement rises up like a wall whenever opportunity approaches. I should be better off, I sometimes think, if I had disposed of my virginity and shyness several years ago. (*L1*, 82)

Eliot was 26 when he made these references to 'nervous sexual attacks' and missed opportunities; the longing for an earlier still-innocent romance is palpable. That romance involved Verdenal, to whom Eliot dedicated *Prufrock and Other Observations*. For the 1925 edition, Eliot added to the dedication the words spoken by the Roman poet Statius, at the climax of Dante's *Purgatorio* XXI, to the shade of his beloved Virgil: 'Or puoi la quantitate / comprender dell'amor ch'a te mi scalda, / quando dismento nostra vanitate, / trattando l'ombre come cosa salda' ['Understand how great the love that burns in me for you, to make me forget our vanity and treat a shade as a solid thing'].

However oblique, this is a remarkable declaration on Eliot's part. It is reinforced by another comment, made ten years later in an editorial for the *Criterion*: 'I am willing to admit that my own retrospect is touched by a sentimental sunset, the memory of a friend coming across the Luxembourg Gardens in the late afternoon, waving a branch of lilac, a friend who was later . . . to be mixed with the mud of Gallipoli'.[7] That friend was Verdenal, and Eliot's image immediately recalls the Hyacinth Garden in *The Waste Land*, in which the single flower, proffered to the poet-narrator, makes for a moment he cannot forget: 'I was neither / Living nor dead, and I knew nothing, / Looking into the heart of light, the silence' (*CPP*, 62). The epiphany is recalled in part 5 of the poem as 'The awful daring of a moment's surrender / Which an age of prudence can never retract' (*CPP*, 74).

The avant-gardism of the poems Eliot began in Paris represents just such a moment of surrender. The carefree Eliot who wandered around the streets of Paris with Jean Verdenal was, as his letters indicate, curious about the lives of others – 'lonely men in shirt-sleeves, leaning out of windows' (*CPP*, 15) – even if he was not inclined to participate in avant-garde soirées or frequent the galleries. In London, the carefree life seemed impossible. If, as he told Aiken, petty worrying 'kills your inspiration', then '*tragic* suffering' would do 'exactly the reverse', for such suffering takes one out of oneself 'to look at one's life as if it were somebody's else' (*L1*, 63). About such suffering Eliot was soon to learn: by the time he wrote his quatrain poems published in *Poems* (1920) – most of them short, satiric third-person telescoped narratives – the avant-garde utopian phase of Eliot's career had culminated in the 'tragic suffering' of *The Waste Land* and in a new concern for what he called, in his most famous critical essay, the relationship between 'Tradition and the Individual Talent.'

All the more ironic, accordingly, that the most famous avant-gardist of the century, Marcel Duchamp, singled out Eliot's essay for praise in one of his own rare critical statements. The occasion was a round-table with a group of illustrious art historians at a Federation of the Arts meeting in 1957, and it was, so Eric Cameron tells us, 'the only time Duchamp ever quoted the opinion of a critic word for word':[8] 'T. S. Eliot, in his essay on "Tradition and the Individual Talent", writes: "The more perfect the artist, the more completely separate in him will be the man who suffers and the mind which creates; the more perfectly will the mind digest and transmute the passions which are its material." '[9] The doctrine of poetic autonomy adumbrated here – and developed in Duchamp's essay – was to become the cornerstone of High Modernism, as distinct from the avant-gardist drive to equate art and life. But this distinction has always been more apparent than real. Like Eliot, Duchamp regarded the artist as medium and designed his readymades – for example, *The Bicycle Wheel* – so as to give them a life of their own, freed from all signs of the creator's touch. The artwork, so Eliot and Duchamp both believed, must speak for itself; it cannot be judged by the author's intention, which may, in any case, be only dimly understood: 'The progress of an artist is . . . a continual extinction of personality' (*SE*, 17).

But in his post-war public persona, the newly minted English Eliot had 'To prepare a face to meet the faces that you meet' (*CPP*, 14). The avant-garde experimentation of the Paris years was a thing of the past. The editor of the *Criterion* who turned down for publication Gertrude Stein's 'Composition as Explanation' was no longer a Francophile avant-gardist. 'Now as to Paris', he writes to Wyndham Lewis in 1921, 'I can't feel that there is a great deal of hope in your going there permanently. Painting being so much more important in Paris, there are a great many more clever second-rate men there … to distinguish oneself from. Then you know what ruthless and indefatigable sharpers Frenchmen are' (*LI*, 552). Paris the city of 'clever second-rate men'? Eliot had attained the Age of Prudence.

NOTES

1. Ezra Pound, *Gaudier-Brzeska: A Memoir* (1916) (New York: New Directions, 1970), pp. 90–2.
2. 'The Love Song of J. Alfred Prufrock' appeared in *Poetry* (Chicago) at the same time as *Blast* 2.
3. 'Ezra Pound', *Poetry* (September 1946), 326.
4. 'The Art of Poetry, I: T. S. Eliot', *Paris Review* (spring/summer 1959), 56.
5. Quoted in C. K. Stead, *The New Poetic: Yeats to Eliot* (London: Hutchinson, 1964), p. 52.
6. For a discussion of these effects, see Marjorie Perloff, *21st-Century Modernism* (Oxford: Blackwell, 2002), pp. 19–28.
7. 'A Commentary', *Criterion* (April 1934), 452.
8. Eric Cameron quoted in *The Definitively Unfinished Marcel Duchamp*, ed. Thierry de Duve (Cambridge, MA: MIT Press, 1992), p. 1.
9. *The Essential Writings of Marcel Duchamp*, ed. Michel Sanouillet and Elmer Peterson (London: Thames & Hudson, 1975), p. 138.

PART FOUR

Politics, society and culture

CHAPTER 26

Politics

David Bradshaw

The more the gap widens between Eliot's time and our own, the more abrasively his socio-political pronouncements and ideological affinities rub against his name. His exclusionary sympathies (with authority, elitism, Anglo-Catholicism and royalism, for instance) hardly lie flush with our predominantly secular, egalitarian and multicultural values, while, as Roger Kojecký noted as long ago as 1971, 'the number of those who have been shocked or repelled by his irreverent attitude towards ideals such as liberalism and democracy is greater than the number who have set themselves to discover what, positively, Eliot did believe.' Kojecký added: 'Frequently only two or three phrases ... have sufficed to convince that his views on social matters were thoroughly reactionary, or highly eccentric, or both'.[1] Most damagingly of all, Eliot has been branded an anti-Semite, a fascist and eugenicist, all notably serious charges in the aftermath of the Second World War, and although it has also been recognised that each accusation demands more nuanced calibration, if not qualified rejection, Eliot's politics were too tightly bound up with the charged polarities and post-Darwinian bugbears of his epoch ever to be wholly free of censure. Ultimately, however, if his political opinions and alignments are to be deplored for their obnoxiousness and excoriated for their occasional extremity, then they also need to be understood as coterminous with his profound sense of cultural exclusion. Eliot's values and those of his age rarely overlapped and were mostly at loggerheads.

When he dismisses the mid nineteenth century as 'an age of bustle, programmes, platforms, scientific progress, humanitarianism and revolutions which improved nothing, an age of progressive degradation' (*SE*, 427), Eliot lays out his own stall of prejudices in relief. Like many intellectuals of his time, he rejected the post-Enlightenment banner of progress and was instead convinced that 'the forces of deterioration are a large crawling mass, and the forces of development half a dozen men'.[2] The innumerable 'muddy feet that press / To early coffee-stands' and 'all

the hands / That are raising dingy shades / In a thousand furnished rooms'
(*CPP*, 22) in 'Preludes', and 'The red-eyed scavengers ... creeping / From
Kentish Town and Golder's Green' and the 'Weeping, weeping multitudes' (*CPP*, 45) of 'A Cooking Egg', spotlight the 'forces of deterioration'
at work in but two of his poems,[3] just as they haunt so much of his prose:
one way or another, Eliot would focus on the ongoing struggle between
the embattled few and the inimical masses time and again in his work. As
late as 1960, for example, five years before his death, he argued that the
term 'fascist' had been 'falsely applied to [Wyndham] Lewis, but flung by
the *massenmensch* at some who, like Lewis, choose to walk alone',[4] and it is
tempting to imagine that Eliot had himself in mind, as well as his fellow
writer, when he penned these words.

   In attempting to anatomise 'the particular torpor or deadness' of
literary London in 1922, Eliot claimed that it was partly 'facilitated ...
by democracy (in the vague habitual sense of the word)'. Further on in
this article he derides 'the so-called modern democracy which appears to
produce fewer and fewer individuals',[5] while his early writings as a whole
monitor the 'debility', 'barbarity', 'degeneration' and 'degradation' of
mass society with sustained contempt. Taking up the editorship of the
Criterion in 1922 was a pivotal moment in Eliot's cultural fight-back:
it was not a political appointment, but it increasingly marked a deep
political commitment on his part. The *Criterion* gradually morphed into
an organ of cultural revanchism, and through its pages, as the years
unfolded (it ceased publication in 1939), Eliot hoped to recover at least
something of the lost order and lost certainties of the past and to vigo-
rously oppose liberalism and romanticism in general and the flaccidity of
'modern democracy' in particular. Accordingly, in defiance of the political
and cultural shibboleths of his day, Eliot's *Criterion* set about promoting
'classicism' and in 1924 he defined this 'new attitude of mind' with
reference to the posthumous writings of the poet and critic T. E. Hulme
(1883–1917): 'Hulme is classical, reactionary, and revolutionary; he is the
antipodes of the eclectic, tolerant, and democratic mind of the end of the
last century'.[6] In the same year, in a circular for prospective subscribers,
Eliot claimed in a rather more graspable fashion that the *Criterion*
'expounds the philosophy of pure Toryism' as opposed to the 'antiquated
principles of suburban democracy'.[7]

   Works by Hulme and the equally influential Irving Babbitt, Eliot told
the *Criterion*'s readers in January 1926, were among the books that had
helped him arrive at his own political mindset, while in the same article he
drew special attention to Charles Maurras, whose writings he had first

encountered as a student in Paris in 1910/11 (see Chapter 3 above). As Kenneth Asher has pointed out, Maurras's intellectual complexion had been described in 1913 'as "classique, catholique, monarchique," a constellation Eliot would later adopt as his own coat of arms'.[8] Later in 1926, Eliot remarked that if the modern artist 'finds himself unable to realise his art to his own satisfaction ... he may be driven to examining the elements in the situation – political, social, philosophical or religious – which frustrate his labour',[9] while his examination of his own predicament resulted in the most striking and provocative pronouncement of his life, when, in the preface to *For Lancelot Andrewes* (1928), he declared that he had arrived at an ideological conjunction that was 'classicist in literature, royalist in politics, and anglo-catholic in religion'. Eliot continued, 'I am aware that the second term is at present without definition, and easily lends itself to what is almost worse than clap-trap, I mean temperate conservatism', before revealing that among the volumes he had in preparation was one called '*The Outline of Royalism*' (*FLA*, ix–x). It never appeared.

For all its apparent abruptness, the foundations of this dramatic announcement had long been in place. In the outlines of his 1916 Oxford University Extension Lectures on modern French literature, for example, Eliot made it clear that he would be attacking both the Romantic outlook and its legacy, while at the same time drawing sustenance from the writings of French reactionary thinkers, such as Maurras, in promoting 'the ideals of classicism', which he went on to characterise 'as *form* and *restraint* in art, *discipline* and *authority* in religion, *centralization* in government (either as socialism or monarchy). The classicist point of view has been defined as essentially a belief in Original Sin – the necessity for austere discipline.'[10] Eliot's celebrated declaration of his political new bearings in 1928, therefore, should be seen as a key moment of ideological stocktaking rather than a sudden epiphany. Nevertheless, for all its patently Maurrassien roots and its measured gestation, Eliot's public embrace of royalism in the late 1920s did have a more immediate and home-grown stimulus. On 15 November 1928, five days before the publication of *For Lancelot Andrewes*, an anonymous review entitled 'Augustan Age Tories' appeared in the *Times Literary Supplement*. It was written by Eliot, and in the course of his essay he praises the political philosophy of Sir Robert Filmer (*c*. 1588–1653), author of *Patriarcha: A Defence of the Natural Power of Kings against the Unnatural Liberty of the People*, which was published posthumously in 1680. In particular, as I have argued elsewhere, it was 'Filmer's insistence on an indefeasible royal prerogative and his belief in political obligation which struck a profound chord in Eliot'.[11] In his *TLS* review, Eliot explained that Filmer 'was opposed to the type of political doctrine that developed later in [Jean-Jacques] Rousseau, he was opposed to humanitarian Liberalism ... His views have never been adopted, and the tide was already strong against him; but neither have his views been refuted or replaced'.[12] This was an extraordinary claim even in 1928, but its blinkered peculiarity merely adds to the likelihood that only a short while after he declared that the Bolshevik revolution of 1917, Benito Mussolini's Fascist revolution of 1922 and the condemnation of Maurras's royalist Action Française movement by the Vatican in 1926 'compel us to consider the problem of Liberty and Authority, both in politics and in the organization of speculative thought. Politics has become too serious a matter to be left to politicians',[13] Eliot's critical engagement with a study of Filmer's political philosophy and his sense of Filmer standing lonely but adamant against the tide of his time was a major impetus behind his 1928 avowal of royalism. After the crisis surrounding the abdication of Edward VIII in 1936, Eliot's public support for royalism became considerably more muted, but he was to be pigeonholed as a royalist for the rest of his life. And not unreasonably. In his preface to the 1962 edition of *Notes Towards the Definition of Culture*, for example, though Eliot felt obliged to confess that he 'should not now ... call myself a "royalist" *tout court*, as I once did', he quickly added that he was 'in favour of retaining the monarchy in every country in which a monarchy still exists' (*NTDC*, 7), while in a 1961 lecture, 'To Criticize the Critic', he remarked that although he had been dogged by his 1928 declaration of royalism, he was still 'strongly in favour of the maintenance of the monarchy in all countries which have a monarchy' (*TCC*, 15). So even if Eliot's preface to *For Lancelot Andrewes* is not quite the watershed it is often made out to be, it did mark a significant turning point in the way his politics were perceived by his contemporaries, while Asher asserts that after the publication of *For Lancelot Andrewes* 'Eliot comes to posit religion as the generating substructure that his congeries of values had always lacked; reactionary politics and classical art ... are reduced to epiphenomena'.[14]

In 'The Humanism of Irving Babbitt' (1928), Eliot argues: 'As forms of government become more democratic, as the outer restraints of kingship, aristocracy, and class disappear, so it becomes more and more necessary that the individual no longer controlled by authority or habitual respect should control himself' (*SE*, 476). 'A man is essentially bad', Eliot declares in 'Baudelaire' (1930), 'he can only accomplish anything of value by discipline – ethical and political. Order is thus not merely negative, but creative and liberating. Institutions are necessary' (*SE*, 430). 'Liberty is good; but more important is order', he writes in his 1927 essay on Niccolò Machiavelli, 'and the maintenance of order justifies every means' (*FLA*, 58). By today's standards these remarks are disconcerting, but by the standards of Eliot's time, a period (especially after the 1929 Wall Street Crash) of increasing social, political and economic turmoil when anti-parliamentary sentiments were far from exceptional, they are not. 'Any form of order is better than chaos', Aldous Huxley told listeners to BBC radio in January 1932, without causing even a whisper of protest.[15]

However, it is undoubtedly Eliot's readiness to countenance order being 'imposed' unconstitutionally and his repeated animadversions on liberal democracy that have led to him being tarred with the 'fascist' brush, while the fact that he concluded a 1929 essay, 'Mr Barnes and Mr Rowse', by 'confess[ing] to a preference for fascism [over Communism] in practice' has not gone unnoticed. He added that he was unprepared to 'admit that this preference is itself wholly irrational. I believe that the fascist form of unreason is less remote from my own than is that of the communists, but that my form is a more reasonable form of unreason.'[16] Six years earlier, moreover, in January 1923, he had written to the editor of the *Daily Mail* to express his 'cordial approval' of the newspaper's highly complimentary 'series of articles ... on Fascismo' (*L2*, 7–8). But as time moved on it became more and more clear, as it did for W. B. Yeats, that fascism of any kind was far too populist a political creed for a man with such pronounced leanings towards elitism. In 'The Literature of Fascism', Eliot wrote that he was

all the more suspicious of fascism as a panacea because I fail so far to find in it any important element, beyond this comfortable feeling that we shall be benevolently ordered about ... Most of the concepts which might have attracted me in fascism I seem already to have found, in a more digestible form, in the work of Charles Maurras.

He concludes his article with these reflections: 'A new school of political thought is needed, which might learn from political thought abroad, but not from political practice. Both Russian communism and Italian fascism seem to me to have died as political ideas, in becoming political facts.' Although Eliot refers to himself in this article as 'a political ignoramus', he cannot resist, yet again, making plain his disbelief in liberal democracy (he calls it a 'silly idea' and claims that it is no more than a front for 'government by an invisible oligarchy', a not uncommon allegation at the time) yet, significantly, he does not repudiate 'the *idea* of democracy' before adding, more controversially, 'a real democracy is always a restricted democracy, and can only flourish with some limitation by hereditary rights and responsibilities'.[17]

Just as he came to see that Christianity and eugenics were incompatible, so Eliot recognised that his Christian faith could not be accommodated with extremist politics on either the left or the right. 'What is to be the attitude of a royalist towards any system under which absolute submission to the will of a leader is made an article of faith or a qualification for office?', he asked in July 1934. 'Surely the royalist can admit only one higher authority than the throne, which is the Church.'[18] He developed this point in another article published in the same month, a piece which underlines how his intense religious devotion helped save him from the kind of vilification that would in time be directed towards Ezra Pound and Wyndham Lewis on account of their enthusiasm for fascism:

The Churches cannot, of course, pick out any one political form and maintain that it is essential for the Christian Life; but they can and should denounce any political form which is either hostile to or subversive of the Christian Life … Both Fascism and Communism exhibit a diversion, to material ends, of passion which should only be devoted to religious ends.[19]

There is one further aspect of Eliot's attitude to fascism that requires clarification. In April 1931 he wrote in qualified support of Oswald Mosley's radical and widely discussed plan to reform the British economy. 'It recognises that the nineteenth century is over', Eliot stated, 'and that a thorough reorganisation of industry and agriculture is essential. The fundamental objection to it, of course, is that it is not fundamental enough. The changes are propounded in the same old cautious and sensible, and at the same time catchy, phrasing, as any other political manifesto.'[20] Mosley had recently left the Labour Party to create his breakaway New Party, and he went on to launch his British Union of Fascists on 1 October 1932. Eliot showed no interest at all in the BUF, but there is further evidence that he was momentarily attracted to the comparatively radical political initiatives that the Mosley manifesto, published in December 1930, promoted. On 2 March 1932 the journalist and New Party member Harold Nicolson had lunch with Eliot and James Strachey Barnes, who had been appointed by Mussolini as Secretary-General of the International Fascist Centre at Lausanne and who would continue to advocate fascism at every turn in the interwar period before ending up, like Pound, resident in Rome and broadcasting for *Il Duce* after the outbreak of the Second World War. 'We discuss the making of a symposium on modern politics', Nicolson recorded in his diary. 'I say that unless we tell our contributors that the book is New Party or fascist in tendency we are not playing fair.'[21] This meeting was part of an effort to create what Robert Skidelsky has called a 'respectable fascism' in England, but nothing came of it and Mosley's BUF soon took off in its distinctly unrespectable direction.[22] Care needs to be taken, therefore, in how Eliot's passing interest in Mosley's programme is represented: he was briefly attracted to the ideas of the visionary Member of Parliament in 1931, during a time of national crisis, but not to the posturing of the increasingly ludicrous and anti-Semitic leader of the BUF. And although he was to remain on good terms with men such as 'Jim' Barnes, Douglas Jerrold and Lord Lymington, all of whom were either openly fascist or full-hearted fellow travellers of the extreme right, Eliot was never affiliated to either camp. So Michael North's claim, for example, that 'there was apparently a flicker of interest in Oswald Mosley, *the indigenous British fascist*' (emphasis added) is misleading.[23]

It was in the early 1930s that Eliot began to adumbrate his own vision of the ideal state, and it is in this context that the infamous offensiveness of *After Strange Gods* (1934) needs to be considered. Speaking in 'the role of moralist' and declaring that his age was 'worm-eaten with Liberalism' (*ASG*, 12, 13), Eliot told his audience at the University of Virginia in 1933 that the 'population should be homogeneous' (*ASG*, 19): 'free-thinking Jews', therefore, and 'a spirit of excessive tolerance' were to be 'deprecated' (*ASG*, 20), prompting William Chace to contend that '*After Strange Gods* is a political work because of the prejudices it expresses, not for the political vision it establishes'.[24] North comments persuasively that behind Eliot's racial slur 'lurked the practicalities of [his] own historically, politically, and geographically anomalous position as an urbanised expatriate preaching settled habits, traditional pieties, and the healthy influence of the land',[25] but while Eliot's remarks may be contextualised, they are much harder to excuse. Many years later, Eliot told Pound that *After Strange Gods* was not a good book and that he had been 'sick' when he wrote it.[26] It has certainly done his reputation nothing but harm, and he never allowed it to be reprinted.

Despite the growth of totalitarianism in Europe, Eliot's opposition to liberalism only deepened during the 1930s, and it is even more pronounced in *The Idea of a Christian Society* (1939):

By destroying traditional social habits of the people, by dissolving their natural collective consciousness into individual constituents, by licensing the opinions of the most foolish, by substituting instruction for education, by encouraging cleverness rather than wisdom, the upstart rather than the qualified ... Liberalism can prepare the way for that which is its own negation: the artificial, mechanised or brutalised control which is a desperate remedy for its chaos. (*ICS*, 16)

The only alternative to this chaos, Eliot proposes in 1939, is a tightly controlled and profoundly conformist Christian society where order has been imposed: his notorious prejudice in favour of a 'homogeneous' Christian culture in *After Strange Gods* is transmuted into a visionary aspiration. As the citizens of a Christian society would have no real option but to abide by Christian dogma, Eliot's *Idea of a Christian Society* comes, indeed, perilously close to promoting a totalitarian theocratic state. In Michael Levenson's eyes, 'it is plain that the imminent catastrophe [of the Second World War] released a more aggressive refusal of the reigning social consensus. *The Idea of a Christian Society* is a book which imagines and *desires* the uprooting of secular democratic politics.'[27]

Notes Towards the Definition of Culture (1948) was to be Eliot's final blueprint of what a British polity might look like if only the British would recognise the Christian truth before their eyes. 'The writer himself is not without political convictions and prejudices', he discloses in the 'Introduction', 'but the imposition of them is no part of his present intention' (*NTDC*, 16), before going on to argue that the state must be hierarchical and that 'an aristocracy should have a peculiar and essential function' (*NTDC*, 48) within it, and condemning, in his conclusion, the 'headlong rush to educate everybody' and so 'make ready the ground upon which the barbarian nomads of the future will encamp in their mechanised caravans' (*NTDC*, 108). Eliot's cataclysmal idiom indicates not just how prominently 'those hooded hordes swarming / Over endless plains' (*CPP*, 73) and the pullulating masses of his early poems still loomed large in his mind, but is part and parcel of how *Notes Towards the Definition of Culture* as a whole 'is a rearguard action nipping at the heels of a triumphant liberal society. The conservatism it advocates does not really conserve, but attempts to retrieve the lost.'[28] Levenson observes that in this work, 'Eliot constructs an alternative to the millenarian politics of the thirties and devises his last political testament, the post-apocalyptic vision of corporate equilibrium, which no longer makes bold to ask what may be achieved, only what may be preserved.'[29] It was only in 1950, in a series of lectures entitled 'The Aims of Education', that Eliot finally came out unequivocally in favour of liberal democracy and against totalitarianism, but even here he felt compelled to point out that the problem of 'how to get the best men as rulers is one which remains to be solved' (*TCC*, 72).

'The temptation, to any man who is interested in ideas and primarily in literature, to put literature into the corner until he has cleaned up the whole country first, is almost irresistible' (*SW*, xi–xii), Eliot had written in the 1920 introduction to *The Sacred Wood*. He never quite succumbed to this temptation himself, but a good few of his *Criterion* editorials and essays, alongside his books of social criticism, bear witness to his inability entirely to resist the urge. He never joined or supported a mainstream political party (though he once or twice expressed mild approval of the Liberal Party and the Conservative Party), but a student of his work will have no difficulty feeling the heat of his political sympathies and anti-pathies. And if Eliot was being strictly factual when he said in a 1955 lecture that 'as a man of letters' he had played two political roles, 'that of a voter – a walking-on part, and that of a reader – a sitting-down part' (*TCC*, 137), he was also understating his lifelong engagement with socio-political questions. Even if they often had a somewhat improvised air, Eliot's politics changed very little during the course of his life and have been neatly summed up by Stephen Spender as 'essentially those of a man who thought that political activity should derive from abstract principles, that principles should be based on dogma, that dogma should be based on supernatural authority. Supernatural authority should be guaranteed by institutions of Church and monarchy.'[30] While Eliot's reactionary allegiance to notions of authority, orthodoxy and order and his loathing of liberal democracy and humanitarianism ran against the grain of British politics, his religious principles were always firmly rooted in tradition and held in earnest defiance of the world around him. Both his religious views and his politics will always be an impediment to his wider reputation, but they are utterly intrinsic to his vision as a poet and writer.

NOTES

1. Roger Kojecký, *T. S. Eliot's Social Criticism* (London: Faber & Faber, 1971), p. 11.
2. 'Observations', *Egoist* (May 1918), 69.
3. For a provocative discussion of this issue, see Michael Tratner, *Modernism and Mass Politics: Joyce, Woolf, Eliot, Yeats* (Stanford University Press, 1995), pp. 97–115.
4. Foreword to Wyndham Lewis, *One-Way Song* (London: Methuen, 1960), p. 10.
5. 'London Letter', *Dial* (May 1922), 510–11.

6. 'A Commentary', *Criterion* (April 1924), 231.
7. Circular for the *Criterion, c.* December 1924.
8. Kenneth Asher, *T. S. Eliot and Ideology* (Cambridge University Press, 1995), p. 36.
9. 'A Commentary', *Criterion* (June 1926), 420.
10. Quoted in Asher, *Eliot and Ideology*, p. 38.
11. See David Bradshaw, 'Lonely Royalists: T. S. Eliot and Sir Robert Filmer', *Review of English Studies* (August 1995), 375–9.
12. 'Augustan Age Tories', *Times Literary Supplement* (15 November 1928), 846.
13. 'A Commentary', *Criterion* (November 1927), 386.
14. Asher, *Eliot and Ideology*, p. 58.
15. Quoted in *The Hidden Huxley: Contempt and Compassion for the Masses, 1920–36*, ed. David Bradshaw (London: Faber & Faber, 1994), p. 111.
16. 'Mr Barnes and Mr Rowse', *Criterion* (July 1929), 690–1.
17. 'The Literature of Fascism', *Criterion* (December 1928), 280–90.
18. 'A Commentary', *Criterion* (July 1934), 629.
19. 'In Sincerity and Earnestness: New Britain As I See It', *New Britain* (25 July 1934), 274.
20. 'A Commentary', *Criterion* (April 1931), 483.
21. Harold Nicolson, *Diaries and Letters 1930–1939*, ed. Nigel Nicolson (London: Collins, 1966), p. 111.
22. Robert Skidelsky, *Oswald Mosley* (London: Macmillan, 1990), p. 286.
23. Michael North, *The Political Aesthetic of Yeats, Eliot and Pound* (Cambridge University Press, 1991), p. 117.
24. William Chace, *The Political Identities of Ezra Pound and T. S. Eliot* (Stanford University Press, 1973), p. 161.
25. North, *Political Aesthetic*, p. 110.
26. Quoted in Kojecký, *Eliot's Social Criticism*, p. 94.
27. Michael Levenson, 'Politics', *A Companion to T. S. Eliot*, ed. David Chinitz (Chichester: Wiley-Blackwell, 2009), p. 383.
28. North, *Political Aesthetic*, p. 114.
29. Levenson, 'Politics', p. 386.
30. Stephen Spender, *Eliot* (London: Fontana, 1975), p. 215.

CHAPTER 27

Economics

Adam Trexler

If there is a difficulty describing T. S. Eliot's economic context, it is that it spans micro-economic events almost invisible to historians and macro-economic events far larger than any individual. Eliot's relationship to economics involves the monetary struggles of a single newly wed couple, the fate of small circulation, almost voluntary literary journals and the serendipity of a personal career, as well as the rise and fall of national currencies, the emergence of labour politics effecting the decisions of the British parliament, the post-war dismantling of Germany's economy, the severe economic depressions of the 1920s and 1930s and Britain's long historical movement from an agrarian to a manufacturing and then a consumer society. Although no single individual could comprehensively understand the economic forces in play, writers across the political spectrum tried to diagnose and prescribe solutions for Britain's economic ills. Eliot's poetic, critical and editorial work records both the material impact of these events and the responses of intellectuals to them, even as economics shifted the ground of aesthetics, creative production, identity, politics and society.

Although Eliot's early poetry was concerned with social class, it was his initial experiences of living in London that ensured a deeper concern with economics. In America, he had grown up in an elite family and was educated at the best schools, with degrees and accolades from Harvard University preparing him for a successful career. However, when the outbreak of the First World War interrupted a grand tour of European universities, Eliot rather impulsively decided to pursue a writer's life. In 1915 he married an Englishwoman, Vivien Haigh-Wood, and settled in London, effectively abandoning his American familial and institutional connections. From September 1915 to December 1916 he was a school-teacher, but he found the work and the pay unrewarding. He also wrote book reviews and critical essays for money, and later described reviewing as 'one of the most corrupting, degrading and badly-paid means of livelihood that a writing man can ply'.[1] Although from 1917 onwards Eliot had a succession of editorial jobs, these were helpful as means to market the poetry of friends and to pass on commissions for articles, rather than for the £12 per year he expected to earn from literary journalism (see Chapter 10 above). It was only in 1922 that Eliot began to be paid significant amounts for his poetry (and even then not enough to live on), and in 1925 that he was employed full time as a publisher at Faber & Gwyer (later Faber & Faber) (see Chapter 8). Despite some financial assistance from both their families, Tom and Vivien found themselves living in a 'wilderness' between middle-class respectability and genteel poverty: Vivien described their London flat in Crawford Mansions as situated in an area 'with slums and low streets and poor shops close around us – (and *yet* within a stone's throw of great squares with big houses and one of the most expensive residential districts)' (*L1*, 207).

These tensions between elitism and working-class identity found expression in Eliot's employment, between 1916 and 1919, as an extension lecturer for the University of London, in which he delivered a series of courses to women and working-class students. Although he was ostensibly teaching literature, Eliot carefully revised economic ideas for his lectures, expanding the curriculum to include John Ruskin and William Morris, notable Victorian critics of laissez-faire capitalism; John Stuart Mill, another Victorian writer on economics and political philosophy, who had sought to temper the extreme liberalism of his father's generation; and radical French political and social theorists. While Eliot's letters home reveal a certain condescension towards his students, he also identified with the intellectual enthusiasm and social conservatism of the English working class and displayed outrage at what he conceived to be the ignorance of the middle class. In 1917 he went so far as to call himself 'a Labourite in England, though a conservative at home' (*L1*, 188). This striking combination of economic radicalism and cultural conservatism would set the pattern for much of Eliot's social thought over the next twenty years.

Eliot began working at the head office of Lloyds Bank in Cornhill in March 1917. His first job was in the Colonial and Foreign Office Department, tracking the balance sheets of foreign banks, based on investments, 'cash in hand', advances and discounts. This work enabled Eliot to learn the basic mechanisms banks used to create credit, control capital and real estate and influence government policy. He liked the job and the sense of playing a small part in the fate of great companies and nations. Within two years, he was promoted to a position that involved economic research, exploring how international exchange rates affected industry. Eliot found his work at the bank absorbing, leading him to study 'the science of money' and 'the theory of banking' (*LI*, 193–5) in classic economic texts. Soon after the Armistice, Eliot found himself 'trying to elucidate knotty points in that appalling document the [Versailles] Peace Treaty' (*LI*, 446) as it involved the entitlement of Lloyds Bank to German reparation debts. In 1923 he was made head of the Intelligence Department, writing a monthly article on 'Foreign Exchanges'.[2] Eliot was embittered by what he saw as the international struggle carried on by economic means, which demanded that Germany pay for nearly the entire cost of the war, crippling that country's economy for generations to come. In retrospect, Eliot claimed that his 'apprenticeship in the City' had taught him that 'accomplished economic specialists' were divorced from 'our simple human principles and convictions', calling into doubt the 'unquestioning loyalty' his colleagues at Lloyds Bank paid to the world of finance.[3] Throughout 1921, Eliot's articles show a steadily increasing anger and incredulity that financial considerations were overwhelming public cultural institutions, including churches and theatres.

Although *The Waste Land* is most often read in terms of spiritual and cultural dissolution, the poem is underpinned by a post-war crisis in the economic system. Eliot's vantage point at Lloyds Bank gave him a deep insight into the disintegration of the basic mechanisms ordering the international economy. While France and Britain sought to extract the maximum penalty from the German economy, John Maynard Keynes, an acquaintance of Eliot's, charged the Allies in *The Economic Consequences of the Peace* (1919) with the imposition of punitive war reparations that impaired 'the delicate, complicated organisation, already shaken and broken by war, through which alone European people can employ themselves and live'.[4] In a footnote to *The Waste Land*, Hermann Hesse observed that half of post-war Europe was on the way to chaos, while the offended bourgeoisie failed to understand the consequences of this chaos. The opening section of *The Waste Land*, 'The Burial of the Dead', instantiates this economic breakdown, showing failed transactions between German, French and English voices. Other traders are lost in the economic turbulence – 'the profit and loss' (*CPP*, 71). The one-eyed merchant, Mr Eugenides, and the Phoenician sailor melt indistinguishably into one another as the Ottoman Empire disintegrated after the war. At the same time, observers could see that the European empires were beginning to disintegrate: associated with national, racial and imperial vanity, the historical basis for international economic order was dissolving. Thus, the imperial inheritance of India speaks in the final section,

'What the Thunder Said', but cultural distance renders it unintelligible. After the war, Britain's economy suffered a precipitous decline of its banking sector, caused by the 'loss of investments during the war, disruptions to international finance due to war debts and reparations, [and] the devaluation of sterling'.[5] Great symbolic importance was attached to Britain's suspension of the gold standard in 1919: sterling and all the international currencies dependent on it were now unsecured from value. This loss of symbolic value is dramatised in *The Waste Land* by the woes of the Thames daughters and the Rhine daughters, who are charged with guarding the gold that secures the nations of Britain and Germany. In 1919, Lloyds Bank played an important part in the economic breakdown, extending easy credit, which in turn led to high inflation and the devaluation of sterling.

The Waste Land dramatises the modernisation of British production. During the war, companies producing motor vehicles, rubber, pharmaceuticals, artificial fibres, cotton, tobacco, biscuits, chemicals, electrical goods, glass, petroleum, iron and steel, and shipbuilding and shipping made immense profits, accompanied by a public outcry against what could be perceived as immoral 'profiteering'. The evidence of this commercial expansion can be seen throughout *The Waste Land*, for example in the excessive luxury of the woman's dressing-table in 'A Game of Chess'; in the 'empty bottles, sandwich papers, / Silk handkerchiefs, cardboard boxes, cigarette ends' (*CPP*, 67) and the absentee City directors of 'The Fire Sermon'; in new machines like typewriters and gramophones; and the image of the war profiteer or 'Bradford millionaire'. The 'taxi throbbing waiting' (*CPP*, 68) had immediate resonance for *The Waste Land*'s first readers, as the number of motor vehicles had dramatically risen from 100,000 in 1910 to 500,000 in 1921. Many contemporaries viewed the rise in industrial production, mechanised labour and the preoccupation with the profit motive as undermining traditional economic and cultural values. Eliot's poem also registers the corresponding decline of Britain's agricultural economy. During the war the British government took unprecedented control of agriculture, setting production targets for farmers, fixing prices and expanding by 30 per cent the land under cultivation. At the same time, the use of tractors greatly increased the productivity of farms. After the war, these artificially high levels of domestic farming, combined with the resumption of large-scale grain imports, led to a severe fall in prices. From June to December 1921 the price of wheat was halved. The government refused to honour the guaranteed prices, 'the Great Betrayal' according to many observers. This situation, in which agriculture was nearly ruined by an overabundance of cheap grain, was a major news story during the period Eliot composed *The Waste Land*. It was also a time of record unemployment – 2 million in 1921. The fertility rituals drawn upon in *The Waste Land* emerged from periods of drought and infertility, a magical attempt to reinstate agricultural and sexual production. However, Eliot's poem captures the distinctly modern crisis of overproduction. April's fertility, sprouting excessive vegetation, makes it the cruellest month; floods and drowning recur as themes; Lil is almost killed by her own fertility; while typists and clerks are bored by the mechanical repetition of sex. The Victorian public moralists that Eliot lectured on in his extension courses were inspired by medieval agriculture's interdependence with natural abundance, cyclical and social order. Post-war overproduction turned these idylls into nightmares.

Observations of mechanised overproduction and the related phenomenon of under-consumption (particularly of workers) were the basis of the economic critiques proposed by Ruskin and Morris and their twentieth-century followers. In general, these movements for economic reform argued that inadequate wages, high unemployment, gaps between the rich and the poor, industrial waste, inferior disposable goods and warfare brought about by competition for markets, were endemic to capitalism. C. H. Douglas's theory of Social Credit was the most important diagnosis of under-consumption in the interwar period. Douglas had developed the technical side of the theory during the war, and his movement was taken up and promoted by A. R. Orage, the socialist editor of the *New Age*. Douglas's analysis of capitalist accounting demonstrated that profitable businesses would never pay workers enough for them to gain financial control of the means of production, ensuring the existence of two classes in capitalist societies. Banks controlled the monetary supply, in the form of credit, allowing them to dictate their own profits as well as the social ends of industry. Thus, both workers and creative business owners were subservient to the profit motive. Douglas's theory of Social Credit argued that public control of technology and the means of production was not an illegitimate seizure, since they were a society's 'cultural inheritance' (this idea appealed to artists) that had been paid for by the innovations and labour of ancestors and the profit generated to pay for them. Douglas and Orage proposed adjusting accounting practices to allow for direct subsidies to factories and the democratic control of those financial institutions giving credit, reforms designed to revolutionise the economy.

Douglas's Social Credit theory attracted a number of supporters from the arts, notably Ezra Pound, and Eliot referred to the theory several times throughout the interwar years. While technical definitions of 'money' kept orthodox economists from acknowledging the importance of credit, Eliot's own experience of working at Lloyds Bank confirmed his sense that banks created credit through cycles of lending, allowing them to control production. Eliot's work on the details of the Versailles Treaty had eroded his loyalty to the current economic system, leading him to take an interest in the literature of Social Credit. He met Douglas personally and recommended his work to others, although in 1920 he confessed that he found Douglas's *Economic Democracy* 'fearfully difficult and obscurely written' (*L1*, 455). At the same time, Pound was creating a Social Credit scheme, called Bel Esprit, to finance the production of poetry. Bel Esprit was designed to free individual writers from market forces by setting up private endowments. Literature could be privately financed as a 'public utility' (comparable to electricity, water and railways), providing a social service and realising only a long-term profit. Pound nominated Eliot to be the first recipient of the scheme, but when he advertised Bel Esprit in radical terms, the *Liverpool Daily Post and Mercury* gossiped about Eliot receiving money from it while continuing to work in the bank. Eliot was obliged to publicly dissociate himself from Bel Esprit in order to protect his salary and pension at Lloyds (essential to pay for Vivien's very expensive health care). Although Pound's scheme was effectively sunk, Social Credit was discussed in the *Criterion* throughout the 1920s and 1930s: Eliot himself seems to have agreed with its condemnation of commercialism, the profit motive as a social ideal, the exploitation of labour and natural resources, usury and 'the misdirection of the financial machine' (*ICS*, 33). In 1934 he signed a letter to *The Times* urging consideration of Social Credit and calling for credit reform. However, he remained unsure of Social Credit's prescriptions and publicly disagreed with Pound, in an exchange printed in the *New English Weekly*, as to whether Douglas's economic proposals were enough to solve society's problems.

Whatever his final opinion of Social Credit, Eliot's preoccupation with the financing of literature was repeatedly expressed in articles and reviews for the *Criterion* exploring the complex economics of modern literary production, which could frustrate the labour of the artist. The *Criterion* promoted those small, private publishers and university presses which made experimental texts and obscure classics available to readers and it criticised the capitalist practices of mainstream publishers who pushed the inferior bestseller at the expense of works of higher quality. Eliot also targeted daily newspapers, arguing that the rapid turnover of news encouraged a superficiality that was deleterious to both writers and the general public. Underlying these criticisms were concerns over the time involved in producing good literature and the worry that it would never be fairly recompensed. Writers were vulnerable to financial necessities. These concerns led Eliot to explore new means of financing art: he rejected proposals for a national theatre, but was interested in the ways in which subscriptions and endowments could allow for sliding scales of pricing in order to cater for those with modest means. The *Criterion* examined the international commercialisation of literature, translating and reviewing foreign publications in order to provide 'a local forum of international thought'.[6] Similarly, Eliot analysed various schemes for cultural exchange proposed by the League of Nations and by Communist states. He campaigned to remove various loopholes in international copyright law that allowed unscrupulous publishers to exploit authors. Eliot hoped that his work in these causes would allow authors to return to the business of writing.

As editor of the *Criterion*, then, Eliot sought to provoke a public debate about the interrelations of economics and culture. In the twentieth century academic economists began to formalise a professional discipline intended to provide scientific solutions to society's ills. However, after the First World War, Eliot observed a groundswell of public interest in the profound international economic transformations of the period, calling on artists and men of letters to resist the demagogy of science that characterised economic debates. Eliot gradually expanded the scope of his nominally 'literary' journal in order to examine the connections between culture and political economy, although it remained aloof from daily politics and avoided purely technical economics. These restraints were designed to allow the *Criterion* to speak to a broader, more general readership than sectarian political or academic economic periodicals, although in fact it isolated the journal from the topical conflicts essential to democratic political reform. During the interwar years, economic radicalism in Britain could not be confined to either the political right or left. In the Labour Party, ameliorists sat uncomfortably alongside revolutionary Marxists. Liberals ran the gamut from ardent social reformers (even Fabian socialists) to those who warned against any economic interventions. There was also a broad range of economic opinions among conservatives, from defenders of aristocratic privilege to radicals calling for the redistribution of the land to empower the poor. In an article of 1927, Eliot reviewed economic proposals in the aftermath of the General Strike, which had seen the solidarity of 4 million workers bring the country to a temporary standstill, but had provoked hostility from those among the non-striking majority who resented the ransoming of the country by less than a tenth of the population. In his article, Eliot praised Anthony Ludovici's *A Defence of Conservatism* for advancing a 'myth or idea for the Tory Party' which encompassed a better organisation of workers, pure food and better housing. Eliot considered the work of another radical conservative, Hilaire Belloc's *The Servile State*, which argued that property, concentrated by capitalism in a few hands, had to be immediately redistributed more widely across society if political and economic freedoms were to be defended. Otherwise, according to Belloc, capitalism would devolve into a society divided between employers and slavish employees, or into a collectivist state in which citizens had no economic rights. Eliot, however, insisted on the analysis of the liberal economist J. A. Hobson, who argued that economic directors 'who have the knowledge' would actually consolidate their power if 'ownership' were diluted, no matter whether ownership was held by small capitalist share-owners or socialist 'self-ownership' of the means of production. Finally, Eliot praised the moral and revolutionary fervour of a group of Christian Social Credit supporters who appeared in the collection *Coal*, although he doubted whether their specific proposals were compatible with consti-tutional 'popular government' or the Anglican Church.[7] Overall, Eliot's article suggests that he envisioned radical economic reform based on collective deliberation and social conscience rather than measures that enriched the capitalist few.

Despite his commitment to broad economic reform, Eliot's economic position was increasingly influenced by political conservatism. However, his political and theological conservatism has rarely been adequately understood as a specific response to Britain's post-war political situation. The Liberal and Conservative parties had formed a wartime coalition government, temporarily suspending the ideological struggles that char-acterised the Victorian period. The war also interrupted the momentum of the Labour Party. After 1919, however, Conservative and Labour politicians were united in their opposition to Lloyd George and the Liberal Party. From 1921, Eliot argued that the decline of liberalism necessitated a shift in political and economic thought: 'At the very point when the middle class appears to be on the point of perdition – beleaguered by a Coalition Government, the Three Trades-Union, and the Income Tax – at this very moment it enjoys the triumph, in intellectual matters, of being able to respect no other standards than its own.'[8] In the general election of 1922, the Labour Party polled a larger vote than the Liberal

Party, leading to the dissolution of the coalition government and widespread acrimony. The new Labour prime minister, Ramsay MacDonald, complained the capitalists had ganged up against him, while the Conservative Party blamed the disarray of the Liberal Party for allowing the Labour Party to gain power. After the election, the Conservative leadership claimed that it stood above class conflict, unlike the Liberal and Labour parties, who represented sectarian class interests. Accordingly, Eliot's persistent attacks on middle-class liberalism should be understood as an attempt to draw a line under the once dominant progressive political forces of the nineteenth century and, armed with a vision of social unity, as a response to class conflict.

As Eliot's economic thinking developed, he came to believe that any science of economics could only be critiqued from an elevated ethical position. In his 1927 article on political theorists, Eliot argued that neither the 'revival meetings' advocated by Ruskin and Thomas Carlyle, nor the statistical approach of Adam Smith and David Ricardo was able to effect meaningful change. Worse, the description of economic 'mechanisms', central to scientific models of the economy, masked the moral choices facing real people and which demanded a reinterpretation of the human motives at work in the economy. Eliot's economics, like his politics, sought to connect his critique to a long-standing cultural tradition. An unsigned notice in the *Criterion* asserted that the 'behaviour of the markets of the world' emerged from a conflict between conservative habits (which could be described by anthropologists and historians) and the material revolutions enacted by technology.[9] This claim necessitated both scientists and men of letters working together to reform the current economic system. Eliot himself forcefully argued that the desire for financial profit was an inadequate motive to destroy churches in the City of London; the traditions and beauty they preserved should be protected until it could be demonstrated that their destruction would lead to demonstrably better lives for the parishioners. Thus, his conservatism worked towards the preservation of social and cultural space.

Eliot's political conservatism also prevented him from sympathising with those revolutionary economic forces associated with Soviet Communism and Italian Fascism: political and cultural forces precipitating command economies. The drafts of *The Waste Land* record Eliot's horrific nightmare of 'hooded hordes' of Russian revolutionaries swarming across 'Polish plains' (*WLF*, 75). In his editorial 'Last Words' of January 1939, he admitted that the *Criterion* had been too preoccupied with the threat of Communism, although he insisted that a British Communism could have been a natural development from nineteenth-century liberalism. The danger of British Fascism seemed more remote. Eliot ridiculed British Fascists in the *Criterion* for trying to dress up British traditions 'in an Italian collar'.[10] The idea that a fascist state would defend the British constitution was dismissed as incoherent. Neither Communism nor Fascism presented desirable economic reform, and Eliot lamented the way in which their political extremism threatened the disintegration of a common European culture encompassing local political differences (see Chapter 6 above). The polarisation of European politics increased after the stock market crash of 1929 and the onset of the Great Depression. Eliot chose to investigate the home-grown theories of Douglas's Social Credit, as well as John Maynard Keynes's radical proposals for government-backed credit and spending to offset disastrous cyclical downturns in the capitalist economy. During the Spanish Civil War, he pointedly refused to 'take sides' on a polarised choice between the extreme right and the Communist left. Yet on the outbreak of the Second World War, it was clear that an era of open debate about economic reform had come to a close.

NOTES

1. Quoted in Donald Gallup, 'T. S. Eliot and Ezra Pound: Collaborators in Letters', *Atlantic Monthly* (January 1970), 54.
2. These monthly 'Foreign Exchanges' have been discovered by Ronald Schuchard in the archives of Lloyds Bank.
3. 'A Commentary', *Criterion* (January 1931), 310.
4. John Maynard Keynes, *The Economic Consequences of the Peace* (London: Macmillan, 1919), pp. 1–2.
5. B. W. E. Alford, *Britain in the World Economy since 1880* (London: Longman, 1996), p. 120.
6. 'Last Words', *Criterion* (January 1939), 271.
7. 'Political Theorists', *Criterion* (July 1927), 69–73.
8. 'London Letter', *Dial* (April 1921), 451.
9. [anonymous review] *Criterion* (August 1927), 182.
10. 'A Commentary', *Criterion* (February 1928), 97–9.

CHAPTER 28

Anti-Semitism

John Xiros Cooper

Today when people are asked what they know about T. S. Eliot, most mention three things: he was the librettist of the enormously popular Andrew Lloyd Webber musical *Cats*; he wrote one of the most celebrated and difficult poems of the twentieth century, *The Waste Land*; and he was an anti-Semite. This last tag, fastened to him after the end of the Second World War, has been the focus ever since of a sometimes acrimonious debate among critics, scholars, and, occasionally, in the popular press. Although Eliot's offending works were written before the Second World War, it wasn't until after the war that anyone thought the anti-Semitism was significant enough to make it the topic of public argument. It seems that before the war, the incidental anti-Semitism of many Europeans and Americans camouflaged attitudes that after the war took on a more sinister and menacing colouring. Two things contributed to the appearance and persistence of the charge against Eliot: firstly, the new position of Jewry in the public sphere after the Holocaust and, secondly, Eliot's own fame and celebrity as a poet and cultural spokesman. After his Nobel prize in 1948, he was a leading public intellectual in the English-speaking world. It did not help that he spoke for a conservatism that some people mistook for the virulent, right-wing authoritarianism of Fascist Germany, Italy and Spain. Although his visibility as a public figure brought greater attention to his work, it also made him a target. An attack by another poet, Emanuel Litvinoff, made the whole matter of his anti-Semitism an issue that has stuck ever since.

The episode occurred at the inaugural poetry reading of the Institute of Contemporary Art (ICA) in London in 1951. With Eliot in attendance, Litvinoff, an Anglo-Jewish writer, read a bitingly mordant poem addressed directly 'To T. S. Eliot'. There he chided the Nobel laureate for several negative references to Jews made in verse he had published three decades earlier. The poem also reminded listeners of the recent history of genocide in Europe and that anything that smacked of anti-Semitism was

285

no longer acceptable, even from a great poet. As soon as Litvinoff finished reading there was silence, followed by scattered applause; yet several persons jumped to Eliot's defence. Stephen Spender and Herbert Read were particularly agitated and assailed the younger man in the course of supporting the senior poet. Eliot himself, no doubt embarrassed by the stir, kept his calm but was overheard by another poet, Dannie Abse, saying the poem was 'good, very good'.[1] Litvinoff's public reading was provoked by the publication in 1948 of Eliot's *Selected Poems*, including the offending lines about Jews. Litvinoff, and others, thought it was insensitive and irresponsible of Eliot to reprint these poems only three years after the horrors visited on European Jewry had become public knowledge. Of course, he was right.

Was it to Eliot's credit that he was not about to go back and alter his early work in order to make it more palatable in new circumstances? He was not about to sanitise the past for political reasons in the way W. H. Auden, for example, removed the traces of pro-Communist bravado from 'Spain 1937' and 'A Communist to Others' to make them fit his later opinions. In the course of these editorial dexterities, Auden removed himself as a possible target during the anti-Communist witch hunts of the Cold War. Eliot's reluctance to revise the past can probably be put down to two things: one, he was not about to repudiate work that reflected the truth of his experience at the time and, second, he seemed to honestly believe that the offending passages were not anti-Semitic. After the events at the ICA, however, the matter of his alleged antipathy to Jews became, at first a minor note in Eliot criticism, rising to a higher pitch of interest in the late 1980s and 1990s. In the 1940s, J. V. Healy and Lionel Trilling confronted Eliot in correspondence over the problematic nature of his treatment of Jews. Trilling raised the issue of prejudice in his 1943 review in the New York *Nation* of Eliot's *A Choice of Kipling's Verse*; in particular, he queried the selection of 'The Waster', in which lurks an implicit but obvious anti-Semitic sentiment. Trilling politely condemned the inclusion of the poem. Eliot defended himself in an equally courteous manner and the matter was laid to rest. From the 1960s onwards, literary scholars, among them George Bornstein and Ronald Bush, probed a little more insistently into the matters of race, anti-Semitism and prejudice in Eliot's poetry and prose (although Bush remarks that he raises 'these questions with great diffidence').[2] However, there was no broader consideration of all the available evidence and very little effort made to read the transgressive utterances in their appropriate contexts until Christopher Ricks took on this task in his book-length study, *T. S. Eliot and Prejudice*

(1988). Not only does this book have the distinction of being the first major critical intervention on the issue of Eliot's anti-Semitism, it is still the most even-handed examination of the subject.

It was Ricks's very reasonableness about a topic that increasingly arouses intemperate passions that seems to have provoked the professional lawyer and part-time man of letters, Anthony Julius, to publish *T. S. Eliot, Anti-Semitism, and Literary Form* (1995). Here the case for the prosecution is put in its strongest possible form and critics were promptly divided into two hostile camps. With prosecutorial single-mindedness, Julius insisted that Eliot was an anti-Semite: his poetry was silent about the suffering of Jews. Yet, although Julius put Eliot in the dock, in an unusual manoeuvre, he claimed that Eliot had made great poetry out of this dark material. Julius's book had the effect of inciting others to disparage Eliot. The poet-critics Tom Paulin and James Fenton were particularly robust in their condemnations. Fenton, speaking with the authority of Oxford University's Professor of Poetry, publicly pronounced Eliot a 'scoundrel' in 1996, to some applause. Many others, however, leapt to Eliot's defence. It fell to Ronald Schuchard, one of the most discerning Eliot scholars, to lead a counter-attack. In his essay 'Burbank with a Baedeker, Eliot with a Cigar: American Intellectuals, Anti-Semitism, and the Idea of Culture' and in a response to critics of this essay 'My Reply: Eliot and Foregone Conclusions' (both published in 2003), Schuchard attempted to answer Julius's indictment. In the course of that defence he brought to light new archival material detailing Eliot's contacts with Jews throughout his lifetime that he felt completely exculpated Eliot from the charge of anti-Semitism. Since the publication of Julius's book others have contributed to the debate, but the controversy remains largely dominated by partisans and there is very little hope of resolution. The divisions in the scholarly and critical community are deep and resolute.

When we consider the amount of heat that the controversy has generated, it is rather surprising to find that the offending passages in Eliot's work are, notwithstanding what his as yet unpublished post-1925 correspondence might contain, few in number. There are no sustained anti-Semitic diatribes as one finds in Ezra Pound's work. Nor is there a complete text hostile to the Jews, such as Mark Twain's 1898 essay 'Concerning the Jews'. Nor is there a fully developed Jewish caricature, such as Charles Dickens's portrait of Fagin in *Oliver Twist* (1838). The case for Eliot's anti-Semitism rests, in fact, on isolated lines in a few early poems and a passing reference to Jews in one of his prose texts. Until all the projected volumes of Eliot's post-1925 correspondence are published, discussions of his anti-Semitism will have to return again and again to these textual fragments.

And what exactly is the nature of the offending passages in the poetry? They cluster in the collection Eliot published in 1920 as *Ara Vos Prec* in London and as *Poems* in the United States. This collection heightened the satirical force of his first book, *Prufrock and Other Observations* (1917). Indeed, these poems went much further than satire. They explored certain extremes of experience, language and emotion that readers found both shocking and disturbing. One might even think of them as the punk or grunge phase of his oeuvre. Disgust with the purely animal side of human nature, decay, depravity, delirium and adultery identify the emotional terrain covered by the first poem in the collection, the dramatic mono-logue 'Geronion'. Although there are negative portraits of Iberians ('Mr Silvero'), Japanese ('Hakagawa'), Scandinavians ('Madame de Torn-quist'), Germans ('Fräulein von Kulp') and others of a less determinate nationality or ethnicity, it is the character in the poem referred to as 'the Jew' (*CPP*, 37), the owner of the house in which the speaker Gerontion lives, who usually receives the greatest amount of attention. The second poem in the collection, 'Burbank with a Baedeker: Bleistein with a Cigar', also puts the two Jewish characters, Bleistein and Sir Ferdinand Klein, in a derogatory light, dimly suggesting that the Jews are responsible for the decline of Venice as a vital civilisation. The poem is an intricate colloca-tion of references, allusions and echoes of other literary works, including Shakespeare, Ben Jonson, Wilkie Collins, Henry James and others. Of course, the lines

> On the Rialto once.
> The rats are underneath the piles.
> The Jew is underneath the lot.
> Money in furs ...   (*CPP*, 41)

have stirred a great deal of comment. To make matters worse, in the original publication, and every reprinting until 1963, the word 'Jew' in both this poem and in 'Geronion' was not capitalised. In 'Sweeney Erect', it is the turn of the Irish, especially the Irish-American title character Sweeney, who is characterised not only as an 'orang-outang' (*CPP*, 42) but is also abused throughout the poem. In 'A Cooking Egg', the chairman of the chemical firm ICI, Sir Alfred Mond, is mentioned in a satirical light, but it is not clear whether this is because he is Jewish or due to the fact that he came to England from Germany, or because his company profited handsomely from the manufacture of armaments during the First World War. In the years immediately following the war there was a great deal of public resentment, fuelled by the popular press, against war profiteers. Later in this poem, Eliot writes: 'The red-eyed scavengers are creeping / From Kentish Town and Golder's [*sic*] Green' (*CPP*, 45). Golders Green is a north London suburb that has a large population of Jewish residents. The four poems in French in this collection take us on a world tour that heaps scorn on Omaha and Terre Haute, Indiana, in the United States, the burning coasts of Mozambique and the Low Countries. The invective in these French poems trades in ugly images and a kind of sweaty disgust; for example, 'La sueur aestivale' ['summer sweat'] (*CPP*, 48) in 'Lune de miel'. In these poems, Eliot seems to find everything about the human animal repugnant. The collection closes with 'Sweeney Among the Nightingales', which contains the lines 'Rachel *née* Rabinovitch / Tears at the grapes with murderous paws' (*CPP*, 56). By suggesting that Rachel has cast off her Jewish origins by marrying a gentile whose surname she has adopted, these lines have also been read as an insulting remark.

There are two other textual fragments that have provoked considerable discussion. One is a cancelled funeral lament from the manuscript drafts of *The Waste Land* that did not come to public notice until the appearance in 1971 of a facsimile edition of Eliot's drafts for the poem edited by his widow, Valerie Eliot. The offending lines come in a poem called 'Dirge', described by Christopher Ricks as the 'ugliest touch of anti-Semitism in Eliot's poetry'.[3] The lines describe Bleistein, no longer a gawping tourist in Venice, but drowned, sunk to the bottom of the sea. The passage begins by adapting a line from a stanza in Ariel's song in *The Tempest*, 'Full fathom five thy father lies'. Eliot replaces 'thy father' with 'your Bleistein' and continues by describing the drowned man as lying 'under' a variety of sea creatures. Indeed, he is so far down, 'wharf rats' cannot reach him. The corpse is also said to suffer from a form of hyperthyroidism (Grave's Disease) and has lost his eyelids to crabs. The final lines in the passage continue reworking Ariel's song, but now evoke the ethnic stereotype of Jews as 'expensive rich and strange' (*WLF*, 121). Eliot cancelled 'Dirge' from the poem that found its way into print as *The Waste Land* in 1922. Ricks comments wisely that 'it does not become us to claim assuredly to know why' Eliot suppressed this draft.[4]

The second fragment is found in a work of cultural criticism entitled *After Strange Gods: A Primer of Modern Heresy*, published in 1934 but never reprinted. It is still out of print. It is an ill-tempered book and perhaps an ill-mannered one. The treatment of D. H. Lawrence, for example, borders on insolence. The book was the revised text of a series of lectures Eliot gave at the University of Virginia in May 1933. In making the case that the population of a nation 'should be homogeneous' in culture, Eliot goes on to state a further point. More important, he declares, is the need to ensure what he calls 'unity of religious background'. This desired 'unity', due to 'reasons of race and religion', makes 'any large number of free-thinking Jews undesirable' (*ASG*, 19–20). Eliot always insisted that the emphasis in his argument about homogeneity should be laid on 'free-thinking' rather than the 'Jews' and that he could just as easily have said free-thinking Welsh or free-thinking Eskimos (itself a terminological error, which could be interpreted as an ethnic slur by, say, the Inuit and Dene peoples).[5] But those already convinced of his animus towards Jews will not be persuaded by this defence.

Peter Ackroyd, one of Eliot's unofficial biographers, reports that he came across four instances of questionable references to Jews in Eliot's private correspondence, dating from 1917 to 1929. He terms these references 'supercilious' rather than derogatory. He then goes on to quote Leonard Woolf's remark: 'I think T. S. Eliot was slightly anti-Semitic in the sort of vague way which is not uncommon. He would have denied it quite genuinely.'[6] And Eliot did deny it: 'I am not an anti-Semite and never have been. It is a terrible slander on a man.'[7] Mention of Leonard Woolf might also remind us that his wife Virginia was not above making (in the words of one of her biographers) 'casual, unsystematic and apparently thoughtless' remarks about Jews, even though she was married to one.[8]

However, the anti-Semitic remarks of others, casual or otherwise, do not excuse Eliot from responsibility for his own utterances. This is the principal point of Ricks's discussion of Eliot's anti-Semitism: namely, that Eliot made these remarks and he was wrong to make them. But Ricks does not stop there. To understand his further thoughts on the matter, an awareness of appropriate contexts is necessary. The years of the First World War and the 1920s were a very difficult period in Eliot's personal life, and much of the poetry he wrote at this time seems deliberately designed to offend, provoke and disturb his readers. This has something to do with the combative, at times ranting, mood in which a new movement in literature – modernism – began. But there was also something more personal and biting about Eliot's anti-Semitism in *Poems* (1920) that can be seen as part of a larger antipathy: a ferocious misanthropy that had its roots in Eliot's adulterous marriage, physical illness and the despair occasioned by the catastrophe of a brutal war and a dishonourable peace, and the gnawing worry about a literary career that had not yet found a secure footing in the London literary world. Ricks is right to say that these factors do not excuse Eliot's lines, but they do, however, go some way in explaining the malevolence that pulses through them. They also suggest, Ricks argues, how Eliot used 'prejudice' in a more general sense as an odd kind of literary resource when other sources of creative vigour were flagging. One might say, then, that Eliot's creative juices, unable to find more positive routes in which to run, found the path of least resistance in disgust.

In his turn, Julius's argument has certain affinities with this view. He claims that Eliot's anti-Semitic poetry manages to be art of high quality, though it is an art made from disgusting materials. The references to Jews cannot be swept under the carpet, ascribed to a general low opinion of humanity. They are specific, deeply personal and historically grounded by centuries of persecution, including the pogroms in Eastern Europe that took place at the end of the nineteenth century and led to waves of Jewish immigrants arriving in London and the United States. The 'mind of Europe' (*SE*, 16), to use Eliot's resonant phrase, has, according to Julius's cultural history, the clear impress of anti-Semitic prejudice upon it that could, and often did, take a murderous turn. Eliot's disparagement of Jews is seen as part of the pattern of abuse and terror, even a poetic extension of it, visited upon Jews after the diaspora. But Eliot was not some racist thug incapable of sufficient self-reflection to get to grips with his own deepest intellectual and emotional impulses. After all, no one doubts he was a very intelligent man, a talented man. A man, indeed, who spent a good deal of his time after 1927, the year he joined the Anglican Church, examining his conscience, reflecting on his sins and on the possibility of atonement, and hoping for redemption. So, to say that all of his work is imbued at every point by a simple animus towards the Jews, and that it can be accurately described by Julius's favourite phrase as 'anti-Semitic poetry', is to say the offence was deliberate, cunningly thought out and then, after its occasional display in the early 1920s, shrewdly camouflaged so as not to arouse animosity in the new historical circumstances; namely, the tragedy that overcame European Jewry in the late 1930s and 1940s. By this account, then, Eliot is as guilty as Ezra Pound, perhaps even more despicable, since unlike this outspoken anti-Semite he cannot be dismissed as either insane or a buffoon.

It is Julius's more serious accusation that Ronald Schuchard took it upon himself to answer. In 'Burbank with a Baedeker, Eliot with a Cigar', Schuchard fills in the detail of the complex web of personal and domestic scenarios and relationships that make up Eliot's experience of misery in the late 1910s and early 1920s. He also sketches the intellectual background of the idealising liberal pluralism in the American academy that Eliot found abhorrent as a young man. Reluctant immersion in 'Emersonian-Unitarian philosophy' set him on a path of fierce opposition to what he considered the corrosive sublimate of latter-day Puritan thought in America – 'religious liberalism, individualism, optimism, sentimentalism'.[9] But none of this material appeared convincingly exculpatory to Julius, who was determined not to dismiss Eliot's anti-Semitism. Schuchard believed that his trump card was the record of Eliot's convivial relationships with a number of Jews in the immediate social and intellectual circles in which he moved. These included Leonard Woolf, John Rodker, Sydney Schiff, Jacob Isaacs, Mark Gertler, Ada Leverson and others. It may be convenient for Eliot's opponents to deride the 'some of his best friends are' argument as nugatory, but in this heated debate, where a man's convictions are the subject of intense and sometimes unsympathetic scrutiny, his friendships with people he is supposed to have despised do have some relevance. Schuchard is right in bringing these relationships to scholarly attention. Even more importantly, he brings forward research done by Ranen Omer-Sherman in the American Jewish Archives at Cincinnati, Ohio. In these archives, Omer-Sherman discovered a hitherto unknown correspondence between Eliot and an American Zionist intellectual, Horace M. Kallen, a founder of the New School for Social Research in New York. Eliot's friendship with Kallen stretches from the 1920s to the 1960s, with the possibility that there was intimate contact between the two going back as far as 1906, when they first met as students at Harvard University.

Kallen was a leading intellectual figure in the American-Jewish community and a champion of a secular humanist theory of society that diverged radically from Eliot's own idealised conception of a Christian society. Yet, in spite of their differences, the two men kept up a cordial relationship for decades. Because the Atlantic Ocean divided them, their relationship is recorded in their correspondence. Omer-Sherman suggests that there is 'compelling' evidence of 'Eliot's compassionate humanism', especially in his 'concern for Jewish refugees' fleeing persecution in Nazi Germany. Although Eliot and Kallen had deep philosophical differences in their assessments of culture, their friendship never wavered and Eliot's 'activism' on behalf of European Jews, which Omer-Sherman points out 'included meetings with Jewish philanthropists'[10] during the Second World War, underlined Eliot's freely offered efforts to find ways to help

German Jews and 'thousands of teachers and men of science in concentration camps'.[11] Their correspondence also reveals that Eliot was more zealous in upholding Judaism as a religion than Kallen, for whom a secular liberal humanism was the greater social good. Omer-Sherman comments: 'Kallen had spent so many years advocating a secular Zionism that he grew to be callously dismissive of both Reform and Orthodox [Jewish] belief'.[12] It turns out that Eliot defended this Orthodox Jewish belief against his friend. It may surprise many to learn that after the Second World War, Eliot's thinking underwent important changes. His approval of cultural homogeneity gave way to other convictions. He came to recognise 'diversity and disagreement' as providing 'a more satisfying variety and richness of experience' than the narrower cultural orthodoxy he had championed in the past.[13]

Many voices have contributed to this ongoing debate and many more will no doubt intervene in the years to come. But given the evidence we have so far, the baldly stated indictment of Eliot as an anti-Semite seems difficult to sustain without qualification. Yes, there is some evidence to suggest that he was, but there is plenty on the other side as well. Perhaps the collected editions of Eliot's prose and letters will yield further ammunition for the battles ahead and cast new light on this controversy.

NOTES

1. Quoted in Dannie Abse, *A Poet in the Family* (London: Hutchinson, 1974), p. 132.
2. Ronald Bush, *T. S. Eliot: A Study in Character and Style* (Oxford University Press, 1983), p. 226.
3. Christopher Ricks, *T. S. Eliot and Prejudice* (London: Faber & Faber, 1988), p. 38.
4. Ibid., p. 39.
5. 'I am no more anti-semitic than I am anti-Welsh or anti-Eskimo.' T. S. Eliot to Edward Field, 17 March 1947. Quoted in Ronald Schuchard, 'Burbank with a Baedeker, Eliot with a Cigar', *Modernism/Modernity* (January 2003), 17.
6. Peter Ackroyd, *T. S. Eliot* (London: Hamish Hamilton, 1984), pp. 303–4.
7. Quoted in William Turner Levy and Victor Scherle, *Affectionately T. S. Eliot: The Story of a Friendship, 1947–1965* (London: J. M. Dent, 1968), p. 81.
8. Victoria Glendinning, 'Features and Reviews', *Guardian* (9 April 2005), 12. In this review, Glendinning finds Julia Briggs's *Virginia Woolf: An Inner Life* is a little disingenuous in its treatment of Woolf's casual anti-Semitism.
9. Schuchard, 'Burbank with a Baedeker, Eliot with a Cigar', 2–3.
10. Ranen Omer-Sherman, 'Rethinking Eliot, Jewish Identity, and Cultural Pluralism', *Modernism/Modernity* (September 2003), 441.

11. Schuchard, 'Burbank with a Baedeker, Eliot with a Cigar', 16.
12. Omer-Sherman, 'Rethinking Eliot, Jewish Identity, and Cultural Pluralism', 443.
13. Richard Shusterman, *T. S. Eliot and the Philosophy of Criticism* (New York: Columbia University Press, 1988), p. 74.

CHAPTER 29

Gender

Rachel Blau DuPlessis

'The sex-gender system . . . is both a sociocultural construct and a semiotic apparatus, a system of representation';[1] it is also historical, imbedded in personal subjectivity and general ideology, and the site of multiple contradictions. Yet throughout significant decades of modernist literary criticism, no one examined sex-gender materials in particular, although sexuality often incurred comment. This was despite fervent debates and social politics about war, suffrage, the new woman, professions opening to women, and many socio-political manifestations of change around gender and sexuality in modernity: sexology, the criminalisation of homosexuality, transgressive feminine masculinities, lesbianism, homoeroticism, eugenicist schemes and fears about virility. Further, no 'gendered' reading exists in isolation from other social materials – in the case of T. S. Eliot, consideration of nationality (twofold), religious culture, sexuality, class and ethnic materials intersect with gender; each inflects the other.

Eliot's biography provides one zone for gender/sexuality readings. Lyndall Gordon points to maternal influence, noting Charlotte Eliot's upstanding late Victorian poems of religious and moral conviction and Eliot's admiration for her work. The singular, strained and even 'possum-like' treatments of women in Eliot's life are striking: from the creatively vibrant but unstable Vivien Haigh-Wood, his first wife, to the woman he admired from afar, Emily Hale, who wanted more than Eliot could give, to Mary Trevelyan, his pal in later life, up until the safe harbour of the marriage of his last seven years with Valerie Fletcher, a figure of love, care, comfort, posthumous editing and executorship. Eliot's early sex-gender attitudes involve torment and yearning: his painful, shaming and aversive bonds with his first wife and his own attitudes (of distaste, recoil, conflict, so far as they may be surmised) to the female body and sexuality. Although Gordon points to the persistence of spiritual crisis and mystical arousals in Eliot's career, she offers temperate, moving summaries of the relations of gender to personal suffering. Other poignant tales, some

with the fervent conviction to 'out' Eliot, track the impact of the death in
the First World War of his French friend Jean Verdenal. There is no doubt
over Eliot's deep attachment to Verdenal and his sense of loss, but what this
means in terms of Eliot's sexuality is unclear. This material and other
motifs in his poetry (notably the latter-day gay icon St Sebastian) may
suggest that Eliot evinced homoerotic yearnings, struggles and structures of
feeling. In Colleen Lamos's formulation from queer theory, the apparently
natural binary division between heterosexuality and homosexuality, as well
as the apparent ease of identifying objects of desire, are rigid sexual myths,
undone by literary works central to modernism such as Eliot's poetry,
whose own gender and sexual identifications are complex and 'errant'.[2]
The sex/gender/erotic pressures that Eliot so forcefully and strikingly
depicts in the diction, textures and motifs of his poetry are illuminated,
but hardly solved, by speculation about his biography.

Some critics have resisted recent sex-gender interpretations and biographical readings with enraged dismissal, seeing these investigations as
an unseemly, even prurient revolt against this iconic, canonical writer. But
in truth explorations of modernism and sex-gender materials have been
critically productive in discussions of Eliot's work.

Eliot began as a modernist and ended as an anti-modernist; in both
positions, he diagnosed modernity. Eliot did not champion women's
sexual freedoms (as did, variously, Ezra Pound, William Carlos Williams,
and D. H. Lawrence when it suited them), though he was for liberty
of literature in *The Well of Loneliness* case (see Chapter 9 above), and
he sponsored, as publisher and editor, some bold women writers (Djuna
Barnes, Marianne Moore, and, up to a point, Vivien Eliot). Eliot's
depictions of female figures often reveal hostility, shock, distaste and
manifest a mordant masochism at female sexual energy and power. Eliot
also puts seriously and sympathetically into his poetry transgressive male
figures who suspect both their manhood (defined by Eliot as potency and
loutishness) and their heteronormativity. 'Eeldrop and Appleplex' (1917)
shows an urbane brace of males dismissing a female figure (an amalgam-
ation of H.D. and Katherine Mansfield); this repositioning of the female
from considerable cultural producer to – both – muse figure and pretentious fake is a cutting response to a new literary marketplace. This, along
with the parallel Fresca-writer-'bitch' materials (excised from *The Waste
Land* by Pound), Eliot's retrograde bluster about female professionals in
his correspondence, and his association of females with debasements of
'romanticism', contribute to these repeated, sexist attitudes. In short, Eliot
was absolutely haunted by sex-gender materials throughout his life and

career, and constructed a variety of resolutions in works that, if personally expressive and even therapeutic, also had a considerable – sometimes unpleasant – socio-cultural impact on Anglo-American modernism.

Indeed, the misogyny and sex-gender agony of Eliot's early poems was both productive for him and culturally decisive within modernism. The deep pain of his early erotic and affective life led Eliot to religious motifs (sin, purgation, humility) and in part motivated his Anglican conversion. However, the universalising, anti-modernist attitudes of his Christianity were less productive precisely because they were less overtly conflicted. When Eliot self-consciously became a spokesperson, notably for an elite leadership of a moral community and a civic (if narrowly constructed) 'idea of a Christian society', he is more studied, hedged, repressive of errant, sordid and sardonic energies and of gender materials.

The early work is richly modern in its formal use of collage and ironic juxtaposition, in the themes of alienation and hidden trauma, in its heteroglossia, mixture of different levels of diction, including jargons, and in a subject matter dealing with the city and male and female hysteria. The mocking urbanity of many early poems – exacerbated sensation and irritation, arid gender relations – opens out to an uncontainable yearning mixing the sexual, spiritual and the existential, which is as quickly closed up or ironised. Impotent connections, incomplete sensations, defensive resistances, frustrating sexual encounters, urban loneliness, self-lacerating crises of being among the obscure and marginalised are his vital modernist themes. This early work also includes the roaring, randy, mannered verses of King Bolo in which cartoonish male figures are uniformly priapic, perverse and scatalogically productive. Sometimes with difficult sex/ gender material, Eliot chose to write in French – with a sour and painful portrait of a honeymoon spent in sexual despair, and an ecstatic self-revealing story told by a dirty, shambling waiter about children who are sexually aroused.

His characteristic mode and findings are captured by the condensed Jamesian stories in verse, 'The Love Song of J. Alfred Prufrock' and 'Portrait of a Lady' as well as in 'Hysteria' and 'Gerontion', dramatic monologues of voices trying to contain an abyss of desire mixed with fear and resistance, splenetic stasis and the failed quest for any exit from being locked in one's own life. The transgressive dandy J. Alfred Prufrock, who cannot manifest the potent will to speak his philosophic/sexual question, the aggressive over-eager, temptingly manipulative lady in 'Portrait', as well as the male figures unable to contain the spill of female hysteria and (dental/vulval) excess in the prose poem 'Hysteria', make all sexual options appear as impossible traps. The instabilities of the conversations and observations offered in patter-song, irregularly rhythmic, closural stanzas are assisted by the extraordinary light verse rhymes translocated from Laforgue. Such rhymes as 'marionettes/cigarettes' precipitate themes, attitudes and tones – ironic control beyond anguish and guarded undercurrents of judgement.

The quatrain poems of 1917–20 had their origin in a bargain between Ezra Pound and Eliot to 'call to order' the flatness of free verse, which, not coincidentally, they viewed as being weakened because appropriated by poeticising females (most notably, Amy Lowell) and their flaccid, if popular, poetic rivals (for example, Edgar Lee Masters). The grand diagnosis of a 'feminisation' of literature is their motif at this time, demanding resistance to both the effete and the feminine. Eliot thereupon presented satiric treatments first of the churchly forces of order; then of an *über*-male figure of exaggerated proportions and appetites (Irish-inflected Sweeney); and of predatory demi-mondaines; fastidious, denatured *flâneurs* (Burbank) being displaced – even physically tainted – by Jewish bankers (Klein) and by Jewish thugs (Bleistein). The sexual licence of uncontrolled females, impotence of struggling men, mongrelised, cosmopolitan predators, and a failing social hegemony are linked together. The verbal condensation, the attraction/repulsion the author feels towards his mongrel louts and the allusions to socio-cultural tropes give these poems a snap and an energy that make them not only politically charged but aesthetically rich and strange.

On *The Waste Land* (1922) there are myriad observations to make from a sex-gender perspective, including the melodramatic erotic and parturitional metaphors used by Pound as 'midwife' of the poem he helped to shape. It is a social poem trying to penetrate the urban plethora that, in relation both to the horrors of the First World War and to personal grief, was saturated with a sense of doom, devastation and despair. It is a haunted poem, filled with broken tokens of past beauties, systems, myths, in disembodied, mysterious citations. It is a poem of desire, frustration, blockage and sexual cross-purposes, with virtually no release. Fertility has been damaged; a wounded male is limned in the quest myth, intermittently used, of the Fisher-King with a Parsifal-like hero (which Eliot had encountered in Jessie Weston's *From Ritual to Romance* [1920]). The semi-narrative juxtapositions offer cut-off glimpses and vignettes of bumbling, burned out, grieving or malicious searchers, of the living dead, and of blighted hopes, in a symphonic montage now so classic that one forgets its shocking brilliance.

The fierce problematic of sex-gender in *The Waste Land* is literally everywhere: the Woman Question and neuraesthenia, incompatibility and desperation, hysteria, impotence, male wounds, homoeroticism, failures of desire and failures of nerve, commonplaces of abortion, grungy loss of virginity, perversity, degradation, rape, rancour, conflicted passion. To make a site in which a fertile heterosexuality is returned as a centre-piece is the overt (and underachieved) aim; this is wrenched and inter-rupted by homoerotic yearnings and propositions that do not come from the hegemonies of heterosexuality. The heightened sensibility and arousal of desire (the hyacinth girl – perhaps Jean Verdenal transposed, whom Eliot recalled greeting him with flowers) sometimes takes on a spiritual-ised not a sexual dimension, but mostly sexuality is just sordid and sorrowful. Finally the sheer unfulfilled burningness of sexual desire seems heightened and beautiful in the regal past, but completely passive, beaten down and 'supine' in the low-life present. In many of the vignettes, the speaker proposes an emphatic picture of female figures whose hopeless acquiescence or depressed resistance to sexual contact is a symptom of the morbid lack of fertility that is mourned – and suffered. The poem travels through loss by its séance-like calling up of half-alive voices and half-dead, unrecognised emotions.

The debate as to whether or not Tiresias is the central consciousness of *The Waste Land* involves each reader's attitude towards being told what to think by Eliot's own controlling notes and by his ideologically motivated attempt to assert an organising figure. To propose Tiresias as 'the most important personage in the poem', despite the poem's gaps, fragments, plethora and vectors, seems tendentious when figures emerge and with-draw as sporadic presences, revenants and irruptions. Eliot's statement gathers gender materials up and universalises them ('all the women are one woman' [*CPP*, 78]) to the point of overgeneralising. On the other hand, Tiresias connects the sexual to the spiritual/prophetic aspects of the poem. In Classical myth, Tiresias is given the punishment of blindness and the gift of prophecy for answering 'Woman' to the gods' probing question about whether men or women derive the most pleasure from sex. However, in Eliot's poem this figure does not bear witness to extremes of sexual pleasure, but rather to sexual pain – indifferent, casual, cruel and anguished. Modernity is, again, loss. Yet as a hermaphroditic, bisexed figure, Tiresias is evidence of how important transgressive sex-gender materials and desires are to this poem.

The shards of citation that stud the text are a constant reminder of our pathetic cultural capital and spiritual imcompleteness. Eliot uses the citations to make it seem as if there is some 'secret' that, if one could just decode it, would reveal an answer. Thus the reader is put in interpretative situations of yearning, seeking and urgency that are constantly frustrated, mirroring, in a different zone, the frustrations of the speakers of the poem. Part of the power of this poem lies in the evanescent sense of a final, always postponed answer, due to the contrastive gap between the poem and the notes. These notes are thus a parallel discourse to the poem, rather than extraneous, gratuitous or accidental. It is a discourse in which another authorial voice intones his allusively comprehensive engorgement of the masterworks of European culture, in part by omitting such contributors as Ellen Kellond, the Eliots' maid, who was the principal source for the Cockney dialogue in 'The Game of Chess' section. The notes thus encourage thematically extractive and universalising high cultural readings, saving the poem from its own grotesque display, domestic horror and ecstatic heightening.

These thematic summaries emphasising only sex-gender are incomplete without pointing to a universal mythic nexus that, for Eliot, is fundamental. Given dessication and hopelessness, other – past – cultures may have had better solutions with a traditional ritual order; modernity is left with the 'immense panorama of futility and anarchy' (*SP*, 177) whose diagnosis points to Eliot's developing social and religious conservatism. For him, cultural fullness and renewal depended on sexuality and gender being rightly organised – that is, normalised and sublimated unto repression.

The tonality of the spiritual poems of the late 1920s differs stunningly from the montage of *The Waste Land* and from the sardonic minstrel-vaudeville of 'Sweeney Agonistes'. The absolute resistance to anything smacking of the chaotic, the modern, the sexual, the sordid, is as soothing as it is unexpected. This new tonality makes a spiritual remix of the Book of Common Prayer, medieval allegory, genres of psalm, prayer, liturgy, meditation and pilgrimage, and uses the most familiar, oft-evoked female topos – woman as intercessor. In 'The Hollow Men' (1925), male figures reveal spiritual hopelessness, reduced to the physical level of dried bits and the rhetorical level of insoluble riddling paradox, from which a quester moves, as in *Ash-Wednesday* and 'Marina' (both 1930) via the calm spiritual leadership of a female figure, in an allegorical ascent that passes through both devilish ugliness and earthly beauties. This figure is the idealised obverse of those sexualised seductresses who appear in the earlier work. Like a wraith, this female (designated variously sister, mother, Virgin, daughter) seems to precede various speakers into an illuminated landscape of prayer and watchfulness. The transmutations and translations of religious motifs from Dante and others construct the remarkable 'always already' sound of this work, both uplifting and gender normative. Or almost. In the Ariel Poems, with a rhythm of maternal rocking, Eliot is remothering himself into rebirth. However, the contradiction between the lulling sound and the spiritual anguish is remarkable.

These religiously inflected poems are in dialogue with two poems written in the same period that move in other sex-gender directions. Perhaps because they are called 'Unfinished Poems' in his *Collected Poems*, 'Sweeney Agonistes' and 'Coriolan' have been neglected. 'Sweeney Agonistes' is a negative print of *The Waste Land*, full of posturing sexuality and threat, homosocial jocularity, threatening men, hand-wringing demi-mondaines, tonal potpourri and panache, mocking narration of femicide (getting away with murder), Africanist cannibal-missionary by-play, and the conviction that crime and guilt in relation to females are every *man's* heritage. This work is emphatically Eliot's literary road not taken. 'Coriolan' is a meditation on apparent male power, hidden male powerlessness (with needy cries of 'Mother mother' [*CPP*, 129]), a sense of sacramental or sacrificial doom and, touchingly, the presence of littleness and beauty in nature. These may or may not provide a spiritual or ethical counter-tendency to the robotic, mechanical, parodied – and ominously militaristic – activities of governance. The final demand 'RESIGN RESIGN RESIGN' (*CPP*, 130) goes to the heart of the political–spiritual dilemma of the male hero: does this command finish off his political power or accept a potent spiritual passivity? Among other elements, these poems face Eliot's own growing cultural power combined with a gnawing sense of his unworthiness, thus exemplifying one paradox of masculinity: a sense of powerless power. From the 1930s forward, Eliot's thought became 'politically' (that is, religiously) correct, even theocratic, a measure of his prior anguish.

After Strange Gods (1934) constitutes a moralist's paean to racial and religious purity and to the American South, praised for its resistance to modernisation, heterogeneity, urbanisation, immigration and to certain 'undesirable' groups, notoriously 'free-thinking Jews' (*ASG*, 20) and out-of-place blacks. The modernists who encourage a bad heterodoxy are also those who focus intensively on sex and gender issues; this fastidious touchstone designates their moral limitations. Sheer femaleness produces only the 'feminine', defined by Eliot through consideration of one story, 'Bliss', by Katherine Mansfield, which he describes as a perfect handling of the most 'limited' and '*minimum* material' (*ASG*, 36). No other female modernist is mentioned (not Gertrude Stein, Marianne

Moore, H.D., Djuna Barnes, with whom he had varied but serious literary dealings, not even Virginia Woolf, whom Eliot knew well). One thereby sees a desire to segregate women authors to a 'feminine' mode already disparaged as miniature and therefore culturally and morally inadequate. One also sees a canon being shaped and crafted by careful exclusion of significant practitioners. Such pertinent moments help to explain how, up to about 1975, the modernist canon was mainly mono-gendered, virtually mono-ethnic, and generally hetero-normative.

In *After Strange Gods*, Eliot resisted authors' focus on sexuality. In his discussion of the works of Thomas Hardy and D. H. Lawrence, the driving narrative force of passionate sexuality is dismissed as reductive. The 'sexual morbidity' (*ASG*, 58) of Lawrence, in particular, in which the female characters might have sex with 'savages' or 'plebeians' (*ASG*, 61), is disdained. (Bearing *The Cocktail Party* in mind, female characters who are crucified by savages are presumably a better narrative bet.) 'Morbidity' is a very striking term for these matters as it is a crossing point for general mental states (gloomy, unwholesome, extreme, unreasonable) and, as a technical medical term, for diseased parts or structures, corrupted, vitiated and infected. From the vantage point of sex and gender issues, the rest of Eliot's career might be seen as avoiding any such 'morbidity' in his work: *Four Quartets* (1943) is post-sex and the later plays are post-gender.

Secular modernism is, for Eliot, hampered by its sexual, materialist focus. *Four Quartets*, an alternative spiritual eternalism, is restrained on the issue of sexuality and normative on gender, devoting more space to mentioning flora and fauna than females. In 'East Coker', 'matrimonie' becomes a vision of dancing, old-fashioned folk, and a good sacrament; a terse 'coupling' – whether of 'beasts' or of 'man and woman' (*CPP*, 178) – has its proper time and uses, noted with acerbic distance. Readers of this poem are addressed as a general set of sinners; further specificity produces lists of males – often 'old men' (*CPP*, 179) or those who are important in the secular world ('the statesmen and the rulers, / Distinguished civil servants' [*CPP*, 180]) but who lack spiritual goals. Otherwise in 'The Dry Salvages', one female is again used as a traditional intercessor. Compared to the anguished, mordant early work, it seems that Eliot uses special restraint to produce these apparently unimpeachable sex-gender 'truths'. Laughing children in a garden present another unquenchable moment of Eliot's unreadable, primal yearning. The mutable public world of men and the fire bombing suffered during the London Blitz are noble tests, and are treated with the sacrificial solemnity of a divine plan revealed. However, the key male figure encountered in 'Little Gidding' is a fascinating, shimmeringly ambiguous psychic double, combining civic *virtù*, purgatorial resignation and a disenchanted self-critical literariness.

The plays, too, are made in the wake of 'morbidity', focusing on post-worldly realisations and spiritual struggle. These plays are exacting rather than exciting. Spiritual crises are their topics; their goals are didactic. All the plays concern soul-intense questers, knowers and fulfilled foreknow-ledge. While they also show conflicts, dialogues and some argument, the foregone conclusions make each drama earnest but far less powerful than the rancid, ambiguous, energetic sexual rage and fear of 'Sweeney Ago-nistes'. Like the elegantly constructed *Four Quartets* (whose materials involve career synopses and self-allusions), the plays also rewrite many motifs from Eliot's works. The gender extremism – including polarised gender binarism, anger at females, homosexual panic and striking hints of sadism and masochism – of the earlier poetry and *The Waste Land* seem to have been put in the past of the characters, alluded to but impalpable. Shocking events such as the possible murder of a female by a male are not performed, but they do haunt the back story of *The Family Reunion* (1939) and are played out in the shadowy aftermath of family reformation and spiritual allegory.

Notable in all the plays (with the exception of *Murder in the Cathedral*) is the sense that the real action is taking place elsewhere. The plays exist in a haunted zone of barely named horrors, anxieties, crimes, guilts, and they proceed in a somewhat therapeutic spirit. These are passion plays, not 'well-made' West End dramas, despite being cloaked in the garb of the drawing-room and family discoveries (for example, of adoption); the works enact a pre-plotted religious-spiritual redemptive narrative man-aged by figures who guide the action but stand outside it. That kind of narrative tends to be gender neutral; the main division occurs between those who 'see' and those who cannot perceive. *Murder in the Cathedral* recounts the historical-spiritual story of the assassination of Thomas Becket, Archbishop of Canterbury. By making the chorus of common folk female, some of Eliot's gender assumptions are revealed. The females are only stunned witnesses. This explicit gendering cuts off their capacity for protest and action; they are caught in an Eliotic limbo of horror and valueless emptiness. The chorus of women is also that group through which sin is verbalised, as great physical disgust and a swoon of spiritual debasement. The male knights are political thugs; they speak a common-sense prose to justify murder. The tempters of Thomas Becket are more poetic and subtle, but as with all the secular figures, the face of action and political decision is made disgusting. This has indirect lessons for all insurgent groups – of class, gender or ethnicity – and is parallel to the pageant *The Rock* (1934), where the bitterness of the unemployed will be solved by giving them work building and repairing churches, literally and allegorically.

In other plays, families often are doubled: an apparently normal one (rancorous, manipulative and inadequate) and the authentic family based on temperate understanding and spiritual realisation. The plot runs on two planes, rumination and meditative reflection on the past coming to a crisis of transformative action (for example, martyrdom); this is intercut with a plane of superficial characters and their uncomprehending, ironic chatter. Gender does not divide the searchers from those mired in temporal banality; a sense of quest and spiritual acumen is given to a select few of all sorts and conditions – something Eliot symbolises as much with class (even a rich man's chauffeur can see deeply enough) as with gender. In *The Cocktail Party* (1949) daimonic but benevolent spirits – knowing more, seeing more, producing forgiveness – guide the action. These are therapist/priest figures, an obliquely gay male figure of witty compassion and a ditzy older woman who is treated with a kind respect by the author. All of the knowers in all the plays are engaged in giving spiritual help, in mentor–sufferer relationships that dramatise a pilgrimage out of sin or confusion and towards salvation. This pilgrimage starts when characters distinguish true paths and redemptive values from the morass of social and familial webbings. Any former sense of gender hierarchy is put away. In *The Cocktail Party*, the Christ figure of suffering and sacrifice is female. However, Eliot's pious account of Celia's sacrifice gets inflected with primitive natives; this imperialist melodrama somewhat undermines the well-meant Christian mythography. Eliot's plays certainly move beyond the earlier sexual and gender conflicts and revulsions. In his last works, Eliot took seriously the austere, hegemonically anointed responsibilities of a cultural priest, a position offering him humble yet redoubtable authority. Despite an expiation or exorcism of his former demons, Eliot could (fortunately) never expunge his earlier sex-gender ferocities, which forcefully framed his powerful version of modernism within modernity.

NOTES

1. Teresa De Lauretis, *Technologies of Gender: Essays on Theory, Film, and Fiction* (Bloomington: Indiana University Press, 1987), p. 5.
2. See Colleen Lamos, *Deviant Modernism: Sexual and Textual Errancy in T. S. Eliot, James Joyce, and Marcel Proust* (Cambridge University Press, 1998).

CHAPTER 30

Religion

Barry Spurr

T. S. Eliot's declaration of his Anglo-Catholicism was made in the preface to *For Lancelot Andrewes* (1928): 'my present position . . . may be described as classicist in literature, royalist in politics, and anglo-catholic in religion' (*FLA*, ix). It is commonplace to refer to the poet's 'conversion' to Anglo-Catholicism, which is useful for marking his formal commitment of 1927 when he received, in private, the Christian sacraments of baptism and confirmation (on 29 and 30 June, respectively). And Eliot occasionally uses the word himself, of his own experience and more generally: 'scepticism', he wrote in 1932, 'is the preface to conversion'.[1] But he also noted: 'No one ever attempted to convert *me*; and, looking back on my pre-Christian state of mind, I do not think that such a campaign would have prospered.'[2] Where 'conversion' is misleading, with regard to Eliot's faith, is in its suggestion of those instantaneous events, as a result of which converts are changed utterly and a breach is made with their previous, unregenerate lives. They are 'born again'. This is where Anglo-Catholic tradition and Eliot's own spiritual experience part company from Protestant, evangelical ideas of conversion, about which (especially the emotional element, which can play a powerful role) he was deeply suspicious. Accordingly, even when Eliot had become the best known of Anglo-Catholic writers, he was at pains to point out that, as no one ever attempted to convert him, so, in his Christian writings, he was not 'attempting to convert' (*ICS*, 21) his readers.

The term 'conversion', in Eliot's case, tends to diminish the importance of the diverse elements that led up to his baptism and confirmation over so many years and, by implying certitude and finality, contradicts Eliot's conception of the individual Christian's experience (especially in the modern age) as a much more complex phenomenon, shot through with doubts and backslidings, throughout one's earthly pilgrimage. The 'Catholic should have', Eliot wrote (after some six years as an Anglo-Catholic), '*absolute* ideals – and moderate expectations'.[3]

In Eliot's fullest formal statement about the stages of his conversion, we note the emphasis placed on the intellectual process that leads to belief:

The Christian thinker – and I mean the man who is trying consciously and conscientiously to explain to himself the sequence which culminates in faith ... – proceeds by rejection and elimination. He finds the world to be so and so; he finds its character inexplicable by any non-religious theory: among religions he finds Christianity, and Catholic Christianity, to account most satisfactorily for the world and especially for the moral world within; and thus, by what [Cardinal] Newman calls 'powerful and concurrent' reasons, he finds himself inexorably committed to the dogma of the Incarnation. (*SE*, 408)

What is notable here is that full Christian commitment is specifically understood by Eliot in terms of acceptance of the Incarnation – that is, God becoming man in Christ. He has repeated recourse to this doctrine, in prose and poetry:

I take for granted that Christian revelation is the only full revelation; and that the fullness of Christian revelation resides in the essential fact of the Incarnation, in relation to which all Christian revelation is to be understood. The division between those who accept, and those who deny, Christian revelation I take to be the most profound division between human beings.[4]

In 'The Dry Salvages', Eliot affirms that 'The hint half guessed, the gift half understood, is Incarnation' (*CPP*, 190) where the capitalisation draws attention to the specific event and dogma. Emphasis on the theology of the Word made flesh, and the idea of the seven sacraments of Catholic Christianity (most importantly, that of the Mass) as extensions of the Incarnation, are at the heart of the Catholic revival in the Church of England, dating from the early nineteenth-century Oxford Movement. They had found their full doctrinal and liturgical expression in the Anglo-Catholicism of the twentieth-century interwar period, when Eliot embraced the faith. This is the essential context in which his life and work must be set and interpreted, from 1927 until his death in 1965.

Further back, these theological and liturgical principles can be discerned in the Anglican Church of the early seventeenth century, which resisted the Protestantism of the Puritans, in doctrine and worship, and particularly in the learned spirituality of Bishop Lancelot Andrewes. Eliot expresses his indebtedness to this older tradition in his first works as an Anglo-Catholic poet and literary critic: in 'Journey of the Magi' of 1927 (which begins in quotation from Andrewes) and in the essay collection, *For Lancelot Andrewes*, of the following year. In relation to that first poem of his Christian period, we can see, again, how misleading is the term 'conversion' when applied to Eliot's poetry. 'Journey of the Magi' focuses, repeatedly, on the difficulties of faith and the elusiveness of transcendental experience, while urging that it is always necessary to strive towards these things. The poem closes inconclusively, with a solitary Magus, years after the event, yearning for a further death to worldliness and for the new birth in Christ. Eliot's poetry is no more attuned to the evangelical goal of converting his readers than his Christian life, at large, was directed by this intention. To the Episcopalian priest who suggested to him that *The Cocktail Party* (1949) was 'covertly all about the Mass', Eliot responded: 'I really wanted to write a damn good play, and I hope I did.'[5]

Of paramount importance, in religion, for Eliot, was 'the love of God and a sound Catholic doctrine'. The former (fulfilling the First Commandment) was insufficient, as, relying on our own perceptions, we may fail to determine matters correctly. A 'fixed point' is needed, to prevent 'our deflecting from the ideal course'. Catholic doctrine makes it possible that 'we may at any moment determine our position' by reference to it.[6] We discern the antithesis here, familiar in Eliot's earlier literary criticism, between personality and impersonality, subjectivity and objectivity, the Romantic and the Classical world-view. He identified Catholicism with the impersonal, objective, Classical critique of the individualistic, Romantic and Protestant 'inner voice' (*SE*, 27). So far from heeding this unreliable counsel, Catholic Christians, Eliot insisted, should be convinced of the 'vast importance of adhering to, and developing, our dogmatic theology'. Theology was, for Eliot, a 'science',[7] the discipline of faith which the humanists and liberal Protestants had abrogated by divorcing themselves from this repository of impersonal wisdom of the ages to pin their hopes on spiritual whims and fancies – 'undisciplined emotions'.[8] He traced the decline in theology not merely from the Enlightenment or even the theological developments of the Reformation, but from the end of the Middle Ages (for him the epoch of Aquinas and Dante). Since then, there had been a 'progressive spiritual deterioration'.[9]

Faith and its practice were inextricably linked; practice was the incarnation of belief (as the 'culture of a people', he argued, was 'an *incarnation* of its religion' [*NTDC*, 33]). Such locutions sound formulaic, but Eliot never underestimated the difficulty of living a Christian life true to these principles, noting, after more than twenty years as a devoted Anglo-Catholic, that

The reflection that what we believe is not merely what we formulate and subscribe to, but that behaviour is also belief, and that even the most conscious and developed of us live also at the level on which belief and behaviour cannot

be distinguished, is one that may, once we allow our imagination to play
upon it, be very disconcerting. It gives an importance to our most trivial
pursuits, which we cannot contemplate long without the horror of nightmare.
(*NTDC*, 32)

Eliot repeatedly rejected the idea that becoming a Christian provided an
easy solution to (or an escape from) the world's problems, or made one's
own personal life simpler. Writing in the 1930s of young people who were
submitting themselves to Communist ideology ('the faith of the day') and
were discovering, thereby, a 'godsend' in finding something in which to
believe, he warned:

Once they have committed themselves, they must find (if they are honest, and
really growing) that they have let themselves in for all the troubles that afflict the
person who believes in something ... They have joined that bitter fraternity
which lives on a higher level of doubt; no longer the doubting which is just play
with ideas ... but that which is a daily battle.[10]

Eliot remembered that it was in the autumn of 1933, the year of the
centenary of the Oxford Movement and of a great Anglo-Catholic congress to celebrate it, that 'I first attended Mass at St Stephen's
[in Gloucester Road, South Kensington]' – a fashionable West End church
and one of the leading Anglo-Catholic shrines in England. Eliot came to
know his new vicar, the Reverend Eric Cheetham, 'and not long afterwards
he offered me rooms, which had become available, in his presbytery in
Grenville Place'.[11] Eliot remained in the clergy house until 1940, when the
circumstances of the war led to all the occupants departing. Cheetham
appointed him his warden just a year after the poet had come to the parish,
in 1934, and Eliot remained in that position until April 1959 and continued
worshipping at the church until his death six years later.

   Central to Eliot's Christian life at St Stephen's was a regime of
attendance at Mass that was fervent even by Anglo-Catholic standards.
His worship expressed the commitment of someone who especially valued
'ritual and habit', which, he said, are 'essential to religion' (*FLA*, 134).
It was a practice that had no purpose, so far as he was concerned, in terms
of witness for others, let alone their conversion:

I do not go out to an early communion on a cold morning in order to convert my
housekeeper, or to set a good example to the night porter of my block of flats
before he goes off duty. If this was my motive, I had better not, for my own sake,
go at all; and if the housekeeper and the porter suspected that this was my
motive, they would – far from being softened – merely be justifiably irritated by
my trying to interfere with their lives.[12]

He rigorously kept the Eucharistic fast, from midnight, prior to receiving communion, so that the Sacrament might be the first food to pass the communicant's lips that day. He also observed the Friday fast, when Roman and Anglo-Catholics used not to consume any meat. Eliot's friend and former Faber colleague, the poet Anne Ridler, recalled for me how Eliot would warn prospective Friday hostesses of the necessity (in his case) for fish. This would have been an exceptional request from an 'ordinary' Anglican. But Eliot was adamant that others should be aware of his position and the implications of his faith. Herbert Read noted of his friend: 'a statement of differences he could respect; what he could not tolerate was any false interpretation of the position he himself held'.[13] The climax of Eliot's worshipping week (which included daily private prayer, often using the rosary – he had had two blessed by Pope Pius XII – and attendance at weekday Low Masses and on all Holy Days of Obligation) was High Mass, late on Sunday morning, at St Stephen's. The climax of his worshipping year were the Holy Week and Easter ceremonies, which were celebrated at St Stephen's in accordance with the elaborate rubrics of *The English Missal* and *Ritual Notes*, the 'bibles' of Anglo-Catholic worship throughout the interwar period, when Anglo-Catholicism was enjoying its heyday as the dominant party in the Church of England.

As the Incarnation accomplished 'the intersection of the timeless moment' (*CPP*, 192) with time, so the Real Presence of the Lord in Holy Communion and in the tabernacle on Anglo-Catholic high altars extended that timeless moment into 'Time present' (*CPP*, 171). The essential thesis of *Four Quartets*, advanced in such phrases and in its most important metaphor of the 'still point of the turning world' (*CPP*, 173), has its source in Eliot's Eucharistic faith, even as it is articulated, in the poetry, in a non-specific expression in terms of the desire for a 'further union, a deeper communion' (*CPP*, 183). This Anglo-Catholic context has been insufficiently recognised by most commentators on Eliot's poetry because they have been uninformed about the centrality of Incarnational theology in Anglo-Catholic faith and practice and of Eliot's unswerving devotion to it.[14]

Of similar importance in Eliot's Christianity, and one of those hallmarks of Anglo-Catholicism which differentiates it from mainstream Anglicanism, was his commitment to the sacrament of penance, or 'confession'. 'Penitence and humility', Eliot declared, 'are the foundation of the Christian life'.[15] Certainly, they are intimately connected, as the recognition of the need for penitence is contingent upon the humbling process of facing up to one's sins. On 15 March 1928, three weeks into the annual penitential Lenten season, Eliot told the priest who had baptised

him, Father William Force Stead, that he had made his first confession
'and feel as if I had crossed a very wide and deep river: whether I get much
further or not, I feel very certain that I shall not cross back, and *that* in
itself gives one a very extraordinary sense of surrender and gain'.[16] The
ascetic discipline was central to his rule of life, as Eliot revealed in an
unusually public expression (in a BBC radio broadcast) of the private
persuasion of his faith: 'the Christian scheme seemed the only possible
scheme which found a place for values which I must maintain or perish
(and belief comes first and practice second), the belief, for instance, in
holy living and holy dying, in sanctity, chastity, humility, austerity'.[17]
A fortnight later – in another BBC broadcast – Eliot confesses to 'low
appetites' and 'vulgar tastes' and how they have been assuaged in his life:
'I have perceived their transience, their unsatisfactoriness, and the horror
of satiety which is far beyond the famine of deprivation ... Without the
love of God there is no love at all.'[18] Eliot's regular use of the sacrament
expressed the deep-seated sense of sin in his personality (not newly
discovered in his Anglo-Catholicism, but deriving from his Calvinistic,
Puritan heritage – severely watered down, doctrinally, in Unitarianism,
but with the scrupulous moral consciousness preserved intact). Yet Eliot
also regarded the issue matter-of-factly, in the Catholic way:

I shall no doubt do and say the wrong thing again and again; but the important
thing is to be conscious of the error or weakness and of its nature, and then to be
sorry for it ... We show our Christianity in the way in which we are aware of our
faults and shortcomings, and the way in which we are sorry for them.[19]

Eliot preferred to have, as confessor, a priest distinct from his vicar at
St Stephen's.[20] The first of these was Francis Underhill, cousin of Evelyn
Underhill, the author of *Mysticism* (1911). The phrase, 'Bless me father',
which Eliot (like all penitents) would have uttered on having knelt down
in the confessional, is woven into the final section of Eliot's Lenten and
most liturgical poem, *Ash-Wednesday* (1930), as the speaker refers to the
ongoing temptations of the sensual world which continue to bedevil him
(and, it is implied, always will) in spite of all that he has accomplished,
in the foregoing sections of that poem, in the purgative discipline of
ascent.

It is in Eliot's plays, however, that the necessity for the expiation of
sin is most evident. Several figures are portrayed as types of father-
confessor, while others are in the role of the penitent engaged in
rigorous preparatory searching of conscience in a personal desire for
absolution and atonement. At the very core of *The Family Reunion*

(1939), which can serve as just one example of this phenomenon, we find a concentration of attention on the process of the recollection of sin and the desire for repentance: it is, to use Agatha's term, a theatrical 'pilgrimage of expiation' (pilgrimage itself, in Catholic tradition, customarily involving recourse to confession). Harry retreats to Wishwood for a contemplative experience of self-discovery (retreats, also, being an important feature of Anglo-Catholic spirituality to which Eliot had recourse, in monastic communities, several times each year). Harry is haunted by the faces and circumstances of a traumatic past and he needs, if he is ever to be freed from the despair they are daily imposing on his spirit, to encounter them courageously and (in humility) to be purged from their influence. Agatha (the name of the virgin martyr who is listed in the Canon of the Mass and who is invoked against fire) promises that, at this moment of grace, all time will be gathered together and stand still: 'When the loop in time comes – and it does not come for everybody – / The hidden is revealed' (*CPP*, 289). Harry's situation is given dramatic force by his impatience for confession and, hence, liberation from his sinfulness. As in *The Cocktail Party* where the penitents turn to a psychologist as their 'confessor', so in *The Family Reunion*, Harry would bare his soul to Warburton, the family's doctor: 'I don't know why, but just this evening / I feel an overwhelming need for explanation' (*CPP*, 318).

This is not merely a desire to discuss the experience of evil, but a determination that is driven by an unpredictable and inexplicable infusion of grace. Agatha discerns this mystery, in mystical and biblical terms:

> Accident is design
> And design is accident
> In a cloud of unknowing.
> O my child, my curse,
> You shall be fulfilled:
> The knot shall be unknotted
> And the crooked made straight.　(*CPP*, 337)

Her reference here to the 'cloud of unknowing' recalls the concept of man's separation from God described in the famous fourteenth-century mystical treatise (upon which Eliot draws again in the final part of 'Little Gidding'). The unknown author encourages the contemplative to meekness, and insists, when referring to counsel, on the necessity for the penitent to follow his confessor's advice.[21]

Agatha reflects:

> What we have written is not a story of detection,
> Of crime and punishment, but of sin and expiation.
> . . .
> It is possible that sin may strain and struggle
> In its dark instinctive birth, to come to consciousness
> And so find expurgation.   (*CPP*, 333)

The Family Reunion concludes with a simulation of the ceremony of *Tenebrae* – the Good Friday service in which all church lights are gradually extinguished in symbolic anticipation of the rising of the Sun of Righteousness on Easter Day and which Eliot attended every year at St Stephen's.[22] It is an ambiguous close to the play – penitential, by virtue of its quasi-liturgical reminiscence of Good Friday, but pregnant with hope. By setting *The Family Reunion* in the Anglo-Catholic context of the sacrament of penance, I am not arguing that it is, explicitly, an exploration and commendation of that ordinance, any more than *Four Quartets* is a versified celebration of the doctrines of the Incarnation and the Real Presence. What I am arguing is that, in order to fully appreciate the world-view and interpret the remedies that Eliot proposes (however, contingently, tentatively and through metaphor) to the profound problems of human existence in the modern age, we are best equipped if we are familiar with the Christian context of faith and practice in which Eliot had immersed himself and which, in various ways, emerges throughout his poetry and prose in the last forty years of his life.

In Eliot's works of Christian social commentary, principally *The Idea of a Christian Society* (1939) and *Notes Towards the Definition of Culture* (1948) – but in many other shorter articles and chapters too – he explains his thesis about the culture of a people being the incarnation of their religion. Eliot's own commitment to the Church of England was determined by his appreciation of the fact that the cultural life of the country that had become his home was inextricably bound up with Anglicanism: 'culture and religion . . . [are] when each term is taken in the right context, different aspects of the same thing' (*NTDC*, 29). Eliot catalogues something of that '*whole way of life* of a people, from birth to the grave', in a much quoted catalogue: 'Derby Day, Henley Regatta, Cowes, the twelfth of August, a cup final, the dog races, the pin table, the dart board, Wensleydale cheese, boiled cabbage cut into sections, beetroot in vinegar, nineteenth-century Gothic churches and the music of Elgar' (*NTDC*, 31). This shows, he contends, that 'the actual religion of no European people has ever been purely Christian, or purely anything else', and he does not deny the spiritual impurity of such interaction: 'It is inconvenient for Christians to find that as Christians they do not believe enough, and that on the other hand they, with everybody else, believe in too many things ... bishops are a part of English culture, and horses and dogs are a part of English religion' (*NTDC*, 32). Having such cultural roots but tolerating a theological and ritual diversity without parallel in any other Christian communion, Anglicanism was scarcely well placed to be always attuned to the orthodox Catholic interpretation and expression of human life and civilisation which Eliot also profoundly valued. He was prepared to admit the combination of 'unity and diversity in religion', while insisting that the essential teachings of the Catholic faith must be maintained. There may be, 'that is, universality of doctrine with particularity of cult and devotion' (*NTDC*, 15) which will include 'many variations of order and ritual' (*NTDC*, 29). Obviously, nowhere is this more the case than in the Church of England, which 'has comprehended wider variations of belief and cult than a foreign observer would believe it possible for one institution to contain without bursting' (*NTDC*, 73). The guarantee of the Catholic character of the Church of England depended upon its recognition of an authority transcending its national boundaries and traditions. Anglo-Catholicism was constantly reminding the Church of England of that universal authority.

There was never any question that Eliot would become a Roman Catholic, so long as he was a British citizen. Had the First World War not happened and had he stayed in Europe, and become a Christian, it is beyond doubt that Eliot would have joined the Church of Rome. But, in England, this was an impossible allegiance for him, not because of any doctrinal or liturgical reservations, but because of the disconnection from the cultural life of the nation of English Roman Catholics. So far from being part of the mainstream of English life, that church, since the Reformation, had been a cultural curiosity in England. Eliot certainly regretted this situation. For he acknowledged that 'When we consider the western world, we must recognise that the main cultural tradition has been that corresponding to the Church of Rome', noting that, at the Reformation, 'the separation of Northern Europe, and of England in particular, from communion with Rome represents a diversion from the main stream of culture' (*NTDC*, 73). And when Eliot was on the Continent, he would fulfil his religious obligations in Roman Catholic churches. But he was convinced that the Catholic Church in any nation must not only hold fast to orthodox doctrine, but be the religious expression of the culture of its people and, indeed, 'representative of the finest spirit' (*FLA*, 15) of its people. The Church of England was, as he often observed, the Catholic Church in England and it was precisely in its Anglo-Catholic movement that the combination of Englishness with the faith and practice of Catholic orthodoxy was most actively and wholeheartedly pursued. So, once again, we see the necessity of setting Eliot's Christianity explicitly in the context of the tradition he espoused – in this case, with regard to his extensive body of published work on social and cultural theory.

Eliot's Anglo-Catholicism belongs to an Anglicanism that no longer exists, as his idea of English culture and society is redolent of an Englishness that has passed. Those who are keen to understand his life, thought and work will need to recover the contexts of these ecclesiastical and cultural circumstances and conditions with an ever-increasing awareness of their historical character.

NOTES

1. 'Christianity and Communism', *Listener* (16 March 1932), 383.
2. *A Sermon Preached in Magdalene College Chapel* (Cambridge University Press, 1948), p. 5.
3. 'Catholicism and International Order', *Christendom* (September 1933), 176.
4. 'I By T. S. Eliot', *Revelation*, ed. John Baillie and Hugh Martin (London: Faber & Faber, 1937), pp. 1–2.
5. Quoted in David Chinitz, *T. S. Eliot and the Cultural Divide* (University of Chicago Press, 2003), p. 130.
6. 'The English Situation', *Christendom* (June 1940), 108.
7. Ibid., 102, 103.
8. 'Catholicism and International Order', 175.
9. 'Religion and Science', *Listener* (23 March 1932), 429.
10. 'A Commentary', *Criterion* (April 1933), 472.
11. 'The Panegyric by Mr T. S. Eliot', *St Stephen's Parish Magazine* (May 1959), 5.
12. *Sermon Preached in Magdalene College Chapel*, pp. 6–7.
13. Herbert Read, *T. S. E.: A Memoir* (Middletown, CT: Wesleyan University Press, 1966), p. 19.
14. See Barry Spurr, *'Anglo-Catholic in Religion': T. S. Eliot and Christianity* (Cambridge: Lutterworth Press, 2010).
15. *Sermon Preached in Magdalene College Chapel*, p. 8.
16. Quoted in Ronald Schuchard, *Eliot's Dark Angel: Intersections of Life and Art* (Oxford University Press, 1999), p. 152.
17. 'Christianity and Communism', *Listener* (16 March 1932), 383.
18. 'The Search for Moral Sanction', *Listener* (30 March 1932), 446, 480.
19. *Sermon Preached in Magdalene College Chapel*, p. 6.

20. Information provided by George Every (1909–2003), a member of the Society of the Sacred Mission, Kelham.

21. See *The Cloud of Unknowing*, ed. Dom Justin McCann (London: Burns, Oates & Washbourne, 1924), p. 9n.

22. Information provided by Mary Trevelyan, Eliot's friend and fellow parishioner at St Stephen's in the 1940s and 1950s.

CHAPTER 31

Philosophy

Manju Jain

Looking back upon his study of philosophy, Eliot ruefully concluded that if he had turned to philosophy instead of to poetry, he might have achieved only a very modest place as a philosopher, becoming perhaps a sort of minor Edmund Husserl or Martin Heidegger. He also acknowledged though that if a poet has pursued philosophical studies, these will have played an important role in his formation and will have informed his poetry.[1] This chapter will explore Eliot's study of philosophy within the context of the major philosophical debates that prevailed at Harvard University during the years he was a graduate student of philosophy there, in a period that has come to be known as the golden age of American philosophy, and will suggest how, despite his reservations about the philosophical theories with which he grappled – idealism, pragmatism and neorealism – his philosophical studies profoundly shaped his creative and critical vision.

When Eliot entered Harvard in 1906, it was dominated by the left-wing Unitarianism of President Charles William Eliot, which gave to Harvard its liberal ethos and its progressive and pragmatic character. Two teachers who played a vital role in shaping Eliot's views on the prevailing philosophical trends, as well as on literary issues, were Irving Babbitt and George Santayana. Both Babbitt and Santayana were opposed to President Eliot's elective system, as well as to Romanticism, liberalism, and the notion of progress, advocating instead Classicism and tradition. Babbitt, in particular, waged a relentless polemic against the anti-intellectualism of the prevailing philosophies of the flux, such as those of William James and Henri Bergson, which exalted intuition at the expense of reason and the intellect. Although Eliot later came to disagree with Babbitt on several important issues, notably with Babbitt's view that humanism could be a substitute for or an alternative to religion, Babbitt's ideas acted as a catalyst for his own and continued to be one of his major preoccupations. Some of these were: the importance of tradition; the unification of thought and feeling; the necessity for the poet and the critic to mediate between the past and the present; the opposition between Classicism and Romanticism; the distinction between 'lower' and 'higher' levels of intuition; and the need for order and control. In fact, it was perhaps as a result of his exposure to these ideas at Harvard that when Eliot intervened in the modernist movement, he gave it a conservative orientation.

Like several students of his time, Eliot was probably under the spell of Santayana's personality and temperament, with his Spanish-Catholic heritage, his hostility to the dominance of Unitarianism at Harvard, his critique of Harvard liberalism as exemplified by the elective system, and its pragmatist ethos. Santayana's colleagues in the philosophy department at Harvard, G. H. Palmer, Josiah Royce, William James and Ralph Barton Perry, disapproved of his aestheticism, his aloofness and his detachment. In fact, when it came to the question of Eliot's appointment at Harvard at 1919, some of his former teachers had reservations about him 'as an attenuated Santayana'.[2] Eliot's own comments on Santayana, scattered over the years, are often acerbic or ambivalent. Despite this ambivalence, however, Santayana's personality and views played an important role in helping Eliot to define the nature of his own discontent with the Harvard of his time and in exploring the relationship between philosophy and poetry, then as well as later. When, in 1935, Eliot recapitulated the development of philosophy during his student years, he admiringly cited Santayana's critique of the older idealism, which his teacher had characterised as 'the Genteel Tradition'.[3]

In October 1910, Eliot arrived in Paris for a year to read French literature and philosophy (see Chapter 3 above). There he encountered the antithetical philosophies of Bergson and Charles Maurras, to whose ideas he had been introduced in Babbitt's course. Eliot attended Bergson's lectures at the Collège de France. He continued to scrutinise the implications of Bergson's views on time, memory, intuition and consciousness from the period when he wrote 'Rhapsody on a Windy Night' in Paris in March 1911 to his later exploration of these notions in *Four Quartets* (1943). Eliot did not accept Bergson's concept of *la durée réelle* [real duration], his view that its unity could be intuited by an act of pure perception, or his notion of an *élan vital* [vital impulse]. In his paper on Bergson, written after his return to Harvard, Eliot dismissed *la durée réelle* as being simply not final and he concluded that some of Bergson's statements tended towards an Absolute, leading some of his critics to call him a mystic.[4] These critics were Eliot's mentors, Santayana and Royce, both of whom had criticised Bergson's concepts of immediate feeling

and pure perception. In his 'Preludes', written at Harvard a few months
after Eliot had attended Bergson's lectures in Paris, he opposed the philosopher's theory of creative evolution. The cosmos is not shown as evolving
progressively forward, animated by a vital impulse, but as revolving cease-
lessly, devoid of meaning and virility. Later, in 1924, Eliot criticised
Bergson's optimism articulated in his theory of creative evolution.[5]

Bergson's influence on Eliot was counteracted by that of Maurras,
whose philosophy was reactionary and opposed to Bergson's notion
of progress. Maurras advocated order, discipline, hierarchy, reason,
willpower and Classicism, as opposed to intuition, impulse and Romanticism. He also favoured the restoration of absolute monarchy, supported
the Catholic Church as an embodiment of the Roman virtues of order,
authority and tradition, and was opposed to the Jewish and mystical
elements in Christianity. As with his response to Bergson, while Eliot
did not accept Maurras's views uncritically, they exercised a lasting influence on him. The conflicting pulls, therefore, that both Bergson and
Babbitt exerted on Eliot epitomise the lifelong tension that he experienced between a fascination with the forces of flux and the need to
subjugate those forces.

On his return to Harvard in 1911, Eliot enrolled as a graduate student
in philosophy. The major concern of the Harvard philosophers during
this period was the justification of religious and spiritual beliefs against
the challenge of Darwinism and the reconciliation of these with the
new scientific, materialist view of the universe. In attempting a synthesis
of science and religion, the Harvard philosophers were influenced by
German idealism and defended religion on a priori Kantian grounds.
The chief exponent of idealism in America was Josiah Royce. Royce
attempted to resolve the conflict between science and religion on the
basis of his monistic idealism. He posited an Absolute, a world soul that
reconciled the antithesis between the finite and the infinite, the temporal
and the eternal. He perceived evolution as the form in which the temporal
constantly yearned to overreach itself, and with the increasing growth of
consciousness, strove for the eternal. Royce took the nature of error as
the starting point to reach the certainty that there is an Absolute. Error
and evil, he believed, are finite, incomplete fragments, which are overcome and transcended in the Absolute. They are logical necessities for
the perfection of the universe and of God, the Absolute Being, although
the perfection of the Absolute is never wholly attained by the temporal.
Eliot did not accept Royce's monistic idealism, nor did he believe with
Royce that error and evil could be absorbed into a higher whole.

In fact, Eliot's dissatisfaction with the efforts of the Harvard philosophers to reconcile science and religion is most evident in the papers he wrote for Royce's seminar on logic in 1913/14. By the first decade of the century, the core of the graduate curriculum in philosophy was Royce's course in logic and epistemology. For if philosophy was required to defend religion against scientific materialism, it would have to re-examine the basis of epistemology, and logic would more convincingly demonstrate the validity of religion. Eliot's papers for Royce's seminars record his attempts to take an independent stand on the issues of the genesis and the foundation of religious experience and its place in a scientific, secular society, the nature of belief and the validity of interpretation. He rejects the notion that a scientific definition of religion is possible, questioning the theories of the older anthropologists such as Max Müller, Edward Tylor, J. G. Frazer and Andrew Lang, as well as the supposedly more scientific work of the French sociologists Émile Durkheim and Lucien Lévy-Brühl, all of whose works displayed the same confusion between definition and interpretation. Eliot's questions are framed within the wider context of early anthropological attempts to establish a scientific, positivist basis for the study of religion and to explain it on the basis of empirical data, thereby subsuming it within rational discourse.

The question of interpretation was one Eliot repeatedly returned to in the course of his writing. Royce believed that the self, community and tradition are formed by the process of interpretation. Following C. S. Peirce, he viewed interpretation as a social cognitive process. Peirce believed, in opposition to Bergson, that there is no direct perception of the given, and that all our cognitions are interpretations. Thinking consisted of a never-ending interpretation of signs without origin or end. The 'real' was the object believed in by the consensus of the community, whose investigations constantly eliminated error and approximated more closely to the truth. Peirce's paradigmatic community was the scientific one. The goal of science was unity with the divine mind and the absorption of all individual egos into an absolute self. Royce adapted Peirce's model of a scientific community to his ideal of a Christian community, progressively and indefinitely realising itself through an infinite series of interpretations.

Eliot, in Royce's seminar, rejected the possibility of there being a community of interpretations, arguing that there can be no congruity between religious experience and scientific attempts to interpret it. Peirce and Royce made Eliot aware that interpretation is necessary and inescapable, but he did not agree with their teleological view of interpretation.

He also countered their belief in the consensus of the community with F. H. Bradley's theory of degrees of reality in order to argue that the difference between truth and error, the real and the unreal, is one of degree. For Eliot, therefore, interpretation is relative and leads to an endless regress. Over the years, he maintained a consistent stand on the question of interpretation, insisting on its subjectivity, temporality, historicity and finitude, and upon the essential fact of error in all interpretation, be it of reality, of history or of literature. It is remarkable that through his engagement with the debates arising from the work of Peirce and Royce, Eliot points forward to later developments in hermeneutics on such issues as interpretation, the critique of foundational or presuppositionless knowledge and the status of the social sciences.

Other philosophers at Harvard also subscribed to idealistic tenets. Palmer, for instance, called himself a moderate idealist and believed that mechanism and teleology were allied. He believed in an ethic of self-realisation formulated in Germany; namely, that the ultimate aim of moral action was self-realisation. Hugo Münsterberg, too, an experimental psychologist, believed that science and religion were compatible. Like Royce, he propagated a voluntaristic world-view, and like Palmer, he advocated an ethic of self-realisation while retaining his scientific positivism. Eliot, in his early unpublished essays on the ethics of T. H. Green and Henry Sidgwick, was critical of the ethic of self-realisation as well as of the moral exhortation implicit in this variety of idealism.

William James's position in this idealistic consensus is more complex. Although he had died in 1910, his influence on Harvard philosophy continued to be very strong during Eliot's student years. In fact, in a 1917 book review, Eliot delineated James's dilemma at Harvard as being caught between the 'oppression of idealistic philosophy' and the 'oppression of scientific materialism'.[6] James was opposed to the absolute idealism of Royce as well as Bradley. As a way out of the conflict between idealism and materialism, and in order to reconcile science and religion, James evolved a voluntaristic idealism and a pluralistic view of the universe according to which order was always in the process of being gradually won and always in the making. His philosophy of pragmatism emphasised the role of action in formulating belief, the practical function of knowledge as an instrument for adapting and controlling reality, the nature of reality as flux and change, and the priority of actual experience over fixed principles. The meaning of any idea is to be found only in the practical consequences to which it leads. Truth is what works, and the religious life must be judged exclusively by its results. Eliot was critical of pragmatism because of its relativism, its anti-intellectualism, its anthro-pocentrism, and for its view of reality as flux. He was also sceptical of James's explorations in psychical research. However, James's speculations on the psychology of religious and mystical experience and on patho-logical states of mind, and his defence of anti-rationalism, deepened Eliot's insights into the nature of the mind and had important reper-cussions on his thought and on his poetry, especially in his poems on pathological mysticism such as 'The Burnt Dancer' and 'The Love Song of St Sebastian'. Also, despite his reservations about pragmatism, Eliot's concerns in his early philosophical work continued to be the pragmatic ones of the indeterminacy of knowledge and the contingency of values and theories. He shared James's distrust of philosophical abstraction and systems, and his sense of the heterogeneity and finitude of experience.

Philosophy had become increasingly technical and specialised during Eliot's years at Harvard. This trend was exemplified in the work of the new realists, represented by Ralph Barton Perry and Edwin Bissel Holt. Perry accepted the results of the natural sciences although he was ignorant of the sciences himself, and he regarded the mathematical sciences as the best model of exact thinking. He opposed the idealistic tenets of subject-ivity and egocentricity as well as its vague and emotive vocabulary serving religious objectives. He advocated a more scientific philosophy, a more technical vocabulary, and the separation of philosophical studies from the history of philosophy. However, despite his scientific and technical priorities, Perry believed that philosophy should serve moral objectives and illuminate current public issues. Therefore, despite belonging to the new, more professional generation of philosophers, Perry continued the Harvard tradition of liberalism and moral fervour.

Eliot deplored this specialisation and professionalisation of philosophy, demonstrated in the work of the new realists. During his student years he had contemptuously described the movement as a spontaneous burst of feeling, as song without words.[7] He later acknowledged the importance of the new realism in displacing idealism, but was critical of its scientific orientation, its neglect of the philosophy of history, and its failure to work out the implications of its philosophy for theology.[8] He also recalled the resentment that he had felt as a student because it had been necessary to acquire a great deal of their vocabulary in order to pass his examinations.

The new realists admired the work of Bertrand Russell, who was a visiting professor at Harvard in the spring of 1914. Eliot attended Russell's courses in Advanced Logic and Theory of Knowledge. In his criticism of the prevalent philosophical theories in 'The Relationship Between Politics and Metaphysics', Eliot had described Russell as directing an unearthly ballet of bloodless alphabets with passionate enthusiasm. He later recalled that Russell's symbolic logic did not seem to have anything to do with reality, but that it gave him 'a sense of pleasure and power manipulating those curious little figures'.[9] He also equated Russell's concept of sense-data (a concept that Russell himself later rejected) with the Absolute of Bradley and the immediate experience of James as the flux that enters philosophy in various forms.[10] Despite his dismissive comments, though, Eliot engaged extensively with Russell's theory of knowledge in his doctoral dissertation. Eliot is critical here of Russell's theory for the assumption of a world of real and independent objects. He argues that the supposedly 'real world' of epistemology is constituted by points of view: it will be 'an essentially indefinite world of identical references of an indefinite number of points of view' (*KEPB*, 91).

While at Harvard, Eliot also studied Sanskrit and Pali, probably on Babbitt's advice, and he took several courses in Indian philosophy. In 1911/12 he studied elementary Sanskrit with Charles Lanman, founding editor of the *Harvard Oriental Series*, which included the reading of classical texts, including the *Bhagavad Gita*. In 1912/13 he took Lanman's course in Pali, which included selections from the sacred texts of Buddhism; he also took James Haughton Woods's course in philosophical Sanskrit, which included a study of Patanjali. In 1913/14 he attended a course entitled 'Schools of the Religions and Philosophical Thought of Japan, as compared with those of China and India', given by Masaharu Anesaki, a visiting professor at Harvard. Over the years, Eliot testified to the influence of Indian thought upon his poetry. Images, references and themes from his study of Indian philosophy and literature recur in his work. However, Eliot also experienced an intolerable tension in his study of Indian philosophy. He recalled some years later that it was impossible to be on both sides of the looking-glass at once, even the best interpreters of Indian philosophy, such as Paul Deussen, had merely translated Indian thought into Schopenhauerian terminology. Eliot was discriminatingly aware of the differences between Indian and western philosophy, and of the difficulty of translating one tradition of thought into the terms of another. The only way he could ever come to understand Indian thought would be to erase not only his own education in western philosophy but also the traditions and mental habits of Europe that had developed over the past two thousand years; that is, by 'forgetting how to think and feel as an American or European' (*ASG*, 41). He was also dissatisfied with superficial appropriations of Indian thought. He was drawn to the ascetic, intellectual aspect of Indian philosophical systems and to their emphasis upon spiritual and intellectual disciplines. However, Eliot also tended to subsume Indian philosophy within his Christian discourse.

Eliot's doctoral dissertation on F. H. Bradley was begun at Harvard and completed in April 1916. Harvard awarded Eliot a Sheldon travelling fellowship in 1914, he went to the University of Marburg in Germany in July, and from there he moved first to London in August and then in October to Merton College, Oxford, to continue his study of philosophy with Bradley's disciple, Harold Joachim. Eliot's discussion of Bradley takes place within the context of the debates about Harvard philosophy and its idealistic consensus. He had explored and formulated many of the views expressed in his doctoral dissertation in his graduate papers on Immanuel Kant, Bergson and Green and the ones he had read at Royce's seminar.

Bradley's metaphysical system is constructed on the basis of the immediately given, immediate feeling, or immediate experience, which is the starting point for knowledge before distinctions and relations, such as those of subject and object, have developed. Facts come to us in this immediate unity, which is broken up before inner unrest and outer impact into relations and divisions through thought and reflection. These relations and divisions are absorbed into the higher unity of the Absolute by a process that Bradley acknowledges is inexplicable. This Absolute, or Reality, is a perfect, harmonious, all-inclusive system that contains in itself all experience. Viewed from the perspective of the Absolute, the parts – such as time, space, self, God – are finite, incomplete, contradictory, and are therefore appearances in contrast to the reality or the Absolute into which they are absorbed, although the Absolute is immanent in all its appearances. These appearances are true or false, real or unreal, by degrees, relative to the Absolute. The degree of truth and error is determined by the amount of correction needed to convert them into reality. Thus religion is truer than morality.

Eliot upholds Bradley's doctrine of degrees of reality as he had done in his seminar papers. He sees the apparently fundamental distinction between the ideal and the real, the unreal and the real, subject and object, as being tenuous, provisional and relative, practically useful but metaphysically baseless. Eliot is aware, though, that degrees exist only from a particular point of view, and that as in any judgement, the interest of the author is implicit. It may be recalled that it was on the basis of Bradley's theory of degrees of truth and reality that Eliot had criticised the positivist explanations of religious and mystical experience given by anthropologists and sociologists. Bradley's relativism also heightened his perception that the self is tenuous, illusory and not a unified entity. However, Eliot had deep reservations about the postulates on which Bradley's relativism was based – immediate experience and the Absolute which, in turn, were based upon Bradley's own presuppositions about the nature of reality.

In discussing immediate experience, Eliot focuses on one of his central literary and critical preoccupations: the relationship of thought and feeling. In his doctoral dissertation, first published in 1964 as *Knowledge and Experience in the Philosophy of F. H. Bradley*, he criticises the concept of immediate experience because it is a rejection of thought, reflection and analysis; like Bergson's *durée réelle* and James's 'pure experience', it is an intellectual construction abstracted from experience which cannot be taken as the foundation of knowledge, whether it is knowledge through intellect or intuition. For Eliot, reality is encountered neither in immediate experience nor in the Absolute: 'nowhere can we find anything original or ultimate' (*KEPB*, 146). For Eliot emphasises that Bradley's Absolute, as the all-inclusive whole representative of ultimate reality, does not exist. It is merely Bradley's postulate, resting upon his assertion that it does. Bradley's Absolute for Eliot is a void, a state of nothingness, 'the absolute zero' (*KEPB*, 202), and not the ultimate goal of his religious and spiritual quest, as has often been supposed. The fear of the void, in fact, recurs frequently in Eliot's poetry.

Bradley's scepticism exercised a lifelong influence on Eliot, but his own scepticism went even further than Bradley's, because though Bradley had shown the necessity of doubting all first principles and presuppositions, Eliot realised that Bradley's own system was a construct, based on his own presuppositions, as are all metaphysical systems. While Eliot's study of philosophy, then, played a vital role in forming his creative and critical vision, it did not provide him with a mainstay in his search for a defining belief; rather, it deepened his awareness of the inadequacy of all philosophical and metaphysical systems, thereby preparing the way for his later acceptance of the dogmas of theology, although this acceptance was tempered by the scepticism that had been fostered and deepened as a result of his philosophical studies.

NOTES

1. 'Scylla and Charybdis', lecture delivered at Nice, February 1952. Hayward Bequest, Modern Archive Centre, King's College, Cambridge.
2. For a discussion of the controversy regarding Eliot's appointment, see Manju Jain, *T. S. Eliot and American Philosophy: The Harvard Years* (Cambridge University Press, 1991), pp. 30–6.

3. 'Views and Reviews', *New English Weekly* (6 June 1935), 151.
4. Paper on Bergson, T. S. Eliot Collection, Houghton Library, Harvard University, MS, fol. 22.
5. See 'A Prediction in Regard to Three English Authors', *Vanity Fair* (February 1924), 29.
6. 'William James on Immortality', *New Statesman* (8 September 1917), 547.
7. See 'The Relationship Between Politics and Metaphysics', T. S. Eliot Collection, Houghton Library, Harvard University, MS, fol. 11.
8. See 'New Philosophers', *New Statesman* (13 July 1918), 296–7.
9. Quoted by Brand Blanshard, 'Eliot in Memory', *Yale Review* (June 1965), 637.
10. See 'Cause as Ideal Construction', T. S. Eliot Collection, Houghton Library, Harvard University, MS, fol. 1.

CHAPTER 32

Social science

Jewel Spears Brooker

The last three decades of the nineteenth century and the first two of the twentieth were golden for the social sciences, due in part to the restructuring of knowledge precipitated by the publication in 1859 of Charles Darwin's *On the Origin of Species*. With men such as William Robertson Smith in comparative religion, James G. Frazer in anthropology, Émile Durkheim in sociology and Sigmund Freud in psychology at the height of their achievements, the first decade of the new century was a rousing time in European intellectual circles. Eliot grew up during this flowering and from 1906 to 1916 he studied the social sciences at three prestigious universities – Harvard, the Sorbonne and Oxford – which were in the vanguard of the best new work. As an undergraduate, he focused on comparative language and literature, and as a graduate student on philosophy and comparative religion. As indicated by his graduate essays and early book reviews, Eliot absorbed the philosophy which is an indispensable element of the social sciences – historicism. He explained his version of historicism in 'Tradition and the Individual Talent' (1919) and explored the meaning of the past in his major poems, beginning with 'Gerontion' (1920) and culminating in *Four Quartets* (1943). He also internalised the social scientists' methodology: namely, the comparative analysis of fragments. In *The Waste Land* (1922), begun soon after completing his graduate work, he adapted the method for his poetry, and in reviewing James Joyce's *Ulysses* in 1923, he outlined this adaptation and christened it the 'mythical method' (*SP*, 178). His appropriation of the philosophy and methodology of the social sciences enabled him to deal with what seemed to be an impasse for modern artists – the requirement that art should reflect both order and chaos, that it should simultaneously be true to an ideal and to contemporary history.

Historicism is the theory that history is a living whole, the two main principles being organicism and holism. Organicism means that the pieces of history – moments, epochs, persons, events – are all interconnected, related as limbs are in a body, not as cogs in a machine, and also, that all pieces are evolving in time. As Eliot's Sweeney suggests in *Sweeney Agonistes*, life consists of recurring cycles of 'birth, and copulation, and death' (*CPP*, 122). Holism means that history is a whole and includes everything that is, or has been or will be – all people, classes, institutions, events small and large. Historicism emphasises life in time, with the old constantly being transformed into the new:

> Old stone to new building, old timber to new fires,
> Old fires to ashes, and ashes to the earth
> Which is already flesh, fur and faeces　　(*CPP*, 177)

Although never merely a historicist (he acknowledged a vertical, spatial dimension), Eliot consistently maintained that life is conditioned by time and place and that its parts are subject to continuous and reciprocal modification. In 'Tradition and the Individual Talent', he insisted that the past should not be taken as a 'lump, an indiscriminate bolus' or fixed as an 'ideal order' of monuments (*SE*, 16), but as a living whole that includes the present. No artist has his 'complete meaning alone ... what happens when a new work of art is created is something that happens simultaneously to all the works of art which preceded it' (*SE*, 15). The past and present have 'a simultaneous existence' and compose 'a simultaneous order'. The mind of Europe 'changes, and that this change is a development which abandons nothing en route, which does not superannuate either Shakespeare, or Homer, or the rock drawing of the Magdalenian draughtsmen' (*SE*, 16). In explaining the relation between history and truth in his 1926 introduction to the dramatic poem *Savonarola* by his mother Charlotte, he remarked: 'Every period of history is seen differently by every other period; the past is in perpetual flux, although only the past can be known.'[1] After his conversion to Christianity, which one would think would have tempered his historicism, Eliot said that even the Incarnation is 'A moment not out of time, but in time, in what we call history: transecting, bisecting the world of time' (*CPP*, 160).

Eliot also made historicism the backdrop for his poetry. In 'Gerontion', he brilliantly explores the historicist principle that history has a history, that contexts have a context. The basic image is that of houses within houses, all interconnected. History is a house with 'many cunning passages, contrived corridors' (*CPP*, 38) and within this house are other houses, including the house of Greece during the battle of Thermopylae in 480 BC, the house of Israel during the time of Christ, the house of Europe at the end of the First World War, and many others, all contained as tenants in the brain of a withered Socrates named Gerontion. In *Four Quartets*, the most important philosophical poem of the century, Eliot intertwines what many thinkers attempt to separate: past and present, being and becoming:

> Time present and time past
> Are both perhaps present in time future
> And time future contained in time past.   (*CPP*, 171)

The exploration continues, as words slip, slide and perish, as patterns in life and art coalesce and dissolve, creating patterns that are 'new in every moment' (*CPP*, 179):

> That the past experience revived in the meaning
> Is not the experience of one life only
> But of many generations – not forgetting
> Something that is probably quite ineffable:
> The backward look behind the assurance
> Of recorded history, the backward half-look
> Over the shoulder, towards the primitive terror.   (*CPP*, 187)

Only a committed historicist could imagine a line of sight stretching from today to prehistory, from present assurance to primitive terror.

Eliot's historicism is a version of the theory of history at the heart of nineteenth-century intellectual life, particularly in the social sciences. Its context includes two sequential elements: (1) the change around the turn of the nineteenth century from a mechanical to an organic view of the universe; and (2) the change around the middle of the century from the view that the earth and its inhabitants are relatively young to the view that they are immeasurably old. The first, part of Romanticism and its idealism, is primarily literary and philosophical; the second, part of Positivism and realism, is primarily scientific. Both include the quest for origins that was to culminate in the rapid maturation of anthropology, sociology and psychology in the last quarter of the century.

The background of the philosophical change lies in the Enlightenment. In the seventeenth century many accepted the biblical account of history as consisting of linear dispensations, beginning in Genesis with the Creation and ending with the Second Coming as described in Revelation. However, this view was undercut by two powerful thinkers. In a landmark essay, 'Natural History of Religion' (1757), the Scottish rationalist David Hume argued that the Garden of Eden should be treated as a story that existed within history. He maintained that even religion has a history and should be studied as existing in time. In *The New Science* (1725), the Italian philosopher Giambattista Vico argued that all societies pass through three cycles or ages associated with gods, heroes and men. His evolutionary theory of history, though not appreciated in his own day, influenced the Romantics, especially in Germany, and his triadic paradigm, with an emphasis on an upward evolution, became a commonplace in the social sciences. The Positivist Auguste Comte, a founding father of sociology, maintained that all societies move through three phases – theological, metaphysical and scientific. Analogously, Frazer argued that all societies pass through stages of magic, religion and science. These thinkers believed that history moved from abstract to concrete, from irrational to rational, from worse to better.

Most credit for the success of organicism, however, is due to the Romantic Movement. In the late eighteenth and early nineteenth centuries, first-generation Romantics, such as William Wordsworth in England and Johann von Herder in Germany, discarded the Enlightenment model of the universe as a perfectly oiled Newtonian machine and substituted instead an organic model of the universe. Turning Enlightenment values upside down, they emphasised temporality, change, motion, interconnection and wholeness. The venerable Chain of Being, in which all of life was represented as a hierarchy of immutable categories, was taken out of space and placed in time. In this ninety-degree turn, boundaries were softened or dissolved, and man (the middle link in a spatial and finite chain arranged from lowest to highest) became a point in a temporal and infinite process arranged from primitive to modern. God was deposed from his lofty throne and resettled in some distant future kingdom towards which all creation was moving. In philosophical terms, Becoming trumped Being, a point elaborated by post-Kantian idealists such as J. G. Fichte and G. W. F. Hegel.

The temporalisation of the Chain of Being was liberating for scientists, whose breakthroughs were built on the assumption of an organic universe evolving in time. Charles Lyell, the century's most distinguished geologist, argued in *Principles of Geology* (1830–3) that the past should not be taken as a lost 'lump' of history but as forming part of the present. In his quest for the origin of the earth, he concluded that it resulted from the accumulation of minute changes occurring over enormously long periods of time, a theory that influenced Charles Darwin, who hypothesised in *On the Origin of Species* that human beings originated in a remote prehistory and evolved from lower to higher forms through a process of natural selection. The theories of Lyell and Darwin provided a scientific foundation for the quest for origins that was already well under way, especially in Germany, where it was associated with the attempt to define national identity. Their work also led to a redefinition of the past, which in the second half of the nineteenth century came to include not only primitive history, but prehistory. This scientific work was in many ways congruent with Romantic historicism, but in one significant way it was different. The Romantics believed in a lost golden age and imagined that the change from the Classical world of Greece and Rome to medieval and modern Europe was a process of degeneration. By arguing for natural selection, dubbed the 'survival of the fittest' by the evolutionist Herbert Spencer, Darwin flipped this Romantic view of decline, substituting a Positivist view of ascent. These views of history as degeneration or as progress remained in conflict for the remainder of the century.

Eliot flashes his awareness of these ongoing debates in a 1920 vignette describing the Hellenism of Gilbert Murray. With a touch of irony, he describes the current phase of Classical study:

> The Greek is no longer the awe-inspiring Belvedere of Winckelmann, Goethe, and Schopenhauer, the figure of which Walter Pater and Oscar Wilde offered us a slightly debased re-edition. And we realise better how different – not how much more Olympian – were the conditions of Greek civilization from ours. (*SW*, 76)

In the late eighteenth century, when Rome was considered the pinnacle of civilisation, the German art historian J. J. Winckelmann fathered a Greek revival with his *History of Ancient Art* (1764). Dividing art into periods, he elevated Classical Greek work above all others. He defined the essence of Greek art as noble simplicity and rapturously described the Belvedere, a Roman imitation of a Greek statue of Apollo, as the standard for absolute beauty. His work ushered in a century of scholarship on Greek philosophy and ideals. In Germany, he influenced such figures as Herder, Johann Wolfgang von Goethe, Gotthold Lessing and Arthur Schopenhauer, and in England Byron and Shelley, and, to stay with Eliot's shorthand, the aesthetes Pater and Wilde. In the middle of the century, as the quest for origins intensified, the Greece of Winckelmann gave way to that of Homer; the age of philosophers to that of heroes. In the anthropology of polymaths such as Frazer and in the sociology of Durkheim, the study of pre-rational Greece was extended further back into the dark recesses of prehistory. For the Romantics, the Greeks had been awe-inspiring residents of Olympus; for contemporary Hellenists, they were simply different. In mock despair Eliot laments that the modern critic is flummoxed, not knowing whether to model his prose on Romans such as Cicero or

Greeks such as Thucydides. In regard to poetry: 'If Pindar bores us, we admit it; we are not certain that Sappho was *very* much greater than Catullus; and we hold various opinions about Vergil; and we think more highly of Petronius than our grandfathers did' (*SW*, 76–7). The past is in motion, and Petronius, exiled by the Romantics, returns as the gatekeeper of the twentieth century's signature poem, *The Waste Land* (see Chapter 17 above).

The historicism which served Eliot as a philosophical backdrop also gave him and other modernists a method they were able to adapt for their contemporary art. In working their way back to origins, historicists focused primarily on language and mythology, both of which were considered repositories for the oldest and deepest intuitions of human experience. In approaching these two areas as 'science', they developed the 'comparative method'. Stated simply, the comparative method is the comparison of fragments in order to reconstruct larger and older fragments that can then be used to hypothesise even older fragments and eventually to reach an original – an ur-language or ur-myth. It assumes a primitive unity that has shattered into pieces which have then evolved, and it attempts to reverse the process of evolution by systematically undoing modifications and reconnecting fragments. It was developed by Danish and German philologists whose search for both national and universal origins was built upon intensive language study. In *Investigation of the Origin of the Old Norse or Icelandic Language* (1818), which compared inflectional systems and word endings, Rasmus Rask had the brilliant insight that most European languages were descendants of an extinct common ancestor. The German philologist Franz Bopp added Sanskrit to the mix, discovering that Indic and European languages were part of the same family. These scholars traced modern languages back to Indo-European roots and modern European peoples back to the so-called Aryans of India.

For most modernists, however, the comparative method was not a product of comparative linguistics, but of comparative mythology. In 1856, Max Müller, a native of Germany trained in Sanskrit, connected linguistics and mythology in a watershed essay 'Comparative Mythology'. His thesis was that the method that had been so successful in philology should be applied to mythology. Instead of comparing fragments of language, scholars should compare fragments of myths, with the aim of reconstructing older and older stories until they eventually recovered a parent myth. Müller's ur-myth, known as 'solarism', associated origins with worship of the sun.

In his final year at Harvard (1913/14), Eliot took a capstone seminar for which the announced topic for the year was 'A comparative study of various types of scientific method'. His essay for that seminar, 'The Interpretation of Primitive Ritual', is a study of the comparative method in religion. When he finished his studies at Harvard, he adapted this method for literary use. In his review of *Ulysses*, he says that the 'mythical method' has been made 'possible' by the social sciences, specifically 'Psychology . . . ethnology, and *The Golden Bough*' (*SP*, 178). He describes it as a method that enables the artist to manipulate 'a continuous parallel between contemporaneity and antiquity', adding that it is a 'way of controlling, or ordering, of giving a shape and a significance to the immense panorama of futility and anarchy which is contemporary history' (*SP*, 177). The artist, like the social scientist, juxtaposes cultural and literary fragments from different times and places, but unlike the scientist, he leaves the work of reconstruction largely to the reader. This is the method of *The Waste Land*, a poem that includes fragments of contemporary life, several languages (including Sanskrit) and numerous myths (including the agricultural myths contained in Frazer's *The Golden Bough* [1890]). The fragments of contemporary life (taxis, songs, pubs, war) are particularly important, for as Lyell had argued a century earlier, the present is always the key to understanding the past.

The immediate context for the emergence of the mythical method was the burgeoning of the social sciences in the wake of Müller's 1856 essay, with the added impetus of the 1859 publication of *On the Origin of Species*. In the first half of the century the main breakthroughs had occurred in Germany, but in the second half the major achievements came from Britain, and at the end of the century from France. In Germany the foci had been on the Greeks and on language, and this scholarship had a strong nationalistic bent associated with the desire to find the origin of the German *Volk* [nation]. In Britain, the emphasis shifted to studies of primitivism, notably anthropology and mythology, and this scholarship had a religious flavour created by the desire to reconcile evolutionary science with Christianity. British scholarship was much broader in scope, in part because scholars did fieldwork throughout the British Empire, including in Australia and India. Müller was the pivotal scholar connecting the first and second halves of the century. Settling at Oxford University while he was in his twenties, he combined his German linguistic concerns with the anthropological interests of the British. He remained in Oxford for the rest of his long career, becoming one of the most eminent figures in the first generation of social scientists. The focus in France was more theoretical than in Germany or Britain; coming later in the development of the social sciences, French scholars, including those associated with Durkheim's periodical *L'Année Sociologique*, were able to build on the accomplishments of their predecessors.

The scholarship of the second half of the century is brilliantly encapsulated in Eliot's 1920 article, quoted earlier, on a performance of Gilbert Murray's translation of *Medea*. Murray was one of the Cambridge Ritualists, a group of Classical scholars that included Jane Harrison, Francis Cornford and A. B. Cook. In a playful paragraph, Eliot provides a bird's-eye view of the late nineteenth-century landscape in the social sciences:

[This day began] with Tylor and a few German anthropologists; since then we have acquired sociology and social pyschology ... we have read books from Vienna and heard a discourse of Bergson ... Few books are more fascinating than those of Miss Harrison, Mr Cornford, or Mr Cooke [*sic*], when they burrow in the origins of Greek myths and rites; M. Durkheim, with his social consciousness, and M. Lévy-Brühl, with his Bororo Indians who convince themselves that they are parroquets, are delightful writers. A number of sciences have sprung up in an almost tropical exuberance ... and the garden, not unnaturally, has come to resemble a jungle. Such men as Tylor, and Robertson Smith, and Wilhelm Wundt, who early fertilized the soil, would hardly recognise the resulting vegetation ... it is this phase of classical study that Professor Murray – the friend and inspirer of Miss Jane Harrison – represents. (*SW*, 75–6)

One of the wittiest aspects of this paragraph is the use of the agricultural metaphor, for it reveals the ghost of Frazer in the branches of the oaks below. In *The Waste Land*, published soon after this article, Eliot brings Frazer out of the shadows, remarking in the 'Notes' that the poem includes reference to 'vegetation ceremonies' (*CPP*, 76) and is more generally indebted to *The Golden Bough*. And in a 1924 essay Eliot lists the same figures in the development of social science, with the addition of Frazer, to whom he gives pride of place, as well as Wilhelm Mannhardt, whose studies in agricultural myth influenced Frazer, and Jessie Weston, whose own work on the Grail legends drew on Frazer's work.[2]

This context that includes *The Golden Bough* can easily be fleshed out from Eliot's tongue-in-cheek genealogy of the Cambridge Ritualists. He begins his survey with an allusion to the fruitful but troubled mid-century marriage of German and British scholarship. Müller not only brought the comparative method to Britain, he also brought the romantic view that history is moving from unity to disunity, from better to worse, a milder version of which was also part of English Romanticism. As was the case with most linguists, his view of history as devolution was tied to the Indo-European thesis, which postulated a parent race and language now in ruins. The first generation of British social scientists, E. B. Tylor and Andrew Lang, accepted the comparative method but rejected the focus on philology and the view of history as degeneration. In *Primitive Culture* (1871), Tylor argued that evolution occurred in natural stages, forward and upward, uniformly, regardless of language and culture, a position also defended by Lang. The principle of uniformity allowed Tylor and Lang to consider primitive peoples, such as the Australian Aborigines, as representatives of an earlier stage of the evolution of modern Europeans.

The Scottish biblical scholar and Semitist William Robertson Smith, included in Eliot's vignette, reorientated the social sciences and was a powerful influence on Frazer and Durkheim, both in turn direct influences on Eliot. Most British anthropologists, including Frazer, did not know ancient languages (Müller's main complaint about them) and they did not collect their own data by conducting fieldwork. They relied on missionaries, explorers and others who travelled within the Empire. Smith, on the other hand, was a brilliant scholar of Semitic languages who spent years in the Near East trying to reconstruct the social context of the biblical religion. Other anthropologists had theorised that religion and mythology originated as attempts by primitive peoples to explain natural phenomena. In Tylor's phrase used in *Primitive Culture*, the creators of myths were 'savage philosophers'. Others, the euhemerists, argued that myths could be traced to historical events or real persons. Conversely, Smith argued that myths originated as the explanation of rituals, the meanings of which had been lost. Ancient people did not make up rituals to support doctrines or to preserve accounts of heroes; rather, they invented stories to explain rituals which had arisen as coping mechanisms in social contexts. Smith's work on social structures, essentially a sociology of religion, is reflected in Durkheim's idea of group consciousness outlined in *Elementary Forms of the Religious Life* (1912), which was reviewed by Eliot in 1916 and again in 1918. Smith's position that sacrifice was the ur-ritual, explored at length in *Religion of the Semites* (1889), gave Frazer the myth of the dying god. In the preface to the first edition of *The Golden Bough*, he acknowledged that Smith's work provided the central idea of his book, the conception of the slain god. Smith also provided the main idea of the Cambridge Ritualists about the priority of ritual, and with Durkheim as a mediator, shaping their understanding of social structures. Smith's legacy, in addition, includes Eliot's poetry and criticism, which prioritises ritual and treats social experience as originary.

Each of the French figures mentioned in Eliot's 1920 article – Durkheim, Lévy-Brühl and Bergson – have a special place in the context treated in this chapter: Durkheim as the main figure in sociology; Lévy-Brühl, author of *Mental Functions in Primitive Societies* (1910), as an explorer of the primitive mind; and Henri Bergson as the thinker who in *Creative Evolution* (1907) integrated the historicism of the social sciences into philosophy proper. As a graduate student in Paris in 1910/11, Eliot heard Bergson lecture and, on his return to Harvard, wrote an essay about Bergson's inconsistencies.[3] He also learned about Durkheim, Lévy-Brühl and the psychologist Pierre Janet in Paris and studied them in greater depth when he returned to the United States, referencing them in graduate essays and book reviews.

Eliot continued to mention the social scientists encountered in his youth, praising the 'brilliant theories of human behaviour' espoused by Durkheim and Lévy-Brühl and remarking that Freud had shed valuable light on the 'obscurities of the soul'. He reserved his most lavish praise, however, for Frazer, who had 'extended the consciousness of the human mind into as dark a backward and abysm of time as has yet been explored'.[4] Eliot's mind, like the mind of Europe, changed over the years, but it abandoned nothing en route, neither the prehistoric Sibyl nor the pre-Socratic Heraclitus. The first presides over *The Waste Land*, a monument to the comparative method, the second over *Four Quartets*, a monument to historicism. Both the early and late masterpieces reveal the quest for origins that is the essential context not only for Eliot's work, but of his life: 'In my beginning is my end' (*CPP*, 177).

NOTES

1. 'Introduction', *Savonarola* by Charlotte Eliot (London: Cobden-Sanderson, 1926), p. vii.
2. See 'A Prediction in Regard to Three English Authors', *Vanity Fair* (February 1924), 29, 98.
3. Unpublished address to the Harvard Philosophical Club (December 1913).
4. 'Prediction in Regard to Three English Authors', 29.

CHAPTER 33

Natural science

Michael H. Whitworth

Context is a matter of weaving together, but there is more than one way of weaving. When considering Eliot's relation to natural science, is a metaphor of human weaving appropriate, one in which science forms part of the warp and weft of Eliot's thinking? Or might the spider's web offer a better metaphor for an antagonistic relationship, a metaphor in which fragments of science are not threads in the web, but the bodies of insects? Of course, both models might be equally true: the thread that flows from the spider's spinneret contains the digested bodies of past victims. Contemporary science was readily available to Eliot through many sources, but it would be a mistake with a writer so alertly critical of the culture in which he lived to assume that he uncritically absorbed it. Equally, it would be a mistake to assume that he was uniformly hostile to it, though some models of modernism have assumed this to be the case.

In Eliot's first published volume of poetry, science is immediately present as a source of vocabulary which disrupts the reader's expectations: the patient 'etherised' (*CPP*, 13) in the third line of 'The Love Song of J. Alfred Prufrock'. In one of his most significant early essays, 'Tradition and the Individual Talent', the comparison of the poet's mind to a platinum catalyst is likewise placed prominently; in the original publication, the metaphor concluded the first instalment in the September 1919 issue of the *Egoist*, and, having hung in the air for a few months, was resumed at the start of the next instalment. While the early poems do not repeat the ear-catching trick of employing a term like 'etherised', there are smaller shocks such as the reference to a pianist who will 'Transmit the Preludes' (*CPP*, 18) of Chopin through his hair and fingertips, as if he were a telegraphic system; or of Mr Apollinax compared to an 'irresponsible foetus' (*CPP*, 31). In the quatrain poems of *Poems* (1920), Eliot's vocabulary grows more knotted, and the introduction of scientific terms is one of the means by which he achieves a distinctive verbal texture.

In 'Burbank with a Baedeker: Bleistein with a Cigar', an eye stares from 'protozoic slime' (*CPP*, 40), and Princess Volupine's hand is 'phthisic' (*CPP*, 41). In 'Mr Eliot's Sunday Morning Service', 'superfetation', 'staminate and pistillate' (*CPP*, 54, 55) help to create the jagged verbal surface of the poem. However, given that the same poem works extraordinary effects with invented terms such as 'polyphiloprogenitive' and theological terms such as 'piaculative' (*CPP*, 54), it appears that Eliot deployed the scientific terms less for their scientific content than for their ability to disrupt the verbal texture of the poem. From this point of view, the theological and the scientific are of equal value, and Eliot might equally have employed any other technical jargon.

That Eliot employed a scientific vocabulary suggests that he might have been following the French poet Jules Laforgue. In *The Symbolist Movement in Literature* (1899), the book which directed Eliot towards late nineteenth-century French poetry, Arthur Symons defined the Symbolist Movement as one in revolt against scientific materialism, and consequently, against descriptive, referential language. Laforgue's puppet-like characters were his means of reacting against science: 'They are, in part, a way of taking one's revenge upon science, by an ironical borrowing of its very terms, which dance in his prose and verse, derisively, at the end of a string.'[1] However, it is not clear that Eliot deploys scientific terminology quite so programmatically. It is true that the very obtrusiveness of the unexpected word generates an irony around it; indeed, any specialised vocabulary, when transplanted from its natural discursive environment, has the potential to appear ironic. But the irony need not be at the expense of science, or not exclusively so. Poems that self-consciously juxtapose specialised vocabularies are gesturing at the incommensurability of any linguistic system with the complexity of reality. If the opening lines of 'The Love Song of J. Alfred Prufrock' juxtapose Romantic longing with a surgeon's instrumental view of the human body, it is to demonstrate the inadequacy of both.

While the scientific vocabulary in the poetry indicates Eliot's interest in science, it does not tell the whole story. Scientific ideas may be drawn into a poet's ideas of poetic form and of the poetic vocation, without featuring explicitly in the poems themselves. To understand what science Eliot might have known and how well he might have known it requires a reconstruction both of his own reading and contacts, and a reconstruction of the literary cultures of the day. To say that scientific ideas were part of the atmosphere is not sufficient: in an era characterised by intellectual specialisation from a relatively early age, one person's atmosphere can have a very different composition from another's. Despite the tendency to specialisation, Eliot inhabited a literary culture that was still receptive to scientific ideas presented in a non-technical form. Moreover, in the course of his graduate education at Harvard University, he was given a broad introduction to some of the latest ideas in the physical sciences and in the philosophy of science.

What Eliot encountered at Harvard in Josiah Royce's graduate seminar in 1913/14 is documented in great detail, thanks to the notes kept by Eliot's contemporary Harry T. Costello. One of the set texts was Karl Pearson's *The Grammar of Science* (1893), a non-technical work which, as well as surveying the current state of scientific knowledge, advanced a distinctive position on matters such as the nature of a scientific law. Although Pearson's text was twenty years old by the time Eliot came to it, Pearson's view of scientific law was influential on Eliot's scientific peers, and in that respect was in the mainstream of advanced scientific thinking. Pearson developed the ideas of the 'empirico-critical' or 'descriptionist' school of Ernst Mach: scientific laws were not the truth about reality, but provided a convenient and economical formula for the description of nature. A description, however, is not an explanation. For Pearson, the task of science was to say how things happen, not to explain why. If we describe the acceleration of a falling object, either with measurements, or, more economically, with an equation, we have not explained why it falls. If we were animists, we might believe acceleration was due to the desire of the object to be reunited with the earth; if we were Newtonians, we would explain it by reference to gravitational force; if we were Einsteinians, we would explain it as due to a distortion in space-time. Eliot took the distinction between description and explanation as the theme for one of his papers for Royce's seminar, and he began by arguing that 'Explanation is more primitive, description more sophisticated'.[2] Given that scientific explanations seem to build upon mere descriptions, Eliot's evaluation appears surprising, but his point is rooted in Pearson's analysis: explanations frequently invoke a hidden first principle. Just as primitive man 'placed a sun-god behind the sun ... because he did not see how and why it moved', so modern science invokes a principle such as 'force' to cover its ignorance.[3]

Royce's seminar also introduced Eliot to fragments of the very latest ideas in physics. In November 1913, Leonard Troland, a physicist, introduced Albert Einstein's 1905 theory of special relativity. (Einstein's general theory, which includes gravitation, was not published until 1916.) Costello's notes are fragmentary, but intelligible:

Relativity asserts motion completely relative, no body is absolute. Out of harmony with ether hypothesis. Both observers are right ... To the stationary observer the moving body contracts in line of motion. Is contraction apparent and not real? ... What do you mean by saying the contraction is only apparent? New conception of contraction: contraction from a point of view ... Standards of measurement are a function of a point of view.[4]

Physicists upholding the ether hypothesis maintained that all space, even 'empty' space, was permeated by a mysterious medium known as the ether or aether (quite distinct from the physicians' anaesthetic 'ether'). Ether was the medium through which electromagnetic waves rippled, and it provided a fixed point in the universe against which other movements might be measured. With the advent of Einstein's theories, it was not so much disproved as rendered unnecessary, though 'the ether' remained part of popular speech as the medium through which radio broadcasts were heard. *The Waste Land*'s reference to 'aethereal rumours' (*CPP*, 74) suggests broadcasting, but Eliot clearly knew of the ether hypothesis and its fate; moreover, he knew of 'relativity' in its broadest sense. In a later seminar, in April 1914, Troland provided an exposition of statistical approaches in physics and of Max Planck's 1900 quantum theory. The statistical method changed the basis for knowledge: although predictions about masses of particles could be made with a high degree of probability, they could not be made with complete certainty. Planck's quantum theory changed physicists' understanding of the nature of reality at its smallest level: energy was not infinitely subdivisible. Though the quantum theory of atomic structure was not articulated until the 1920s, Eliot had already heard of two of its basic components.

Costello also recorded his own speculations, confessing in his notes that the relativity theory had 'a certain appeal to the imagination': 'Suppose you took a ride on a light wave: the earth would rush past you with the speed of light and thus flatten up like a pancake, and what would things look like then?'[5] While Eliot may not have been privy to such thought experiments, they suggest how a strict scientific account could lead to more imaginative thought experiments. The new scientific thinking undermined established ideas about the structure of reality and about the reliability of our knowledge. If light has a finite velocity, and if light can be curved in its path, then not only might an object not appear to be where it is, but two events that appear to be simultaneous might actually have occurred at very different moments. The consciousness of the presence of the past that Eliot mentions in 'Tradition and the Individual Talent' has many tangled intellectual roots, but physics was prominent among them. Physicists' discussions of light and its movement provided a point of contact between traditional metaphors of illumination and new thinking in science.

As well as having opportunities to learn about science which were peculiar to his educational path, once he settled in England Eliot was part of a literary subculture that continued to take a discriminating interest in science. In 1913 Bertrand Russell distinguished between science as represented in newspapers, where it consisted of 'sensational triumphs', mysteries and technological breakthroughs, and science as an unsensational, non-utilitarian discipline which could help to form a 'scientific habit of mind'.[6] Such a view influenced the representation of science in weekly political or generalist periodicals such as the *New Statesman*, to which Eliot contributed between 1916 and 1918, and the *Athenaeum*, under the editorship of John Middleton Murry, to which Eliot frequently contributed in the period 1919–20 (see Chapter 10 above). While such periodicals had little to say about technological discoveries, they were receptive to pure science and to debate about the place and value of science within culture. The *New Statesman* ran regular articles on biology by J. Arthur Thomson and by the eugenicist C. W. Saleeby (who used the pseudonym 'Lens'); the chemist Alexander Findlay occasionally contributed articles on chemistry, and on the place of science. The *Athenaeum*'s science articles were primarily written by J. W. N. Sullivan, a writer of popular science and the deputy editor of the journal, and they typically concerned physics and mathematics; but there were occasional contributions from Julian Huxley on biology, and from Geoffrey Keynes on medical matters. Though Eliot modelled the *Criterion* on literary reviews such as *Art and Letters* and the *Nouvelle Revue Française*, he envisaged it being an outlet for articles 'as unliterary as possible' (*LI*, 776), not only from Sullivan, but from the anthropologist Sir James Frazer, the social psychologist Wilfred Trotter, the physicist A. S. Eddington and the neurologist Charles Sherrington (although none turned out to be contributors).

In his critical prose throughout 1918 and 1919, Eliot frequently invokes science as a reference point for his ideal of poetry. Science offered a model for four interconnected ideas: that the poet must be professional in his approach to his craft; that poetry must be international in its outlook; that the poet must build on and yet modify the tradition; and that the poet must have an impersonal relation to the poem. There are broad similarities with Pound's critical rhetoric, but Eliot did not share Pound's interest in a vocabulary of energy and force. If he took a hint from

Pound, it was from 'A Few Don'ts for Imagists' (1913), where his contemporary had compared the poet to the scientist: 'The scientist does not expect to be acclaimed as a great scientist until he has *discovered* something. He begins by learning what has been discovered already. He goes from that point onward.'[7]

In April 1918, Eliot argued that the British distrust of specialists was the cause of the British 'worship of inspiration'; he rejected the idea that poetry could come naturally to the amateur, untutored poet. To Eliot, British amateurism implied insularity, 'an avoidance of comparison with foreign literatures, a dodging of standards'.[8] He returned to this theme a few months later, invoking science more explicitly. It was necessary, he insisted, that a poet writing in English who wished to be taken seriously should know French poetry since the 1870s. There was more to a poet's education than 'reading, writing, and ciphering'. He continued: 'The analogy to science is close. A poet, like a scientist, is contributing toward the organic development of a culture: it is just as absurd for him not to know the work of his predecessors or of men writing in other languages as it would be for a biologist to be ignorant of Mendel or De Vries.'[9] Both examples are drawn from evolutionary biology. Gregor Mendel (1822–84) was an Austrian monk whose work on inheritance in plants had long been neglected; its rediscovery in the early twentieth century, pioneered by the Dutch botanist Huge de Vries, prompted significant developments in evolutionary biology. Eliot had used genetic metaphors in an earlier article to deplore the 'inbred' quality of Georgian poetry (see Chapter 22 above), and in the present article he again insisted on the necessity of 'cross-breeding' in poetry. Eliot draws on science here both for its ideas and for an ideal of international co-operation. Later in 1918, he noted that literary criticism suffered from similar disadvantages to 'creative art', and again science was the point of comparison: science had the advantage of being 'internationalised'. In this article he made finer distinctions between kinds of scientist, and, by analogy, kinds of critic. Though both science and literature required immersion in the work of predecessors and contemporaries, they also depended on 'the occasional appearance of a man of genius who discovers a new method'. Eliot acknowledged that there was 'useful work' done in science by scientists 'who are only clever enough and educated enough to apply a method', and he suggested that in literature there ought to be a similar place 'for persons of equivalent capacity'. In this article, Eliot, while extending the scope of tradition, was also finding a place for the individual talent.

Although the essays of 1918 advance the ideas of professionalisation, internationalism and tradition, the idea of impersonality fully emerges only in Eliot's essay of late 1919, 'Tradition and the Individual Talent'. Here, Eliot claims that, in 'depersonalization', 'art may be said to approach the condition of science' (*SE*, 17). It seems likely that Eliot's thinking was influenced by several articles in the *Athenaeum* concerning the relations of science and the arts. The contributors included an art critic and a literary critic (Roger Fry and I. A. Richards), but the most significant contributions came from J. W. N. Sullivan.[10]

Einstein's general theory of relativity and its experimental proof prompted Sullivan's discussions. Einstein had published the general theory in 1916, but it was only after the war had ended that experimental tests could be made. Einstein's theory predicted that a massive body such as the sun would distort space-time and cause the deflection of a ray of light, and the deflection his theory predicted was measurably different from that given by previous theories. The British Astronomer Royal, A. S. Eddington, organised two expeditions to measure the deflection of starlight during the eclipse on 29 May 1919; in November 1919 he announced results that proved Einstein's theory. In the *Athenaeum* in May and June, Sullivan published a series of five articles on Einstein's theory, apparently to coincide with the expeditions. More importantly, though, he dwelt upon what it would mean for the existing Newtonian theory of gravity if Einstein's theory were proved correct. In May 1919 he noted an apparent paradox about science: 'if the scientific method is infallible why are the results reached by it provisional? To judge from the history of science, the scientific method is excellent as a means of obtaining plausible conclusions which are always wrong, but hardly as a means of reaching the truth'. In the same article he mentioned in passing 'that Newton's theory is very probably not exactly true'. Newton's theory had provided plausible conclusions for centuries, but it had turned out to be unreliable when dealing with very large scales. Sullivan resolved the paradox by noting that each newer, more powerful theory incorporated parts of the older one. Sullivan's approach allowed the superseded theories to retain some value. The basis of such value was aesthetic: theories were beautiful because they brought harmony to a large range of observed facts. The motives that guide the scientific man, Sullivan claimed, 'are manifestations of the aesthetic impulse'.[11]

If a superseded theory could remain valuable because it was beautiful, then an as yet untested theory could also have aesthetic value. The general theory of relativity was greeted as a great work even before it had been experimentally verified: many mathematicians and physicists remarked on the beauty and elegance of Einstein's reasoning. In this respect, then, it appeared to many that a scientific theory could resemble a work of art. Yet according to popular ideas of art since Romanticism, an artist should express himself or herself through the work of art. This problem prompted Sullivan to discuss impersonality. He began the discussion in an article on the recently deceased mathematician, Lord Rayleigh. Although Rayleigh was not the greatest of the Victorian scientists, his papers were a pleasure to read, 'because his instinctive sense of form makes his treatment aesthetically as well as logically satisfying'. Sullivan developed the idea in more general terms in the article 'Science and Personality'. He began with a conventional contrast between art and science: science 'rests on the obliteration of personality, whereas a cursory reading assures us that art is an emphasis and expression of individuality'.[12] He conceded that if art were to communicate with an audience, then it could not be utterly idiosyncratic, and that, to that extent, it was impersonal, but as general tendencies the distinction of art and science appeared valid. More importantly, he asserted that analysis could discover 'the personal element in the great scientific work': one might speak of the 'individual quality' in a mathematical essay just as in a piece of music. Nevertheless, these two arguments were concessions in an argument that championed the impersonality of science and suggested that the decadence of art was due to the excessive cultivation of personalities.

The relation of Eliot's thinking to Sullivan's is most readily apparent in 'Modern Tendencies in Poetry', a lecture given on 28 October 1919. The text, published the following year, has many similarities to 'Tradition and the Individual Talent'. Many literary figures from London attended the lecture, and Eliot specifically invited Sullivan.[13] Unlike 'Tradition and the Individual Talent', Eliot's lecture refers explicitly to the debate about art and science in the pages of the *Athenaeum*, and its ideal reader appears to be someone conversant with that debate. At one point, Eliot asserts that when one studies the work of a 'great scientist', it becomes apparent that what he achieved was done 'not through a desire to express his personality', but through 'a complete surrender' to the work. The surrender to the work is also a surrender to the tradition, and not only to what has gone before, but what will come afterwards: 'he is continuing a work which will be continued after him'. Yet Eliot also wishes to find a space for individuality. If the scientist is a 'great scientist', 'there will be – I believe scientists will corroborate this statement, a cachet of the man all over it. No one else could have drawn those inferences, constructed those demonstrations, seen those relations.' Sullivan's assertions about Rayleigh are exactly the kind of evidence Eliot was referring to, and Eliot no doubt had Sullivan in mind as one of the scientists who would corroborate his claims. Eliot hints at there being an elegiac compensation to the scientist's sacrifice: 'His personality has not been lost, but has gone, all the important part of it, into the work'.[14] The transformation of the personality into a quality of impersonal individuality is crucial to Eliot's model of what a literary work of art could be. Eliot's lecture implicitly refutes Sullivan's assertion that modern art is exclusively concerned with the cultivation of personalities, but at the same time draws upon Sullivan's idea of science as something with aesthetic motivations.

Although in the years leading up to *The Waste Land* Eliot was receptive to the adoption of science as a model, soon afterwards he began to question it. In editorials for the *Criterion* in 1924, he remarked that men of letters were 'too easily impressed and overawed'[15] by the authority of science and later he warned against the danger of non-scientists 'making use of scientific generalisations'.[16] Eliot's certainty on this point grew stronger with his conversion to Christianity. Several scientists had made prominent remarks on the relation of religion and science: Eddington, a Quaker, had done so in *Science and the Unseen World* (1929), and another Cambridge scientist, James Jeans, had ventured in the final chapter of his bestselling work *The Mysterious Universe* (1930), that 'the Great Architect of the Universe' appeared to be a mathematician.[17] In 1932, Eliot remarked that while he had read such works 'with pleasure', he felt that 'outside of their special field' men of science were just as ignorant as anyone else. The spectacle of their attempting to create a theology was likely to appear comic, though, he added 'not so comic as I should be if I tried to improve upon the quantum theory in physics'.[18] However, science may have retained some imaginative utility for Eliot in his poetry: the way that light connects past and present in the opening section of 'Burnt Norton' (1936) suggests the imagery of earlier popular accounts of relativity. Though in his earlier poetry Eliot had used scientific terminology to create estranging effects, scientific ideas and imagery were now more readily woven into the texture of his poetry, and more readily absorbed into his thinking about his vocation.

NOTES

1. Arthur Symons, *The Symbolist Movement in Literature* (London: Dutton, 1919), p. 59.
2. Harry T. Costello, *Josiah Royce's Seminar, 1913–14*, ed. Grover Smith (New Brunswick, NJ: Rutgers University Press, 1963), p. 52.

3. Karl Pearson, *The Grammar of Science* (London: A. & C. Black, 1900), p. 120.

4. Costello, *Royce's Seminar*, p. 52.

5. Ibid., p. 56.

6. Bertrand Russell, 'Science as an Element in Culture', *New Statesman* (24 May 1913), 202, 203.

7. Ezra Pound, *Literary Essays of Ezra Pound*, ed. T. S. Eliot (London: Faber & Faber, 1954), p. 6.

8. 'Professional, or ...', *Egoist* (April 1918), 61.

9. 'Contemporanea', *Egoist* (June/July 1918), 84.

10. For a discussion of this topic, see Michael H. Whitworth, '*Pièces d'identité*: T. S. Eliot, J. W. N. Sullivan and Poetic Impersonality', *English Literature in Transition* (1996), 149–70.

11. J. W. N. Sullivan, 'The Justification of the Scientific Method', *Athenaeum* (2 May 1919), 275.

12. J. W. N. Sullivan, 'Science and Personality', *Athenaeum* (18 July 1919), 624–5.

13. For details, see Michael H. Whitworth, 'Enemies of Cant', *Oxford Critical and Cultural History of Modernist Magazines*, vol. 1, ed. Peter Brooker and Andrew Thacker (Oxford University Press, 2009), p. 374.

14. 'Modern Tendencies in Poetry', *Shama'a* (April 1920), 10.

15. 'A Commentary', *Criterion* (April 1924), 233

16. 'A Commentary', *Criterion* (October 1924), 3.

17. James Jeans, *The Mysterious Universe* (Cambridge University Press, 1930), p. 134.

18. 'Religion and Science: A Phantom Dilemma', *Listener* (23 March 1932), 429.

PART FIVE

Reception

CHAPTER 34

Contemporary reviews

Martin Dodsworth

Eliot's early poetic reputation was made thanks to a network of his friends, the first of whom in importance is his fellow student at Harvard, the poet and critic Conrad Aiken. Early in 1914 Aiken took a copy of 'The Love Song of J. Alfred Prufrock' with him to London. He showed it to Harold Monro, English poet and proprietor of the Poetry Bookshop; Monro, he claimed, thought the poem 'insane'.[1] On the other hand Ezra Pound, American poet and publicist, 'recognised *Prufrock* instantly'.[2] When Eliot arrived in England from Marburg a few months later, he met Pound. Impressed by its author, Pound then sent 'Prufrock' off to Harriet Monroe for her Chicago-based magazine, *Poetry*. She was not eager to publish, and delayed eight months before it appeared at last in June 1915. In the following month, 'Preludes' and 'Rhapsody on a Windy Night' appeared in the second number of Wyndham Lewis's magazine *Blast*. Judging by the coolness of Lewis's response ('very respectable intelligent verse'),[3] he was deferring to Pound's judgement.

Pound's exertions did not end here. 'Prufrock' appeared again, with 'Portrait of a Lady', in his *Catholic Anthology* in November 1915, and attracted favourable attention not only from the loyal Aiken in *Poetry Journal* ('psychological character-studies, subtle to the verge of insoluble idiosyncrasy, introspective, self-gnawing' [Brooker, 3]) but also in the London *Nation*, which singled it out for special attention. Eliot was drawn into the orbit of the *Egoist*, a little magazine with which Pound had been associated for some time, and in June 1917 the Egoist Press brought out *Prufrock and Other Observations*. Pound, who had in fact paid for the book's publication, reviewed it in both the *Egoist* and *Poetry*. He linked Eliot's work with that of Jules Laforgue and praised 'its fine tone, its humanity, and its realism' (Brooker, 8). In another magazine with which Pound had contacts, the *Little Review*, May Sinclair wrote favourably, following Pound's line (not uncongenial to Eliot) in representing the poet as the enemy of 'the comfortable and respectable mind' (Brooker, 11).

Aiken did his bit in the New York monthly *Dial*: 'psychological realism, but in a highly subjective or introspective vein' (Brooker, 9).

The 'comfortable' mind belonged in particular to Arthur Waugh, who had attacked the *Catholic Anthology* in the *Quarterly Review* (October 1916). Doubtless he considered Pound a bad thing in himself; his attitude was intensified by the wartime patriotism of a man whose son, Alec, was just about to go into the British Army. Waugh's natural sympathies lay with the decent pieties of the officer class represented in the *Georgian Poetry* anthology, which he reviewed alongside Pound's volume. Eliot, clever, English-speaking, but a non-combatant, was dubbed a 'drunken slave' (Brooker, 4) after the practice in ancient Sparta of displaying the disgraceful insobriety of helots that their betters might learn, by contrast, the value of responsibility and breeding. At least, Pound took it that Eliot was specifically Waugh's butt in the 'drunken helot' (Brooker, 5) gibe, and accordingly capitalised on it to stress the revolutionary nature of Eliot's achievement. Marianne Moore, writing in *Poetry* for April 1918, pretended to sympathise with 'the good English reviewer whom Ezra Pound quotes' but concluded that Eliot was 'a faithful friend of the objects he portrays; altogether unlike the sentimentalist who really stabs them treacherously in the back while pretending affection' (Brooker, 15).

Pound also lay behind an article on 'Recent United States Poetry' published in the *English Review* for May 1918, whose author, Edgar Jepson, used Eliot's poetry as a stick to beat the mediocrity of other American poets (like Valery Larbaud in the *Revue de France* in 1921, he considered Eliot emphatically an *American* poet). This did not get by without dispute – Monroe had to advise Jepson (in the pages of *Poetry* later that year) to get to know some *real* Americans, 'our boys in the trenches'.[4] The question of Eliot's American qualities was to recur many times in his career. William Carlos Williams stubbornly resisted Eliot's Old World habits of mind until Robert Lowell apparently won him over to a grudging appreciation in 1952.[5] In the 'Prologue' to *Kora in Hell* (1920), Williams objected to Jepson's praise of 'La Figlia Che Piange': 'IT CONFORMS! *Ergo*, here we have "the very fine flower of the finer spirit of the United States"'.[6] In *Poetry* in March 1923, Monroe put *The Waste Land* ('a masterpiece of decadent art' [Brooker, 104]) much on a par with the book she reviewed alongside it, *The Box of God*, by Lew Sarett, a poet of the American West who, she felt, made up in healthiness for any want of sophistication.

Aiken and Pound were powerfully persuasive on Eliot's behalf, in America at least, even if it took a while for some people to distinguish

Eliot's individual talent from mere discipleship of Pound. (In *Poetry* for May 1916, Max Michelson had described 'The Love Song of J. Alfred Prufrock' as a 'very interesting attempt to bring vorticism into poetry by breaking up thoughts, moods, scenes, into fragments, and making them play on one another'. 'Prufrock', however, had been composed before Eliot met Pound and well before Pound had launched his 'vorticist' movement.) By 1921 it was possible for Louis Untemeyer to offer a parody of Eliot, amongst others, in the pages of *Vanity Fair*. The pace had been set by the *Dial*, undoubtedly the most intelligent journal of the time. Its editor, Scofield Thayer, had been at school with Eliot and followed him to Harvard before going on to invest substantially in the magazine; naturally he was himself an admirer of Eliot's work. Eliot often published prose contributions and *The Waste Land* had its first American printing in the *Dial*. Its readers were proud to recognise Eliot as an American author of distinction. Hart Crane, who seems to have come across Eliot's work alongside Pound's as early as 1918, refers to him frequently (though often in an 'English' context); he encouraged Allen Tate in his reading of him. Tate's review of *Poems 1909–1925* for the *New Republic* (30 June 1926) is an important study of Eliot as a poet of ideas: 'His collected poems [*sic*] is the preparation for a critical philosophy of the present state of European literature. As this criticism becomes articulate, the poetry becomes incoherent' (Brooker, 143). The whole essay, which unobtrusively makes the case for the essentially American quality of the poetry, is essential reading. It is the forerunner of distinguished work by R. P. Blackmur, Cleanth Brooks and others in America associated with the 'New Criticism', which was to have a profound impact on the academic study of Eliot's work.

Eliot's growing success complicated his relationship with his earliest American admirer, and this explains, if need be, the sharper tone which Aiken adopted in his reviews of *The Sacred Wood* (in the *Freeman*) and *The Waste Land* (in the *New Republic*). Of the criticism, he observed: 'He is meticulous without being clear; he passes quickly from one detail of analysis to another ... he appears to believe that mere fineness of analysis will constitute, in the sequence of his comments, a direction' (Brooker, 63). He is equally acute on *The Waste Land*: 'the poem succeeds ... by virtue of its incoherence, not of its plan; by virtue of its ambiguities, not of its explanations' (Brooker, 102). Edmund Wilson, in his piece for the *Dial* (December 1922), had also noticed the 'lack of structural unity', but his emphasis was more positive: 'we feel that he is speaking not only for a personal distress, but for the starvation of a whole civilization'

(Brooker, 86). Like Aiken, Wilson stresses the element of feeling in the poem; the subtext is the tendency of other reviewers to depict Eliot as intellectual and satiric.

Naturally, there was no complete agreement, even in America, as to the stature of Eliot's poetic achievement. It was possible for Mary Colum in *Scribner's Magazine* (4 April 1926) to describe Eliot's work as 'on the margin of emotion, on the margin of thought, on the margin of profundity', dealing only 'with thin super-refinements which are undoubtedly the real presentments of certain contemporary neuroticism of feeling'. She was, however, comparing Eliot adversely with James Joyce, and very much, one suspects, from the point of view of an Irish writer praising Irish genius. In doing so, she did not scruple to borrow from a range of negative views more characteristic of England than America. The English literary establishment was hostile to modernism. The *Times Literary Supplement* treated *Prufrock and Other Observations* with contempt, regretted Eliot's '"phobia" of sentimentality' (Brooker, 21) in *Poems* (1919) and castigated the cleverness of *Ara Vos Prec* (1920). *The Waste Land* received short shrift. J. C. Squire in the *London Mercury* (October 1923) was 'unable to make head or tail of it': 'it is a pity that a man who can write as well as Mr Eliot writes in this poem should be so bored (not passionately disgusted) with existence that he doesn't mind what comes next, or who understands it' (Brooker, 115). It was Squire who, reviewing *Poems 1909–1925* in the *London Mercury* (March 1926), described the poet as 'Baudelaire without his guts' (Brooker, 141).

Nevertheless, Eliot made headway in England from the start, and not merely thanks to Pound and Aiken. Pound was a gifted publicist, but it took something else to get an *entrée* to the indigenous intelligentsia. The person who did this for Eliot was Bertrand Russell. He had taught Eliot for a brief while at Harvard (he was the subject of the poem 'Mr Apollinax') and had evidently found him interesting. Their paths crossed again shortly after Eliot's arrival in England, and he was responsible for the poet's introduction to Lady Ottoline Morrell, at whose country house near Oxford the group of Bloomsbury artists and writers gathered at weekends (see Chapter 23 above). Leonard and Virginia Woolf were to publish *The Waste Land* at their Hogarth Press in 1923. Aldous Huxley was already recommending his brother Julian to read Eliot's work in December 1916: he found the man 'overwhelmingly cultured' and an inspired commentator on French literature.[7] The favourable notice that 'Prufrock' got in the *Nation* earlier that year has already been mentioned. A delighted Eliot enclosed a copy of it in a letter to his mother

(6 September 1916), remarking: 'Bertie [Russell] thinks it is due to the fact that Massingham, the editor, visited Lady Ottoline Morrell lately, and probably had the things called to his attention there' (*L1*, 164). As Russell was conducting an affair with Morrell at the time, he should have known.

Yet Bloomsbury's Eliot did not have the challenging newness of Ezra Pound's. The Woolfs' 'melancholy suspicion that he is a product of a Silver Age' even left room for accommodation with the *Times Literary Supplement* and its complaints of 'cleverness' (Brooker, 22). The Woolfs were anonymously reviewing *Poems* (1919), published by the Hogarth Press, in the *Athenaeum* (20 June 1919); the editor was John Middleton Murry, another frequenter of Morrell's weekend parties – Eliot had already published several reviews in his weekly magazine. The 'melancholy suspicion', of course, might simply be an attempt to avoid the imputation of something incestuous in promoting such a slim and esoteric volume. More telling is the weight they place, in however contradictory a fashion, on Eliot's way of being modern: 'Poetry to him seems to be not so much an art as a science' (Brooker, 22). They keep up the scientific analogy throughout the review; it cannot have been uncongenial to Eliot who himself in 1919, propounding his theory of poetic impersonality, makes use of scientific analogy. Favourable reviewers of *Prufrock and Other Observations* had been prepared to praise only so long as they need not take the book seriously. The *Southport Guardian* (18 August 1917), for example, could not feel that certain of the poems were 'quite worthy of inclusion even in an Imagist book', though it was on the whole positive. When Clive Bell wrote in a review of *The Waste Land* for the *Nation and Athenaeum* (22 September 1923) that Bloomsbury thought 'The Love Song of J. Alfred Prufrock' 'better than anything of the sort that had been published for some time', the 'sort' of poem he had in mind was apparently *vers de société*, in the manner of Praed, an early nineteenth-century writer of light verse. Bell thought that Eliot had written 'nothing wittier, more brilliantly evocative of a subtle impression, than "Mr Apollinax"' (Brooker, 112). In 'Shakespeare and the Stoicism of Seneca' (1927), Eliot implicitly dismisses this view of his early work. Bell asserted that Eliot 'lacks imagination' (Brooker, 113), and he accused him of doing nothing but repeat himself since 'Prufrock'.

Eliot's pre-eminence as a critic, realised in a long series of reviews for the *New Statesman* (where he had been introduced by Russell's friend Sydney Waterlow), the *Athenaeum*, and finally the *Times Literary Supplement*, was generally recognised (see Chapter 10 above). Bloomsbury, too, was willing to admit the brilliance of his criticism – *The Sacred*

Wood (1920) was well received by them and their friends in the *New Statesman* and the *Athenaeum*, for example. But praise for the criticism led to talk of the 'narrow' limits of the poetry, so dependent on books, so short on experience. This attitude was influential: it is, for example, reflected in an essay by Edwin Muir in the *Nation and Athenaeum* (29 August 1925) subsequently reprinted in his book on modern literature, *Transition* (1926). Far more appreciative of the criticism than Clive Bell (whose review of *The Waste Land* judged scathingly: 'He has an *a priori* theory, which is no sillier than any other *a priori* theory, and he applies it unmercifully' [Brooker, 114]), Muir nevertheless concludes that Eliot is 'definitely a poet of inferior range', his poetry 'lacks immediacy and importance'.[8]

The review by I. A. Richards of *Poems 1909–1925* in the *New Statesman* (20 February 1926) has, therefore, a special significance for the English scene, since it rejected the notion that Eliot's allusions were the product of pedantry or a shortage of 'experience'. The poems, he said, were held together by 'the accord, contrast, and interaction of their emotional effects, not by an intellectual scheme that analysis must work out' (Brooker, 138). He concluded strikingly, in tones by far the most positive so far encountered: 'some readers find in his poetry not only a clearer, fuller realisation of their plight, the plight of a whole generation, than they find elsewhere, but also through the very energies set free in that realisation, a return of the saving passion' (Brooker, 140). Richards, whose 'generational' reading of *The Waste Land* echoes Edmund Wilson's, had made Eliot's acquaintance upon reading *Ara Vos Prec*: he came to Eliot through the poems and did not pay much attention to the criticism. In England this was probably a good thing.

Eliot did have both English admirers and English imitators beside Richards, and outside Bloomsbury (Herbert Read, for example), and his work *was* paid considerable attention. In 1919, Arnold Bennett was so struck by Eliot's work in the little magazine *Art and Letters* that he made his acquaintance. But beneath much of the praise there may be discerned a diminishing doubt, timidity or condescension. Only after the publication of *Poems 1909–1925* do things begin to change – the reactionary Sir Henry Newbolt included Eliot in his anthology *New Paths on Helicon* in 1927. 'Prufrock', he said, brought the reader 'pure delight' of a kind suggesting Henry James and George Meredith.[9] Not surprisingly, there is in the crucial early years little contact between Eliot's own thinking about poetry and what other people said about him, except in the rare cases where a critic tried to use the criticism to throw light on the verse.

In particular, Eliot's interest in drama, so evident in his criticism, failed to attract notice. The alternative to seeing *The Waste Land* as summing up the experience of a generation was to see it as the expression of *personal* feeling.

Richards seems to be the only critic to have radically affected the direction of Eliot's thinking about literature. (Many critics served in the less rewarding role of Aunt Sally – Middleton Murry being foremost.) Richards claimed that in *The Waste Land* Eliot had effected 'a complete severance between his poetry and all beliefs'.[10] Eliot's reply, 'A Note on Poetry and Belief' in the *Enemy* (January 1927), shows that he considered Richards wrong both on the particular count and the general one: that is, he thought that *The Waste Land* embodied a form of belief, even if that belief was only implied by doubt, and he refused in general to admit an antinomy of art and life. Great art was moral, and hence bore directly on the concerns of life. But in what sense could art effectively do this when it was based on premises that were philosophically or religiously unacceptable? Eliot's entry into the Church of England in 1927 was a statement of belief; and the hardening of attitude expressed in the preface to *For Lancelot Andrewes* (1928) was a prelude to a deflection of interest to more strictly philosophical and religious issues in his criticism, and presented difficulties for those who wished to take the same line as Richards. But by this time, or a little thereafter, Eliot's friends had done their work; his reputation was made. By and large, his American proponents, friendly to his 'realism', come off better than the English. Critics like the Woolfs stumble like people in a dark room who know where the light switch is, but somehow can't find it. The tone of criticism now changes; Eliot is still a puzzling figure, but he is a well-established critic, publisher and editor, as well as a poet. There is a tendency to question his achievement in poetry and prose just as staid members of the literary community come to accept him.

His newly avowed religious and political principles resulted in appreciably cooler reviews for Eliot's new poetry of the 1930s. Edmund Wilson's piece on *The Waste Land* was updated for inclusion in *Axel's Castle* (1931). Wilson hesitates over the later prose, finally judges *Ash-Wednesday* (1930) 'a not unworthy successor' to *The Waste Land*, though its imagery 'less vivid because more artificial' is 'a definite feature of inferiority', and he calls the first three Ariel Poems 'comparatively uninspired'.[11] In *Poetry* (September 1930), Morton D. Zabel found 'The Hollow Men' bad, and disliked the Ariel Poems. He identified 'a conciliatory attitude' in the more recent poetry, which 'deprives his art of its once incomparable distinction in style and tone' (Brooker, 185). Allen Tate's account of *Ash-Wednesday* for *Hound and Horn* (January–March 1931) is more appreciative. He emphasises moral achievement in the abandonment of the irony employed in *The Waste Land* in favour of humility: 'His [new] form is simple, expressive, homogeneous, and direct, and without the usual elements of violent contrast' (Brooker, 191). Tate's description minimises the modernist aspect of the poem without at all slighting it. It was not necessary, however, to sympathise with Eliot's religious views (as Tate did) to admire *Ash-Wednesday*. By 1935, Richards could be found saying that it was 'better poetry even than the best sections of *The Waste Land*'. The reason was that it showed 'less dread of the unknown depths' (Richards was alluding to a passage in Joseph Conrad's *Lord Jim*) than its predecessors.[12]

The solid nature of Eliot's reputation by the mid 1930s is reflected in the fact that, whereas the first Faber edition of *Poems 1909–1925* had consisted of only 1,460 copies, 6,000 made up that of *Collected Poems 1909–1935*. The first American edition of the latter was only of 4,700 copies, confirming Eliot's establishment (in England) as an English poet. The success of *Murder in the Cathedral* (1935) played its part; it was seen by twenty thousand people in its first year in London. *Collected Poems 1909–1935* ends with 'Burnt Norton', the first part of *Four Quartets*, which was not published as a whole until 1943. 'Burnt Norton' was not received with universal praise; the reviewer in *New Verse* described it as 'rather a dull meditation on time and God and love, which breaks only a few times from a thin monotony into richness'.[13] Eliot was always a controversial poet, and did not cease to be as he grew older. When Delmore Schwartz reviewed the completed sequence for the New York *Nation* (24 July 1943), he dissented from the 'unmixed admiration' (Brooker, 479) that others had given the volume. He objected especially to the 'blocks of long lines very close to the rhythm of prose ... the crucial instant of insight is betrayed by the language'. He disliked, too, the lyrics in conventional form: 'the images seem *made*, self-imitative, forced; they have the look of the artificial' (Brooker, 480). In the end, it seems that only the sestina and the passage in imitation of *terza rima* please Schwartz.

The Cambridge academic journal *Scrutiny* reviewed almost all Eliot's books from 1933 to 1952, sometimes to adverse effect. Martin Turnell found *The Family Reunion* (1939) to have 'no centre and no significance. The confusion leaves its mark on every line of the verse; it is apparent in the looseness of the texture, the preference for vagueness and abstraction and in the muddled images'.[14] (In the *New Republic* [3 May 1939], Louis

MacNeice thought the verse 'most successful' and the play as a whole 'very moving' [Brooker, 389].) Turnell disliked 'Burnt Norton', but some of the most appreciative accounts of *Four Quartets* appeared in *Scrutiny*. Before Turnell's throwaway dismissal, the psychologist-critic D. W. Harding had discussed 'Burnt Norton' at length (September 1936): 'the poem takes the place of the ideas of "regret" and "eternity" … this poem is a newly created concept, equally abstract but vastly more exact and rich in meaning' than the 'ideas' it replaces (Brooker, 372). F. R. Leavis developed Harding's view in his review of 'The Dry Salvages' (summer 1942): the poetry from *Ash-Wednesday* onwards 'is a searching of experience, a spiritual discipline, a technique for sincerity' (Brooker, 447). These judgements are all the more remarkable for coming from a self-consciously non-Christian point of view, but its very subtlety made it difficult to maintain. George Orwell, for example, was more forthright. He dealt unenthusiastically with the first three Quartets in an essay for *Poetry (London)* (October–November 1942), complaining at the lack of memorable lines. His view of the early poetry owes much to the Marxist critique of the 1930s (the most notable example is the 1931 essay by D. S. Mirsky). That early poetry only had 'room for *rentier* values, the values of people too civilised to work … that was the price that had to be paid, at any rate at that time, for writing a poem worth reading' (Brooker, 453). Fundamentally, Orwell objected to the Christianity of the Quartets: 'the negative Pétainism, which turns its eyes to the past, accepts defeat, writes off earthly happiness as impossible, mumbles about prayer and repentance and thinks it a spiritual advance to see life as "a pattern of living worms in the guts of the women of Canterbury" – that, surely, is the least hopeful road a poet could take' (Brooker, 455).

After *Four Quartets*, Eliot's creative energies were channelled into the theatre, where he had considerable success with *The Cocktail Party*, which ran for 400 performances in London and for the same number in New York in 1949 and 1950. *The Confidential Clerk* (1954) did less well. *The Elder Statesman* (1959) was not seen at all in New York. The critical response was also one of diminishing returns. With *The Cocktail Party*, for example, the original response of reviewers stressed the play's comedy. Only later does the gruesomeness of Celia's martyrdom attract negative criticism. The play won over William Carlos Williams, who in the *New York Post* (12 March 1950) wrote that it was 'a very thrilling play' and builds to 'a tremendous emotional climax' (Brooker, 527).

Eliot's reputation was secured largely thanks to his friends. The apparent incestuousness of this is not to the point. They were intelligent people who knew that he deserved their support. But the diversity of their views is surprising. They were unable to promote a single line on his behalf. Even when their efforts were no longer needed, he continued to provoke an extraordinarily wide range of views. This explains some of the excitement that reading Eliot brings with it still. When one has done with the critical record, there is always more to be said.

NOTES

1. Quoted in Charles Norman, *Ezra Pound* (London: Macmillan, 1960), p. 166. Aiken told the story in different versions; Dominic Hibberd questions their veracity in *Harold Monro: Poet of the New Age* (London: Palgrave, 2001), pp. 153–4.
2. Conrad Aiken, *Collected Criticism* (Oxford University Press, 1968), p. 196.
3. *The Letters of Wyndham Lewis*, ed. W. K. Rose (London: Methuen, 1963), p. 68.
4. Harriet Monroe, 'Mr Jepson's Slam', *Poetry* (July 1918), 212.
5. *The Selected Letters of William Carlos Williams*, ed. John C. Thirlwell (New York: McDowell, Obolensky, 1957), pp. 311–13.
6. *Selected Essays of William Carlos Williams* (New York: Random House, 1954), p. 22.
7. Quoted in *Letters of Aldous Huxley*, ed. Grover Smith (London: Chatto & Windus, 1969), p. 117.
8. See Edwin Muir, 'Contemporary Writers: Mr T. S. Eliot', *Nation & Athenaeum* (20 August 1925), 644–6.
9. See Sir Henry Newbolt, *New Paths on Helicon* (London: T. Nelson & Sons, 1927), p. 403.
10. I. A. Richards, 'A Background for Poetry', *Criterion* (July 1925), 520n.
11. See Edmund Wilson, *Axel's Castle* (London: Fontana, 1961), pp. 80–110.
12. I. A. Richards, *Science and Poetry* (London: Routledge, 1935), p. 71.
13. 'New Books', *New Verse* (June/July 1936), 19.
14. See Martin Turnell, 'Mr Eliot's New Play', *Scrutiny* (June 1939), 108–14.

CHAPTER 35

Contemporary and post-war poetry

Stephen Regan

The 'new bearings' in English poetry that F. R. Leavis wrote about so positively and authoritatively in 1932 were essentially those established by T. S. Eliot in the poetry up to and including *Ash-Wednesday* (1930). Leavis is acutely responsive to a poetry that 'expresses freely a modern sensibility, the ways of feeling, the modes of experience, of one fully alive in his own age'.[1] The epilogue to *New Bearings in English Poetry* records 'the decisiveness of Mr Eliot's achievement' in revising and reordering the tradition of English poetry, but it also harbours reservations about the 'great deal of discipleship of varying degrees of *naïveté* and subtlety' that Eliot has suffered. The imitation of Eliot, he concedes, has 'become a nuisance and even something of a menace'. Eliot's achievement has cleared the way for serious work, but it has also 'beguiled a certain amount of young talent into something worse than waste of time'.[2] The likeliest successors are William Empson and Ronald Bottrall, both of whom exhibit an intellectual sophistication and technical control derived from Eliot's example. In 'Retrospect 1950', however, Leavis ruefully acknowledges the failure of these poets to develop in any significant way, and he grudgingly observes the popular success of W. H. Auden and his near contemporaries. A general failure of 'the function of criticism' and an implied lowering of critical standards are offered as an explanation of 'why the influence of T. S. Eliot, out of which a poetic revival seemed so likely to come, should have been so sadly defeated'.[3]

Taking his cue from Leavis, A. Alvarez further sanctioned the idea that Eliot's influence, even after the publication of *Four Quartets* (1943), amounted to very little. In *The Shaping Spirit* (1958) and then in his highly influential anthology, *The New Poetry* (1962), Alvarez claimed that the experimental techniques of Eliot 'never really took on in England because they were an essentially American concern'.[4] Caught in a process of 'negative feed-back', experimental verse was replaced in the 1930s by 'traditional forms, in a chic contemporary guise', but Auden and the poets of the 1930s were in turn displaced by the anti-intellectualism of Dylan Thomas and the new romantics.[5] This led to a further reaction, with the so-called 'Movement' poets offering a rational, ironic corrective to the emotional excesses of their predecessors. Despite its mechanical simplicity, this version of literary history gained widespread assent and authority. It was driven by a fundamental conviction that post-war poetry needed to move beyond the limiting 'gentility' of Philip Larkin and the Movement, and that it might do so by fruitfully combining the best of British and American modernism: the psychological acuity and openness to experience of D. H. Lawrence and the technical proficiency and critical intelligence of T. S. Eliot. That eager hope for a merging of poetic traditions was strikingly registered in the cover design of *The New Poetry*, based on Jackson Pollock's 1952 painting, *Convergence*.

The urgent, vitalistic poetry that Alvarez called for is well represented in *The New Poetry*, with 'The Americans', John Berryman, Robert Lowell, Anne Sexton and Sylvia Plath, ushering in the promising talents of 'The British', among them Ted Hughes, Thom Gunn, R. S. Thomas, Charles Tomlinson and Geoffrey Hill. By 1962, however, the Movement poets had already exercised considerable sway over the direction of post-war British poetry and had come to be associated with anti-modernist prejudice and a concerted reaction against the influence of Eliot in particular. The Movement stood for retrenchment rather than innovation, with the careful cultivation of regular, disciplined verse forms offered in place of modernist fragmentation. The poets associated with the Movement seemed intent on making poetry more accessible to a post-war generation of readers. Eliot, like Pound, had come close to 'scrapping the contracts traditionally observed between poet and reader'.[6] As Donald Davie noted, it sometimes seemed that the Movement was part of 'a conspiracy to pretend that Eliot and Pound never happened'.[7] Larkin's 'Statement', accompanying a selection of his poems in D. J. Enright's anthology *Poets of the 1950s*, is frequently cited as an exemplary instance of a deliberate turning away from Eliot: 'As a guiding principle I believe that every poem must be its own sole freshly created universe, and therefore have no belief in "tradition" or a common myth-kitty or casual allusions in poems to other poems or poets'.[8] Many of Larkin's readers suspected that the statement concealed a genuine admiration for Eliot's poetry, borne out by his judicious selection of Eliot's work for *The Oxford Book of Twentieth-Century English Verse* (1973). Although the Oxford anthology is still seen to epitomise an English line of poetry, with Thomas Hardy leading the way, Larkin's choice of poets, including Austin Clarke, Louis

MacNeice, Basil Bunting and Derek Walcott, is far more eclectic and adventurous than he is given credit for. Commenting on his selection of poets for the book, Larkin admitted the language of the Georgian poets was 'stale', and that 'It was Eliot and Yeats, and perhaps even Pound, who sharpened up the language'.[9]

The powerful and pervasive influence of Eliot in Larkin's early poems and juvenilia makes the Movement's rejection of modernism seem all the more contrived and misleading. In the summer of 1939, at the age of 16, Larkin began to write an ambitious series of experimental lyrics in which the nocturnal urban imagery, the ironic mode of address, the deflationary bathos and the subtle play of consciousness are all derived from Eliot. 'The Ships at Mylae', with its windswept empty streets, has the imagistic precision of 'Preludes' and 'Rhapsody on a Windy Night', though the title and the exclamatory voice clearly suggest the influence of *The Waste Land*:

> Stanley!
> You who serene from unsung argosies
> Gazed on the mounting foam!

As well as standing in for Stetson, Stanley appears to be modelled on Eliot's Sweeney and is subject to the same kind of satirical treatment of human foibles and failings. 'Stanley en Musique' and 'Stanley et la Glace' are composed in the quatrains Eliot employed for 'Sweeney Among the Nightingales' and 'Sweeney Erect', and their comically pretentious French titles suggest that Larkin was alert to Eliot's borrowings from Charles Baudelaire and Jules Laforgue (see Chapter 21 above). A note that Larkin attached to 'Stanley en Musique' reveals a high degree of critical self-reflection, confirming that the teenage poet was not content simply to imitate his elders: 'Eliotian but amusing'.[10]

Larkin's versions of Eliot are never weakly imitative. In every case, they demonstrate a critical independence, even if it tends towards parody. Sometimes these early poems appear to be exaggerating stylistic tendencies and thematic obsessions in Eliot's work, intensifying familiar ironic moods and perspectives, but always they bear a complex relationship with the texts that prompted them. 'Street Lamps' is an experimental sonnet that initially recalls the spluttering streetlamps of 'Rhapsody on a Windy Night', but then modulates into a supple and sinuous syntax reminiscent of the opening of 'The Love Song of J. Alfred Prufrock':

> When night slinks, like a puma, down the sky,
>   And the bare, windy streets echo with silence,
> Street lamps come out, and lean at corners, awry ...[11]

Larkin's response to Eliot, then, is not one of outright rejection, but one of excited emulation followed by a more restrained process of absorption and assimilation. Even before the publication of his first full-length book of poems, *The North Ship* (1945), Larkin had acquired from Eliot a valuable repertoire of rhetorical effects.

It should come as no surprise that some of the most celebrated Movement anthology pieces are poems by Larkin that show deep and continuing affinities with Eliot. On closer inspection, the 'Bored, uninformed' speaker of 'Church Going' who takes off his 'cycle clips in awkward reverence' seems less an attempt to show that the poet is 'just like the man next door' than a knowing cultivation of a modernist angst and alienation typified by J. Alfred Prufrock. The comic fumbling awkwardness prepares us for the deep-seated existential dilemma of one who ends 'much at a loss like this, / Wondering what to look for', taking us back through Eliot to Laforgue.[12] The discomfiture of the alienated intellectual generates the social drama of 'The Whitsun Weddings', a poem surprisingly complicit with *The Waste Land.* The caricature of working-class culture and the effortless condescension ('The nylon gloves and jewellery-substitutes') derive from Eliot, but so too does the powerful search for some redeeming vision amidst the chaos and contingency of contemporary civilisation. The magnificent closing image of 'an arrow-shower / Sent out of sight, somewhere becoming rain' might well look back to Laurence Olivier's 1944 film version of *Henry V* in a nostalgic display of post-war nationalist sentiment, but it is also in keeping with the poem's symbolic apprehension of regenerative processes. The depiction of marriage as 'a happy funeral' and 'a religious wounding' is a potent reminder that what Eliot and Larkin share is a profoundly mythic and anthropological interest in rituals and rites of passage.[13]

Like Larkin, Seamus Heaney could hardly avoid Eliot's presence, working closely on the production of his poems with Eliot's Faber colleague, Charles Monteith. Heaney, however, confesses to having been 'daunted by the otherness of Eliot and all that he stood for', and he admits that it was some time before he 'began to grow up to Eliot'. Although 'the schoolboy in a Catholic boarding school in Derry' in the mid 1950s could readily identify with the Christmas imagery, the notions of conversion, and even the reek of 'vegetation' in 'Journey of the Magi', the formal complexity and imaginative strangeness of Eliot's verse eluded him. 'The Hollow Men' was understood in the terms required by school examinations, as an exploration and manifestation of loss of faith in the modern world, and its 'rare music' only fully appreciated later. The aspiring poet in Heaney was stirred by the sensuous passages in *Ash-Wednesday*, but only later perceived 'the finer tone and stricter disciplines of Eliot's poetry'.[14] Heaney's reading of Eliot's essays during his undergraduate years at Queen's University, Belfast, was clearly decisive in terms of alerting him to his own complex relationships with tradition and in fostering within his own critical instincts an acute appreciation of 'the "auditory imagination" ... the feeling for syllable and rhythm, penetrating far below the conscious levels of thought and feeling' (*UPUC*, 118–19). It was Eliot's meditations on the music of poetry that drew Heaney's attention to the 'undulant cadences and dissolvings and reinings-in' of the 'Death by Water' section of *The Waste Land*, and later taught him to listen to 'the interweaving and repetition' of words that went round 'like a linked dance through the ear' in the opening lines of 'Burnt Norton'.[15]

Given the rural life and labour to which the young Heaney was accustomed, it should come as no surprise that his earliest poetic influences were Patrick Kavanagh, R. S. Thomas and Ted Hughes. By his own admission, what he heard in the work of these poets was 'more in tune with the actual voices of my own first world than the ironies and elegances of MacNeice and Eliot could ever have been'.[16] The transition from *Death of a Naturalist* (1966) to *Door into the Dark* (1969) is enabled by a changing conception of poetry based on Eliot's notion of the 'dark embryo' which forms in the poet's consciousness and gradually takes on the form and speech of a poem.[17] A strong psychological interest in the processes of composition is accompanied by a new, exploratory way of thinking about poetry and place that probably derives from a reading of *Four Quartets*. The 'tall' sky in 'The Peninsula' recalls Larkin's tall light ('Deceptions') and tall heat ('The Whitsun Weddings'), but the mode of address is surely Eliot's: 'so you will not arrive / But pass through, though always skirting landfall'.[18] If the controversial Bog Poems in *Wintering Out* (1972) and *North* (1975) owe a debt to W. B. Yeats and his search for 'Befitting emblems of adversity' in *The Tower* (1928),[19] they also suggest Heaney's positive response to 'the mythical method' (*SP*, 178) described by Eliot in '*Ulysses*, Order, and Myth' (1923): 'a way of controlling, of ordering, of giving a shape and a significance to the immense panorama of futility and anarchy which is contemporary history' (*SP*, 177).

In 'Learning from Eliot', Heaney writes of how Eliot's 'dream processes' fed upon Dante's visionary art in the *Divine Comedy*, and his own turning to Dante by way of Eliot finds its most creative expression in the purgatorial 'Station Island' (1984).[20] Heaney's conversations with the dead show the unmistakable imprint of Eliot's encounter with a ghostly figure

'In the uncertain hour before the morning' (*CPP*, 193) in 'Little Gidding'. Heaney returns to the same 'Dantesque set-piece of the dawn patrol' in an essay in *The Government of the Tongue* (1988), this time presenting 'Little Gidding' as an exemplary instance of how the imagination might endure the impact and destruction of war, invigorated and sustained by tradition. He notes how the 'matutinal airs' of the passage float from Dante to Shakespeare in their recollection of Hamlet confronting the ghost of his father.[21] In the poems written after *North*, Heaney the 'inner émigré', having 'Escaped from the massacre', turns more and more to the meditative timbre of *Four Quartets*, especially 'Little Gidding'.[22] The hope and anticipation, as well as the trepidation, that Heaney experienced after leaving Northern Ireland and settling in County Wicklow in the Republic are powerfully registered in his 'Glanmore Sonnets': 'And I am quickened with a redolence / Of farmland as a dark unblown rose'.[23] If Yeats and James Clarence Mangan find a well-ploughed furrow in Heaney's *Field Work* (1979), so too does Eliot. Thereafter, the presence of Eliot is altogether more pervasive and assimilated. It manifests itself most powerfully in those poems that seem to bear out Eliot's belief in poetry as the 'concentration' of experience ('a concentration which does not happen consciously or of deliberation') rather than a Wordsworthian 'emotion recollected in tranquillity'.[24] 'From the Frontier of Writing' might well have been written to demonstrate this distinction. What initially looks like the recollection of a routine 'stop and search' at an army checkpoint is startlingly transformed into pure concentration as the poem asserts its own countervailing reality:

> And suddenly you're through, arraigned yet freed,
> as if you'd passed from behind a waterfall
> on the black current of a tarmac road
>
> past armour-plated vehicles, out between
> the posted soldiers flowing and receding
> like tree shadows into the polished windscreen.[25]

Here is that 'new thing resulting from the concentration', the poem itself 'adjacent and parallel to lived experience'.[26] As Heaney has 'grown up' to Eliot, he seems increasingly to have accommodated and emulated the mystical qualities of *Four Quartets*, most obviously in the visionary, transcendental poems of *Seeing Things* (1991). More recently, however, in *Electric Light* (2001) and *District and Circle* (2006), Heaney has circled back on his own coming to consciousness as a writer, and a different side of Eliot's legacy has emerged. In the title poem of the earlier volume,

'Electric Light', Heaney records a visit to London and counts among the voices of his education the unmistakable voices of *The Waste Land*: 'To Southwark too I came, / From tube-mouth into sunlight, / Moyola-breath by Thames's "strange stronde"'.[27]

In 'Stern', Heaney remembers asking Ted Hughes what it was like meeting Eliot:

> 'When he looked at you,'
> He said, 'it was like standing on a quay
> Watching the prow of the *Queen Mary*
> Come towards you, very slowly.'[28]

The title cleverly catches Eliot's stern demeanour, the Stearns in Thomas Stearns Eliot (his mother's side of the family), and the stern of the boat of death in which Heaney imagines Hughes's recent departure. In one of his best-known critical essays, 'Englands of the Mind' (1976), Heaney listens to the sounds of Hughes's poems and seeks to understand them in terms of Eliot's notion of 'the auditory imagination'. Eliot prompts a careful 'thinking of the relationship between the word as pure vocable, as articulate noise, and the word as etymological occurrence, as symptom of human history, memory and attachments'.[29] Here, Eliot serves as the critical medium enabling a creative dialogue between contemporary poets. However long it took Heaney to 'grow up' to Eliot in his poetry, it is clear that his critical faculties were strongly influenced by Eliot as early as 1972, when he composed an essay on Hugh MacDiarmid titled 'Tradition and the Individual Talent'.

The influence of Eliot is not so evident in the work of Ted Hughes as it is in the poetry and prose of Heaney, but there is ample evidence of Hughes's high estimation of 'the master' in the occasional speeches given in honour of Eliot collected as *A Dancer to God: Tributes to T. S. Eliot* (1992). The most instructive and revealing section in this strange and astonishingly arcane work is Hughes's intense appreciation of 'The Death of Saint Narcissus' as an objective correlative for Eliot's tortured poetic self. If Hughes succeeds superbly well in showing how the poem embodies Eliot's 'curious neurasthenic self-awareness of himself as a thing', he also inadvertently reveals how Eliot, as much as Lawrence, prompted his own erotic primitivism in the sensuous appeal of lines like this:

> Then he knew that he had been a fish
> With slippery white belly held tight in his own fingers,
> Writhing in his own clutch, his ancient beauty
> Caught fast in the pink tips of his new beauty.

If these lines sound uncannily like the early naturalist Hughes, there is also a prefiguring of the later, hieratic Hughes in the lines that Eliot transplanted from 'The Death of Saint Narcissus' to *The Waste Land*: 'Come under the shadow of this gray rock – / Come in under the shadow of this gray rock' (*CPP*, 605).

Having read Hughes through Eliot's concept of 'the auditory imagination', Heaney was to turn his attention to the work of Sylvia Plath in the final instalment of his T. S. Eliot Memorial Lectures in 1986. There, Heaney reads Plath in the light of Eliot's conviction that 'poetry housed older and deeper levels of energy than those supplied by explicit meaning and immediate rhythmic stimulus'.[30] The lecture is exemplary in its attention to the vocal qualities of the poetry, subtly aligning Plath with Eliot in their shared raid upon the inarticulate. The idea that a supposedly 'confessional' poetry might be a sophisticated development, rather than a simple rejection, of an earlier modernist emphasis on impersonality has been thoughtfully considered by Clive Wilmer.[31] His essay does not propose that Plath's work was directly influenced by Eliot, but there is no shortage of intertextual echoes and allusions to support the case. Plath's biographer, Anne Stevenson, has provided a comprehensive account of how 'deeply she was indebted to T. S. Eliot'.[32] Plath's first book of poems was initially titled 'The Devil of the Stairs' (a phrase taken from *Ash-Wednesday*) and an early story, 'The Daughters of Blossom Street', was initially titled 'The Earth Our Hospital' (an allusion to 'East Coker'). Stevenson claims that many of the distinctive 'Plathic familiars' derive from *Four Quartets*: 'the surgeon, the nurse, Adam, mental wires (nerves), fever, roses, flames, and the Eucharistic blood and flesh of Eliot's hymn'. She notes how Plath frequently draws upon the Christian iconography of Eliot's verse, giving it her own iconoclastic twist, and she argues that Plath both emulates and parodies Eliot's tonal qualities and rhetorical effects, as with the preponderance of hissing noises reminiscent of 'The Love Song of J. Alfred Prufrock'. As if wilfully ignoring the interjection, 'Oh, do not ask, "What is it?"' (*CPP*, 13), she asks in 'The Bee Meeting': 'is it the hawthorn that smells so sick? / . . . / Is it some operation that is taking place?' Eliot's presence is pervasive in the sacrificial myths that haunt Plath's poetry, but it is clearly there at the local level of diction as well, in the curious verbal 'etherizes' in 'The Bee Meeting', or the title of her 1965 collection, *Ariel*, recalling Eliot's Ariel Poems as much as *The Tempest*. It might even be, as Stevenson claims, that Eliot underwrites Plath's feminist determination to recast tradition: 'What any and every aspiring woman poet ought to learn from Sylvia Plath, it seems to me, is how to overhear, imitate, play variations on, and eventually transmute the English tradition in a wholly original and affective way.'[33]

Surprisingly, perhaps, Eliot also underwrites the recasting of tradition for poets in the Caribbean and elsewhere, especially those contemplating the challenges of writing about a difficult and divided post-colonial inheritance. Derek Walcott's *Epitaph for the Young* (1949), an experimental free verse poem in twelve cantos, takes its bearings from Baudelaire's 'Le Voyage' but opens into a quest for cultural authority strongly reminiscent of Eliot. There are unmistakable echoes of 'The Love Song of J. Alfred Prufrock', *The Waste Land* and *Ash-Wednesday*, and very likely the title derives from *Four Quartets*: 'Every phrase and every sentence is an end and a beginning, / Every poem an epitaph' (*CPP*, 197). The teenage poet both laments the passing of his younger 'island' self and invokes the spirit of his dead father, Warwick, as he looks out towards new beginnings and poetic geographies. There are moments of Prufrockian self-consciousness and self-doubt, such as those recalling the reception of Walcott's privately published *25 Poems* (1949), though the poet's soul is afflicted by post-colonial politics as much as by metaphysical abstractions:

> Suffering is applauded, encouraged, and dissolves
> In a kind Englishwoman's smile among the olives,
> My soul, neatly transfixed in toothpick proportions
> Is spread among the lenient, lovely patrons.
> By 25 gestures of a lame mind,
> The privately prejudiced pretended to be tamed ...

In the fifth canto of *Epitaph for the Young*, Walcott looks back to Dante, as Heaney does, with Eliot as a mediating presence. Recalling 'The Dry Salvages', Walcott's disillusioned young speaker tells us: 'We had had enough of the Lady on the promontory, / *Figlia del tuo figlio*'. The reference is to St Bernard's prayer in Dante's *Paradiso*, but Walcott casually subverts the declaration of religious belief both here and in Eliot's poem, partly as a way of emphasising his own speaker's quest for redemption and therefore preparing us for the return to the promontory and 'the will of Heaven' in canto XII. These two examples of Walcott's indebtedness to Eliot suggest that, even at this very early stage in his career, his technique involves intelligent assimilation rather than simply imitation.

Again, as with Heaney, the most powerful engagement with Eliot's example involves an encounter with a spirit guide reminiscent of Dante's meeting with Brunetto Latini in the *Inferno* and of Eliot's meeting with 'some dead master' (*CPP*, 193) in 'Little Gidding'. In canto 8 of *Epitaph for the Young*, Walcott's poetic persona speaks with the shade of his dead father, but asks amidst the smoke and shadows, 'Are you here, Ser Brunetto?' The imagery of 'the thrush in the rose garden' and 'the desert where there is no water' speaks emphatically of Eliot's influence, but the general tenor is towards outrageous parody rather than obedient reverence:

> Say this not out of time, but in time, not timeless
> But rhymeless and out of time.
> For the
> For the wheel turns and the impatient suffer
> And the peasant passes distracted by insinuations
> Here and now in Castries and Hampstead, burnt nothing,
> A Little Giddying,
> But where was I?[34]

Parody, in this instance, has a post-colonial political significance. If it registers respect and admiration for the great achievements of Anglo-American modernism, it simultaneously announces the urgent need for writers in the Caribbean and elsewhere to create a new and authentic poetic idiom of their own. As John Thieme points out, *Epitaph for the Young* shows Walcott 'embarking on the project of evolving an appropriate tradition and in so doing transcending colonial mimesis'.[35] In more recent work, including *The Prodigal*, Walcott has continued to draw confidence from the example of the American expatriate poet in Europe, confronting tradition and rethinking it in the light of his own New World experience. If Eliot's example has been a salutary one for English poets such as Larkin and Hughes, helping to revitalise poetic forms and ideals, it has also had far-reaching consequences for non-English poets such as Heaney and Walcott, for whom the English lyric tradition is a more problematic inheritance.

NOTES

1. F. R. Leavis, *New Bearings in English Poetry* (1932) (London: Chatto & Windus, 1950), p. 61.
2. Ibid., pp. 144–5.
3. Ibid., p. 171.
4. A. Alvarez, ed., *The New Poetry* (1962) (Harmondsworth: Penguin, 1966), p. 21.
5. Ibid., pp. 22–3.
6. Donald Davie, *Articulate Energy* (London: Routledge & Kegan Paul, 1955), pp. 128–9.

7. Donald Davie, *The Poet in the Imaginary Museum* (Manchester: Carcanet, 1977), p. 67.
8. Philip Larkin, *Required Writing: Miscellaneous Pieces 1955–1982* (London: Faber & Faber, 1983), p. 79.
9. Philip Larkin, *Further Requirements: Interviews, Broadcasts, Statements and Book Reviews*, ed. Anthony Thwaite (London: Faber & Faber, 2001), p. 96.
10. Philip Larkin, *Early Poems and Juvenilia*, ed. A. T. Tolley (London: Faber & Faber, 2005), p. 21.
11. Philip Larkin, *Collected Poems*, ed. Anthony Thwaite (London: Marvell Press and Faber & Faber, 1988), p. 230.
12. Ibid., pp. 97–8.
13. Ibid., pp. 114–16.
14. Seamus Heaney, 'Learning from Eliot', *Finders Keepers: Selected Prose 1971–2001* (London: Faber & Faber, 2002), pp. 26, 29.
15. Ibid., pp. 34, 35.
16. Quoted by Neil Corcoran in *Seamus Heaney* (London: Faber & Faber, 1986), p. 20.
17. 'Critical', *The Collected Poems of Harold Monro* (London: Cobden-Sanderson, 1933), p. xiii.
18. Seamus Heaney, *Opened Ground: Poems 1966–1996* (London: Faber & Faber, 1998), p. 21.
19. W. B. Yeats, *Poems*, ed. A. Norman Jeffares (London: Macmillan, 1989), p. 310.
20. Heaney, 'Learning from Eliot', p. 31.
21. Seamus Heaney, *The Government of the Tongue* (London: Faber & Faber, 1988), p. 43.
22. Heaney, *Opened Ground*, p. 144.
23. Ibid., p. 163.
24. Heaney, *Government of the Tongue*, p. 124.
25. Heaney, *Opened Ground*, pp. 297–8.
26. Heaney, *Government of the Tongue*, p. 125.
27. Seamus Heaney, *Electric Light* (London: Faber & Faber, 2001), p. 81.
28. Seamus Heaney, *District and Circle* (London: Faber & Faber, 2006), p. 46.
29. Seamus Heaney, *Preoccupations: Selected Prose 1968–1978* (London: Faber & Faber, 1980), p. 150.
30. Heaney, *Government of the Tongue*, p. 148.
31. See Clive Wilmer, 'The Later Fortunes of Impersonality', *T. S. Eliot and the Concept of Tradition*, ed. Giovanni Cianci and Jason Harding (Cambridge University Press, 2007), pp. 58–71.
32. Anne Stevenson, *Between the Iceberg and the Ship: Selected Essays* (Ann Arbor: University of Michigan Press, 1998), pp. 40–1.
33. Ibid., pp. 41–2, 45, 50.
34. Derek Walcott, *Epitaph for the Young* (Barbardos: Advocate, 1949).
35. John Thieme, *Derek Walcott* (Manchester University Press, 1999), pp. 3–4.

CHAPTER 36

Eliot studies

Benjamin G. Lockerd

T. S. Eliot shocked his Bloomsbury friends when he entered the Anglican Church in 1927, and these shock waves still roll through Eliot Studies today. The animus against Eliot's religious and political traditionalism motivates a good deal of academic commentary, as does the reaction against Eliot's fame and authority; for example, Cynthia Ozick's sophomoric declaration of independence from the master, or Harold Bloom's recollection that he entered a profession 'virtually enslaved' by Eliot's 'preferences and prejudices'.[1] While contemporary reviews (see Chapter 34 above) opened up most of the issues that we still debate – nor should we forget the engagement with Eliot represented by the work of many modern poets (see Chapter 35 above) – academic criticism made Eliot's oeuvre central to the growth of a school of literary criticism, New Criticism, which became a dominant force in American universities by the mid twentieth century. Eliot's allusive and difficult style was particularly suited to intensive university study and it encouraged source hunting: Grover Smith's encyclopaedic *T. S. Eliot's Poetry and Plays* (1956) remains a work that must be consulted by Eliot scholars. Excellent monographs by academic critics, such as Helen Gardner's *The Art of T. S. Eliot* (1949) and Hugh Kenner's *The Invisible Poet* (1959), helped to raise Eliot to the peak of his prestige and, in the decades following the poet's death in 1965, further general studies and detailed analyses by many first-rate critics – including Denis Donoghue, Frank Kermode, Christopher Ricks, A. D. Moody, Ronald Bush, Ronald Schuchard and others too numerous to mention – have not been superseded by later critics: to adapt Eliot's essay on tradition, 'they are that which we know' (*SE*, 16). In the following survey of recent trends in Eliot Studies, the question of tradition will be a leitmotif in the examination of a number of key critical contexts, although in addressing such a voluminous and controversial terrain this account must necessarily be somewhat partial and argumentative.

BIOGRAPHY

Although Eliot advanced an 'Impersonal theory of poetry' (*SE*, 18), it has long been clear that his poetry is intensely personal. Biography is legitimately the first critical context. Herbert Howarth's *Notes on Some Figures Behind T. S. Eliot* (1964) gives some extremely useful biographical information, such as details about Eliot's Harvard professors. Perhaps the best introduction to Eliot's life and work is Russell Kirk's *Eliot and his Age* (1971; second edition 2008). This is the work of a man who knew Eliot and was deeply sympathetic to his ideals and beliefs. There are many reminiscences by people who knew Eliot, including two collections published during his lifetime, edited by Richard March and Tambimuttu (*T. S. Eliot: A Symposium* [1948]) and by Neville Braybrooke (*T. S. Eliot: A Symposium for his Seventieth Birthday* [1958]), as well as memoirs by Robert Sencourt (*T. S. Eliot: A Memoir* [1971]) and E. W. F. Tomlin (*T. S. Eliot: A Friendship* [1988]). A special issue of the *Southern Review* (autumn 1985) collects first-hand accounts. Anne Ridler's 'Working for T. S. Eliot' (*PN Review* [March 1983]), written by Eliot's Faber secretary, remembers him as a good-humoured, considerate and generous colleague; the aloof and arrogant Eliot seems to be largely a caricature drawn by those who did not know him.

The first attempt at a biography, *Great Tom* (1974) by T. S. Matthews, was rightly subtitled *Notes Towards a Definition of T. S. Eliot*. Peter Ackroyd's *T. S. Eliot* (1984) was far more successful and remains an important resource today, although, to a certain extent, it has been superseded by Lyndall Gordon's larger and thoroughly researched *T. S. Eliot: An Imperfect Life* (1988). Her subtitle indicates the tendency to find fault in Eliot's life. Making effective use of a wide range of sources, published and unpublished, Gordon's biography reveals new details about Emily Hale, including a statement from an unnamed source that Eliot had been in love with Hale shortly before his marriage to Vivien. This biography looks at Eliot primarily in relation to the women who were closest to him, an engaging approach but one that at times occludes other dimensions of his life. Of course, the eventual lifting of restrictions on archive material, including Eliot's correspondence with Hale, will occasion a revision of this biography. The most recent biography is James Miller's *T. S. Eliot: The Making of an American Poet* (2005), which, although learned and interesting, returns obsessively to the question of Eliot's putative homosexuality (a topic Miller first addressed thirty years earlier). Carole Seymour-Jones's biography of Vivien Eliot, *Painted*

Shadow (2001), provides new perspectives on the Eliots' marriage (her research reveals they were not as poor as they maintained). However, this book also presses conjectures about Eliot's sexuality too far, suggesting, for instance, that Eliot experienced a vicarious sexual intimacy with Bertrand Russell by colluding in Vivien's affair with him.

SEXUALITY

In 1952, John Peter published an article in *Essays in Criticism* suggesting that Eliot had a homosexual passion for a young man. Eliot's solicitor threatened to bring a suit for libel and the editors of the magazine were obliged to pulp the issue. George Watson examined the evidence that this lover was Jean Verdenal (*Sewanee Review* [summer 1976]), concluding that there is no reason to suppose that these friends had a sexual relationship. However, James Miller elaborated upon Peter's speculation in *T. S. Eliot's Personal Waste Land* (1977) and his recent biography advances the theory again, albeit in a more muted way. With the aid of postmodern theory, Colleen Lamos argues that Eliot was both homosexual and homophobic: she asserts that Eliot's allusions to male poets are homoerotic. More persuasively, Richard Kaye has suggested in an article published in *Modernism/Modernity* (May 1999) that Eliot's treatment of St Sebastian, an icon of homosexual desire, was a case of experimental decadent posturing. As mentioned above, Carole Seymour-Jones's biography of Vivien Eliot pushes the theory about Eliot's homosexuality further than the evidence will allow. Gabrielle McIntire also makes too much of too little in an article in *Modernism/Modernity* (2002), seeing homoeroticism in Eliot's Bolo poems rather than the use of all kinds of naughtiness for comic, if shocking, effect. Her *Modernism, Memory and Desire* (2007) is more subtle and engaging.

Eliot clearly had difficult relationships with some women, but the recent charges of misogyny levelled against him seem to me another aspect of the negative reaction to his traditionalism. Tony Pinkney's *Women in the Poetry of T. S. Eliot* (1984) highlights a pattern of violence against women in the poetry. Carol Christ's chapter in Ronald Bush's collection of essays, *T. S. Eliot: The Modernist in History* (1991), presents an interesting discussion of the feminine voices in the early poems. A refreshingly nuanced and supple interpretation of sexuality in Eliot's poetry is offered in Laurie MacDiarmid's *T. S. Eliot's Civilized Savage: Religious Eroticism and Poetics* (2003). There are also some very good essays in the collection edited by Nancy Gish and Cassandra Laity, *Gender, Desire and Sexuality in T. S. Eliot* (2004). Cyrena Pondrom has published articles from a forthcoming book reading Eliot's poetry through the lens of Judith Butler's theory of the performativity of gender. Although her work is always enlightening, Pondrom's use of Butler's radical theory is in danger of turning an insight into an absolute. In contrast to Pondrom's subtle and engaging articles, Sharon Stockton's *The Economics of Fantasy: Rape in Twentieth-Century Literature* (2006) starts from the oversimplified notion that to be female is to be liable to rape. She finds rape everywhere in Eliot's poetry, including the sexual intercourse between the clerk and the typist in *The Waste Land,* which, however devoid of affection, is depicted as consensual.

AMERICAN ELIOT AND THE FRENCH CONNECTION

For many years it was customary to ignore the expatriate Eliot's American roots; he was not even included in the annual review of criticism, *American Literary Scholarship,* until 1974. Eventually, however, scholars began to pay attention to this context. Ronald Bush's *T. S. Eliot: A Study in Character and Style* (1983) investigated the links to Ralph Waldo Emerson. Eric Sigg's *The American T. S. Eliot* (1989) was the first book-length study of Eliot's American background and sources, including examination of the influence of such figures as Henry Adams and Henry James. The first book to give an extended analysis of Eliot's relations with American poets is Lee Oser's excellent *T. S. Eliot and American Poetry* (1998), which considers Eliot's debts to Emerson, Edgar Allan Poe and Walt Whitman and also takes account of Eliot's mother, Charlotte. Oser turns his attention towards several younger American poets who were influenced by Eliot: John Ashbery, Elizabeth Bishop and Robert Lowell. These American critics have opened up a rich vein in Eliot scholarship.

Eliot scholars have been well aware of the enormous importance of several French writers to his poetic development. One fine book-length treatment is *The Road from Paris* (1974) by Cyrena Pondrom. The French scholar William Marx has written on Eliot's association with a wide range of French intellectuals, particularly those associated with the monthly magazine *La Nouvelle Revue Française.* On the centenary of Eliot's year in Paris (1910/11), new approaches to this subject are being made. In *T. S. Eliot's Parisian Year* (2009), Nancy Hargrove presents her extensive research into the cultural scene in Paris at that time – examining music, opera, ballet, painting and much else. Two recent scholarly works have broken new ground: John Morgenstern has written a thesis on Eliot and the Catholic literary revival in France in the early part of the twentieth century, and James Matthew Wilson has researched Eliot's engagement with the writings of the neo-Thomist philosopher Jacques Maritain.

CULTURE AND POLITICS

Two of the best books on Eliot's cultural and political ideas were first published in 1971: *T. S. Eliot's Social Criticism* by Roger Kojecký and *Eliot and his Age* by Russell Kirk. Anyone who has a serious desire to understand Eliot's views must, in addition to reading what Eliot actually wrote, read these two books. Kojecký carefully explores the many and varied influences on Eliot's ideas. Kirk examines all of Eliot's editorials in the *Criterion*, where many of his responses to contemporary social and political issues are to be found. Both studies are learned and balanced, in contrast to tendentious assertions of 'elitism' or the charges of 'reactionary' voiced in other writings on the subject. William Chace's *The Political Identities of Ezra Pound and T. S. Eliot* (1973) sees Eliot rejecting modernity by retreating into the Church. Marxist critics have also treated Eliot's social and political ideas unsympathetically. The most blatantly ideological assertions in Terry Eagleton's *Criticism and Ideology* (1978) – he sneers at Eliot the capitalist banker, cultural elitist and high churchman – can appear as dated as the fashions of the 1970s. John Xiros Cooper's *T. S. Eliot and the Politics of Voice* (1987) gives a more persuasive account of Eliot's thinking, though his interpretation of the passage on the typist and the clerk in *The Waste Land* reductively sees only class disdain rather than a satirical attack on the social order. Critics have consistently failed to acknowledge that Eliot was himself a radical critic of the materialism and individualism of modern industrialised economies. A recent exception is Edward Comentale's *Modernism, Cultural Production and the British Avant-Garde* (2004), which refuses to assume that Eliot's Classicism is reactionary. Similarly, Michael North's brilliant explication in *The Political Aesthetics of Yeats, Eliot, and Pound* (1991) examines the way in which both Christianity and Marxism offered alternatives to liberal capitalism. He concludes that Eliot was too conservative to be a supporter of Fascism.

The debate about Eliot's politics has often revolved around Charles Maurras, the French writer who seems to have inspired Eliot's tripartite credo: monarchist, classicist and Catholic. Balanced assessments of

Maurras and Eliot can be found in the studies by Kojecký and Kirk, as well as in a 1995 article by Father Shunichi Takayanagi. All of these commentators agree that Maurras's influence on Eliot was replaced by that of various Christian thinkers, including Jacques Maritain, Christopher Dawson and colleagues in the 'Moot' (an ecumenical sociological discussion group). Nevertheless, Kenneth Asher's *T. S. Eliot and Ideology* (1995) asserts that Maurras was the main source of Eliot's political ideas from beginning to end. He irresponsibly quotes Eliot's 1948 statement that Maurras was 'a sort of Virgil who led us to the gates of the temple'[2] without noting that Maurras (a non-believer who used Catholicism for political ends) must part company with Eliot, just as Virgil leaves Dante in *Purgatorio*. Denis Donoghue's comments on the complexity of Eliot's dealings with Maurras – advocating 'an exposition that would include nuances of appreciation, liking and disliking, repudiation of one aspect, respect for another' – offers a corrective to Asher's thesis.[3] Jason Harding's *The 'Criterion': Cultural Politics and Periodical Networks in Interwar Britain* (2002) shows that Eliot's journal was not, as has often been assumed, 'predictably conservative, even proto-fascist'.[4] Harding points out that Eliot's editorial policy in the *Criterion* was to seek intelligent debate; for example, the symposium he organised on the competing political theories Fascism and Communism, with contributions by the fascist J. S. Barnes and the socialist A. L. Rowse.

Eliot was so often viewed as an icon of classical decorum that it took some time for critics to notice that he loved popular culture. Grover Smith's *T. S. Eliot and the Use of Memory* (1996) suggested that the 'rattle of the bones' (*CPP*, 67) in *The Waste Land* owes something to the figure of 'Mr Bones' in contemporary minstrel shows. Michael Coyle has examined Eliot's many radio broadcasts for the BBC and he concludes that Eliot was interested in reaching a large audience through this mass medium. John Xiros Cooper's collection of essays, *T. S. Eliot's Orchestra* (2000), includes chapters on Eliot and popular music. The most comprehensive work on the subject of Eliot's relation to popular culture is David Chinitz's *T. S. Eliot and the Cultural Divide* (2003), a book that combines fine scholarship and critical tact. Chinitz quotes Eliot's lucid remark: 'fine art is the *refinement*, not the antithesis, of popular art'.[5] His book shows that Eliot's attempts to write drama were motivated by a desire to reach a large and varied audience through a communal medium, and he points out that Eliot's plays were indeed popular with theatregoers. Todd Avery returns to the subject of Eliot's BBC broadcasts in *Radio Modernism* (2006), while David Trotter has considered the influence of cinematic techniques on Eliot in *Cinema and Modernism* (2007).

Since Eliot's doctoral dissertation was on the idealist philosopher F. H. Bradley, critics have naturally focused attention here. Anne C. Bolgan's *What the Thunder Really Said* (1973) read *The Waste Land* in this Bradley-an context, and A. D. Nuttall wrote a chapter on Eliot and Bradley in *A Common Sky: Philosophy and the Literary Imagination* (1974). Louis Freed's *T. S. Eliot: The Critic as Philosopher* (1979) is an astute analysis of Eliot's understanding of Bradley. But the definitive explication of the relevance of Bradley's philosophy to Eliot's poetry is given in Jewel Spears Brooker and Joseph Bentley's *Reading 'The Waste Land': Modernism and the Limits of Interpretation* (1990), which situates Eliot in a modern epistemological dilemma, searching for objective knowledge.

Walter Benn Michaels was perhaps the first critic to discuss Eliot's familiarity with American pragmatism, a prominent school of thought in Harvard philosophy during Eliot's time as a graduate student there. Piers Gray widens the topic considerably in *T. S. Eliot's Intellectual and Poetic Development, 1909–1922* (1982) to include Henri Bergson, Josiah Royce, and the anthropologists Émile Durkheim and Lucien Lévy Bruhl. Another authoritative work of elucidation is Sanford Schwartz's *The Matrix of Modernism* (1985), examining William James, Edmund Husserl, Friedrich Nietzsche, and, with admirable cogency, Bradley and Bergson. Richard Shusterman made a significant contribution to Eliot studies with *T. S. Eliot and the Philosophy of Criticism* (1988), arguing that Eliot turned from Bergson to Bradley, and that he was influenced by the American pragmatists and by Russell's analytic philosophy. Shusterman notes Eliot's continuing adherence to Aristotle, a fact lost in the critical preoccupation with Bradley; his attempt to align Eliot with Richard Rorty's postmodern relativism, however, downplays Eliot's (Aristotelian) philosophical realism.

Eliot studied eastern philosophy and mysticism while at Harvard. Eloise Knapp Hay's *T. S. Eliot's Negative Way* (1981) emphasises the influence of Irving Babbitt on Eliot's eastern studies and traces a move-ment in his work from Bradleyan scepticism, through Buddhist teaching, to the Christian *via negativa*. Paul Foster's *The Golden Lotus* (1977) and P. S. Sri's *T. S. Eliot, Vedanta, and Buddhism* (1985) examine the Buddhist aspects of Eliot's poetry. Cleo McNelly Kearns's *T. S. Eliot and Indic*

Traditions (1987) presents a wide-ranging investigation of Eliot's studies, under the guidance of James Woods, of the *yoga-sutras* attributed to Patanjali; his reading of the Pali texts in Henry Clarke Warren's *Buddhism in Translation*; and the influence of the philosophers Babbitt, Royce and Paul Elmer More, and the poets Walt Whitman and W. B. Yeats, on Eliot's understanding of eastern thought. Kearns's masterful study is the best starting point for anyone interested in this context. Paul Murray's *T. S. Eliot and Mysticism* (1991) further explores the eastern and western mystical traditions evident in Eliot's work.

By the 1990s critics were viewing Eliot in relation to cross-currents generated by several philosophies. Manju Jain's *T. S. Eliot and American Philosophy* (1992) examined the interactions between pragmatism and anthropology at Harvard during Eliot's time as a graduate student, and suggested that neither of these schools of thought offered him a total understanding. Gail MacDonald's *Learning to be Modern* (1993) takes a similarly eclectic approach to Eliot's university studies in philosophy. My own *Aethereal Rumours: T. S. Eliot's Physics and Poetics* (1998) highlights Eliot's attack on Cartesian dualism and its connection with the 'dissociation of sensibility' (*SE*, 288) he traced back to the seventeenth century, as well as his lifelong commitment to the Pre-Socratics (especially Heraclitus) and to Aristotelian realism. (Edna Rosenthal's study *Aristotle and Modernism* [2007] goes so far as to call Eliot a modernist Aristotle.) In the last decade it has become possible to integrate various studies of Eliot's philosophy in order to give an overview of the topic. M. A. R. Habib's *The Early T. S. Eliot and Western Philosophy* (1999) opens up discussion of Eliot's graduate school essays on Immanuel Kant. Habib argues that Eliot's return to the classical realism of Aristotle and Thomas Aquinas establishes a harmony between subject and object in his aesthetic theory. The introductory chapter of Donald Childs's *From Philosophy to Poetry* (2001) offers a thorough and judicious overview of the scholarship to date.

Childs notes Eliot's fascination with the occult, an enthusiasm that had previously been examined in Leon Surette's *The Birth of Modernism* (1993) and Timothy Materer's *Modernist Alchemy* (1995). Childs points to Eliot's attendance at the séances organised by P. D. Ouspensky and the importance of Madame Sosostris to the structure and symbolism of *The Waste Land*, a subject that bears upon Eliot's engagement with the new science of anthropology and its study of primitive ritual. Grover Smith edited the notes from *Josiah Royce's Seminar* (1963) taken by a classmate of Eliot's. Robert Crawford's *The Savage and the City* (1987) is the authoritative study of the relation of anthropology and notions of the 'primitive' to Eliot's work. There have been useful contributions to this field by Marc Manganaro, David Spurr, Tatsushi Narita and Caroline Patey.

As regards Eliot's reaction to the 'new physics', Marion Montgomery's article 'Eliot and the Particle Physicist' (*Southern Review* [July 1974]) opened up discussion of this topic. Michael H. Whitworth has explored Eliot's connections with J. W. N. Sullivan, a science writer who contributed to the same journals as Eliot. Daniel Albright brilliantly examines Eliot's work in relation to the new physics in *Quantum Poetics* (1997) and in *Aethereal Rumours: T. S. Eliot's Physics and Poetics* (1998) I attempt to show that the early poetry exposes falsifications inherent in the scientific materialist view of the world. Lois Cuddy's *T. S. Eliot and the Poetics of Evolution* (2000) demonstrates that Eliot knew several works of evolutionary theory. Cuddy also suggests that Eliot was a proponent of eugenics, a view seconded by Donald Childs in *Modernism and Eugenics* (2001), although the evidence for this supposition is thin. Robert Crawford, for example, concludes that Eliot was opposed to eugenics.

POSTMODERN THEORY

Eliot's work has been an obvious choice for postmodern critics, but they have had some difficulty in deciding whether he is to be deconstructed or admired for his own deconstructive moves. (Can we avoid the binaries and have it both ways?) Psychoanalytic interpretations of Eliot's work abound. Gregory Jay successfully employs Harold Bloom's theory of the 'anxiety of influence' in *T. S. Eliot and the Poetics of Literary History* (1983). In the 1980s, Andrew Ross and Jacqueline Rose approached Eliot's work from a Lacanian perspective. In *The Poetics of Impersonality* (1987), Maud Ellmann employed elements of postmodern theory to argue that Eliot offers no coherent theory of personality. Michael Beehler led the way with deconstructive approaches to Eliot, culminating in his virtually unreadable *T. S. Eliot, Wallace Stevens, and the Discourse of Difference* (1987). On the one hand, Joseph Kronick's *American Poetics of History* (1984) attacks Eliot's work for being logocentric (that is, grounded on *logos* [reason]), while on the other hand Scott Christianson's 1990 article on 'Burnt Norton' recruits Eliot to the deconstructionist cause. To my mind, the best use of Jacques Derrida's theories in reading Eliot's poetry is to be found in Cleo McNelly Kearns's 1993 article on *Four Quartets*, but I am still left thinking that there is a significant difference between Eliot's way of holding opposites in tension and Derrida's theorising of aporia. A good sampling of postmodern essays on Eliot has been collected in Harriet Davidson's *T. S. Eliot* (1998). Davidson's introduction offers a frank and incisive assessment, concluding that an outpouring of postmodern theory has left Eliot largely untouched – ignored or dismissed by most theoretical critics. In *Eliot's Dark Angel* (1999), Ronald Schuchard voices a critique of postmodern approaches to Eliot, concluding: 'In view of the swelling barrier reef of reductive and formulaic criticism, we may never hear the low and high registers of despair and love, horror and vision.'[6]

RELIGION

I want to close by returning to the question of Eliot's Christian faith, which has made some academic critics deeply suspicious of him. Eliot himself says that one need not share Dante's beliefs to appreciate how they inform his poetry, and many critics (believers and non-believers) have written sympathetically about the religious aspects of his work. Barry Spurr's *'Anglo-Catholic in Religion': T. S. Eliot and Christianity* (2010) is a long-awaited attempt to see Eliot's work in the light of his daily practices as a Christian. Others have questioned the sincerity of Eliot's faith. William Skaff, Adam Kirsch and the Catholic writer Joseph Bottum have even gone so far as to doubt Eliot's belief in Christian dogma. Others have condescendingly suggested that Eliot only believed in Christianity out of a weak and neurotic need for certainty (they are certain about Eliot's need for certainty). The best answer to this is provided by Denis Donoghue's *Words Alone: The Poet T. S. Eliot* (2000), which argues that Eliot's turn to the traditional in literature, politics and religion was not a neurotic quest for straightforward answers. Rather, this commitment went against the grain of Eliot's philosophical scepticism and idealism. Donoghue challenges the anti-Christian prejudice freely displayed in much contemporary criticism and asks his secular colleagues how they can continue to espouse Enlightenment rationalism after the horrors of the twentieth century: 'I am not blaming our modern philosophes for these horrors, but I remain bewildered by their insistence on the adequacy of Enlightenment thinking.'[7]

NOTES

1. Harold Bloom, 'Introduction', *T. S. Eliot: Modern Critical Views* (New York: Chelsea House, 1985), p. 1.
2. 'L'Hommage de l'étranger', *Aspects de la France et du Monde* (25 April 1948), 6.

3. See Denis Donoghue, *Words Alone: The Poet T. S. Eliot* (New Haven, CT: Yale University Press, 2000), p. 226.

4. Jason Harding, *The 'Criterion': Cultural Politics and Periodical Networks in Inter-War Britain* (Oxford University Press, 2002), p. 177.

5. 'Marianne Moore', *Dial* (December 1923), 595.

6. Ronald Schuchard, *Eliot's Dark Angel: Intersections of Life and Art* (Oxford University Press, 1999), p. 20.

7. Donoghue, *Words Alone*, p. 182.

CHAPTER 37

Legacies: from literary criticism to literary theory

Patricia Waugh

> To us he is no more a person
> Now but a whole climate of opinion
> (W. H. Auden, 'In Memory of Sigmund Freud')[1]

No doubt W. H. Auden did not intend any reference to T. S. Eliot's theory of impersonality in his famous poem 'In Memory of Sigmund Freud'. But even in 1940, Eliot's distinction between the man who suffers and the mind that creates (the mind that created the mind, in Freud's case) was a linchpin of twentieth-century criticism: its influence had already reoriented criticism towards the poem and away from the poet and would stimulate W. K. Wimsatt's more philosophical exposition of 'The Intentional Fallacy' (1946). Soon after, Harold Bloom's 'anxiety of influence' more pugnaciously continued the textual conversation with the dead, though in a rivalrous and agonistic vein only hinted at in Eliot's understanding of tradition (and disavowing any influence of Eliot himself). Finally, in the post-structuralist intertextualities of the 1980s, the theory that had begun life on the tide of Eliot's early desire to secure a more communitarian ground for the practices of authorship than the disembodied and individualistic Romantic theory of inspiration, was now exposed, in the most paradoxical swerve of all, as the distal cause of the death of all authors. The question of authorship, of who or what produces poems, and of legacies, of who or what continues the conversation with them, would emerge as one of the major chords of modern literary theory, continuing to sound through feminist, New Historicist and cultural materialist discussion for the rest of the century. Auden's phrase is as apt a description of Eliot and his influence, as of Freud and his, supplying a performative witness to the depth and extent of Eliot's assimilation into almost every school of twentieth-century poetics.

For just as the Freudian unconscious is now an assumption in any thinking about the self, so Eliot's ideas – about authorship, creativity,

impersonality and tradition – are still the literary air we breathe, even as
post-structuralism and its heirs seem to have demolished the author,
demystified the Romantic organicist roots of impersonality, and put
tradition to bed as the fantasy of a Eurocentric neo-imperialism. But
Eliot's influence does not stop with the theory of impersonality, for his
central mythopoetic conceit, the idea of a 'dissociation of sensibility' (*SE*,
288) and a poetically redeemable fall into modernity, along with the
related concept of the 'objective correlative' (*SE*, 145), would provide, in
the revisionism of his academic contemporaries and immediate legatees,
the very justification for and integrity of English Studies as a modern
university discipline, built on the practices of literary criticism. Eliot's
early essays had aimed to introduce a new rigour into the former 'Sunday
park of contending and contentious orators' (*SE*, 25), and his ability to
create a series of provocative, teasing and immensely resonant mythopoetic conceits and motifs quickly attracted the attention of such figures as
F. R. Leavis, I. A. Richards, Cleanth Brooks and John Crowe Ransom.
Eliot appealed enormously to these academic critics as an appropriate
authority – a thinker, but of a peculiarly literary kind – able to provide an
appropriate and legitimating voice for the establishment of the distinctive
integrity of literary studies in an academy underpinned by a positivist
'research' framework.

Indeed, the seeds of almost every preoccupation of later criticism and
literary theory lay germinating in the dark embryo of Eliot's poetically
expressed ideas of the 1920s and early 1930s, and in their more pedagogic-
ally oriented dissemination in the work of his academic contemporaries.
Even the generation of academic critic-theorists that followed in North
America – Northrop Frye, Harold Bloom, Paul de Man and J. Hillis
Miller – and in Britain – Raymond Williams, Richard Hoggart, Terry
Eagleton and early British cultural studies – began their revolt within the
terms laid down by Eliot. And the generation that followed them either
unwittingly perpetuated Eliot's 'influence' in reductionist caricatures as
the whipping boy of the post-structuralist critique of 'aesthetic ideology'
or attempted to rescue him as an 'historical critic' (Ransom's description
of Eliot)[2] through co-options into Gadamerian hermeneutics, American
neo-pragmatism or varieties of broadly phenomenological reception
theory. Only in the ideologically driven 1990s did Eliot's star as a critic
almost entirely fade. But as the preoccupations of the twenty-first century
emerge as those of religion and belief, cultural identity and belonging, the
significance of emotion and affect in rational thought, and an ongoing
communitarian and multicultural critique of liberalism, interest in Eliot's

criticism has once again begun to pick up, refocusing on hitherto occluded aspects of his thinking, such as the intense concern with the capacity of poetry to refine feeling and its place in thinking, and in the relationship between language, affect and belonging.

Leavis was the first academic who took forward Eliot's ideas into a programme for English Studies, though also struggling for almost his entire career to escape the influence of his master. But although Leavis placed Eliot's dissociation thesis at the centre of his mission for criticism, where it remained until the end of his career, he never accepted the theory of impersonality, aligning it with Richards's 'pseudo-statement' and detecting an ironising effect at odds with Leavis's own ethics of passionate conviction. Eventually, he even used the theory as the means to discredit Eliot the man by arguing *ad hominem*, in his essays of the 1960s and 1970s, that Eliot was a 'case' and that the theory of impersonality was simply a screen constructed to hide Eliot's own emotional instability, revealed in the evasions of his 1919 essay on *Hamlet* and in the uncharacteristically personal note at the end of *The Use of Poetry and the Use of Criticism* (1933) with its description of the creative process as the unburdening of unbearable emotional anxieties.[3] Yet, despite this ambivalence, Eliot furnished Leavis's pedagogic mission with a justified canon, a critical method and a disciplinary ethos.

But it was the 'dissociation of sensibility' thesis of the 1921 essay on 'The Metaphysical Poets', and the supporting concept of the 'objective correlative' in the essay on *Hamlet*, that provided Leavis with the crux on which he would rest his re-evaluation of the English literary canon, and the ground on which to build his grand moral vision of cultural rejuvenation through the restoration of literary sensibility. Between them, Leavis and the New Critics, especially Brooks and Ransom, elevated the dissociation conceit into a grand declinist theory of modernity and a redemptive programme for modernist literary studies. The main outline of the thesis was that in the seventeenth century, and for reasons left tantalisingly vague in Eliot's original argument, cultural life, language and customary living in Britain fell into a generalised 'dissociation of sensibility', a severance of thought and feeling whose unification might only now be experienced through the reading and writing of an appropriately complex literature, the true heir to a buried but still dormant tradition (both timeless and temporal), to be restored in the practice of a professionalised modern literary criticism. Already in the bare concepts of dissociation and impersonality, Eliot provides the most important foundation for the methods, ethos and, indeed, *mythos* of the discipline of academic literary criticism. As the deferential literary critical cultures of the first half of the century seceded to the more insubordinate, democratic, fuzzy and nomadic cultures of the post 1960s, it is hardly surprising that Eliot's criticism would become a significant point of orientation for most of the new movements in theory and criticism: 'the death of the author', intertextuality, the decentering of the self, instrumental rationality, structures of feeling and the hermeneutic 'fusion of horizons'.

Literary historical advocates of the idea of a 'theory revolution' tend to believe in a watershed between a (supposedly) theoretically naive pre-1960s era of practical criticism, devoted to the defence and rigorous appreciation of the autonomy and distinctive ontology of literary texts as well-wrought urns and, sometime around 1968, the breaking of such sacred vessels in the sudden explosion of (another mysterious universal) 'Theory'. Eliot may have given birth to the idea of literary impersonality, but his heirs would refine and theorise its full implications or foster more permissive variations on its theme. Bloom's 'anxiety of influence' read impersonality against itself as a ploy to protect the egotistical sublime of Eliot's own personality; yet his thesis may be viewed as an extended formal and psychological working through of the (half-conscious) influence of Eliot on Bloom himself. Bloom's is the first sustained attempt to slay the demon of Eliot and to give birth to a new era of more theoretically developed criticism. In his 1920 essay on Philip Massinger, Eliot had argued: 'Immature poets imitate; mature poets steal … The good poet welds his theft into a whole of feeling which is unique, utterly different from that from which it was torn; the bad poet throws it into something which has no cohesion' (*SE*, 206). Bloom steals, rewriting Eliot's doctrine of impersonality as the expression of a psychoanalytically revived Romantic theory of authorship, now conceived as a 'dread of threatened autonomy'.[4] The *ephebe* struggles for poetic life against the ghostly infiltration of his soul and style by the 'strong' precursor who must be 'defeated' through a variety of strategic textual 'swerves' which empty out the earlier poet's immortality by displacing his uniqueness as the effect of something always beyond and anterior to himself. Though Bloom's account is openly agonistic, the hermeneutic encounter always a confrontational battle for survival, he also implies that the concept of tradition was ever a kind of feint, a coy screen for such aggressive evacuative activity. In Bloom's strong grip, impersonality is the modern means of continuing to assert the Romantic personality of the poet in an age of democratic threats to its existence.

If Bloom is the Oedipal son of Eliot, Roland Barthes is his Dionysian alter ego, the one who seeks liberation from filiation, and liberation, too, of the theory of impersonality into a fully post-structuralist and promiscuous textual *jouissance* that not only finally slays the father but is shown to give birth to him again and again in a textual remembrance of a past whose ground was only ever figural. As the monotheistic authority of the author/parent/God gives way to the multiple drives and desires of a democratised readership, the fundamental generative causalities are reversed so that, in a neat swerve from Eliot's account, the text is seen to give birth to its author. Thralldom to authorial antecedence as a placeholder term for divine authority is also overcome as intentionality is conferred upon writing itself as a play of intertextualities, the product of a vast textual interplay: 'Did he wish to *express himself*, he ought at least to know that the inner "thing" he thinks to "translate" is itself only a ready-formed dictionary, its words only explainable through other words, and so on indefinitely'.[5] There is actually little in either Bloom or Barthes that is not at least strongly implied by Eliot. But by the 1980s, Eliot was all too often presented by postmodernists exclusively in the terms of a formalist or neo-Kantian modernism founded on the cult of literary autonomy, impersonality, spatial form, and invoked in order to safeguard the revolutionary claims to difference of the postmodern. Much of this work indirectly refers to Eliot's own early statements about the importance of 'facts' in criticism, or his description of the literary work as 'autotelic' or the need to recognise the 'autonomous' frontiers of criticism: little attention is paid to the linguistic texture and rhetorical art of his arguments. What is overlooked in almost all of these reconstructions of Eliot, however, is what Ransom referred to as the 'Socratic irony' with which Eliot speaks 'of his own disinterest in theory'.[6]

For surely what is distinctive about Eliot's criticism, in large part accounting for the tentacular persistence of his ideas in later literary theory, is not simply the mythopoetic power and perfect timing of motifs such as impersonality and dissociation, but also the peculiar force of his language. Eliot's non-academic poetic-critical language of wit broke down distinctions between theory and criticism and magnetised his contemporaries and later critics in his discursive performance of understanding and knowledge beyond the confines of positivistic enquiry. Eliot was in the fortunate position of being able to develop his thoughts about literature outside of the restrictions and conventions of the academy and through the economical and understated vehicle of a more poetic mode of delivery. In the 1921 essay on Andrew Marvell, he argues that wit consists neither of

erudition nor cynicism, but 'involves, probably, a recognition, implicit in
the expression of every experience, of other kinds of experience which
are possible' (*SE*, 303). Significantly, he describes it as an 'impersonal
virtue ... something precious and needed and apparently extinct' (*SE*,
304) that also functions, in Eliot's own critical writing, as a resistance to
criticism (and theory) as modes of closure: the reductive 'explanation' and
the exclusive interpretation that unwittingly pin the text to a single
historical moment. Eliot's ideas have shaped later literary theory, but
inseparably from his perfection of the art of criticism as a mode of wit
inspiring an admiring and sometimes envious desire to imitate his
authoritative but restrained, ironic but also passionate, rhetorical performances. This is a language able to fight off, in one moment, the desire not
to live in uncertainties and ambivalences, but to seek premature closure;
and in the next, able to restrain the impetus to egotistical brilliance that
might also result in a betrayal of the work. Eliot's language of criticism
prompts imitation and repudiation in equal measure, but renders him
finally unassailable, irreducible to the philosophic or historic packaging.
Ransom recognised this only too well and was irritated by it, preferring
that Eliot should position himself more openly and explicitly, wearing his
theoretical stripes on his sleeve, for it was his view that 'the good critic
cannot stop with studying poetry, he must also study poetics. If he thinks
he must puritanically abstain from all indulgence in the theory, the good
critic may have to be a good little critic'.[7] Eliot is clearly not a 'good little
critic' in Ransom's eyes, but a great one: he recognised how Eliot's wit so
ingeniously disguises the driving force of its own theoretical power.

For the mode of wit, above all, opposes bare assertion in criticism, as in
literature. In numerous essays, Eliot argued against the notion of literature
as simply a vehicle for ideas open to sociological or philosophical con-
tainment. In *Dante* (1929), in particular, Eliot foregrounds the nature of
this resistance, praising Dante for writing which is the poetic equivalent
of a state of mind, through the perfection of a common language where
ideas – 'philosophy' – appear only as the embodied visual perception of a
world. Instead of reading Thomas Aquinas's *Summa* as preparation for
understanding the medieval world picture of the *Divine Comedy*, he
recommends that the modern reader should simply cultivate the kind of
humility of a person visiting a new world and allow the language to do its
work in transporting him or her into a largely affective and sensory
experience that is the perception of an entire universe. In Eliot's essays,
wit becomes the equivalent means of circumventing the tyranny of the
explicit and the assertive, staying close to the text but leaving open a

world that will remain brimful of possibility. 'Wit' thus enabled Eliot's writing to be seen to provide unique resolution to perennial problems and dilemmas in the professionalisation of English. For early practitioners recognised that the language of criticism must provide something different to other subjects in the humanities; history, for example, whose methods and ethos are comfortably accommodated within the broad carapace of positivism or 'research'; or philosophy, committed either to a systematic world-view built on questionable if substantive premises, or to a mode of scepticism which, though it may never lie, many never affirm either. Neither of these central disciplines in the humanities seemed able to address the crisis of values perceived, in the early twentieth century, as the culmination of a dissociated modernity.

But criticism might establish itself in this disciplinary niche, however, only if it rejects the impressionistic or subjective and challenges the positivistic disregard for values with tools other than those of positivism. In a later lecture, 'The Frontiers of Criticism' (1956), Eliot spells this out forcibly, condemning the vogue for positivistic scholarship as 'explanation by origins' (*OPP*, 107) and the critical technicism that tries to overmaster the poem, reducing it to a single definitive meaning. The good critic is never simply a technical expert, but 'the whole man, a man with convictions and principles, and of knowledge and experience of life' (*OPP*, 116), responding in appropriate language to the complex affective thinking and linguistic expression of the work. Eliot's wit is the forerunner of Leavis's more workaday notion of the tacit or ostensive, the idea that the realm of 'value' as engaged by literary criticism, in particular, is underpinned by and inseparable from an alternative kind of knowledge – not the knowledge of 'fact' – but a kind of prereflective knowing that grounds human beings in their cultural worlds and provides that sense of being out of which that other kind of knowledge – the explicit kind of the scientist or historian – has developed and on which it rests. The discipline of literary studies could only make its claims, in its own terms and language, by asserting a complex performative significance and, like literature itself, eschewing the explicit as a version of the 'heresy of paraphrase'.

Eliot's critical essays convey a paradoxical 'resistance to criticism' akin to Paul de Man's later 'resistance to theory', expressing a complex anti-institutionalism that also recognises the power of and necessity for institutions. Both Eliot and de Man are, in different ways, equally fastidious about the language of criticism, and to read de Man's painstaking contestation of 'aesthetic ideology' is already to recognise the closeness of Eliot to the ironising distance defined in the de Manian concept.

Aesthetic ideology, for de Man, is that idea of *presence*, of overcoming in language the necessary and tragic gulf between language and the materiality of the world and the human experience of it that lurks not only in Romantic poetics but also, in modernism, in the account of the poem as a well-wrought urn, a self-begetting organicist plenitude that closes the gap between language and the phenomenal. Similarly, in *The Resistance to Theory* (1986), de Man's argument opposes similar tendencies to plenitudinous circularity in theorising about literature, insisting that if theory is broadly the attempt to ground questions about exegesis and evaluation in some conceptual system then, given that there must always be some a priori definition of literature before such discussion can begin, the very attempt to define theory will always fall down (logically) on the grounds of circularity, and will always rely on assumptions which stand outside the generalised system.

Just as Plato needed to banish the poets in order to found philosophy, so the founders of modern literary criticism and theory, including early deconstructionists such as de Man and Hillis Miller, built on Eliot's authority and example as a poet-critic in their need to oust philosophy in its metaphysical and logical positivist guises, in order to safeguard the distinctiveness of English as a discipline with a unique order of thinking, knowledge and understanding. From the very first, even in his doctoral thesis on F. H. Bradley, Eliot repeatedly took issue with what he saw as the perennial problem of theories from Plato onwards, and his terms and arguments are uncannily close to de Man. He, too, argues that every philosophical system has eventually been forced to acknowledge the impasse of what – after the post-structuralist appropriation of Gödel's Theorem – would be thought of as 'undecidability'. Just as every theory has sought to provide a foundation or origin for its own propositional assertions, this origin has subsequently always been discovered to be an effect or construct of, rather than a ground for, the system of knowledge that is postulated. Any theorist who claims that s/he has crossed the 'frontier' or, to use another of Eliot's favourite metaphors, plumbed and charted the depths, in order to provide such a foundation is simply blind to the circularity of the path which has been traced. In the concluding paragraph of the 1919 essay on tradition, therefore, Eliot pulls up short: 'This essay proposes to halt at the frontier of metaphysics or mysticism, and confine itself to such *practical* conclusions as can be applied by the responsible person interested in poetry' (*SE*, 21–2, my emphasis). And throughout his doctoral thesis Eliot suggests that theory may only exist authentically as practice: 'All of our terms turn out to be unreal abstractions; but we can defend them, and give them a kind of reality and validity . . . by showing that they express the theory of knowledge which is implicit in all practical activity' (*KEPB*, 18).

As a philosopher turned poet-critic, Eliot's critical thinking is developed in a language of wit as complex and dense as the language of his poetry. Its effect is to break down easy distinctions between theory and criticism, so that later theorists who reduce Eliot to shibboleths of New Critical 'objectivity' must either ignore that language and simply manipulate concepts (impersonality, dissociation of sensibility) or, if they do try to read Eliot closely and to expose the linguistic sources of his 'aesthetic ideology', they may never realise their blindness to the extent of his influence or his co-implication in their own theorising. Even in the austere and fastidious linguistic precision of de Man, Eliot's evident ironic awareness of what de Man calls 'aesthetic ideology' remains unacknowledged by de Man himself. What de Man's own feline but affectless prose cannot convey is embodied in Eliot's very performance and in his constant emphasis on the absolute centrality of feeling and emotion in the writing of and response to literature. Curiously, contemporary neuroscience has confirmed Eliot's conviction that the feelings and perceptions used to negotiate the verbal literary world are those employed in the negotiation of the real world outside of art. Though they may combine and fuse to produce an emotion peculiar to each work, there are no categorically distinguishable 'aesthetic emotions' as such. The grounding of aesthetic response in the sensory and affective inevitably engages the phenomenological for Eliot. De Man's textualism, meanwhile, can only condemn such belief in embodiment as an ideological manoeuvre.

For Eliot's notion of 'dissociation' may be read not so much as a Fall myth and justification for a redemptive practice of criticism, but more as part of Eliot's preoccupation with preserving, in the act of critical understanding and appreciation, the feeling of sensuously embodied and affective experience provided in the encounter with great art. Eliot's repeated attacks on 'rumination' as a modern disease are part of his desire to create a model for criticism that avoids that excess of reflection which produces the kind of self-consciousness that radically disembeds the self, or a people, or a poem, as it does Hamlet, or Blake (who has to invent a world picture), or the cultures of modernity, or the literary critic who is too ready to step back out of the work and into something else: 'we should begin to learn to distinguish the appreciation of poetry from theorising about poetry, and to know when we are not talking about poetry but about something else' (*UPUC*, 123). That Eliot might treat with suspicion 'Theory' understood as an attempt to provide a systematic ground for criticism from a position entirely outside of the literary experience is evident in almost everything he wrote. It is suggested in the belief that a true thought is felt on the senses as 'immediately as the odour of a rose' (*SE*, 287); or is an experience that modifies one's sensibility; or occurs as the expression of the highest consciousness at the very tips of the senses. But his writing also raises the possibility that theory may exist in a mode also not detachable from its linguistic embodiment, but woven deep into the experiential encounter between the critic and the poem, similarly eschewing the directly propositional for the oblique and the tropic. If such 'Theory' exists, then it is likely to attract as much interpretative disagreement and playful engagement, and to inspire as many legacies, directions onward, and palimpsestic layerings inward, as the most complex work of literature: like Eliot's own poetry and criticism. Such a practice of 'Theory' has been named in a later era as deconstruction, and if we turn to Jacques Derrida, he too articulates a 'resistance to theory' as disembodied meta-reflection that is uncannily close to Eliot's own: deconstruction is neither a theory nor a movement nor a method, 'it is what happens'.[8]

In 'Shakespeare and the Stoicism of Seneca' (1927), Eliot reflects that 'the influence of any man is a different thing from himself' (*SE*, 132–3). The statement is another version of the impersonality thesis and a continuation of his preoccupation with a contradictory historicism, whereby the past, as tradition, is both there monumentally, in all its quiddity, but also ever alterable, a shifting facade promising a depth that may be ever ineffable and unspeakable, supporting a creaky edifice of perishable words. But it may also be read as an autobiographical reflection on Eliot's own awareness of his likely ghostly legacies and provides, too, a perfect example of the slipperiness of his uses of 'wit' as an alternative to or indirect mode of theoretical pronouncement. Even as a self-professed 'minor poet' he informs the reader, with beguiling modesty, that, like Shakespeare, he too is becoming inured to constant critical reconstruction, *theorisation* by academic critics who take the words out of his mouth and turn them (and him) into something else. Even ten years into a literary career, he is 'used to having cosmic significances, which I never suspected, extracted from my work (such as it is) by enthusiastic persons at a distance … and to having my biography invariably ignored in what I *did* write from personal experience' (*SE*, 127). The essay, purportedly on the 'influence' of Senecan stoicism on Shakespeare, proceeds to build and substantiate its position until, half way through, and perplexingly, it suddenly explodes its own tightly argued case, exposing its own historicity as fictional invention. The scholarly case is revealed as Eliot's hoax, designed to trip up the reader and lay bare the misguided scholarly propensity to look for watertight influences that explain the genesis of a literary work, sidestepping thereby any need for close critical engagement with a text as an ongoing and renewable experience. As if reversing E. D. Hirsch's later historicist argument for intention as the available ground of the 'meaning' of a literary work, Eliot goes on to show how Shakespeare is more Senecan than Seneca (his tragic protagonists constantly stage their own need to 'cheer themselves up' because bereft of the kind of cosmic consolation available to the Greeks). Far from Seneca influencing Shakespeare, Shakespeare influences Seneca to produce another familiar compound ghost who will beguile scholars for generations to come. Influence runs in both directions, defying the arrow of time, and Eliot already signals a prescient sense of his own legacy as a ghostly dissolution.

What begins as a scholarly account of 'influence' finishes by collapsing the positivistic assumptions framing the category into an infinity of mirrors. But it is his earlier essay, 'The Function of Criticism' (1923), that has most often been read as his strongest endorsement of an objective criticism, that 'comparison and analysis' might perform the important if subordinate function of 'putting the reader in possession of facts which he would otherwise have missed' about the work – 'its conditions, its setting, its genesis' (*SE*, 32). The apparently grounded 'facts' to be supplied or excavated by the positivist, however, also go the way of positivist 'influence'. Another devastating volte-face is performed as Eliot finally raises the question of what is meant by a 'fact' while denying that he had ever intended to seek their definition, only to 'find a scheme into which, whatever they are, they will fit, if they exist' (*SE*, 34). The impudence of the series of qualifications is all the more audacious as it reveals the confident positivism of the essay as yet another sleight of hand another mocked-up edifice comes crashing down. Facts are, at best, pragmatic tools, and their definition and existence is dependent on use: but Wittgensteinian insights must be gleaned through the practised and slippery wit of Old Possum.

In a letter written before the completion of his doctoral thesis, Eliot argued that 'all philosophising is a perversion of reality: for, in a sense, no philosophic theory makes any difference to practice ... It invariably involves cramming both feet into one shoe ... The theories are certainly, all of them, implicit in the inexact experience of every day, but once extracted they make the world appear as strange as Bottom in his ass's head' (*LI*, 87). This comment tells us much about Eliot as a philosopher about to embark upon a literary career. Indeed, 'Tradition and the Individual Talent' (1919) may be read as an extension of the implications of this letter into a working practice for literary criticism. Eliot begins the essay by suggesting that 'criticism is as inevitable as breathing', but that we should be 'none the worse' for 'criticising our own minds in their work of criticism' (*SE*, 13–14). He appears to recognise the need to complicate the fantasy of intimacy, the immediate feeling of directly speaking with the dead that criticism as 'breathing' is likely to sustain. He seems to recognise, too, the need for theoretical distance, some second-order or meta-textual position from which to criticise the first-order, breathy voice of criticism as immediate response. For in the rest of this famous essay, Eliot is already setting out to try and develop a mode of theory in practice and a form of critical thinking that allows for tacit theoretical reflection which does not fall into the abyss of an infinite regress in search of metaphysical origins.

In Eliot's writing, both in its earliest and later cultural materialist manifestations, when the mind steps back to criticise itself in the act of criticism, it steps back not into a space of pure rationality or scepticism, but into the very depths from which it has emerged in the first place and in which it has all along continued to be immersed: the literary mind of Europe, a mind which has left nothing behind en route, even 'the rock drawing of the Magdalenian draughtsmen' (*SE*, 16). Critics have noticed a curiously passive account of artistic creativity in this essay, for nothing much seems to happen under the agency of the individual poet; certainly, very little of what we might think of as conscious thinking or deliberate activity. The literary mind, whether critical or creative, appears to be simply a conduit through which the emotions and sensory impressions, already shaped through the refining immersion in the literary mind of Europe, enter into new combinations and 'fuse' in unexpected ways to produce a new 'aesthetic emotion'. Eliot allows into the process a kind of attenuated intentional agency in the shaping of verbal expression, but he is already beginning to challenge the idea of *thinking* assumed in the Cartesian and Kantian traditions, in order to develop the idea of thinking as a practice that might remain embodied even in its critical and appraisive modes. In the essay on tradition, the practice of literary creation is entirely grounded in the body: in the idea of the creative 'fusion' that occurs as the feelings of the body are allowed to enter the 'inert' shred of platinum, the individual mind, and in the idea of that mind as the embodiment of a cultural tradition that has already shaped that mind. The relations between tradition and the individual creative mind are conceived in terms closest to Thomas Aquinas's Aristotelian (hylomorphic) understanding of the paradoxical reality of the soul: that the soul is in the body and yet contains, rather than being contained by, that body.

Eliot was never more than circumspect about the lasting importance of any act of criticism, and always ready to disavow his own inclusion in any purported school or movement; but he was, too, derisory about the fantasy of a '"Pure" artistic appreciation' uncontaminated by critical reflection. Rather, 'There is for each time, for each artist', he says, 'a kind of alloy required to make the metal workable into art; and each generation prefers its own alloy to any other. Hence each new master of criticism performs a useful service merely by the fact that his errors are of a different kind from the last; and the longer the sequence of critics we have, the greater amount of correction is possible' (*UPUC*, 109). Not unusually, Eliot's metaphors carry a scientific resonance not just in the reference to metallurgy, but also, more subtly, in the idea of 'correcting errors' that curiously undoes the very positivism they might seem to avow: after Heisenberg's Uncertainty Principle (1927), quantum physicists acknowledged that they were unable to observe particles directly, but must infer their existence from traces to which statistical corrections are applied, in order to attempt to account for the effect of the observation on the observed. If science cannot directly grasp the fundamental particles of matter, what hope for the critic confronted by a literary work? But for the critic, too, it is suggested, 'errors' become available for successive, equally historicised 'corrections', and so a kind of 'probabilistic' reading emerges running through the canon of criticism. Eliot does not use the term but he is articulating the notion of a 'fusion of horizons', an idea central to the reception theory of the 1970s and 1980s.

Eliot always saw the critic's task as one of 'readjustment' of the work to the age, setting 'new and strange objects in the foreground', and ensuring that those of former eminence now 'invisible to the naked eye' do not drop entirely off the map, preserved in the capacious lens of the 'exhaustive critic' (*UPUC*, 108). This concluding chapter has suggested how many of the 'angles' adopted by modern literary theorists were initially opened up by Eliot's own (wide-angled) critical lens, and how, in turn, they have allowed for the formation of ever renewed Eliotic compound ghosts to occupy the centre ground of contemporary theory and criticism. Given the contemporary neuro-scientific discovery of the role of affect in cognition and judgement and the current philosophical preoccupation with the 'embodied mind', and given too our anxieties about and recognition of the need for cultural belonging and linguistic difference in an increasingly globalised world, there is every likelihood that Eliot's tactful words are poised to undergo further hermeneutic transformation in the near future: for in our own problematically post-theory era, his criticism may still speak to us of our concerns as well as of his own.

NOTES

1. W. H. Auden, *Selected Poems* (London: Faber & Faber, 1979), p. 93.
2. John Crowe Ransom, *The New Criticism* (Connecticut: New Directions, 1941), p. 135.
3. See F. R. Leavis, *The Living Principle: 'English' as a Discipline of Thought* (London: Chatto & Windus, 1975), pp. 248–9.
4. Harold Bloom, *The Anxiety of Influence* (Oxford University Press, 1973), p. 26.
5. Roland Barthes, 'The Death of the Author', *Image-Music-Text*, ed. Stephen Heath (London: Fontana, 1977), p. 146.
6. John Crowe Ransom, *The World's Body* (New York: Charles Scribner, 1938), p. 174.
7. Ibid., p. 173.
8. Jacques Derrida, *The States of Theory*, ed. David Carroll (New York: Columbia University Press, 1990), p. 85.

Further reading

The following bibliographies consist of suggested further reading for each chapter.

1   ST LOUIS

Crawford, Robert. *The Savage and the City in the Work of T. S. Eliot.* Oxford: Clarendon Press, 1987.

Holt, Earl K. *William Greenleaf Eliot: Conservative Radical.* St Louis, MO: First Unitarian Church of St Louis Press, 1985.

Howarth, Herbert. *Notes on some Figures behind T. S. Eliot.* Boston, MA: Houghton Mifflin, 1964.

Howe, D. W. *The Unitarian Conscience: Harvard Moral Philosophy, 1805–1861.* Middletown, CT: Wesleyan University Press, 1988.

Olney, James. 'T. S. Eliot Memorial Lecture', *The Placing of T. S. Eliot,* ed. Jewel Spears Brooker. Columbia: University of Missouri Press, 1991 [60–76].

Reavis, U. L. *St Louis: The Future Great City of the World.* St Louis: C. R. Barnes, 1876.

2   NEW ENGLAND

Bush, Ronald. *T. S. Eliot: A Study in Character and Style.* Oxford University Press, 1983.

Crawford, Robert. *The Savage and the City in the Work of T. S. Eliot.* Oxford: Clarendon Press, 1987.

Howarth, Herbert. *Notes on some Figures behind T. S. Eliot.* Boston, MA: Houghton Mifflin, 1964.

Miller, James E. *T. S. Eliot: The Making of an American Poet, 1888–1922.* University Park, PA: Pennsylvania State University Press, 2005.

Oser, Lee. *T. S. Eliot and American Poetry.* Columbia: University of Missouri Press, 1998.

Sigg, Eric. *The American T. S. Eliot.* Cambridge University Press, 1989.

3 PARIS

Greene, Edward J. H. *T. S. Eliot et la France.* Paris: Boivin, 1951.

Grogin, Robert C. *The Bergsonian Controversy in France: 1900–1914.* University of Calgary Press, 1988.

Hargrove, Nancy Duvall. *T. S. Eliot's Parisian Year.* Gainesville: University Press of Florida, 2009.

Marx, William. *Naissance de la critique moderne: la littérature selon Eliot et Valéry, 1889–1945.* Arras: Artois Presses Université, 2002.

Pondrom, Cyrena N. *The Road from Paris: French Influence of English Poetry, 1900–1920.* Cambridge University Press, 1974.

4 LONDON

Brooker, Peter. *Bohemia in London: The Social Scene of Early Modernism.* Basingstoke: Palgrave Macmillan, 2007.

Crawford, Robert. *The Savage and the City in the Work of T. S. Eliot.* Oxford: Clarendon Press, 1987.

Rainey, Lawrence. *The Annotated Waste Land with Eliot's Contemporary Prose.* New Haven, CT: Yale University Press, 2005.

Ricks, Christopher. *T. S. Eliot and Prejudice.* London: Faber & Faber, 1988.

Zwerdling, Alex. *Improvised Europeans: American Literary Expatriates and the Siege of London.* New York: Basic Books, 1998.

5 ENGLISHNESS

Colls, Robert and Philip Dodd. Eds. *Englishness: Politics and Culture 1880–1920.* London: Croom Helm, 1986.

Ellis, Steve. *The English Eliot: Design, Language and Landscape in 'Four Quartets'.* London: Routledge, 1991.

Gervais, David. *Literary Englands: Versions of 'Englishness' in Modern Writing.* Cambridge University Press, 1993.

Giles, Judy and Tim Middleton. Eds. *Writing Englishness 1900–1950: An Introductory Sourcebook on National Identity.* London: Routledge, 1995.

Gray, Piers. *Marginal Men: Edward Thomas, Ivor Gurney, J. R. Ackerley.* London: Macmillan, 1991.

Grimble, Simon. *Landscape, Writing and the 'Condition of England' 1878–1917: Ruskin to Modernism.* Lampeter: Edwin Mellen Press, 2004.

6 THE IDEA OF EUROPE

Däumer, Elisabeth and Shyamal Bagchee. Eds. *The International Reception of T. S. Eliot.* London: Continuum, 2007.

Harding, Jason. *The 'Criterion': Cultural Politics and Periodical Networks in Inter-War Britain.* Oxford University Press, 2002.

Howarth, Herbert. *Notes on some Figures behind T. S. Eliot.* Boston, MA: Houghton Mifflin, 1964.

Vanheste, Jeroen. *Guardians of the Humanist Legacy: The Classicism of T. S. Eliot's 'Criterion' Network and its Relevance to our Postmodern World.* Leiden: Brill, 2007.

7 THE ROLE OF INTELLECTUAL

Asher, Kenneth. *T. S. Eliot and Ideology.* Cambridge University Press, 1995.
Collini, Stefan. *Absent Minds: Intellectuals in Britain.* Oxford University Press, 2006.
Goldie, David. *A Critical Difference: T. S. Eliot and John Middleton Murry in English Literary Criticism, 1918–1928.* Oxford: Clarendon Press, 1998.
Harding, Jason. *The 'Criterion': Cultural Politics and Periodical Networks in Inter-War Britain.* Oxford University Press, 2002.
Kojecký, Roger. *T. S. Eliot's Social Criticism.* London: Faber & Faber, 1971.

8 PUBLISHING

Du Sautoy, Peter. 'T. S. Eliot: Personal Reminiscences'. *Southern Review* (autumn 1985) [947–56].
Mairet, Philip. 'Memories of T. S. E.'. *T. S. Eliot: A Symposium for his Seventieth Birthday,* ed. Neville Braybrooke. London: Rupert Hart-Davis, 1958 [36–44].
Morley, F. V. 'T. S. Eliot as Publisher'. *T. S. Eliot: A Symposium,* ed. Richard March and Tambimuttu. London: Editions Poetry London, 1948 [60–70].
O'Donovan, Brigid. 'The Love Song of T. S. Eliot's Secretary'. *Confrontation* (fall/winter 1975) [3–8].
Ridler, Anne. 'Working for T. S. Eliot: A Personal Reminiscence'. *Poetry Review* (March 1983) [46–9].
Schuchard, Ronald. 'T. S. Eliot at Fabers: Book Reports, Blurbs, Young Poets'. *Areté* (summer/autumn 2007) [63–87].

9 CENSORSHIP

De Grazia, Edward. *Girls Lean Back Everywhere: The Law of Obscenity and the Assault on Genius.* London: Constable, 1992.
Ernst, Morris L. and William Seagle. *To the Pure . . . A Study of Obscenity and the Censor.* London: Jonathan Cape, 1929.
Lewis, Felice Flanery. *Literature, Obscenity and the Law.* Carbondale: Southern Illinois University Press, 1976.
Rolph, C. H. Ed. *The Trial of Lady Chatterley: Regina v. Penguin Books Limited.* Harmondsworth: Penguin, 1961.
Thomas, Donald. *A Long Time Burning: The History of Literary Censorship in England.* London: Routledge & Kegan Paul, 1969.
Vanderham, Paul. *James Joyce and Censorship: The Trials of 'Ulysses'.* London: Macmillan, 1998.

10 LITERARY JOURNALISM

Goldie, David. *A Critical Difference: T. S. Eliot and John Middleton Murry in English Literary Criticism, 1918–1928.* Oxford: Clarendon Press, 1998.

Harding, Jason. *The 'Criterion': Cultural Politics and Periodical Networks in Interwar Britain.* Oxford: Oxford University Press, 2002.

  'Tradition and Egoism: T. S. Eliot and the *Egoist*'. *T. S. Eliot and the Concept of Tradition*, ed. Giovanni Cianci and Jason Harding. Cambridge University Press, 2007 [90–102].

Sullivan, Hannah. '"But we must learn to take literature *seriously*": T. S. Eliot and the Little Magazines of Modernism, 1917–1920'. *Critical Quarterly* (summer 2004) [63–90].

Vanheste, Jeroen. *Guardians of the Humanist Legacy: The Classicism of T. S. Eliot's 'Criterion' Network and its Relevance to our Postmodern World.* Leiden: Brill, 2007.

White, Peter. 'New Light on *The Sacred Wood*'. *Review of English Studies* (September 2003) [497–515].

11 VISUAL ART

Altieri, Charles. *Painterly Abstraction in Modernist American Poetry.* Cambridge University Press, 1995.

  '"Preludes" as Prelude: In Defense of Eliot as Symboliste'. *T. S. Eliot, a Voice Descanting: Centenary Essays*, ed. Shyamal Bagchee. London: Macmillan, 1990 [1–27].

Cameron, Sharon. *Impersonality: Seven Essays.* Chicago University Press, 2007.

Cianci, Giovanni. 'Reading T. S. Eliot Visually: Tradition in the Context of Modernist Art'. *T. S. Eliot and the Concept of Tradition*, ed. Giovanni Cianci and Jason Harding. Cambridge University Press, 2007 [119–30].

Materer, Timothy. *Vortex: Pound, Eliot, Lewis.* Ithaca, NY: Cornell University Press, 1979.

Trotter, David. 'T. S. Eliot and Cinema'. *Modernism/Modernity* (April 2006) [237–65].

12 DANCE

Bernstein, David. 'The Story of Vaslav Nijinsky as a Source for T. S. Eliot's "The Death of Saint Narcissus"'. *Hebrew University Studies in Literature* (1976) [71–104].

Hargrove, Nancy Duvall. 'T. S. Eliot and the Dance'. *Journal of Modern Literature* (fall 1997) [61–88].

Koritz, Amy. *Gendering Bodies/Performing Art.* Ann Arbor: University of Michigan Press, 1995.

Mester, Terri. *Movement and Modernism: Yeats, Eliot, Lawrence, Williams and Early Twentieth-Century Dance.* Fayetteville: University of Arkansas Press, 1997.

Schuchard, Ronald. *Eliot's Dark Angel: Intersections of Life and Art.* Oxford University Press, 1999.

Seymour-Jones, Carole. *Painted Shadow: A Life of Vivienne Eliot.* London: Constable, 2001.

13 DRAMA

Badenhausen, Richard. *T. S. Eliot and the Art of Collaboration.* Cambridge University Press, 2004.

Browne, E. Martin. *The Making of T. S. Eliot's Plays.* Cambridge University Press, 1969.

Chinitz, David. *T. S. Eliot and the Cultural Divide.* University of Chicago Press, 2003.

Malamud, Randy. *T. S. Eliot's Drama: A Research and Production Sourcebook.* New York: Greenwood Press, 1992.

Sherek, Henry. *Not in Front of the Children.* London: Heinemann, 1959.

Sidnell, Michael J. *Dances of Death: The Group Theatre of London in the Thirties.* London: Faber & Faber, 1984.

14 MUSIC

Acquisto, Joseph. *French Symbolist Poetry and the Idea of Music.* Aldershot: Ashgate, 2006.

Alldritt, Keith. *Eliot's 'Four Quartets': Poetry as Chamber Music.* London: Woburn Press, 1978.

Cluck, Nancy Anne. Ed. *Literature and Music: Essays on Form.* Provo, UT: Brigham Young University Press, 1981.

Cooper, John Xiros. Ed. *T. S. Eliot's Orchestra: Critical Essays on Poetry and Music.* New York: Garland, 2000.

Howarth, Herbert. *Notes on some Figures behind T. S. Eliot.* Boston, MA: Houghton Mifflin, 1964.

15 RADIO

Avery, Todd. *Radio Modernism: Literature, Ethics and the BBC, 1922–1938.* Aldershot: Ashgate, 2006.

Briggs, Asa. *The Birth of Modern Broadcasting 1896–1927.* Oxford University Press, 1995.

Chinitz, David. *T. S. Eliot and the Cultural Divide.* University of Chicago Press, 2003.

Cohen, Debra Rae, Michael Coyle and Jane Lewty. Eds. *Broadcasting Modernism.* Gainesville: University Press of Florida, 2009.

Coyle, Michael. *Ezra Pound, Popular Genres and the Discourse of Culture.* University Park: Pennsylvania State University Press, 1995.

'The Radio Broadcasts of T. S. Eliot, 1929–1963'. *T. S. Eliot and our Turning World*, ed. Jewel Spears Brooker. London: Macmillan, 1997 [203–13].

16 ALLUSION: THE CASE OF SHAKESPEARE

Bush, Ronald. *T. S. Eliot: A Study in Character and Style*. Oxford University Press, 1983.

Litz, A. Walton. 'The Allusive Poet: Eliot and his Sources'. *T. S. Eliot: The Modernist in History*, ed. Ronald Bush. Cambridge University Press, 1991.

Longenbach, James. '"Mature Poets Steal": Eliot's Allusive Practice'. *The Cambridge Companion to T. S. Eliot*, ed. A. D. Moody. Cambridge University Press, 1994 [176–88].

Ricks, Christopher. *Allusion to the Poets*. Oxford University Press, 2002.

Riquelme, John Paul. '"Withered Stumps of Time": Allusion, Reading, and Writing in *The Waste Land*'. *Denver Quarterly* (1981) [90–110].

Smith, Grover. *T. S. Eliot's Poetry and Plays*. University of Chicago Press, 1974.

Southam, B. C. *A Student's Guide to the 'Selected Poems of T. S Eliot'*. London: Faber & Faber, 1981.

17 CLASSICS

Highet, Gilbert Arthur. *The Classical Tradition: Greek and Roman Influences on Western Literature*. Oxford: Clarendon Press, 1949.

Howarth, Herbert. *Notes on some Figures behind T. S. Eliot*. Boston, MA: Houghton Mifflin, 1964.

Kermode, Frank. *The Classic*. London: Faber & Faber, 1975.

Reeves, Gareth. *T. S. Eliot: A Virgilian Poet*. London: Macmillan, 1989.

Sherry, Vincent. *The Great War and the Language of Modernism*. Oxford University Press, 2003.

18 DANTE

Bullaro, John J. 'The Dante of T. S. Eliot'. *A Dante Profile*, ed. Franca Schettino. Los Angeles: University of Southern California Press, 1967 [27–37].

Charity, A. C. 'T. S. Eliot: The Dantean Recognitions'. *The Waste Land in Several Voices*, ed. A. D. Moody. London: Edward Arnold, 1974.

Gervais, David. 'Eliot's Shakespeare and Eliot's Dante'. *T. S. Eliot and Our Turning World*, ed. Jewel Spears Brooker. London: Macmillan, 2001 [114–24].

Litz, A. Walton. 'Dante, Pound, Eliot: The Visionary Company'. *Dante e Pound*, ed. Maria Luisa Ardizzone. Ravenna: Longo, 1998 [39–45].

Manganiello, Dominic. *T. S. Eliot and Dante*. London: Macmillan, 1989.

Praz, Mario. 'T. S. Eliot and Dante'. *The Flaming Heart*. New York: Doubleday, 1958 [348–74].

19 SEVENTEENTH-CENTURY LITERATURE

Brooks, Harold F. *T. S. Eliot as Literary Critic.* London: Cecil Woolf, 1987.

Carpenter, Peter. 'Taking Liberties: Eliot's Donne'. *Critical Survey* (1993) [278–88].

Empson, William. *Argufying: Essays on Literature and Culture,* ed. John Haffenden. University of Iowa Press, 1987.

Kenner, Hugh. *The Invisible Poet: T. S. Eliot.* London: W. H. Allen, 1960.

Ricks, Christopher. *Decisions and Revisions in T. S. Eliot: The Panizzi Lectures 2002.* London: British Library, 2003.

20 ROMANTIC AND VICTORIAN POETRY

Baker, Carlos. *The Echoing Green: Romanticism, Modernism, and the Phenomena of Transference in Poetry.* Princeton University Press, 1984.

Bornstein, George. *Transformations of Romanticism in Yeats, Eliot, and Stevens.* Chicago University Press, 1976.

Kermode, Frank. *Romantic Image.* London: Routledge, 1957.

Lobb, Edward. *T. S. Eliot and the Romantic Critical Tradition.* London: Routledge, 1981.

O'Neill, Michael. *The All-Sustaining Air: Romantic Legacies and Renewals in British, American, and Irish Poetry since 1900.* Oxford University Press, 2007.

Raine, Craig. *T. S. Eliot.* London: Faber & Faber, 2006.

21 FRENCH POETRY

Bush, Ronald. *T. S. Eliot: A Study in Character and Style.* Oxford University Press, 1983.

Davie, Donald. *The Poet in the Imaginary Museum.* Manchester: Carcanet, 1977.

Kenner, Hugh. *The Pound Era.* Berkeley: University of California Press, 1971.

Marx, William. *Naissance de la critique moderne: la littérature selon Eliot et Valéry, 1889–1945.* Arras: Artois Presses Université, 2002.

Moody, A. D. *T. S. Eliot: Poet.* Cambridge University Press, 1979.

Schuchard, Ronald. *Eliot's Dark Angel: Intersections of Life and Art.* Oxford University Press, 1999.

22 GEORGIAN POETRY

Davie, Donald. *Thomas Hardy and British Poetry.* London: Routledge, 1973.

Hibberd, Dominic. *Harold Monro: Poet of the New Age.* Basingstoke: Palgrave Macmillan, 2001.

Howarth, Peter. *British Poetry in the Age of Modernism.* Cambridge University Press, 2005.

Larkin, Philip. *Required Writing.* London: Faber & Faber, 1983.

Ross, Robert H. *The Georgian Revolt*. Carbondale: Southern Illinois University Press, 1965.
Stead, C. K. *The New Poetic: Yeats to Eliot*. London: Hutchinson, 1964.

23 BLOOMSBURY

Bell, Quentin. *Bloomsbury*. London: Weidenfeld & Nicolson, 1968.
Edel, Leon. *Bloomsbury: A House of Lions*. London: Hogarth Press, 1979.
Holroyd, Michael. *Lytton Strachey*. New York: Farrar, Straus & Giroux, 1994.
Hussey, Mark. Ed. *Virginia Woolf A to Z*. Oxford University Press, 1996.
Lee, Hermione. *Virginia Woolf*. London: Vintage, 1996.
Rosenbaum, S. P. Ed. *The Bloomsbury Group*. Toronto University Press, 1975.

24 EZRA POUND

Bush, Ronald. *T. S. Eliot: A Study in Character and Style*. Oxford University Press, 1983.
Davie, Donald. *Modernist Essays: Yeats, Pound, Eliot*. Manchester: Carcanet, 2004.
Gallup, Donald. 'T. S. Eliot and Ezra Pound: Collaborators in Letters'. *Atlantic Monthly* (January 1970) [48–62].
Kenner, Hugh. *The Pound Era*. Berkeley: University of California Press, 1971.
Praz, Mario. *The Flaming Heart*. New York: Doubleday, 1958.
Stough, Christina. 'The Skirmish of Pound and Eliot in *The New English Weekly*'. *Journal of Modern Literature* (1983) [231–46].

25 THE AVANT-GARDE

Bürger, Peter. *Theory of the Avant-Garde*, trans. Michael Shaw. Manchester University Press, 1984.
Duchamp, Marcel. *The Essential Writings of Marcel Duchamp*, ed. Michel Sanouillet and Elmer Peterson. London: Thames & Hudson, 1975.
Levenson, Michael. *A Genealogy of Modernism: A Study of English Literary Doctrine, 1908–1922*. Cambridge University Press, 1984.
Perloff, Marjorie. *21st-Century Modernism: The 'New Poetics'*. Oxford: Blackwell, 2002.
Stead, C. K. *The New Poetic*. London: Hutchinson, 1964.

26 POLITICS

Asher, Kenneth. *T. S. Eliot and Ideology*. Cambridge University Press, 1995.
Chace, William. *The Political Identities of Ezra Pound and T. S. Eliot*. Stanford University Press, 1973.
Kojecký, Roger. *T. S. Eliot's Social Criticism*. London: Faber & Faber, 1971.
Levenson, Michael. 'Politics'. *A Companion to T. S. Eliot*, ed. David Chinitz. Chichester: Wiley-Blackwell, 2009 [376–87].

North, Michael. *The Political Aesthetic of Yeats, Eliot and Pound.* Cambridge University Press, 1991.

Tratner, Michael. *Modernism and Mass Politics: Joyce, Woolf, Eliot, Yeats.* Stanford University Press, 1995.

27 ECONOMICS

Alford, B. W. E. *Britain in the World Economy since 1880.* London: Longman, 1996.

Bradshaw, David. 'T. S. Eliot and the Major'. *Times Literary Supplement* (5 July 1996) [14–16].

Bush, Ronald. 'Eliot and Ruskin: Second Thoughts'. *Ruskin and Modernism,* ed. Giovanni Cianci and Peter Nicholls. New York: Palgrave, 2001 [155–64].

Cooper, John Xiros. *Modernism and the Culture of Market Society.* Cambridge University Press, 2004.

Harding, Jason. *The 'Criterion': Cultural Politics and Periodical Networks in Inter-War Britain.* Oxford University Press, 2002.

Stough, Christina. 'The Skirmish of Pound and Eliot in *The New English Weekly'. Journal of Modern Literature* (1983) [231–46].

28 ANTI-SEMITISM

Julius, Anthony. *T. S. Eliot, Anti-Semitism, and Literary Form.* London: Thames & Hudson, 2003.

Omer-Sherman, Ranen. 'Rethinking Eliot, Jewish Identity, and Cultural Pluralism'. *Modernism/Modernity* (September 2003) [439–45].

Paulin, Tom. 'T. S. Eliot and Anti-Semitism'. *Writing to the Moment.* London: Faber & Faber, 1996.

Raine, Craig. *T. S. Eliot.* London: Faber & Faber, 2006.

Ricks, Christopher. *T. S. Eliot and Prejudice.* London: Faber & Faber, 1988.

Schuchard, Ronald. 'Burbank with a Baedeker, Eliot with a Cigar: American Intellectuals, Anti-Semitism, and the Idea of Culture'. *Modernism/ Modernity* (January 2003) [1–26].

29 GENDER

DuPlessis, Rachel Blau. *Genders, Races, and Religious Cultures in Modern American Poetry, 1908–1934.* Cambridge University Press, 2001.

Ellmann, Maud. *The Poetics of Impersonality: T. S. Eliot and Ezra Pound.* Brighton: Harvester Wheatsheaf, 1987.

Gordon, Lyndall. *T. S. Eliot: An Imperfect Life.* New York: W. W. Norton, 1999.

Laity, Cassandra and Nancy K. Gish. Eds. *Gender, Desire and Sexuality in T. S. Eliot.* Cambridge University Press, 2004.

Lamos, Colleen. *Deviant Modernism: Sexual and Textual Errancy in T. S. Eliot, James Joyce and Marcel Proust.* Cambridge University Press, 1998.

McDonald, Gail. *Learning to be Modern: Pound, Eliot, and the American University.* Oxford University Press, 1993.

30   RELIGION

Davie, Donald. 'Anglican Eliot'. *Eliot in his Time,* ed. A. Walton Litz. Princeton University Press, 1973.

Donoghue, Denis. *Words Alone: The Poet T. S. Eliot.* New Haven, CT: Yale University Press, 2000.

Gardner, Helen. *The Art of T. S. Eliot.* London: Cresset, 1949.

Kirk, Russell. *Eliot and his Age: T. S. Eliot's Moral Imagination in the Twentieth Century.* Wilmington: ISI Books, 2008.

Schuchard, Ronald. *Eliot's Dark Angel: Intersections of Life and Art.* Oxford University Press, 1999.

Spurr, Barry. *'Anglo-Catholic in Religion': T. S. Eliot and Christianity.* Cambridge: Lutterworth Press, 2010.

31   PHILOSOPHY

Childs, Donald. *From Philosophy to Poetry: T. S. Eliot's Study of Knowledge and Experience.* London: Athlone Press, 2001.

Gray, Piers. *T. S. Eliot's Intellectual and Poetic Development.* Brighton: Harvester Wheatsheaf, 1982.

Habib, M. A. R. *The Early T. S. Eliot and Western Philosophy.* Cambridge University Press, 199.

Jain, Manju. *T. S. Eliot and American Philosophy: The Harvard Years.* Cambridge University Press, 1991.

Perl, Jeffrey. *Skepticism and Modern Enmity: Before and After Eliot.* Baltimore, MD: Johns Hopkins University Press, 1989.

Shusterman, Richard. *T. S. Eliot and the Philosophy of Criticism.* London: Duckworth, 1988.

32   SOCIAL SCIENCE

Ackerman, Robert. *The Myth and Ritual School: J. G. Frazer and the Cambridge Ritualists.* New York: Garland, 1991.

Brooker, Jewel Spears. *Mastery and Escape: T. S. Eliot and the Dialectic of Modernism.* Amherst: University of Massachusetts Press, 1994.

Bush, Ronald. 'The Presence of the Past: Ethnographic Thinking/Literary Politics'. *Prehistories of the Future: The Primitivist Project and the Culture of Modernism,* ed. Elazar Barkan and Ronald Bush. Stanford University Press, 1995.

Crawford, Robert. *The Savage and the City in the Work of T. S. Eliot.* Oxford: Clarendon Press, 1987.

Harmon, William. 'T. S. Eliot, Anthropologist and Primitive'. *American Anthropologist* (December 1976) [797–811].

Manganaro, Marc. *Myth, Rhetoric and the Voice of Authority: A Critique of Frazer, Eliot, Frye and Campbell.* New Haven, CT: Yale University Press, 1992.

33 NATURAL SCIENCE

Albright, Daniel. *Quantum Poetics: Yeats, Pound, Eliot and the Science of Modernism.* Cambridge University Press, 1997.

Beer, Gillian. *Open Fields: Science in Cultural Encounter.* Oxford: Clarendon Press, 1996.

Costello, Harry T. *Josiah Royce's Seminar, 1913–14,* ed. Grover Smith. New Brunswick, NJ: Rutgers University Press, 1963.

Montgomery, Marion. 'Eliot and the Particle Physicist'. *Southern Review* (July 1974) [583–9].

Whitworth, Michael H. *Einstein's Wake: Relativity, Metaphor, and Modernist Literature.* Oxford University Press, 2001.

'*Pièces d'identité*: T. S. Eliot, J. W. N. Sullivan and Poetic Impersonality'. *English Literature in Transition* (1996) [149–70].

34 CONTEMPORARY REVIEWS

Brooker, Jewel Spears. Ed. *T. S. Eliot: The Contemporary Reviews.* Cambridge University Press, 2004.

Clarke, Graham. Ed. *T. S. Eliot: Critical Assessments.* 4 vols. London: Croom Helm, 1990.

Grant, Michael. Ed. *T. S. Eliot: The Critical Heritage.* 2 vols. London: Routledge, 1982.

Harding, Jason. 'Prufrock and Prejudice'. *Times Literary Supplement* (22 October 2004) [24].

35 CONTEMPORARY AND POST-WAR POETRY

Corcoran, Neil. *English Poetry since 1940.* London: Longman, 1993.

Däumer, Elisabeth and Shyamal Bagchee. Eds. *The International Reception of T. S. Eliot.* London: Continuum, 2007.

Heaney, Seamus. *Finders Keepers: Selected Prose 1971–2001.* London: Faber & Faber, 2002.

Hughes, Ted. *A Dancer to God: Tributes to T. S. Eliot.* London: Faber & Faber, 1992.

Leavis, F. R. *New Bearings in English Poetry.* London: Chatto & Windus, 1950.

Wilmer, Clive. 'The Later Fortunes of Impersonality: "Tradition and the Individual Talent" and Postwar Poetry'. *T. S. Eliot and the Concept of Tradition,* ed. Giovanni Cianci and Jason Harding. Cambridge University Press, 2007 [58–71].

36 ELIOT STUDIES

Bloom, Harold. Ed. *T. S. Eliot: Modern Critical Views*. New York: Chelsea House, 1985.

Brooker, Jewel Spears. 'Eliot Studies: A Review and a Select Booklist'. *The Cambridge Companion to T. S. Eliot*, ed. A. D. Moody. Cambridge University Press, 1994 [236–44].

Clarke, Graham. Ed. *T. S. Eliot: Critical Assessments*. 4 vols. London: Croom Helm, 1990.

Knowles, Sebastian D. G. and Scott A. Leonard. Eds. *An Annotated Bibliography of a Decade of T. S. Eliot Criticism: 1977–1986*. Orono: National Poetry Foundation, 1992.

Martin, Mildred. Ed. *A Half-Century of Eliot Criticism*. Lewisburg, PA: Bucknell University Press, 1972.

Ricks, Beatrice. Ed. *T. S. Eliot: A Bibliography of Secondary Works*. Metuchen: Scarecrow Press, 1980.

The Newsletter of the T. S. Eliot Society publishes an annual bibliography of secondary criticism on T. S. Eliot.

37 LEGACIES: FROM LITERARY CRITICISM TO LITERARY THEORY

Baldick, Chris. *The Social Mission of English Criticism, 1848–1932*. Oxford: Clarendon Press, 1983.

Harwood, John. *Eliot to Derrida: The Poverty of Interpretation*. London: Macmillan, 1995.

Lobb, Edward. *T. S. Eliot and the Romantic Critical Tradition*. London: Routledge, 1981.

Shusterman, Richard. *T. S. Eliot and the Philosophy of Criticism*. London: Duckworth, 1988.

Waugh, Patricia. *Practising Postmodernism/Reading Modernism*. London: Edward Arnold, 1992.

Waugh, Patricia. Ed. *Literary Theory and Criticism: An Oxford Guide*. Oxford University Press, 2006.

Index